What Happened to the Vital Center?

What Happened to the Vital Center?

Presidentialism, Populist Revolt, and the Fracturing of America

NICHOLAS F. JACOBS AND SIDNEY M. MILKIS

OXFORD
UNIVERSITY PRESS

OXFORD
UNIVERSITY PRESS

Oxford University Press is a department of the University of Oxford. It furthers
the University's objective of excellence in research, scholarship, and education
by publishing worldwide. Oxford is a registered trade mark of Oxford University
Press in the UK and certain other countries.

Published in the United States of America by Oxford University Press
198 Madison Avenue, New York, NY 10016, United States of America.

CIP data is on file at the Library of Congress
ISBN 978–0–19–760352–9 (pbk.)
ISBN 978–0–19–760351–2 (hbk.)

DOI: 10.1093/oso/9780197603512.001.0001

1 3 5 7 9 8 6 4 2

Paperback printed by LSC Communications, United States of America
Hardback printed by Bridgeport National Bindery, Inc., United States of America

Contents

Preface

The book grew out of a relationship formed at the University of Virginia, where the professional ties between mentor and student evolved into warm friendship and fruitful collaboration. We began to collaborate when Nick was working on his PhD under Sid's supervision. But we quickly learned that we shared strong philosophical and empirical interests in presidents and political parties—a curiosity that focused on the convergence of executive power and partisanship from the 1930s to the present. Our determination to parse executive-centered partisanship rose to near desperation when an iconoclastic reality television star captured the Republican Party—a dangerous culmination of political developments that had been wending through political life in the United States for almost a century. We wrote the final words of this book in the aftermath of the post-election assault on the Capitol—the first time a president had sought to prevent the peaceful transfer of power. Our academic arguments had come perilously close to realization.

Donald Trump's right-wing populism confirmed antinomian strains that Sid had been warning about for three decades; but his alliance with Nick opened exciting new avenues of inquiry into the critical and fraught relationship between populism and party politics that added historical depth and institutional nuance to the story of how the vital center fell apart. The tension between mediating institutions like parties and populist uprisings is a hazardous but inevitable feature of a democracy. But the combustible interaction between gatekeepers and insurgents has changed dramatically over the past six decades. Our core argument is that the expansion of executive power since the 1930s combined with the rise of movement politics during the turbulent sixties to unleash an unmediated form of populism that denigrated political parties as collective organizations with a past and a future. The result is a disruptive form of executive-centered partisanship—animated by the unlikely joining of presidential prerogative and social activism—that has fractured the nation and weakened national resolve. As scholars of American political development, we argue that the righteous demands for racial justice and the hazardous infatuation with right-wing authoritarianism that currently roil American democracy are best understood when placed in this broad historical context. There is little hope of remedying the pathologies of what many of our colleagues have identified as a "Cold Civil War" without understanding how we got to this stage of development in the first place.

We are deeply grateful to all the friends and colleagues who helped and inspired us to complete this project. The seeds for the book were planted when Sid gave a talk on the 2016 election at his alma mater, Muhlenberg College. The warm welcome he received from his host Chris Borick, his former teacher Lud Schlecht, and the political science faculty and students was truly memorable—and motivation to keep seeking the answer to the core question of this lecture, which became the title of this book: What Happened to the Vital Center? To Nick goes the credit of offering incisive comments on the "draft" of this talk—and having the vision for a book-length treatment of Sid's very preliminary thoughts. Sid had the opportunity to further test these ideas in delivering various iterations of the "What Happened to the Vital Center?" talk at Trinity College, where he was hosted by a former student Kevin McMahon, and the Tocqueville Forum, which gave him the opportunity to share ideas over a sumptuous dinner with several of the distinguished faculty from Georgetown University's Government Department. Nick had the good fortune to present many of the ideas on party and governmental centralization at a symposium on the political economy of Vincent and Elinor Ostrom at George Mason University. He is especially grateful for the incisive comments from Bobbi Hertzberg, Brian Kogelmann, Peter Boettke, and Jan Volger.

The ideas and evidence that were essential to fleshing out these thoughts were marinated in stimulating and productive collaboration with our colleagues and friends: Laura Blessing, Sean Beienburg, Jordan Cash, Emily Charnock, Connor Ewing, Boris Heersink, Jeffery Jenkins, Desmond King, Michael Nelson, Jesse Rhodes, James Savage, and Daniel Tichenor. Our interlocuters at the University of Virginia and Colby College also helped us confront the thorny issues that emerge in the process of writing: Lawrie Balfour, James Ceaser, George Klosko, Rachel Potter, Barbara Perry, Guian McKee, Mark Selverstone, Russel Riley; Tony Corrado, Carrie LeVan, Sandy Maisel, Joe Reisert, and Dan Shea. Special thanks go to William Antholis, the CEO and president of the Miller Center, who gave our research steadfast support and, with the able assistance of communications director Howard Witt, projected our work on executive-centered partisanship into the public sphere. Sidney Tarrow, a great friend and generous colleague, read the manuscript in draft form and gave several chapters the "Tarrow

Treatment": detailed comments that were unflinchingly honest and unfailingly perceptive. The broader contours of this work owe to conversations over the years with generous and brilliant friends: Marie Gottschalk, Cathie Martin, Bruce Miroff, Jim Morone, Stephen Skowronek; Emile Lester, Kal Munis, and Anthony Sparacino.

It has been a great pleasure to work with Dave McBride, senior editor at Oxford University Press. Dave expressed an interest in this project from the beginning, solicited very helpful reviews at the critical incubating stage of our journey, and waited patiently for us to reach a destination. It is no mean feat to navigate an ambitious manuscript through a peer review process in the middle of the pandemic, and we are very grateful that Dave managed the task with panache. We are also very appreciative of the highly constructive reviews provided by the anonymous readers Dave enlisted. At Oxford University Press, we are thankful that Patterson Lamb, Emily Benitez, and Jeremy Toynbee were there to guide our work to final publication.

Finally, we are deeply thankful for the constant love and support of our families, even as they occasionally tired of the countless hours that we spent laboring on this book. It is only fitting that we dedicate this work to them: Carol, Lauren, David, and Jonathan Milkis (and the center of the family's attention, our beagle Iverson); and Rachel and Benjamin Jacobs. Benji was born during the final tortuous stage of our writing—a blessing that helped both of us put our work, no matter how devoted we are to it, in perspective.

Nicholas F. Jacobs
Vassalboro, Maine
Sidney M. Milkis
Charlottesville, Virginia

1

Populism and American Democracy

By the time he formally declared his candidacy for president, every American already knew his name. For decades, he made national headlines by defying the conventional wisdom and deriding the political establishment—attracting the ire of sitting presidents, disgusting the intellectual elite, and capturing the media's attention. His name was synonymous with a provocative style, distinguished by a thick accent, a clear sign to his followers that he was not a conventional politician. He claimed to speak for the "forgotten" American—the Americans who felt left behind by seismic cultural, economic, and political change.

In running his campaign, he trashed leaders of both parties and national heroes. In front of large banners reading "Stand Up for America!" he taunted bureaucrats, shouting that we needed to "take away their briefcases and throw them in the Potomac River!" He spoke of crime in the streets and promised that "if *we* were president today, you wouldn't get stabbed or raped in the shadow of the White House, even if we had to call out 30,000 troops and equip them with two-foot-long bayonets and station them every few feet apart."[1] His rallies were staged spectacles. Campaign staffers ensured that a couple of demonstrators would always be able to sneak in, so that they could shout down the candidate as a fascist and a neo-Nazi. These protesters were pawns in staged political theater, allowing the leader of "real Americans" to play the strongman his followers craved: "Come on down, I'll autograph your sandals" he would yell back. "All you need is a good barber!" "That's right honey; that's right sweetie pie. Oh, I'm sorry, I thought 'he' was a 'she!' "[2]

George Wallace wanted to be president. And in 1968, nearly 10 million Americans—13.5% of voters—supported him.

Wallace's assault on the "establishment" echoed a rallying cry that is endemic to American politics. As bitter and divisive as modern American politics appears, such eruptions have frequently roiled the country. Farmers in Western Pennsylvania mobilized in the 1790s and violently attacked federal tax collectors who were implementing the new government's excise tax on distilled spirits; rage spilled over this controversial tax issue and galvanized a mob of nearly 7,000 men who marched on Pittsburgh determined to raze the American "Sodom" and loot the homes of its merchant elite.[3] Fifty years later in 1863, at the height of the Civil War, the largest riot in American history broke out in New York City in response to Congress's new draft order. White working-class residents—many of them new, impoverished Irish immigrants—were enraged by the provision that allowed wealthy citizens to buy substitutes for the draft at the cost of an average workingman's yearly salary.[4] Anger swelled as the mob torched the homes of prominent politicians and lynched Black residents throughout Manhattan.[5] A century later, in the 1950s, anti-communist hysteria swept the nation. Lesser-known politicians, including a young congressman, Richard Nixon, took advantage of new television audiences, fabricated lists of suspected communist agents in high-level positions throughout government and society, and subjected them to vindictive hearings on Capitol Hill. Suspicion seeped out of Washington, and by the beginning of the 1960s, 100,000 dues-paying members had joined the John Birch Society—an organization formed to fight communism's spread as evidenced by developments such as the United Nations, water fluoridation, civil rights laws, and even President Eisenhower, whom they considered "a dedicated, conscious agent of the Communist conspiracy."[6] The anger of Wallace and his followers was animated by the civil rights reform and antiwar movement of the 1960s. But like all populists, they were tapping into a deep strain of unmediated protest, which has defined the American experiment in self-government since the beginning.

Donald Trump is just the latest manifestation of populist rage. No doubt many readers who considered the opening lines to this book recognized some of the impulses and rhetoric of George Wallace in 1968, perhaps mistaking it for positions taken in more recent presidential campaigns. Certainly, there are important ideological differences between Wallace and Trump, and between the state-building motivations of 19th-century populists, and the anti-tax, agrarian rebellions of the late 1700s. But populist politics is as much a matter of style as substance. While scholars have gone to great lengths to try to categorize populism's various iterations—reactionary versus progressive, conservative versus liberal, coercive versus democratizing—we see a common refrain. Throughout American history, politicians have routinely exploited the pervasive belief that the country's political system is rigged and illegitimate. The politically ambitious ride those periodic waves of anger, because in tearing down the institutional constraints that stifle the will of the "People," it aids their own selfish aspirations. Populism is an ancient threat to democratic politics and an obstinate problem in the practice of representative government in the United States.

While populism cuts a deep current through American political history, so too does its antithesis. Standing in its path is a form of *constitutional politics*—the practice of persuasion, negotiation, and compromise, the art of acknowledging irreconcilable differences, of appreciating diversity in how people want to live their own lives, and of recognizing the limits to collective action. Populism is vindictive, spurred by the desire to seek revenge on those in power because of a sense of prolonged injustice. Followers are uncompromising in their beliefs, and distrustful of those who do not share their vision of a remade future. As much as cynicism and suspicion are the hallmarks of the populist, faith in institutions and desire to persuade are necessary ingredients of spirited republican debate and resolution. Leaders of populist movements exploit the anger of disaffected citizens and offer simple solutions to complex questions. Patient, sober statesmanship is drowned out by the fury of self-righteousness that makes wise citizens look cowardly, and foolish ones courageous.

Donald Trump's presidency was fueled by a visceral disregard for constitutional politics. The January 6, 2021, assault on Congress to disrupt the legitimate, fair, and peaceful transition of presidential power—one of the most celebrated features of constitutional democracy—may be the most evocative image of the present populist moment. Trump's power, like all populist leaders, emanated from a widespread belief among his followers that the rules of the game were fundamentally rigged against them. Minutes before rioters broke through the windows of the Capitol building, the lame duck president drove home this fundamental point: "If you don't fight like Hell, you're not going to have a country anymore." "When you catch somebody in a fraud, you're allowed to go by very different rules." "You'll never take back our country with weakness." It was a startling call to arms anticipated by remarks he delivered four years earlier at his inaugural address, when the newly inaugurated president sought to rally the "people" to reclaim control over their government: "For too long a small group in our nation's capital has reaped the rewards of government, while the people have borne the cost. Washington flourished, but the people did not share in its wealth. Politicians prospered, but the jobs left and the factories closed. The establishment protected itself, but not the citizens of our country."[7]

To some progressives, even as they abhor his America First vision, Trump's image of politics accurately portrays an "establishment" that denigrates

American democracy. The only way to defeat Trump, or a would-be emulator, they believe, is to beat him at his own game: to denounce more fiercely, mobilize more effectively, and in effect, fight fire with fire. Populism is on the rise in the United States, and globally.[8] Leaders imbued with a populist ethos have taken the reins of power across the world, sometimes inspired by Trump's own assault on constitutional norms and institutions. Right-wing populism has a long history in Europe; but it is startling to see this authoritarian tradition move from the margins of what was once thought to be a moderate constitutional republic to the mainstream of American politics. George Wallace never became president; Donald Trump did. In capturing power and using it aggressively, he and his followers have left an indelible print on the pages of history, charting the path forward for future movements that want to discredit any governing constraints that stand in their way.

As shocking as his presidency and its tumultuous aftermath has been, we do not view Trump or this most recent uprising of populist furor as the cause of the contemporary crisis of American democracy. Trump is a symptom. He and the insurgents who follow him are but the latest eruption in long-standing developments that have transformed politics in the United States. Although unique in many ways, his candidacy and presidency are the consequence of eroding institutional bulwarks that traditionally have contained populist impulses. Moreover, because Trump is a product of deeply ingrained features of American politics, we are certain that he will not be the last populist leader to denounce the "establishment" on behalf of the "people." Always a threat to the existing order of things, populism might now be a more regular feature of politics and government in the United States, because the institutions and processes that once restrained democratic politics from its worst tendencies have been hollowed out over the last fifty years. And in this vacuum of unfiltered democracy rests the potential for another enterprising leader ready to "flatter [the people's] prejudices to betray their interests," as Alexander Hamilton once warned.[9]

Because Trump will not be the last, and because the forces that breed demagogues and populist uprisings have only swelled in recent years, this book is our effort to recover the lost idea of a "vital center" in American politics. We seek to understand why a shared consensus and a belief in American institutions that prevailed from the end of World War II until the late 1960s has devolved into a state of distrust and false hope. In this search for the lost promise of a "vital center," we draw on Arthur Schlesinger Jr.'s classic book of the same title, published in 1949. Schlesinger promoted the idea of a vital center to champion the emergence of a new consensus that would buttress America's experiment in self-government against the debilitating anxieties of economic industrialization and globalization.[10] It was written at a time when Schlesinger feared that support for fundamental principles was fraying, not only on the right but on the left as well. Schlesinger's vital center was a powerful, theoretically rich account of democratic politics rooted in what Louis Hartz called America's "liberal tradition"—that is, the norms of a polity uncommonly dedicated to individualism, diversity, rights, and private property.[11]

Schlesinger's notion of American consensus—along with the hundreds of texts it inspired—is an impressive defense of the virtues traditionally associated with liberalism and the need to contemplate the character of democratic leadership in a "modern" industrialized democracy.[12] However, Schlesinger and others who defended the post-war consensus paid inadequate attention to the institutional framework that sustained liberal virtues amid the rising forces that threatened to pull the center apart.[13] In our own time, there is a similar crisis of faith—globalization, technological automation, and material advances have brought wondrous prosperity to millions of Americans and others worldwide; at the same time, these developments have been joined to an unlimited global war on terror; growing inequalities; and the persistence of racial, gender, and nativist prejudice. It is no wonder that today, as in Schlesinger's day, many believe that their "lives are empty of belief. They are lives of quiet desperation."[14] But if present political conditions do pose a threat to the country's cultural and social commitments—and if a particular method of politicking does disregard and offend some widespread, popular consensus about how pubic officials should behave—we need to place specific actions in a larger context, to take account of what institutional conditions gave rise to the erosion of established traditions. Indeed, intrinsic to this inquiry is a presumption of political development—that a shared consensus on political norms did at one point exist, that institutions once buttressed these shared commitments, and that the onset of centrifugal forces caused the center to fall apart.

We are not alone in contemplating the renewal of a vital center. Joining the clarion call to redefine a "new center" in American politics is a bipartisan alliance, well represented by the partnership of William Galston, a former policy advisor to President Clinton, and William Kristol, the former editor of the conservative magazine the *Weekly Standard*. By the authors' own admission, theirs is an unlikely pair, but they joined hands to express a "shared concern that the basic institutions and principles of liberal democracy are under assault."[15] Bringing to mind the refrain, attributed to Mark Twain, that "history does not repeat itself, but it does rhyme," there is deep theoretical agreement between the Galston-Kristol "new center," predicated on "Opportunity, Security, Accountability, and Ingenuity," and Schlesinger's more than 60-year-old rendition of the vital center.[16] Like Galston and Kristol, we believe that some essential element of our politics has gone awry. But unlike these public intellectuals and the many others who are attempting to renew American democracy—and for that matter, Schlesinger—we argue that the maladies that fracture the nation and weaken national resolve are badly aggravated, if not caused by, the decline of America's two-party system.

Our central argument is that party politics can help produce an energetic democratic politics that nourishes the vital center. We defend this by detailing the collapse of the American party system during the last 50 years, which once sustained the New Deal political order. The vitality of *both* political parties and the party structure as a whole have a fundamental bearing on the type of politics we can practice in the United States. To the extent that many believe there is no principled alternative to the intransigent calls of the far left and the far right, we suggest that such a resolution will be born, not from a soulless splitting of the differences between Democrats and Republicans, but rather from the spirited debate between competing party organizations. Robust party institutions, properly structured, have, and can again, give forceful, but responsible, animation to the country's inevitable political disagreements. Robust parties can encourage candidates running for state and national office to build geographically vast and inclusive coalitions—a necessary ingredient to ensure that all communities are included in the conversation. Robust parties require diffuse leadership; when power is shared by multiple officials within an organization, parties maintain a sense of a collective past and a shared future—both within the halls of Washington and among the public. Finally, robust parties nourish responsible, meaningful, and fulfilling citizen engagement.[17]

To be sure, party organizations have not always provided a salutary check on populist movements; this book does not argue for a return to some golden age of party politics. Sometimes, as during the Civil War, social movements have arisen that raise such fundamental grievances, and seek to resolve these injustices with such dedicated attention to institutional reform, that the party system has been rightfully remade. We reference the Republican Party—an insurgent third party—that arose amid the conflagration over slavery, as a party that gave effect to, rather than "stabilized" the timeless struggle over America's original sin. We are also deeply attentive to the Democratic Party's "Faustian Bargain" with segregationists, which made it a particularly "effective" institution for blunting the long civil rights movement and maintaining the status quo. These struggles over national identity, in particular, have resulted in heated party contests—reckonings—that cannot be resolved by party organizations alone.

One chief aim of our book, however, is to distinguish this variant of movement politics, which has animated democracy in the United States, from the anti-institutionalist strain of protest that diminishes the vital center. There must be a role for the average citizen, and the traditional form of party organization in American political development has not always encouraged active participation. But far from the movement-style politicking that advantages those voices at the extremes of society—be they intellectual elites or those who outwardly disdain liberal values—party leaders can bring more voices into politics, so long as they have the financial capacity and personnel to, at the same time, remove themselves from all the shouting. Politicians must be able to respond to public demands but also to broker compromise, practice cooperation, and cope with inevitable disagreement in society. In short, a reconstituted partisanship—bounded by the renewal of party organizations—can in fact serve as a safeguard against current and future populist challenges to constitutional government.

Aside from a relatively small circle of scholars with an uncommon appreciation of institutions, few believe a strengthened party system is the solution to raw and disruptive partisanship.[18] Most scholars warn that parties have become too strong in the 21st century. Yet, as Daniel Schlozman and Sam Rosenfeld have argued, our polarized age is one of partisan revival within a "hollow" party system. In the mass electorate, "party identification predicts voting behavior better than any time since the dawn of polling." In government, "interparty antagonism and intraparty discipline have reached unprecedented levels." And yet, they point out, "parties do not feel strong." Aside from raising money and offering voters helpful labels on Election Day, party organizations seem inadequate to the tasks of building enduring and stable coalitions and providing a vital connection between the electorate and representatives.[19] We share the view of Schlozman and Rosenfeld that the solution to the puzzle of weak parties and heightened partisanship is the decline of party *organizations*. Vital party organizations, in fact, have historically mediated populist demands and moderated party conflict. Strong party

organizations have the capacity to "mobilize popular participation, to integrate disparate groups, interests, and movements, and to foster meaningful
choice and accountability in policymaking."[20] In V. O. Key's formulation, the
decline of party organizations has also weakened party loyalties in the electorate and diminished the ability of party leaders in Congress and the states
to coopertatively govern.[21]

We do not believe, however, that the return to a "responsible partisanship"
will come by restoring the status of party organizations alone. As Dan Shea
has explained, recent efforts to revitalize party organizations have uninten-
tionally turned voters away from the political process altogether; revitalization has made the two increasingly centralized organizations more likely to
go negative, give priority to campaign contributions, emphasize scandal, and
deliberately diminish the size of the electorate so that it can be more manageable. "Party scorecards tally only wins and losses after election day," he
argues, "rather than any long-term cultivation of voters."[22] So, while strong
party organizations do indeed have the capacity to mobilize popular support,
forge broad coalitions, foster choice, and transform election promises into
government action, more attention needs to be placed on the broader political context in which they operate.

One major part of the political environment, largely neglected among
students of party politics, is the central contribution that presidents
have made to polarization. We argue that the major problem facing both
Republican and Democratic party organizations is that presidents, armed
with the tools of the administrative presidency, make a powerful claim to
mobilize and lead movement-politics. Presidents do not broker; they do
not value prudence. They lead their parties, but they are not, in the traditional sense, party leaders. Without accounting for the fusion of executive
power and partisanship, party organizations will remain in the shadow of a
presidency-centered democracy.

As the chapters below show, the emergence of presidential partisanship
had its origins in the cataclysmic developments of the 1960s. Sparked by
populist revolts on the left and right against an establishment tarnished by
the stubborn tumor of racial injustice and imperialist adventures, polarizing conflicts based on culture, race, ethnicity, and sexuality emerged that
scorned party politics. These social developments raised the stakes of party
politics and cast a moral shadow over contests for the White House, person-
alizing the institution, and diminishing the incentives presidents once had
to manage disagreement. Consequently, as Nancy Rosenblum and Russell

Muirhead have argued, parties dominated by combatants who not only disagree on principle and policy but also consider their opponents enemies have become unable to enforce "the discipline of regulated rivalry."[23]

Parties have at various moments in American history fostered debate and nurtured resolution. However, since the 1960s, Democrats and Republicans have methodically chipped away at the norms, rules, and procedures that sustain them as collective organizations with a past and a future, giving rise to what we call "executive-centered partisanship."[24] Both Democrats and Republicans have adopted a faith in presidential power, which, while promising to fulfill important party commitments, has in actuality sapped both parties of their collective strength. It subjects partisans to the periodic machinations of a single leader, ordained by a minority faction within each party, who commands loyalty, not as a consensus builder but as the vanguard of partisan objectives.

Executive-centered partisanship sits at the crosscurrents of two related phenomena in American political development, which are largely untethered to contemporary policy debates between the left and right. First, the form of party contestation we must now contend with is a consequence of organizational and electoral reforms that both the Democratic and Republican parties embraced throughout the 20th century, undergirded by common pressures to democratize party life. These populist incursions culminated with the McGovern-Fraser reforms, which established a system of open causes and direct primaries by the early 1970s. Both parties altered the rules governing the presidential selection process with the intention of giving more power to "the people" in selecting candidates for office and in determining party priorities. However, the effect of these reforms did not empower the median voter, the average American, the vital center. Rather, the weakening of traditional party organizations enhanced the influence of donors, interest groups, and social activists who scorned the pragmatic politics and compromises hitherto credited with forging majority coalitions.[25]

The institutional consequences of those reforms were enhanced by a second development: the creation of the Executive Office of the President, comprising the White House Office (the West Wing) and important staff agencies such as the Office of Management and Budget. Formed during the New Deal pursuant to the 1939 Executive Reorganization Act—the organic statute of the modern presidency—the White House grew in size and power during the 1960s. The forging of an elaborate executive office has allowed the White House to form alliances with activists and outside groups who disdain the party "establishment," thus subordinating decentralized and pluralistic party coalitions to the more national and programmatic networks that shape contemporary partisan politics.[26] Of course, the diversity and complexity of the American electorate—inherent features in a country as large as the United States—and the institutional rivalry built into the constitutional structure of checks and balances and American federalism have continued to constrain the excesses of presidential partisanship. Yet executive-centered partisanship represents the fusing of presidential prerogative, social activism, and partisanship that both circumnavigates and weakens the traditional guardrails of liberal democracy. The presidency is uniquely situated to respond to popular protest, and the mythology that surrounds the office—that its occupant is a distillation of majority opinion and the voice of the people—gives authority to social activists who can associate themselves with grandeur of the White House. For this reason, it is not enough to focus on just the development of party organizations; we must also account for the changing relationship between presidents and parties over time.

Although both parties have declined as collective and responsible organizations, modern populism has manifested in different ways. Those most sensitive to the changing nature of partisanship in contemporary American politics stress the *asymmetry* between Democrats and Republicans. Simply put, Republicans are more polarized than Democrats on a variety of commonly used measures: Republican primary voters are more ideologically coherent; Republican legislators are further to the right of the congressional median than the average Democrat; within the states, Republican parties are more unified around a central set of animating causes. Our focus on presidential partisanship confirms much of this perspective. Hostile to government and bureaucracy, the Republican Party has been more susceptible to populist currents that disdain constitutional arrangements and pluralistic politics. Less opposed to the administrative state forged during the New Deal and more responsive to the demands of a multiracial nation, Democrats have resisted the xenophobic and nationalist claims that often accompany populist capture.

Nevertheless, both liberals and conservatives, Democrats and Republicans disdain party organizations and rely on presidential candidates to mobilize their base supporters and programmatic causes. Indeed, as we show in Chapter 4, it was liberal activists who first stormed the ramparts of the party establishment and set precedents that rewrote the rules of partisan conflict. Our focus on executive-centered partisanship also challenges the argument of Matt Grossmann and David Hopkins, that Democrats are merely a coalition of interest groups, immune to the movements politics that the Trump presidency has unleashed inside the Republican Party.[27] As Joe Biden's victory in the 2020 nomination contests shows, Democrats are a more diverse party; however, since the 1960s, interest groups like labor and "neo-liberal" business constituents have had to share power with a multitude of social movement organizations—representing the causes of civil rights, environmental protection, gun control, and consumer protection—that disdain pragmatism and the regular party apparatus. It is this conflict between establishment groups and "outside" organizations within the Democratic Party that has galvanized the left's own anti-establishment strain. And so, although the two parties are very different, neither champions the "idea of a party system" that historically has mediated the ongoing conflicts between the establishment and popular uprisings.[28]

Moreover, with the transformation of partisanship, Democrats no less than Republicans have adopted a faith in executive dominion. Where the left yearns for President Obama's unifying message of "Hope," and the right pines for the Trump's promise of "American greatness," we want to understand why either was able to govern with a "popular mandate," when their popular majority (or lack thereof!) was minuscule, or when 40% of the voting eligible population stayed home.[29] More problematic we fear, this presidential partisanship has fueled new waves of populist discontent and demagogic leadership, which disdains constitutional constraints and compromise. While Democrats and Republicans are not symmetrical in their contribution to executive-centered partisanship (Trump is almost farcically paradigmatic), we depart from the bulk of commentaries on American political life, which seek to blame one party over the other. The real danger is when both parties, regardless of intent or goodwill, give credence to and practice a raw and disruptive partisanship.

We recognize that party organizations are likely to be viewed as the problem rather than the solution. Or so the usual commentary goes.[30] Bernie Sanders's "revolution" did not succeed in 2016 in spite of the energy and passion of his followers, because the Democratic National Committee rigged the system. Hillary Clinton lost because she was too timid and calculating; her decades of experience and ties to the party "elite" arrested her desire to promote righteous reforms. In contrast, Donald Trump's supporters praised his disdain for pragmatic party politics. He won because he captured the passions of a distraught minority—a "silent majority" he claimed—that had been waiting for an outsider to give them an awareness of their collective strength.

However, these common narratives overstate just how unique Sanders's and Trump's brazen claims are. Over 50 years ago, the Republican nominee for president, Barry Goldwater, apocalyptically argued that "extremism in defense of liberty is no vice"; and, for good measure, he added that "moderation in the pursuit of justice is no virtue." In 2016, both militant Democratic and Republican partisans voiced a similar mantra.[31] They echoed a disdain for parties that has deep roots in American politics, when "the people" have repeatedly excoriated intermediary organizations that muffle the voices advocating for a purer democracy, or a stronger national state. Significantly, in the wake of Bernie Sanders's provocative insurgency in 2016, the Democratic National Committee scaled back the power of the so-called superdelegates, public officials who were expected to inject a measure of pragmatism into the party counsels.[32] How this fragile balance between pragmatism and insurgency plays out in Joe Biden's administration is something we briefly discuss in the concluding chapter. When considering the fate of the present administration, however, one must recognize that the great challenge for anyone seeking to restore consensus in American politics is that the roar of unfiltered partisanship rejects any attempt to restore a vital center as a sellout; they can always be accused of being against "the people" and for their own privileged position.

Organized party competition, we argue, does not disdain popular discontent; rather, it can moderate the most dangerous tendencies of populist movements and demagogic leaders who incite their fervor. A party system, characterized by enduring and structured competition, is a necessary institution in a country as large and diverse as the United States. Any attempt to recover the vital center requires a defense of the two-party system. The vital center cannot avoid ennui or destructive polarization without healthy political parties that protect all of us—citizens and leaders—from our own worst tendencies.

Theoretical Foundations

The question of how to renew responsible partisanship is an essential problem that must be solved if we are to recover America's vital center. Parties and partisanship force individuals to think about the larger commitments they share, especially the commitment to abide by certain fundamental norms and restraints. As Hugh Heclo argued, it forces those engaged in politics to "think institutionally," to ask a set of questions about their actions that are not solely self-referential or about naked self-interest.[33]

As social scientists, we can, and often do, discuss parties and partisanship in purely positivist terms: who votes for Democrats and who votes for Republicans; how the parties in Congress are organized to facilitate legislative expertise; how parties have developed over time to include or forestall different interests and issue groups. We rely on empirical analysis to make valid comparisons and to generalize about how the political world does, in fact, work. But in suggesting that the vital center has collapsed, we are also making an argument about how the political world *should* work. Before documenting how partisanship has been fundamentally transformed over the last 50 years, we want to make our normative commitments clear. As Heclo warns, "If the normative purposes of institutions are regarded as pure façade, nothing more than masks to be continually stripped away so as to reveal interest group politics, legitimizing myths, self-interested bureaucratic survival strategies, and so on, there is really nothing much of substantive value to talk about. We will end up destroying the very basis for caring about institutions enough to think about them in the first place."[34]

We value political parties because the dignity of the democratic individual depends on empowering communities of like-minded interest, by giving them authority over their own destinies. In admiring self-government, we remain committed to the idea that it is better to be ruled by the collective decisions of our fellow citizens than by the recriminations of a few, or by the oppressiveness of tradition and social class. Democratic politics can be vicious. But as Alexis de Tocqueville warned, popular rule's despotic potential is revealed not only in those moments where an impassioned majority tramples on the rights and dignity of the few. More often, the greatest threat to modern democracies, born of the Enlightenment's celebration of individualism, is rank apathy—the loss of a sense of purpose and a passion for self-government, leading citizens to delegate civic responsibilities to "mild despots" who purport to rule in their interest. "Democratic governments can become violent and even cruel at certain moments," Tocqueville wrote, but more fearful are the times when citizens become "withdrawn and apart [like] a stranger to the destiny of others . . . [when] he is beside them, but does not see them; he touches them and does not feel them; he exists only in himself and for himself alone, and if a family still remains for him, one can at least say that he no longer has a native country."[35] We need restraints not only to protect us from the excesses of majority tyranny but also from the degeneration of individualism to selfishness, to a state of being that Tocqueville calls "egoism."

Faith in the vital center thus depends on a sustainable civic culture—what Robert Bellah and his colleagues, invoking Tocqueville, famously described as the "habits of the heart," which nurture a sense of responsibility that coexists, albeit uneasily, with the powerful demand for rights.[36] Following the 2016 presidential election, our fellow democrats on the political left and right bemoaned the demise of America's civil religion and traditions. David Von Drehle echoed Schlesinger's center-left critique of modern political hubris—the casual way in which militant partisans "assume powers we don't possess," an ambition that sits at the very core of both parties whose "shared goal is to simplify the complexity of politics in a diverse nation."[37] Conservatives such as David Brooks lamented the depreciating value that Americans place on genuine pluralism. "Trumpian nationalists, authoritarian populists and Islamic jihadis are different versions of antipluralism," he writes. "These movements are reactions against the diversity, fluidity and interdependent nature of modern life. Antipluralists yearn for a return to clear borders, settled truths and stable identities. They kill for a fantasy, a world that shines in their imaginations but never existed in real life."[38] Spanning the concerns of pragmatic liberalism and conservatism, E. J. Dionne, Thomas Mann, and Norman Ornstein credit the rise of Trump to a type of civic apathy that Tocqueville might have recognized. In doing so, they identify a potential silver lining to our present discontents: "Precisely because the Trump threat is so profound, he has jolted much of the country to face problems that have been slowly eroding our democracy. And he has aroused a popular mobilization that may far outlast him."[39]

Where Drehle calls for humility; Brooks for tolerance; and Dionne, Mann, and Ornstein for sustained activism, we call for an appreciation of institutions. Contemporary critiques of American democracy that are rooted in culture are meaningful and provocative; however, they often overlook Tocqueville's caution that *mores* are nurtured first and foremost by political associations and institutional arrangements that give them strength. It is oftentimes difficult to find guidance in cultural critiques beyond importunities: "be more humble," "practice greater empathy," "participate more." If our diagnosis of American political development has merit, such sociological prescriptions, which see politics principally rooted in cultural values, are not so much wrong as incomplete.

To these accounts of democratic culture, we seek to add a recognition of how associations and institutions help to cultivate healthy democratic practice. Institutions depend, undoubtedly, on a healthy civic culture that rewards those who practice humility, empathy, and participation. Institutions cannot succeed if they are tarnished with an unreflective distrust toward authority or a cynical view that politics cannot be used to promote the general welfare. Yet even if we succeed in placing the most humble or empathetic leader in office, we might still run up against many of the same problems we face today. In recognizing the need for strong institutions, we do not place our faith in virtuous leaders. As James Madison warned in his justly famous 10th *Federalist Paper*, "Enlightened statesmen will not always be at the helm."[40] Rather, we argue that by requiring those in power to follow certain rules, consider past precedent, and follow *ex ante* processes—to speak to obligation rather than self-interest—we are more likely to build consensus and preserve commitments that allow us to sustain America's experiment in self-government.

Populism

The inherent fragility of norms or culture, and the necessity of institutional constraints, speaks to the reality that populism has been a recurrent force in American politics since before the Constitution was written. Indeed, it is fair to say the Constitution is an outgrowth of the country's first populist insurgency. When the delegates to the Constitutional Convention assembled in Philadelphia in 1787, they were responding not just to the weaknesses of the current federal government but also to the systems of state governments that allowed demagogues and populist leaders to capture power and use it on behalf of an unruly few.[41] Across the states, self-serving elites captured office, inflated currency, and helped to drive a wedge in a fledgling national society, still reeling from the chaos and devastation of the revolution. In western Massachusetts, an enterprising farmhand and veteran of the Continental Army transformed a largely peaceful protest against the state's tax courts into an armed rebellion on behalf of those he thought were the truly deserving Americans: laborers, farmers, and former soldiers. Daniel Shays's 1786 uprising marked a turning point in the country's public philosophy. Thoughts and celebration of revolution, which had animated the independence movement, gave way to deep deliberation over how to sustain free government—how to solve what Samuel Beer described as the essential "dilemma of scale": "If the republic is small enough to govern itself peaceably, it will be too weak to defend itself, while if its numbers are great enough for defense, they will be too many for self-government."[42]

The delegates at the 1787 Constitutional Convention attempted to solve that dilemma, and in doing so, they deliberately acknowledged populism's recurrent force in democratic politics.[43] The framers' system of divided and separated powers in a large and diverse society would moderate but not prevent populist uprisings that would threaten their grand experiment of self-government on a grand scale. American populism has found its greatest nourishment in the country's democratic tradition, which precedes the Constitution—a politics animated by the ideals of social equality and mass enfranchisement.[44] America's exceptional mystique is the story of the common man—the frontier family, the industrious factory worker, the sons and daughters of immigrants—not notable families, stately princes, or heavenly ordainment. For this reason, frustration and discontent have often aroused those who seek to tear down the institutions of privilege, power, and prominence—anything that stands in the way of a true democratic polity and the use of political power on behalf of "the people." Populism has manifested in many different guises. What all these upheavals have in common is a claim that "the people" are in the right: minorities, communists, Washington elites, and corporate America stand in the way of justice. Couched in a language of certitude and unabashed self-righteousness, populists stoke antinomian fervor that poses hard challenges to cultural or institutional restraints that protect democracy from its worst tendencies.

In exploring the origins and development of populism, we discover that our deepest and most enduring political debates are often reflections on just how that political debate should be structured. Much of American history is a story of advancing the idea of "We the People"; and, without question, Americans have a much more capacious sense of "the people" today than the framers of the Constitution did in 1787.[45] The right of suffrage, while by no means monotonic, has expanded to include nearly every American citizen who is at least 18 years old, regardless of race and gender.[46] But as Wilson Carey McWilliams pointed out, focusing merely on popular sovereignty, as important is it is, neglects how self-government presupposes a sense of community that relies on strong political organizations and institutions.[47]

Likewise, it is also helpful to recognize that the promise of self-government has been repeatedly torn assunder by its own internal dynamics and the sharp divisions among "the people" themselves. Celebrating the great advantages and dangerous possibilities of American democracy, Abraham Lincoln, more than anyone of his generation, recognized that "if destruction be our lot, we must ourselves be its author and finisher. As a nation of freemen, we must live through all time, or die by suicide."[48]

Populism, therefore, is an endemic feature of any free society. Different interests arise, and different perspectives are inspired in a community dedicated to open discussion, the free movement of capital, and the protection of different ways of living. In a political regime defined by open and contested elections, every politician must make some attempt to appeal to "the people." Yet populists and their rhetoric are distinguishable from other claims of democratic leadership because their power and legitimacy stems from their direct, special relationship with a homogenous, single-minded group. As one of the foremost scholars of populist movements, Michael Kazin, has described, "Populism [is] more an impulse than an ideology." Throughout American history, self-styled leaders of the people have "employed populism as a flexible mode of persuasion. They used traditional kinds of expressions, tropes, themes, and images to convince large numbers of Americans to join their side or to endorse their views on particular issues."[49] At the same time, diversity, tolerance, the rule of law, and individual rights are formidable bulwarks against the claims of the populist leader; and for that reason, they are the enduring enemy of demagogues and their feverish followers. The label "populism" is often considered to be synonymous with democracy. But it is a highly amorphous concept that eschews an easy definition. In many respects, populism—as we use the term—represents *unmediated* democratic politics. Populism thrives in a democracy, and any institutional regime that can lay claim to eradicating populism would likely fail to meet the standards of self-rule and contested elections.

Populism is also an ideologically contingent phenomenon—at times it is reactionary, other times progressive. Historians' interpretations of various populist movements change: a reflection of their own time and understanding of what constitutes social justice. Richard Hofstadter—a foremost historian of the 20th century—viewed the Populist Movement of the late 1800s as a regressive, unprincipled, and backward-looking band of angry farmers who railed against the rise of modern America.[50] More contemporary scholarship, however, has viewed this movement as the forerunner to the Progressive Movement—as a genuinely egalitarian cause that sought to resolve the most vexing social issue in the United States: racial hierarchy.[51]

Still others have identified the Populists as an early variant of modern American multi-culturalism, especially in breaking down class, gender, and racial barriers.[52]

Likewise, political scientists use the concept of populism to define many discrete, sometimes contradictory, phenomena. Many students of Latin American politics would recognize it to mean, in general, fiscally irresponsible economic policies that lead, on the one hand, to rampant clientelism, and on the other, to periods of radical wealth redistribution to make amends for bad policy.[53] Others connect their study of populist fervor to social movement politics, which are themselves conditional on opportunities provided by new media, changing cultural norms, growing inequality, and general weakness among those charged with the task of governing.[54]

These grassroots movements expose latent ideological cleavages in society and give political parties incentives to tackle new issues—and to propose dramatic reform. For some scholars, in fact, populism might simply denote marginal interests that no major party has yet incorporated into their coalition.[55] And still others might use the term to refer to a particular grassroots movement at the turn of the 20th century. Certainly, as used most often, populism—at least in the American context—refers to the Populist Movement, comprised of agrarian leaders and various organized political interests, that was the first national social movement in American politics to address the injustices of industrial capitalism.

Seeking to cut through the conceptual muddle, Kazin concludes that "populism is . . . a grand form of rhetorical optimism; once mobilized, there is nothing ordinary Americans cannot accomplish."[56] We sympathize with this framing, which views populism as an indigenous form of radicalism. We would suggest, however, that populism involves more than a messianic form of political rhetoric. Populist movements and the leaders that curry their favor also presume to use state power in the name of the people. As a general rule, populists often struggle to specify who "the people" are—perhaps because, in doing so, they would concede that their claims are made not on behalf of a forgotten majority but for a vocal minority. Nevertheless, they readily identify the "anti-people" or "the elite." Populist movements on the left have derided the "malefactors of great wealth," as Theodore Roosevelt famously described the ruling class of the Gilded Age: big bankers, financiers, and powerful corporations are all to blame for virulent economic injustices. Populist movements on the right have excoriated the decay of traditional values: purveyors of political correctness, Hollywood celebrities, and the mainstream media preach from on high about the values of multi-culturalism, as they ridicule the traditional values of "real Americans."

Both radical and backward-looking populists presume that the common interest of a disparate people can be discerned. As Pierre Rosanvallon has argued, "Populists denounce 'otherness' in moral terms (by vilifying the 'corrupt' and 'rotten'), in social terms (by condemning 'elites'), and in ethnic terms (by attacking 'foreigners,' 'immigrants,' 'minorities,' etc.). By contrast, they celebrate 'the people' as unified and pure, undivided so long as outsiders are kept out."[57] In demonizing "the other," populists are distrustful of ruling institutions; their energy is dedicated to tearing down the prevailing order that thwarts the popular will. Expertise, rational debate, and legal processes cannot lead to just outcomes, because they stand in the way of unbridled public expression.[58]

This understanding of populism excludes many seminal figures in American history on the left and right. American abolitionists were un-compromising foot soldiers in the fight against slavery; among them, Anna E. Dickinson—the first woman ever to address Congress—rose to national prominence for her fierce attacks on the "slave catcher" Abraham Lincoln. But she, like many of her female compatriots, did not proffer any simple solutions. She toured the country, brokered talks with leading politicians, and recognized that the only way to transform American democracy was to change the minds of a generation reared to condone America's peculiar institution. Her task was to build an anti-slavery Republican Party.[59] At the turn of the 20th century, urban reformers—none more prominent than the social worker Jane Addams—lamented the scourge of America's cities and the material poverty that immigration inflicted upon their communities. Like Dickinson, Addams was an institution builder. She pioneered the development of new settlement homes where reformers and immigrants developed an incipient social safety net against the ravages of a rapidly changing industrial society. And while Martin Luther King Jr. was an idealistic revolutionary, he had an unparalleled faith in the institutions and traditions of American liberalism even as he insisted on the need to reform them. No moderate, he led a movement schooled in the art of spectacle, rhetoric, and mass protest. But at every step, he acknowledged that the history of race relations was the history of unpersuadable minds and difficult problem solving. Decades later, peaceful protesters would again take to the streets in response to multiple public instances of police violence against African Americans. They did not speak for "the people." They marched in solidarity to demand change for a marginalized, victimized community. Black Lives Matter may, to some, be a radical force, but its proponents are not populist.

In contrast to these movements, there is a common logic that arouses populist leadership today, whether these leaders are found among so-called progressives—who stand on an uncompromising assault on the "establish-ment"—or among conservatives—who sacrifice the difficult work of politics to uncompromising attacks on "un-Americanism," "creeping socialism," or a violation of Judeo-Christian values. Both tend to moralize politics and to see governmental outcomes as unjust or corrupt unless they are fully in agree-ment with their particular set of preferences. While the populist ethos might have beneficial effects when the governing system is, indeed, corrupt or un-just—such sentiments can give voice to the disenfranchised and animate the disimpassioned—too often populism threatens to tear down the cultural and institutional fabric of liberalism that makes mobilization of the dispossessed effective and the forging of a vital consensus possible.

Pragmatism

Just as populism is endemic to American government, so too is its margin-ality. The concern to control the "mischiefs of faction" is at the core of the the nation's founding. Perpetual and heated struggles between citizens would mean that "the *passions* . . . not the *reason*, of the public would sit in judge-ment," Madison argued in the *Federalist Papers*. "But it is the reason, alone, of the public, that ought to control and regulate the government. The passions ought to be controlled and regulated by the government." Madison conceded that factions were inevitable in a free society: "Liberty is to faction, what air is to fire. But it would not be less folly to abolish liberty, which is essential to polit-ical life, because it nourishes faction than it would be to wish the annihilation of air because it imparts to fire its destructive agency." Heated struggle, there-fore, has to be endured; the only recourse is to create institutions and to culti-vate social conditions that might control the consequences of spirited political struggles.[60] A great deal of constitutional scholarship emphasizes the division and separation of powers—as a bulwark against precipitous government ac-tion. Yet is worth recalling that the goal of the Constitution that replaced the highly decentralized Articles of Confederation was to form a government strong enough to control the destructive tendencies of raw and disruptive populism and an ineffectual government. More than two centuries before his debut on Broadway, Hamilton riffed on this fact: "the true test of a good government is its aptitude and tendency to produce a good administration."[61]

Although populism often goes hand in hand with, or exploits, repulsive xenophobic and racist beliefs, populism's defining feature is a distrust of public officials who are viewed as too far removed from those they presume to represent—a vantage point that encourages unprincipled men to sacrifice the interests of the people to feather their own nests. Animating the roar of populist leaders is the widespread—and not unreasonable—fear that the republican government created by the Constitution empowered elites who mistrusted, if they did not scorn, the masses. As much as we may disdain the style and rhetoric of populism, it is important to take seriously the populist's claim that the system is rigged or that a privileged few have power.

Consequently, critics of harsh partisanship should invest faith in pragmatic problem solving cautiously. Politics is about conflict. When leaders and movements try to paper over societal differences and appeal to "common sense" solutions, they disregard, no less than populists, the institutions that are vital for democratic self-government. Indeed, fervent pragmatism might represent a greater danger to the country's vital center. Populists show their hand with moralistic fury; pragmatists ostensibly devote objective analysis and neutral competence to the public interest. In contrast to the raw disruption fomented by populists, it might seem desirable to return to a golden era of cooperation, civility, and a resounding faith in the tools of government management—except that such a by-gone era does not exist.

Indeed, the most ambitious programs that have been interwoven in the fabric of American democracy, such as Social Security, Medicare, and the 1964 Civil Rights Act, were forged amid divisive partisan debate and maneuvers. President Franklin D. Roosevelt (FDR)—the apostle of "bold persistent experimentation"—was, in fact, routinely denounced as a socialist and dictator. While pushing back against these charges, FDR and his political allies trumpeted a militant liberalism that excoriated "economic royalists." The New Deal political order was thus conceived in a harsh partisan environment that did not abate until the post-war years when Eisenhower bestowed bipartisan legitimacy on the welfare and national security states. At the same time, most New Dealers were willing to combine tough partisanship with political maneuvers. As James Q. Wilson recognized, much of the New Deal would have been dead in the water if not for the New Dealers' modus vivendi with professional, material-driven urban machines, which implemented the federal government's new programs.[62] Until the end of his second term, Roosevelt, reluctant to challenge a fragile North-South alliance that he believed was necessary to build a majority Democratic coalition that supported the "economic constitutional order," posed no direct threat to Jim Crow laws in the South, refusing even to support efforts of the National Association for the Advancement of Colored People (NAACP) to enact anti-lynching laws.

Many scholars and pundits who view pragmatism as an essential ingredient for effective government and pluralistic politics must carefully distinguish principled compromise and pragmatism as an end in itself. Nor is principled compromise effective, as Jonathan Rauch has argued, because leaders can capitalize on the "mainstream's acceptance of the give-and-take of transactional politics."[63] There is very little evidence that those most interested and engaged in politics are fervent centrists. Indeed, decades of behavioral research suggests the opposite.[64] We hold that institutions, not public opinion, are necessary to buttress the vital center. Few politicians like to compromise, and fewer still win election on a promise to work the other side of the aisle.[65] But institutional arrangements can make it difficult to construct majority coalitions, so that even presidents and legislatures who promise change are often forced to accept compromise to get things done.

Moreover, defenders of the pragmatic tradition neglect the longer story of party development and coalition building that are the sine qua non of significant change. Legacies of the New Deal and Great Society are heralded as pragmatic solutions to identifiable problems. Yet hindsight clouds just how deeply contentious and ideologically charged those moments were. Transformational change took place because of the enormous efforts exerted by political leaders and their partisan allies, who mixed transactional politics with fraught but effective alliances with passionate movement leaders.[66] As Stephen Skowronek recognizes, the legacies of middle-of-the-roaders are never all that inspiring, or successful: "Historically, no third way has outlasted the president who articulated it. Such leadership efforts have been highly individualized, and the political contests they set up have tended to become radically personalized."[67]

While we sympathize with modern commenters who lament the bold, unrealistic promises that candidates running for office make, there is nothing extraordinary about heated rhetoric on the campaign trail. The country's most transformative presidents all recognized the dilemmas posed by their desire to be great democratic leaders yet still commanded enough authority to navigate the obstacles to fundamental change in a constitutional republic.

In order to leave a legacy of enduring change, America's most important presidents have had to overcome the gravitational pull of constitutional forms without succumbing to the temptation of leading paternalistically.[68] Consequential leadership has had to rely on ideologically charged rhetoric to inspire collective action in the name of something revolutionary. That is hardly the stuff of technocratic problem solving.

Indeed, students of American political development have detailed the myriad ways in which government action is contorted and stifled when pragmatic politicians are at the helm. As Suzanne Mettler has observed, the largest government interventions of the last five decades are actually "submerged" or invisible government policies, enacted by a savvy elite who, constantly running for reelection, are nervous about the image of expanding government.[69] Consequently, few Americans realize just how much government actually does in their day-to-day lives.[70] Likewise, Andrea Louise Campbell and Kimberly Morgan have detailed how extensively American government relies on private corporations and vested interests for the delivery of public services. In order to pass the threshold for effective compromise, politicians distribute government largesse to the well organized.[71] And, most generally, the need to balance programmatic ambition and institutional roadblocks frequently leads Congress to abdicate its responsibility to make the tough choices. Deals made in the spirit of compromise often produce, as Theodore Lowi brilliantly depicted, a set of incoherent and vague instructions to unelected administrators who do the actual work of governing: "At its best the system is a hell of administrative boredom. At its worst, it is a tightly woven fabric of legitimized privilege."[72]

This is not to say that there is no value in expertise. Many of the programs and government services Americans depend on are shaped in important ways by self-styled "pragmatists"—those who were schooled in the art of administration. But we are skeptical that calls to return to a golden era of consensus can temper the bitter partisan divide that fractures the nation. Since the beginning, American politics has required its most consequential leaders to solve the intractable tension built into our system of government between the democratic impulses to inspire, secure equality, and increase participation, and the pragmatists' sensibilities to limit popular control and reduce political conflict to administration.

As such, we identify the origins of contemporary partisan rancor in Franklin Roosevelt's efforts to transcend, rather than navigate, this tension. The expansion of national administrative power—the rise of centralized

government in a country that had stood out among other industrial nations for resisting it—followed from the idea at the heart of the New Deal.
As Franklin Roosevelt argued throughout his long presidency, the Great
Depression and World War II showed that the time had come for the national
government—which was still constrained, if not dominated, by local politics
and a spoils system—to dedicate itself to social welfare programs and national security. And yet, FDR was no technocrat. He lamented the system of
independent regulatory agencies that had sprung up since the end of the 19th
century that owed their allegiance to experts and regulated entities, not popularly elected leaders, namely, the president of the United States.

Yet, as we document, the 1960s marked an era when both distrust of the
government and a passion to expand its responsibilities grew—creating
an impenetrable impasse that neither party could overcome.[73] This ideal
manifested itself most fully in the social causes championed by President
Lyndon Johnson's Great Society. The attempt to realize the Great Society
exposed the pragmatic state's central fault lines, and with violent upheaval
in Vietnam and in the nation's urban core, the hardheaded center that
buttressed the New Deal disintegrated. The 1960s left many social and anti-
war activists feeling alienated from the "establishment"; but they remained
active in government during the 1970s through "public interest" groups
dedicated to remaking, rather than dismantling, administrative politics.
Celebrating "participatory democracy," these public lobbyists gained access to the regulatory process, opened up the courts to further litigation, and
democratized congressional procedures, with the consequence that programmatic liberalism was extended to affirmative action, environmental and
consumer protection, and education.[74] As Paul Pierson argues, these policies
gave rise to an activist and polarized state centered on "a range of profoundly
contentious issues. . . . The character of these issues made compromise difficult and created incentives for polarizing forms of mobilization."[75]

Consequently, by the late 1960s, the center had cracked, the myth of
neutral competence exposed, and the frame of partisanship transformed.
The promise of pragmatic policymaking shifted the locus of party politics
from the states, localities, and Congress to the presidency. The prominent
Democratic Speaker of the House during the 1980s Tip O' Neil coined the
phrase, "All politics was local." In fact, by the end of Ronald Reagan's two
terms, that refrain was confined to the dustbin of history. Democrats and
Republicans depend on presidents and presidential candidates to raise funds,
mobilize grassroots support, articulate the party's message, and advance

party programs through unilateral action.[76] Furthermore, Democrats and Republicans no longer fought over *whether* there should be a large national government, tasked with extensive responsibilities—a struggle that dominated the Roosevelt years. Instead, the parties now were engaged in a battle for the services of the national administrative state forged on the New Deal political order. Conservatives, no less than liberals, as the political scientist Hugh Heclo puts it, became "policy minded," and so they have remained.[77] Put simply, partisanship reflected a populist rejection of New Deal politicking. Conservatives embraced the national security state (transformed into the ubiquitous Homeland Security State in the wake of the 9/11/2001 terrorist attacks on the US Twin Towers and Pentagon)—seeking to uphold what Roosevelt called "Freedom from Fear"—while liberals have devoted more attention to the welfare state—championing what New Dealers dubbed "Freedom from Want."

For all their differences, during the 1960s, both the far left and far right were responses to a bureaucratic New Deal state that appeared to insulate American government from public accountability and to encourage massive indifference in the face of festering problems that perpetuated gross injustices. Although most critics of contemporary partisan rancor blame the Republicans for fracturing America, it was leftists, especially the leaders of the civil rights and anti-war movements, who first threw American politics "off center"—who rejected the working arrangements of the New Deal state for its compromises with racism, with corporate greed, and the imperialism it pursued under the banner of protecting global freedom.[78]

Fast forward 60 years. President Trump appears to mark a reckoning for the bureaucratic torpor of the New Deal state. Consequently, the pendulum between democracy and administration might have swung too far in the other direction—a startling testimony to Lowi's warning that the greatest threat to the modern democratic experiment and its fragmented character, is a plebiscitary politics that promises the "deconstruction of the administration state."[79]

Partisanship

On the one hand, populism threatens to periodically disrupt, if not dismantle, the institutions that can respond to the political, economic, and social problems that citizens want solved. On the other hand, an unreflective commitment to pragmatism and neutral competence undermines popular control and risks cultivating an apathetic citizenry, ripe for exploitation when the experts' plans do not bring what was promised. Accordingly, those who wish to proscribe populism must be mindful that passionate movements do not operate in isolation; they compete within an institutional system that was deliberately designed to moderate populist discontent. The American political party system is a critical intermediary institution that has been tasked with brokering the tension between populism and the "guardrails" that constrain it. For this reason, as much as populist movements have sought to disdain party brokers, they have also fought to change the rules, norms, and procedures governing the two major party organizations.[80] Beginning in the 1960s, attacks on the party "establishment" in the name of democracy have resulted in a more unfiltered partisanship that sharply divides liberals and conservatives. Paradoxically, absent institutions that can constrain populist demands, American politics is now shaped by weak parties and passionate, angry partisanship.[81] Parties were, at one-point, central mediating institutions. Consequently, they played a critical role in maintaining a healthy civic culture during previous periods of populist unrest. Populism is not new, but the hollowed out, institutionally maligned party system that once contained it is.

Madison and the architects of the US Constitution did not view political parties or a party system as essential for moderating the most dangerous passions of self-government; as almost every account of the Constitution's creation makes clear, the framers feared that ongoing conflict between two parties would be more likely to deteriorate into dangerous factionalism that would derogate a free society.[82] Yet no sooner had the new republic come to life than even Madison, noting that the Federalists and Republicans fought over the proper interpretation of the Constitution, conceded that "parties seem[ed] to have a permanent foundation in the variance of political opinions in free states."[83] As we shall see in Chapter 2, the system of ritualized, mass party mobilization that emerged in the early 1800s was an attempt to redefine the relationship of its citizens to the political system— to compensate for the Constitution's failure to cultivate an active and competent citizenry. Echoing this initial debate for the next 200 years, political parties, composing a party system, have captured those variegated impulses of reform and strife and turned them into effective instruments of change. Political parties, mediating between democratic passion and constitutional sobriety, have served to strengthen the democratic potential of the

Constitution while restraining conflict and moderating popular impulses that would destroy it—that would expose citizens to popular demagogues who promise to serve the people by overcoming the gravitational pull of constitutional principles and institutions.

At times, parties have relegated important issues to the sideline of the national conversation, used public resources to maintain their own organizational grip on power, and offered little semblance of choice to an electorate clamoring for a clear vision. Yet precisely because party organizations possess the potential to constrain individual and collective behavior, they can be platforms for consensus building and compromise. Strong parties stand in the way of unbridled ambition by collectively investing an array of independently empowered individuals and the factions they lead with resources. They arbitrate fractious conflict among ambitious actors by channeling their diverse preferences through rules.[84] Consequently, those who desire power and influence often recognize that the party organization is their best, if not only, chance for electoral success.[85]

As independent sites for political contestation, parties have been strongest when they are organizationally diverse and non-centralized.[86] As Daniel DiSalvo documents, the diversity of opinion and contestation within parties is what makes the two-party system as a whole accountable and responsive to changes within the broader public. Non-centralized and loosely structured parties infuse old debates with new ideas, give structure to presidential nominating contests, and devolve power in the Congress to give individual legislators a reason for finding creative solutions to existing problems— problems that emerge because people disagree about what should be done. As institutions with a shared past and a collective future, strong parties can escape the short-term myopia that dominates an individual legislator's focus on the next election campaign. In contrast, Frances Rosenbluth and Ian Shapiro note that when parties are structurally weak, "they might look highly democratic, but they produce coalitions that are held together with money and favors," not principled interests and commitments to the long-term viability of the country.[87]

While not a formal part of the constitutional order, parties and party competition also help to cultivate an active and competent citizenry—a task inadequately provided for in the original constitutional framework of "republican" government. Throughout the course of American political development, parties have been the dominant institutional sites for mediating populist unrest and have often channeled movements' passions into meaningful and sustainable governing reform. They have mobilized voters, given voice to marginalized views, and, as Walter Dean Burnham once noted, served as the "mainsprings of American politics."[88]

Perhaps most important, strong but non-centralized party organizations can constrain presidential ambition. Indeed, the origins of the party system reflected an effort by America's first party builders to ameliorate the despotic potential of unchecked presidential power—and throughout American history executive aggrandizement has been moderated when members of the president's own party have held him accountable.[89] Vital party organizations provide a forum for presidents and their fellow partisans to transcend their own self-interest and to attend to the principles and programs that make collective responsibility meaningful. In contrast, weak parties are nothing more than a collection of personalities and interests, clamoring for power, all eyes set on the next election. By moderating the ambitions of public officials—especially presidents—and by connecting citizens to government institutions, party associations can give politicians and voters a sense of efficacy in a complex political environment with hundreds of independent voices and multiple sites of power. As parties seek to win office, they mobilize the electorate and bring citizens into a political world that isolated individuals can view as distant and threatening.

Strong party organizations thus temper populist unrest by creating an alternative set of incentives for party leaders, potential nominees, and the average citizen. They can transcend the recriminations of any single ambitious individual who desires to supplant collective action—those whom Arthur Schlesinger Jr. called "the political adventurer."[90] Ambitious partisans are coaxed into supporting the institutional vitality of their organization, because no single individual or narrow faction can capture the party label, impose a personal style on its message, or dole out its largesse. The greatest threat to this collective responsibility is a charismatic president who might sacrifice party principle for personal preference—to a cult of personality. But collective partisanship forces potential contenders for high office to recognize that in order to climb the ranks of power, they must demonstrate their aptitude for and loyalty to forging a party coalition.

During times of limited social and economic conflict, party competition might devolve into conflict of interests and personalities; yet during times of heated conflict, which are inevitable in a healthy democracy, partisans find themselves engaged in a common enterprise, animated by a passionate democratic spirit on behalf of their team. When parties filter partisanship, that energy is channeled into campaigns and elections that foster debate and allow for resolution. Yet when unfiltered, that passion sharply fractures the country. Rather than a contest over party principle, contestants distrust their opponents' motives—the opposition is perpetually vilified and demeaned. As Schlozman and Rosenfeld note, this is precisely the dynamic now on display every four years. "The process of nominating a president . . . serves not as a celebration of party," they write, "but as an extended opportunity to bash it, without the parties themselves, or anybody on their behalf, offering principled responses. . . . The primaries and caucuses that now select the delegates provide months-long fodder for candidates and their supporters who feel aggrieved by the process, and parties . . . rarely stick up for the rules that they themselves have chosen. Regardless of whether the party still typically decides the nominee, it wins few friends in the deciding."[91]

Viable parties occupy the middle ground between moderation and agitation. As contenders in a party system, these organizations reject fanaticism and dogmatic certainty as readily as apathy and disinterest. Civic engagement for civic engagement's sake is not enough. Given the high stakes of any election, citizens should be able to reasonably demand that the field of partisan battle be waged more on competing principles than personal recrimination. Principled debate can inspire political participation. But when leaders are demonized as traitors and every decision is discussed as if it poses an existential threat to this diverse, complex society, the vital center cannot hold.

Parties as collective, accountable organizations have provided a critical institutional foundation that makes the vital center possible. But this does not mean that we should lament the passing of some idyllic era of political parties. Just as there is no golden era of pragmatic centrism, so the hope to return to an idyllic party contestation is a chimera. To return to the "smoke-filled backrooms" that dominated American politics until the New Deal in an era of welfare-state capitalism would risk government corruption on an unprecedented scale—something resembling a National Tammany Hall.

However, the origins and development of party politics helps us see that foundational conflicts in American politics have involved lively, sometimes fierce struggles between political parties. Schlesinger's ideal of the vital center presupposes the party system that arose with the forging of the New Deal political order.[92] But this was not a system without its own internal tensions. Indeed, as we trace in Chapter 3, the developmental trajectory set off by the New Deal state weakened the constraining effects of mediated partisanship and highly structured party competition. Ironically, many of the reformist

impulses that gave rise to the modern welfare state—most notably, the celebration of an executive-centered stewardship that transcends parties—also
work to undermine it. The tension between administration and politics
sheds light on the demise of the vital center and the profound challenge we
face in recovering it.

Like Schlesinger, most contemporary scholars of political parties in the
United States have not reconciled such partisanship with a commitment to
the party *system*. Indeed, students of America's party structure often emphasize an institutional political science, more or less detached from the ideological battles waged at any one moment. Some of the finest scholars of political
parties can define their institutional dynamic, speak about their incentives,
and predict voting coalitions all without making a single reference to the
ideas that animate them.[93] And yet, America's two-party system was born of
an *idea* to preserve a particular way of self-government—one that would animate localized and highly mobilized politics that remained within the pur-
view of the American public. As such, the traditional decentralized two-party
system in the United States was in tension with—indeed, an obstacle to—the
development of the New Deal state. By tracing the history of party development through the New Deal and up to the fundamental rift in the 1960s, our
task is to show how the battle of defining a vital center in American political life necessarily implicates a fight over the very "idea of a party system."[94]
At the heart of this inquiry is a deep, probing search of the vital center's demise—an erosion of liberal democratic norms and institutions that has accelerated since the 1960s with the fundamental challenges to America's
two-party system.

Outline of the Book

In subsequent chapters we trace the major developments that have played
out over the 20th and 21st centuries that have tilted the inherent tension between institutional constraints and raw factionalism too far in the direction
of an unmoderated strain of populism. To be sure, consensus-driven politics—or a politics of constraint—does not mean tranquil or unexciting politics. Quite the contrary: the vital center was supposed to be a "fighting faith."
It was, however, a shared faith—a politics of affirmation and a common field
of disagreement on which both liberals and conservatives could wage a contest for America's constitutional soul. It thus had boundaries and a common

belief in how to play the game and, most important, what the objective was. The threats to the party system that have subsequently challenged the pragmatic center of American politics lack this democratic spirit. While, the partisan rancor that roils contemporary politics, for all its ugliness, had its origins in idealistic, insurgent assaults from the left and the right during the 1960s, parties have lost the legitimacy necessary to organize debate, present new ideas, and forge consensus from within.

In celebrating the institutional logic of the Constitution, Madison referred to the complex checks and balances of the Constitution as a system of "successive filtrations." While the formation of the party system represented an effort to buttress the more democratic features of the Constitution, partisan contest reworked rather than eliminated the way popular passions were regulated. Parties are not the only institution that mediates between populism and the Constitution, and they are not the only filtering institution under attack. Neither the establishment, nor especially the anti-establishment, defend the myriad institutions that give structure to our collective causes and restrain us from our own worst inclinations; the media, public schools, organized religion, and law enforcement are all derided as vestiges of privilege and unearned deference.[95]

The bulk of this book is occupied with understanding how the decline of the two-party system has led to the erosion of a democratic center since the mid-20th century. It is a partial project, because recovering the vital center demands a reconsideration and reconstitution of all institutions. But taking account of an institution that is so critical to the framers' imperative of taming vicious factionalism might shed important light on where to move next. The task of renewing our shared commitment to political contestation based on competing political principles, where each side recognizes that it is not always right, is a daunting and bracing challenge.

In Chapter 2, we offer a more detailed account of the American party system through time. We argue that, structured accordingly, party leaders responded to populist protest without allowing it to erode the central pillars of constitutional government that made that response efficacious and sustainable. Many scholars see the era of current partisanship as in tension with some older variant. While true, it is more precise to say older variants. There was no single party system of an older era. The structure of governmental power and party organization has been in flux since the beginning. Indeed, as we show, populist fervor is the mainspring impulse giving rise to new forms of party contestation and demands for government. Populism is endemic to the American experiment, but so too were organized parties that responded to its demands. We survey the course of party development through the 1930s and illustrate the complicated but fruitful relationship between populist protest and party organization that made American politics responsive, but responsibly so. Each of the cases we survey—anti-Masonry in the 1820s, agrarian populism in the late 19th century, and the demagogic leadership of Father Charles Coughlin during the Great Depression—takes place in a time period prior to the full-scale reconstruction of the party system in the late 1930s. Historians have recognized the common features that connect these populist revolts, but scholars of American political development have paid scant attention to the ways they intersected with and transformed the mass party system.

In Chapter 3, we continue the story of populist protest and partisanship to explore the development of an executive-centered partisanship during the later parts of the New Deal. This transformation deserves special attention, because the developments accompanying Roosevelt's remaking of the presidency and Democratic Party so weakened party organizations that it became possible for modern populists to capture governing institutions. The breaking apart of the vital center is related to the emergence of the New Deal party system that was a consequence of, and further advanced, the nationalization of politics and correspondingly, heightened expectations for presidential leadership. But the New Deal party system did not come from nowhere—it was a consequence of a fight over the nature of party government that stretches back to the Constitutional Convention. It helped to inspire its own modern-day Constitutional Convention, which took the form of a 1950 report issued from academic political scientists. *Toward a More Responsible Two-Party System* is often viewed as a blueprint for a post New Deal effort to build a more democratic, party system, and it reflected the country's emerging demands for complete political equity and inclusion.[96] And yet, while many may see this report and the institutional reforms that sprang from it as the beginning of our collective impasse, we interpret it as a post-war call to strengthen collective organizations that might remedy the most dangerous tendencies of the New Deal political order. Far from writing a new rulebook that has magnified populist insurgency, our interpretation takes seriously their early diagnosis of executive-centered partisanship. Any attempt to account for the joining and breaking apart of the vital center must also consider what these early architects of the new, modern party system sought to change, where they succeeded, and why their handiwork came under attack during the 20th century.

Chapter 4 traces the splintering of the Democratic Party beginning in the 1960s with the rise of the "New Left" and the abandonment of its southern constituency to displacement of economic and national security issues by the prepossessing causes of civil rights and anti-imperialism. Beyond these concerns for social justice, the "new" liberals transformed the presidential selection process and the way both parties operated in Congress. Most significant, between the late 1960s and early 1970s, the convention system, which empowered local and state party leaders and national public officials to nominate presidential candidates, came under full-scale attack. As in the larger survey of populist protest in American political development, our goal is not to evaluate or approve of various causes that gave the left its moral force. We are interested in the ways the party system's response to those causes, largely through the vanguard of an empowered White House office, led to the denigration of the Democratic Party as a collective organization.

Chapter 5 analyzes the mass discontent that has weakened the Republican "establishment," culminating in the rise of Donald Trump as the party's nominee and his election as president. Trump's ascendance, especially, highlights the paradoxical development of weak parties and heightened partisanship. For as much as Trump was disruptive inside a party he only recently joined, he just as often echoed the commitments of militant Republican partisans when it came to transforming—or "deconstructing," as his controversial political ally Stephen Bannon put it—the administrative state. Rather than dismantle the executive-centered administrative state forged by the New Deal political order, Trump sought to redeploy the instruments of state power in protecting conservative priorities, such as law and order, homeland security, and "earned entitlements," that have defined Republican administrations since the 1960s. We trace Trump's historic rise inside the Republican Party to a similar internal splintering that has affected Democrats since the 1960s. Conservative activists, too, scorned the vital center. In the wake of 1964's insurgent presidential campaign, that of Senator Barry Goldwater (R-AZ), they joined the attack on party organizations. Viewing partisan insurgency as a double-edged sword that could cut in a conservative as well as a liberal direction, they sought to expose the New Deal state for its failure to uphold private property (or as Herbert Hoover put it, "rugged individualism"), to protect "middle class" values, or to effectively fight communism.

In Chapter 6, we consider what all these historical developments have meant for our current polarized moment focusing, in particular, on the presidencies of Barack Obama and Donald Trump. There was a time when scholars debated whether the hyper-partisanship and bitterness of American politics was a Washington Beltway phenomenon, implying that most American voters occupied the proverbial center of the bell-shaped curve. This may have been the case once—perhaps until the Bush 43 and Obama presidencies, when Bush's contested victory over Vice President Al Gore, the September 11 attacks, and the Great Recession arrived to exacerbate the divisions between Red and Blue America. But recent public opinion polls show that the partisan divide has become all-encompassing. Not only has political rancor increased inside the Beltway, but Republicans and Democrats also have become anchored in distinct regions, states, and communities.[97]

The vital center, eroded from political forces within the Democratic and Republican parties, faced serious challenges during the Trump administration, as the fusion between presidentialism and populist fervor reached its apex. And then, as we were putting the final touches on this book, the United States was infested in the spring of 2020 by a massive world pandemic—COVID-19—which closed a large majority of schools, subjected most of the country to stay at home orders, and shuttered the economy. Many scholars and pundits speculated that the worst national disaster since the Great Depression might change everything, and for a few weeks, the sharp partisan divisions in the country were suspended, with Democrats and Republicans quickly rolling out two huge relief bills in the hope of stanching the effects of the crisis. It soon became clear, however, that the political response to the pandemic further aggravated rather than resolved the partisan warfare that divided Red from Blue America.

If that was not enough, as the coronavirus threatened to overwhelm the public health system and plunge the economy into a deep recession, the nation was further tested in the spring when four Minneapolis policemen murdered George Floyd, an unarmed African American suspected of using a counterfeit $20 bill in a convenience store. There ensued a heated struggle in the streets over policing and whether the demonstrations against systemic racism, which while mostly peaceful were marred by looting and arson, were expressions of righteous anger or, as the president defiantly insisted, a sign that law and order was threatened by radical agitation. With the nation roiled by the pandemic and mass protests against police brutality, the Trump administration, following the playbook of executive-centered partisanship, forged ahead with its broader agenda: extending restrictions on immigration, continuing efforts to undermine the Affordable Care Act, and intensifying its assault on the mythical deep state. The dangerous cultural and geographic splintering of Americans by party, which endured through a national crisis of the highest order, is a testament to just how weak the vital center has become.

In Chapter 7, we seek to come to terms with the denouement of the Trump presidency: the noxious efforts of a defeated president, citing specious evidence and bizarre conspiracy theories, to retain power and to incite his rabid supporters to storm the Capitol, making clear just how difficult it will be to repair the fabric of America's constitutional democracy. In the aftermath of the assault on the nation's capital and the First Hundred Days of Joe Biden's presidency, we offer some reflections for recovering a vital center in a new and highly treacherous political time. Our argument for strengthening the party system does not call for a return to the halcyon days of the early '60s, but stem from the careful historical consideration of why things fell apart and how America has changed over the past half century. As it is rooted in a defense of American liberalism, broadly understood—one that conservatives and liberals can embrace—the idea of a vital center should be of interest to both Democrats and Republicans. The development of mass parties in the 1820s and 1830s made political representation in a large republic possible. Predicated on fears of demagoguery, civic apathy, and majority tyranny, the theoretical underpinnings of the American two-party system offer clues for restoring American democracy's vital center.

The fracturing of our polity is only the latest chapter in an ongoing story of America's quest for national identity—a battle for the soul of American democracy that threatens what is still, in the history of politics, a very young and audacious experiment in the project of *self*-government. At a time when Americans make ever more demands on government and trust it less, it remains very uncertain that they and their representatives might once again come to this realization. But a democracy that is both enlivened and tempered by strong party organizations can help the United States reestablish that sense of personal, political constraint. The Declaration of Independence, as Lincoln recognized in his Gettysburg Address, is our common ground. But Lincoln also recognized that protecting the "jewel of liberty" required strong party organizations and adherence to constitutional principles, without which an appeal to public opinion was impossible. To restore the balance between populism and constitutional constraints— amid historic struggles over America's national identity—requires that we give new thought to the never-ending challenge of forging consensus amid the bitter conflicts that awaken and threaten democracy—that we "think institutionally."[98] Only then will our political leaders be able to collectively celebrate the virtues of prudence and the power of institutional constraint. Only then can we begin the practical but exalted task of renewing the idea of the American party system that may bring about a "new birth of freedom" in the nation.

2

The American Party System and
Populist Upheaval

Mediating Anger and Discontent, 1800–1945

Partisanship has always been rancorous. People do not engage in politics to hold hands and celebrate consensus. There has never been a golden age of American politics when "the people" marched forward with unanimous affirmation of a leader and program. Free society gives rise to clashing interests, sectional struggles, and polarizing conflicts over domestic and world problems. Citizens engage in politics to fight for their understanding of a just society and to find common cause with fellow partisans to achieve electoral success. Their vision might be noble; their wisdom might be the truth; but it is never uncontested. Partisanship is a discordant drama.

Yet, while partisanship has always been acrimonious, parties themselves have looked different over time. Party organizations have had different structures: the rules they impose on fellow partisans have changed; the power given to party leaders to set a unified course has fluctuated; and the parties' relations with a "living" constitutional order have been transformed. Most scholars and historians focus on the ideological substance of the parties as a way of understanding this change: the Jeffersonian Democrats as compared to Roosevelt's Democratic Party, or Lincoln's Republicanism as compared to Reagan's. This reveals much about America's political history and the centrality of party organization to that history. Nevertheless, in this chapter, our focus is on the institutions themselves. The fundamental problem of partisanship in contemporary American politics is not that it is more divisive. The problem is that parties, as institutions, are no longer effective at channeling that dissent toward productive and accountable governing outcomes.

As we made clear in the opening chapter, populist movements are endemic to democratic government. Throughout American history, populist uprisings have been important democratic movements that address political and economic injustices. At other times, they have clearly cut the other direction. While the substantive differences between these types of populist movements is intriguing history, it does not offer much guidance in diagnosing the country's current populist moment. However, in looking at the institutional structure of the party system itself and the various ways in which party competition has channeled populist discontent, we argue that this further reveals the uniqueness and problem of the current party system's structure: a fusion of presidential prerogative tied to a nationalized and highly mobilized partisan base. Equally important, probing the deep historical roots of populist insurgency might offer valuable lessons for ameliorating our Manichean politics.

In contrast to our present moment, there are periods when the American party system constrained the most dangerous tendencies of democracy. The non-centralized parties, which dominated American politics up to the 1960s, while closed off to many parts of the electorate, nevertheless tended to moderate conflict in society and government. They were diverse institutions—ideologically, regionally, and professionally—that waged hard-fought battles for voters' hearts and minds in cities and non-urban areas, on the coasts and in the heartland. Within each party, politicians collided in a war of ideas for the public's imagination. Ambitious office seekers wanting to control the party had to cajole, persuade, and work through the rank and file, learning the skills of coalition management and artful persuasion. More important, there was little semblance of "control." Dissent was the norm, because no loyal partisan owed their power to the authority of a single leader. As a result, these complex organizations erected multiple barriers against petty factionalism and demagogic leaders, even as they remained open to the periodic swells of democratic anger that threatened to upend that system. Partisanship was rancorous, but it was not unfiltered. Parties did not always play a salutary role—a point we stress below, in particular, when we discuss the intransigence of the party system at the end of the 20th century. But parties were independent forces that constrained political actors when they launched antinomian assaults on the country's political and governing institutions; they were not vessels for populist warfare.

By comparison, contemporary partisanship is unfiltered, devoid of the institutional complexity that marked earlier periods. This has led to a paradoxical combination of angry partisanship, weak parties, and strong presidents. We will document in the next few chapters how the 1960s unleashed a wave of unchecked movement politics that succeeded in weakening party organizations. But to better understand "Sixties Civics,"[1] we must first consider the relationship between parties and populism at earlier stages of party development. In this chapter, we consider three cases of populism that the party system mediated: the Anti-Mason movements of the 1830s and 1840s, the "Populist" agrarian protest of the 1880s and 1890s, and the demand for economic nationalism in the 1930s. Each of these movements represents a strain of American populism for its substance and style: although they claimed to speak for the common man, they never had majority support; and while their particular grievances varied, they shared an uncompromising perception that a scheming ruling elite purposefully kept them subjugated and disempowered. There is no gainsaying that American politics has often been dominated by self-serving elites. However, these movements strained against individual freedom, the country's constitutional norms, and, most important, the role robust party organizations played in organizing political life at the time. Anti-Masonry threated to eviscerate the country's fundamental commitment to cultural diversity and economic mobility; the Populists envisioned an expansive national government that would cut against if not destroy the local communal bonds that first animated their grassroots movement; and the cries of injustice heard throughout the 1930s—none louder than those resonating from Father Charles Coughlin—sketched out a pathway that resembled the denigration of liberal government in Italy, Germany, and France—and the rise of a fascist state. Nevertheless, in each case, party organization tempered populism's potentially degenerative pathology.

In suggesting that the populist impulses of these movements were moderated, we recognize that in each instance there was some legitimate claim against the prevailing power structure. However, we argue that in these particular cases, parties played a stabilizing and mediating role, so that partisan organizations and government institutions were reformed rather than decimated. Perhaps the best way to make sense of how "gatekeepers" respond to populist pressure is to recognize the institutional change that these leaders forced on the party organizations themselves.[2] Each of the major party reformers— Martin Van Buren, Woodrow Wilson, and Franklin D. Roosevelt—long-recognized by historians and political scientists alike, formed their views of the party system in the midst of populist revolt. Throughout this chapter, we present primary evidence to demonstrate that there was a direct connection between their proposed reforms and their reflections on the past. Anti-Masonry helped to inspire the creation of the decentralized mass-party system that dominated the mid- to late 1800s; the Populist movement was at the vanguard of the Progressive Era's democratization of the party system at the turn of the 20th century; and as we explore in Chapter 3, FDR's party reform efforts followed from his own engagement with populist furor during his first term. Yet, for all the change that took place over the first 150 years of American history, parties nevertheless possessed the power to respond to populist demands and to maintain a civic culture of trust and widespread political efficacy. In short, unlike the nationalized and centralized party organizations that emerged after World War II and which fueled 1960s-era politics, the party organizations we survey here reconciled populist fervor to institutional features that safeguarded the fragility of American liberalism. In other words, institutions helped encourage party leaders and citizens to respond to popular protest and to sustain the constitutional experiment that limited the demands of an unchecked majority.

Institutional Development: The Fusing of Populism and Partisanship

Although the US Constitution says nothing about the place or purpose of political parties, the periodic battles over the meaning of the Constitution have often centered on the role party organizations play in the republic. Over the past 230-plus years of the Constitution's history, one thing has remained constant: those seeking to change, reform, or restore the nation's governing commitments have sought to do so by reorganizing how political parties operate. As political parties lie at the heart of America's major political developments, changing the form of the party system—how candidates are selected, how the parties structure themselves, how the president relates to his fellow partisans in Congress and the states—produces a different type of politics. In the 19th century, the goal of the party system was to maintain America's commitment to state and local government—to protect a type of politics rooted in place and related to the different social and economic conditions of a small community. The industrial revolution, which advanced a dramatic concentration of economic power, appeared to undercut America's decentralized party system. Indeed, the Progressive movement—excoriating corporate greed, monopoly, and the exploitation of workers—was above all an attack on the localized, patronage-based parties that posed an obstacle to national administrative power that would control national economic forces. Far from enhancing civic life, Progressives argued, party

"bosses" corrupted it. This assault on traditional party organizations eventually gave rise to a more national, programmatic, and presidency-centered
partisanship.

The rise and fall of party orders has not been haphazard. The development of organized political party competition during the Jacksonian era was
constructed by savvy political leaders during the first half of the 19th century
who recognized the defects of a Constitution that discouraged the formation
of strong majority "factions." The party system arose from an effort to forge
a more active and competent citizenry—an objective at the heart of the subsequent stages of party development. This is not to suggest that change in
American politics is produced wholesale. Political leaders must work within
a system already defined by vested interests and entrenched institutions.
And, in order to convince those actors to join a reform effort—often at risk
of losing their own privileged position—elements of the old system must be
retained.[3] It is for this reason that the development of executive-centered
partisanship has been decades in the making. It is also for this reason that
we can turn to history to imagine alternative arrangements of power—to see
how variation in party organizations has intersected with a recurrent strain
of populist revolt and protest.

Populist upheavals have significantly changed the way that decision-
making authority is distributed within the party organizations. Parties form
because ambitious individuals want to secure elected office. Consequently,
the arrangement of governing institutions also matters for understanding
how party leaders and party activists behave. In considering both the control of party organizations and the control of governing institutions, there
are many ways in which political power has been distributed. Most generally,
however, power is either centralized or decentralized. Power is centralized
when it is in the hands of a limited set of interests, subject to few checks on
their authority, and exercised by those who tend to agree on fundamental
issues and strategy. Alternatively, power can be dispersed within an organization so that many independent interests have the capacity and authority
to make decisions, often at odds with one another but always in response
to other empowered groups or individuals within the collectivity. How governing institutions and parties are organized and interact determine how
party organizations mediate populist unrest. In American political history,
we have witnessed four possible configurations between the government and
party (Figure 1), each yielding different forms of populist discontent and dis-
tinctive responses to these uprisings.

Control of Party Organizations

		Centralized Control	Decentralized Control
Control of Governing Institutions	Centralized Control	Executive-Centered Partisanship (Post–1960s) and the Threat to the Vital Center	New Deal Partisanship (1920–1940) and the Threat of Economic Nationalism
	Decentralized Control	"King Caucus" (1820–1840) and the Threat of Anti-Masonry	The State of "Courts and Parties" (1865–1900) and the Threat of Agrarian Protest

Figure 1 Distributions of Power Within Party Organizations and Governing Institutions

Although established during an era of state and local government supremacy, the first party organizations were noted for their relatively high degree of centrality. The selection of presidential nominees was controlled by an insulated cadre of congressional officials who presided over isolated and elitist cliques of elected officials in their respective states. Beginning in the 1820s, populist movements roiled this early party system with repeated challenges to the government's legitimacy. Consequently, parties were reformed during the 1830s and 1840s; this reduced congressional control over party life, but it also established a multitude of independent party-fiefdoms, or machines. Paradoxically, the most decentralized form of party and governmental organization was also the most indifferent to populist protest. At first glance, this is puzzling because it has been argued that this era of decentralized parties was one of effective popular mobilization.[4] However, in a constitutional system of separated and divided powers, these highly decentralized party organizations permitted a single coalition to dominate the levers of power in a particular state or city, and to use governmental authority to protect itself from public pressure, especially, and most notoriously, in the former states of the Confederacy.

At the end of the 19th century, the Populist Movement—the trademark term given to the collection of farmers' organizations and political challenges centered in the South and Midwest—launched an assault on the regnant localized party machinery. Although it failed to dislodge deeply entrenched political machines, certain causes of the Populist crusade influenced mainstream political discourse, once again pressuring party leaders to reform their own selection rules and render political elites more responsive to popular pressure. After the Populist movement fizzled following the election of 1896, a new, Progressive movement seized the momentum and leveraged a partially reformed party system to centralize elements of the American constitutional order—transforming, most importantly, the capacities and expectations placed on the American presidency. Consequently, when populism reared its head once again in the aftermath of a global economic depression, it fell to President Franklin Roosevelt (FDR) to temper its dissonance. Roosevelt, with the support of key party leaders such as James Farley, built an ideologically diverse coalition that responded to the public's demand for government action while remaining sensitive to the enduring place of state and local governments in American political life. As Barry Karl observed about the limits of the New Deal state, "Local government and community control remain at the heart of the most intuitive conceptions of American democracy, even though they may also represent bastions of political corruption and locally condoned injustice."[5]

In the sections that follow, we explore the tense political dynamics that have routinely pitted the governing elite against populist insurgents. While it is common to describe the development of party organization as monotonic, or ever democratizing, we evaluate the change in more precise terms—one period was not more or less democratic than another. Rather, different institutional arrangements created different political incentives for leaders and movements seeking to capture power. Within each institutional context, there are virtues and vices. The vital center is somewhere in between.

The Founding and Unraveling of the First Party System (1800–1840)

It took less than a decade from the ratification of the Constitution—the "Constitution Against Parties," as Richard Hofstadter described it—for party factions to develop in the new governing order. This is surprising since the "compound republic," as Madison termed the Union, was supposed to prevent the rise of party government. The complicated amalgam of different represented interests in a large and diverse society—with the people themselves, state legislatures, and the Electoral College all selecting representatives to the federal government—was supposed to make it nearly impossible, the framers thought, for a strong national party to impose its will on officeholders or society.

Ironically, James Madison—the chief architect of the Constitution against parties—decided that partisan opposition was necessary to strengthen the foundation of republican principles, just eight years after the new government began. The country's first great national party was therefore founded as an attempt to recover that "original" American ideal of republican government. During George Washington's two terms in office, with the able support of Treasury Secretary Alexander Hamilton, the first president began to establish an important role for the federal government in domestic and foreign affairs. To Madison, and his fellow Virginian, Thomas Jefferson, it seemed as though Hamilton's economic plans, especially his proposal for a national bank, and his effective advocacy of Washington's exercise of executive prerogative in foreign affairs—most notably in defense of the first president's unilateral proclamation of neutrality in the war between France and Great Britain—threatened the diverse fabric of American life that Madison prescribed as a critical ingredient of a moderate democracy. These initiatives, they feared, would establish national institutions and policies that exceeded the constitutional powers of the new government, thus subordinating the states and legislative institutions to the national executive, undermining popular sovereignty. Madison had played a leading part in crafting the new government's system of federalism and checks and balances with the idea that "pure democracy" would encourage a raw and disruptive factionalism that would ultimately lead to majority despotism. But Hamilton's centralizing ambitions—and the fact that no strong voices emerged to oppose them—focused his concerns on the mischief of minority factions. A detached, listless citizenry, he now saw, was vulnerable to the machinations of a centralizing, oligarchic minority that had captured the presidency.

The two Virginians, Jefferson and Madison, thus formed an alliance to arouse public opinion in defense of their republican principles—the first of what would become many attempts to return power to the people and save the American experiment in self-government. Together, Madison and Jefferson built a national coalition from myriad opposition groups which had emerged to oppose the new government. Within the small towns and county seats that dotted the American countryside, various clubs and organizations had formed to express their discontent by circulating essays and publishing fierce and scathing newspaper articles opposed to Washington and Hamilton. Increasingly, Madison came to believe that republican government depended on the civic and voluntary associations in local communities, which these clubs seemed to nourish.[6] Absent an animated citizenry, Madison and his political allies warned, the federal government would become vulnerable to a program of "consolidation," the very political disease the Constitution's opponents—the Anti-Federalists—had foretold. Madison and Jefferson helped these detached groups to join ranks and form a new Democratic-Republican party, while their opponents responded and formed their own nascent political party, the Federalists. When Washington's successor, John Adams, began to prosecute political dissenters under the authority of the Alien and Sedition Acts, deep concern turned into alarm. Party government was born.

Still, the initial factionalism that roiled the new nation was short-lived, and intentionally so. Madison and Jefferson's Democratic-Republican party was a faction intended to end factionalism. Once the enemies of popular rule were discredited and removed from the halls of power, they hoped the Democratic-Republican Party might wither away. However, when Jefferson became president in the modern world's first peaceful transition of power in 1801, the "Revolution of 1800," partisan division had already so poisoned the well of American political life that the new president struggled to restore national harmony. Jefferson sought in earnest to dampen, rather than exploit, the bitter partisan divisions that roiled the country.[7] In his first inaugural address—an utterance he considered hardly less important than his draft of the Declaration of Independence—he called on all citizens to recognize that "we are all republicans, we are all federalists," thus reminding Americans that their shared commitment to constitutional government transcended their partisan disputes.[8] And, in some ways, Americans heeded Jefferson's call for reconciliation; by the end of his successor James Madison's tenure (1817), the Federalist party had effectually ceased to exist, having put up no opposition against James Monroe's presidential election. When the French observer Alexis de Tocqueville visited America for nine months in 1830–31, he remarked that there were no *great* parties engaged in meaningful ideological struggles. "This is the time of intrigues and *small* parties," Tocqueville observed. "America has had great parties; today they no longer exist: it has gained much in happiness, but not in morality."[9] Tocqueville saw disagreement, but not the type of grand struggle that characterized the battle between the Democratic-Republicans and the Federalists.

It would appear that organized party dispute had ended almost as soon as it had begun; indeed, scholars refer to this period of political history as the

"Era of Good Feelings." Yet the complete triumph of the Jeffersonians did not give rise to a renewal of the Constitution-against-Parties, resting on a stronger republican foundation. Rather, as Tocqueville recognized, this so-called Era of Good Feelings gave birth to a new form of petty factionalism agitated by regional interests and personal rivalries, which the parties failed to control. Party politics remained a critical force in American life, helping leaders organize support for and opposition to America's war with Great Britain (the War of 1812), in routing the ruling establishment following the 1819 economic depression, and in organizing new social reform movements, notably those led by still disenfranchised women in the areas of penal reform, temperance, and abolition. However, the formal party organizations that emerged from Jefferson and Madison's institutional creation grew highly insulated from public pressure. Family dynasties and elitist "juntos" controlled organized political life from Capitol Hill all the way down to City Hall. In sum, the party system was not a system of competing parties that mobilized voters and cultivated lifelong loyalties; it was a system defined by personal loyalties, unprincipled debate, and vindictive electoral warfare on politically privileged families. At the national level, the centralization of party control defied public accounatablity and diminished the legitimacy of governing institutions. With the collapse of the Federalist Party in the mid-1810s, almost all these disputes took place internally, within the Democratic-Republican Party. Since Jefferson's selection of Madison to be his successor, members of Congress gradually assumed the role of picking candidates for office, including the presidency, and set the agenda through an unopposed, informal assembly of national leaders—excoriated as the reign of "King Caucus." Politics was insulated and structured to keep divisive issues off the table, bottling them up until they erupted.

As personal memories of the American Revolution faded, a new generation of politicians took hold of the country's animating, democratic ethos, but the party system, which had mutated from the principled contests between Jefferson and Hamilton, proved especially inept at capturing and filtering the demands of this renewed popular energy. Indeed, less than a generation after the country had been fractured by the "Revolution of 1800," America was embroiled in another constitutional crisis—a controversy aroused by the 1824 presidential contest, which once again featured a deadlocked Electoral College, this time because four ambitious politicians claimed the mantle of the Democratic-Republican Party and refused to drop out of the race: John Quincy Adams of Massachusetts, James Monroe's secretary of state, came in second with 84 electoral votes; Monroe's secretary of the Treasury, William Crawford, of Georgia, was the nominee of the Democratic-Republican caucus, whose dominance of the presidential selection process was no longer accepted, and came in third with 41 electoral votes; Henry Clay, the favorite son of Kentucky and powerful Speaker of the House, was fourth with 37 votes; and Tennessee's Andrew Jackson, the hero of the Battle of New Orleans, received the most electoral votes, but with 99, fell short of the 131 needed for a majority and election. For the second time in 24 years, a presidential election was decided not by the Electoral College but by the House of Representatives; and once again elite maneuvers within the House resulted in a highly controversial verdict.

This was not a controversy, like the contest between Jefferson and Adams, rooted in principle; rather, it was agitated by opportunism. Under the 12th Amendment, when any candidate fails to secure a majority of electoral votes, the House of Representatives chooses the president from among the three highest vote getters. This procedure eliminated Clay as a candidate. If the 14 delegations from the states in which Jackson finished either first or second only to Clay in the election had supported the Tennessean, he would have become president. But Clay used the influence he still had with his fellow representatives to help secure Adams's election. The dispute stirred by the election was further aroused by its aftermath: Adams's selection of Henry Clay as secretary of state, which the Jacksonians condemned as a "corrupt bargain" to thwart the will of the people. The charge of conspiracy was unfounded. Clay and Jackson knew and respected each other, and both were National Republicans, who prescribed expanding the role of the federal government, rather than Old Republicans like Jackson, who inclined toward a strict construction of the Constitution. Adding salt to the country's wounds, the president's first State of the Union address, which proposed an active role for the national government in the economy and society, was in stark contrast to Jefferson's principles of local self-government, thus aggravating the fractious rivalries that shattered the general harmony of the Era of Good Feelings. The entirety of Adam's presidency operated in the shadow of Jackson's attempts to wrest the presidency from him in the next election.

The debacle of the 1824 presidential election was just one indication of the party system's dramatic failures. Within the states—where most American governance took place—populist insurgency, most notably, a burgeoning Anti-Masonic movement, further threatened to disrupt the new constitutional order. Yet, even as the earlier party organization centralized, strengthening the populists' claims and feeding their protest, the decentralized nature of governing authority thwarted the populists' most dangerous ambitions, by giving party leaders a chance to respond and re-structure American politics.

The Threat of Anti-Masonry

The Anti-Masonic movement arose in the 1820s in the northern United States to champion the causes of popular democracy and rural egalitari-anism. It contributed significantly to the animus against economic and polit-ical privilege that historians associate with the rise of Jacksonian Democracy; but its supporters were obsessed with the conspiracy and antinomian fervor that distinguishes populist uprisings.

Anti-masonic insurgency arose amid developments during the first three decades of the 19th century that aroused hard challenges to the pre-vailing political elite and the party system that reinforced political ine-quality throughout the country. Economically, the American marketplace blossomed, and the country's merchants and farmers burst onto the global trading scene with unconstrained opportunity. Profiting from a revolution in transportation technologies and government investments, the American entrepreneur was no longer confined to his local marketplace but instead encountered a world of potential consumers. A real sense of social mobility permeated the nation's heartland, except in the South, where the growth and spread of chattel slavery was as valuable as nearly all the land in the expanded United States.[10] Jefferson's purchase of the Louisiana territory doubled the size of the country, and westward expansion reinforced the democratizing spirit of the age, as White Americans escaped the trappings of elite rule and tradition simply by setting off west to create their own communities. These jarring dislocations helped spawn a religious revival throughout the country, and a new middle class further transformed the expectations and roles placed on women, who turned toward their communities with ambitious plans to curb alcoholism, reform prisons, and abolish slavery.

Yet, within this democratizing context, state party leaders succeeded in consolidating their power, mimicking the divisive machinations that the country witnessed in 1824. To be sure, the debilitating effects of party cen-tralization would have been greater if not for the country's prevailing con-stitutional structure that limited the scope of federal activity. Federalism, in other words, provided a partial solution to the insularity of "King Caucus" and the national party system. Nevertheless, for much of the early 1800s, true competition did not exist between parties in the states, as strong leaders snuffed out ambitious challengers or small-town heroes seeking to take down the ruling political establishment. Like "King Caucus," individual state-level parties maintained monopolistic control of state governing institutions and the nomination processes that structured elections.[11] Scholars have often overlooked these anti-democratic tendencies in the age of expanding democracy. But, behind the scenes, as Kathleen Kutolowski has documented, "while party leaders adopted egalitarian rhetoric and new, modernizing electoral tactics, they continued to embrace anti-party sentiments characteristic of an earlier period and to recruit traditional, notable types of leaders who dominated local party machines. Celebrating mass participation in the republic's political life, they nonetheless perpetuated old patterns of deference and fused them imperceptibly to new organizational and campaign devices."[12]

While it would take a constitutional crisis in 1824 to spark a national campaign that eventually routed the establishment in Washington, perceptions of elite rule and privilege stirred the public's ire much closer to home and earlier in the century. Often, the results of party dominance and party centralization were more visible at this local level—and with real implications for how Americans led their lives in different states. In both Kentucky and Tennessee, for instance, party leaders responded to the banking crisis of 1819 by levying a tax on banks that were not chartered by the state. While rewarding the economic elite that had enough of a connection to receive a state charter, such action further constrained the amount of credit that banks—including the US national bank—were willing to lend. State courts—responding to elite pressure—ordered the massive forfeiture of property among middle- and lower-class debtors, further consolidating economic power in the hands of a wealthy few. Elsewhere, merchants in Boston suffered a similar fate. Still reeling from the calamitous embargo policy imposed by Jefferson in 1807, the bank panic suffocated the much-needed credit on which Massachusetts's burgeoning middle class relied. However, Massachusetts state politics remained in the hands of three wealthy men—Harrison Gray Otis, William Sullivan, and Thomas Perkins—who stood by as more than 3,000 residents were imprisoned under the state's antiquated debtors' laws. Making matters worse, the responsibility for collecting taxes fell to the much despised "courts of sessions," which remained isolated from public control and which had recently been exposed for favoring the state's "opulent citizens" over disputes in tax assessment.[13]

As Ronald Formisano has argued, in the early 1800s, the initial response from the marginalized and latent populists is best described as an intense "antipartyism." But anti-partyism presupposes a particular form of party competition, not the absence of party organization. "Antipartyism did not simply survive in isolated pockets like guerrilla bands hiding in the mountains," Formisano argues; "it was interwoven into party political culture itself."[14] Massachusetts, Kentucky, and Tennessee were not unique as hotbeds of elite rule and growing populist unrest—and in each case, the local party establishment learned from its initial missteps, suffered some defeats at the ballot box from growing anti-party resistance, and reformed the government's initial response. In Boston, the insurgency against the Federalist Central Committee—a group calling itself the "Middling Interest"—helped to restructure Boston's governing charter, establishing the modern-day ward system, which would "prevent intrigue," "cut up caucuses," and demolish the "coaxing mechanics" that inhibited the people's voice.[15] In Kentucky, a new legislative majority swept to power; and over the wishes of the state's most prominent political leader, Henry Clay, it repealed the banking charter of the "40 Thieves" and issued new laws to temporarily halt the collection of debt. Tennessee voters elected William Carroll as governor, and he helped enact a hard-money policy that virtually destroyed all paper-issuing banks in the state—a victory for the common man out west.[16]

As with many populist movements throughout history, economic catastrophe further galvanized these anti-party, popular revolts. In western New York, however, the Anti-Masonic movement—the largest populist revolt to hit the early republic—was spurred by a conspiracy to commit murder. As rumors spread about the death of a local newspaperman, politically ambitious populists seized on the intrigue over Freemasons and their perceived flagrant violations of democratic principles. These Anti-Masons threatened to topple New York state politics and impose a highly restrictive vision of American life on a diversifying frontier and integrating national market.

Freemasonry was a club—one of many civic organizations that in early American society —which promised friendship, connection, and entertainment. Imported from Great Britain during the 1700s, it proved immensely popular within an egalitarian American society: its mysterious rituals, its emphasis on secular debate and intellectual growth, and its opportunity for individuals to progress through "the Craft" offered many young men an escape from the toils of America's market revolution and growing evangelical fervor. Perhaps most important, Masonry created a sense of status in a country defined by its classlessness. Its membership included some of the most prominent names in contemporary society—President James Monroe, Andrew Jackson, David Crockett—and bore remembrance of Revolutionary heroes; Washington, Lafayette, and Franklin were all early Masons.

Membership in Masonic lodges swelled during the first two decades of the 19th century, especially in the less densely populated frontiers, where membership proved vital for social and economic success. As popular as it became among a prominent group of politicians during the early part of the 19th century, Masonry proved to be just as unpopular among the excluded. Freemasonry was resolutely secular in an age of religious revival, adamantly exclusionary in a time of democratization, and proud of its connections to the Old World just as America was coming into its own. Shrouded in secrecy, members only added to the conspiratorial views as to what really happened in lodge meetings and the power that members exerted over religious leaders, politicians, judges, and military commanders (if they were not Masons themselves!).[17]

In 1826, one Freemason, William Morgan, sought to capitalize on the public's curiosity about Masonic culture and influence by publishing the group's secrets. Local Masons in western New York (Genesee County) pleaded with Morgan to remain quiet, but when their appeals failed, they convinced a local judge to imprison Morgan and the would-be publisher for petty theft. The local sheriff confiscated Morgan's manuscript and destroyed it. When he was finally released, a group of Masons from a nearby county abducted Morgan and took him to another town, where the local magistrate there imprisoned him. As news of Morgan's entanglement with the law and the Masons spread, he suddenly disappeared from his jail cell. Whether he was rescued by friends or dumped into the Niagara River—Morgan became a martyr of a nascent populist movement. Over the next few months the stories over Morgan's disappearance grew in complexity, detailing the complicity of local sheriffs, shopkeepers, and political elites in his alleged murder. Fellow Masons refused to testify, placing brotherhood and loyalty to the secret society above their civic duties and obligations to justice. A few trials were held; but most of the judges themselves were Masons, and little punishment was doled out. Conspiratorial suspicion boiled over into vehement resentment. Guilty convictions were deemed as nothing more than a plot to hide other, more high-profile murders and recriminations perpetrated by Masonic lodges.[18] Enterprising state leaders, eager to capitalize on the public's growing animosity, ordered special counsel investigations, which seemed to confirm the people's anxiety over high-level plots and intrigues. Frontier justice, these reports determined, was a chimera; the reality was a web of jury-tampering, prosecutorial misconduct, rampant obstructionism, and biased sentencing.

The Anti-Mason movement sprang from real and fictionalized acts of frontier injustice. As with most populist movements, Anti-Masonic anger toward the governing establishment quickly boiled over to address a number of social, cultural, and economic issues that had very little to do with the underlying conditions that motivated the movement in the first place. On one level, the Anti-Masons sought to attack growing economic and social inequalities. They condemned disparities in economic opportunity created by the early American legal system, as evidenced by their routine condemnation of debtor-imprisonment laws. Anti-Masons also were distinguished by their resolute views on temperance, and many northern abolitionists cut their teeth as early Anti-Mason leaders. William Lloyd Garrison, editor of the uncompromising and powerful newspaper, the *Liberator*, was a delegate at several Anti-Mason nominating conventions in Massachusetts and argued that slavery was inextricably braided with the presence of Masonic privilege in American society.[19]

Yet Anti-Masonry's collective distrust of the ruling establishment also fed a type of cultural and religious intolerance. Far from simply trying to recover a vision of social and economic mobility celebrated in the American creed, Anti-Masons sought to punish those who had violated Anti-Mason precepts (preventing Masons from joining juries or serving in office), and harbored an intense animosity toward the growing Catholic population inside the United States.[20] Moreover, while the Northeast's localized and participatory democracies kindled the roots of Anti-Masonic passion, most of its leaders promoted reforms that would have subjugated the political independence of townships to the states, if not an activist federal government. The Whig Party that developed in the 1840s was an outgrowth of this impulse, harboring many former Anti-Masons who, while once anxious about political power, now demanded that it be harnessed to enforce a specific vision of American life and economic progress.[21]

The Anti-Masons were most disruptive in New York where the governing political faction at the time offered an indifferent response to the movement's myriad demands. Indeed, the state government's insularity is a testament to the centralized power of the "Albany Regency"—a party organization formed by Martin Van Buren in 1822 as a grand experiment in organizational loyalty and the birth of "machine politics" in the United States. Van Buren formed the Regency to break the reign of New York's traditional governing establishment, more or less controlled by the Clinton family since the 1770s. By centralizing control of party nominations at the state level, the "Holy Alliance" of party leaders rewarded supporters and ambitious would-be candidates with government jobs, contracts, and offices. While they captured governing power, the Regency's initial political success failed to translate into enduring popular support as the tide of Anti-Mason sentiment swelled across New York state. Rather, the Regency put forward plans to restrict suffrage in US presidential elections, supported the proud Freemason, Andrew Jackson, for president, and refused to endorse any constitutional change to the maladministration of justice in New York, such as imprisonment for debt and state-licensed monopolies. Nor did the Regency show any appetite to reduce its control over local political offices, which favored Freemasons. At the New York constitutional convention of 1821, for example, Van Buren opposed the populist demand for direct election of justices of peace, powerful officials whose patronage he thought essential to the New York Democratic Party's dominance. In return for political jobs on the frontier, appointees worked to elect Regency's candidates.[22]

Ironically, it fell to a Freemason and former New York Democratic governor, Dewitt Clinton, to capture the popular passion of the Anti-Mason movement. Van Buren's centralized organization had routed the Clinton establishment wing; however, witnessing the potential influence of Anti-Masonry, Clinton saw a way back into power if he could harness the popular passion that the Regency ignored. Creating a new "People's Party," the Clinton faction spawned a new cadre of organizations at the county level to capture voters' enthusiasm.[23] County conventions nominated Anti-Regency candidates for a wide array of offices; these office seekers had little in common other than the populist rhetoric animating their campaigns. Unable to capture the governorship or extend their legislative victories outside of western New York, a new crop of populist leaders extended the attack on the Democratic establishment, incorporating the concerns of additional marginalized groups, especially those of a nascent union movement (Workingman's parties) and the growing number of tenant farmers. Populism took on a multi-faceted dimension but trained its sights on the perceived elitism of Van Buren, the Masons, and traditional New York politics.[24] These efforts bore fruit in 1824, when Clinton, running under the banner of the People's Party, was swept into the governorship.

For a time, coalition politics supplanted the personalized, intra-organization politicking that was a hallmark of New York governance. The two dominant factions of New York State politics—the Regency and Anti-Mason parties—organized themselves along lines that cut against class and geography, producing real competition for political office across the state for the first time. While Anti-Mason parties were initially a mix of amateurish opposition and unorganized rumor mills, leaders ultimately succeeded in building a formidable organization that transcended more rudimentary populist sentiments. "If Anti-Masonry's leaders initially consisted of ordinary folk from the grass-roots," Formisano argues, "they soon came to resemble . . . the leadership of other political factions—more representative of local and regional economic and social elites."[25]

In order to mount real electoral competition, anti-Masonic parties within and outside New York organized themselves first on the local level, which was no surprise given that most of the movement's grievances were directed toward police powers exercised by the state governments and county magistrates. This gave the movement a decidedly grassroots presence and helped to energize local democracy. Throughout the Northeast, the task of organizing opposition to establishment politicians fell to local leaders, who had to understand the particular contours of populist fervor within their state and local community. In Vermont, Pennsylvania, and Connecticut, Anti-Masonry was infused with a greater dose of religious fervor and moral self-righteousness than found in their New York fraternity; leaders capitalized on these attitudes to push temperance laws, reestablish taxes to support churches, and, in some cases, support the cause of abolitionists. Elsewhere, as in Massachusetts, aspiring partisans used the symbolic villainy of the Masonic lodges to denounce economic elites and promote liberalizing reforms to the state's incorporation codes.[26]

With time, Anti-Masonry fizzled as a form of populist protest. Candidates championed by Anti-Mason parties gradually won office and stifled the perception that the system was perpetually rigged against them; elements of the anti-establishment became a part of the establishment. Burdened with the arduous responsibility of governing, Anti-Mason leaders ceded authority to established political elites who proved successful in redirecting populist anger toward the ballot box and brokering diverse coalitions of interests within the states. Anti-Mason parties still organized themselves as third-party challengers up until 1840, but the scope of party competition expanded beyond the Mason–Anti-Mason dispute. The famed Regency, too, responded to citizen complaints and shed its elitist trappings. Local leaders understood the electoral potential of citizen mobilization, and nomination and patronage decisions were gradually decentralized outside of the Holy Alliance's control. Van Buren and the Regency suffered the consequences for challenging the direct election of justices of the peace in the New York state elections of 1824, which returned Clinton and his allies to power. Two years later, Van Buren and the Regency approved an amendment added to the 1821 constitution giving "the people in their several towns, at their annual elections," the power to choose justices of the peace.[27]

While the "official" Anti-Mason Party was a short-lived experiment, the broader movement's concerns, rhetoric, and democratic demands were, with time, incorporated into the dominant political organizations throughout the northeastern states. Anti-Masons nominated their own presidential candidate, William Wirt, in 1831, at the first national nominating convention. But thereafter, they supported the new Whig Party in presidential campaigns. The Whig Party's elite supporters included many wealthy capitalists; however, the inclusion of Anti-Masons in the Whigs' ranks caused the new party to "adopt far more of a populist posture than their immediate National Republican predecessors." Just as they condemned the power and privilege of Masons and their use of fraternal oath and influence to break the law, so Anti-Mason insurgents indicted Democratic patronage practices for creating a privileged class of officeholders who bestowed legitimacy on Jackson's usurpation of executive power in killing the national bank. Salvation from Jackson's unlawful action rested "IN THE HANDS OF THE PEOPLE,'" Whigs newspapers trumpeted. King Andrew had to be resisted "through the medium of elections."[28]

To be sure, Anti-Masonry was distinct from the other forms of populist insurgency that have threatened the country's institutional structure. Anti-Masonry, especially as we have detailed it here, seems to be missing a token characteristic found among modern populist movements: it lacked a national leader. But part of that was the result of the institutional structure of the party system itself. Given the electoral terrain and the constitutional imperatives imposed by American federalism, it is hard to imagine any single leader of such a disparate, diverse movement. The incorporation of Anti-Masonry in partisan competition was localized and fragmented, preventing the claims of any individual to speak on behalf of the whole people or even the whole movement. Nominating conventions, sponsored by political leaders, and Anti-Mason newspapers increased the number of voices in the arena of democratic persuasion. Ultimately, it fell to local leaders to tap into the grassroots enthusiasm and anger, brokering political alliances across borders in order to capture political office. Forced to forge alliances with regular party organizations, Anti-Masonry did not undermine representative institutions; it had the effect of democratizing the rhetoric and organizations of a burgeoning mass party system.

The State of Courts and Parties (1840–1900)

While scholars tend to celebrate the energetic, participatory form of party politics that dominated the mid-19th century, we should recognize that it was the outgrowth of a party system that was, for too long, isolated and unresponsive to the demands of the common man. Moreover, it was Martin Van Buren—the chief recipient of Anti-Masonic rage—who helped to engineer the new democratic mass party system, in large part as a response to the movement's populist fervor.

Elected to the Senate in 1821, Van Buren was on hand to witness the devastating effects of the 1824 presidential election alongside the Anti-Mason movement closer to home. Believing that he could construct an organization as vigorous and organized as his New York Regency across the country, he ultimately established a ritualized system of two-party competition across and within the several states. While the Regency adapted to the Anti-Masonic threat in the Northeast, Van Buren helped build a new, parallel organization that ushered in the national two-party system that existed for nearly half a century. The new Democratic Party was broad-based, participatory, and highly decentralized. It established, in effect, multiple regencies throughout the states—encouraging partisan loyalty at the local level as a way of constraining national political leadership.

Van Buren's immediate task was to contend with the social turmoil of the age: rising inequality brought about by technological advances led to demands for currency inflation; an anti-establishment sentiment pervaded Western-frontier constituencies, making them ripe for movements like Anti-Masonry; and the expansion of suffrage privileged a common-man style of discourse over an elitist form of politics. Yet egalitarianism, regionalism, and populism were all too abstract to fight head-on. Van Buren understood that the political demands aroused by each of these "isms" were frustrated by a defective political process; and his lasting contribution followed from the recognition that a strengthened political party could not only constrain elite ambitions but also serve as the needed "extraneous force to secure harmony in [the people's] ranks."[29] Party, in other words, could redirect the country's emerging egalitarian proclivities beyond the airing of grievances and toward constructive debate over competing principles and effective government action. As with the first attempt to establish a partisan organization, Van Buren's Democratic Party was committed to a particular type of constitutional arrangement—one that could help channel the political passions of a disaffected and diverse popular movement, and mediate the claims made by their popular champion. The party needed to stand for principles that transcended the passions and personalities of presidential candidates and presidents, and as an organization that strengthened the ties between candidates and voters, could bring much needed stability to the experiment of self-governance on a large scale.

Although it bore strong similarities to the Jeffersonian Democratic-Republican Party, the Jacksonian Democratic Party was not envisaged as a party to end parties. The centralizing ambitions of John Quincy Adams and Henry Clay made clear that the Constitution's tendency toward consolidation had not been corrected merely by banishing the Federalists. Van Buren recognized that the Constitution had inherent flaws that required a party system: enduring competition between two decentralized organizations that could restore and maintain constitutional balance between the presidency and Congress as well as the states and national government. Personalities were fleeting and disruptive, but party organizations could moderate the ambitions of popular leaders and hold them accountable to collective responsibility. As Van Buren wrote to Thomas Ritchie of Virginia, Jackson's popularity revealed the need to "substitute party principle for personal preference."[30] Party democracy was therefore organized with two institutional goals in mind: first, to connect individuals to the political system in a way that forged a coalition of diverse interests; and second, to constrain the ambitions of political elites and force them to work for the good of collective organizations with a past and a future.[31]

Jackson's decisive victories in 1828 and in 1832, and Van Buren's own elevation to the presidency in 1836, provided the crowning vindication for a system of mass parties. In response to the Democrat's collective electoral success at all levels of government, the anti-Jacksonian Whigs organized into an opposition party. By 1840, they succeeded in denying Van Buren reelection; however, having lost three straight elections to Jackson and Van Buren, they used the same partisan campaign tactics that the Jacksonians had pioneered. From then on, "Party life itself would serve as a kind of moral disciple," Hofstadter has noted, "putting a high premium upon loyalty, fidelity, patriotism, and self-restraint. Moreover, controversies were most conducive to the general interest if they were waged between *two* parties, in what could even then already be called the national tradition."[32]

While there were important policy differences between the two parties, they shared similar organizational features and applied similar rules governing the selection of candidates for local, state, and national offices. Both parties embraced the party system, dedicated to organizational loyalty and patronage—government jobs that victors of elections could dispense to their supporters. Furthermore, the Whig and Democratic parties were both federated, with the organizational capacity to compete in every part of the country. Their national appeal followed from the creation of independent state party organizations in the mold of Van Buren's initial Regency in New York. Within the various states, authority for selecting candidates and distributing patronage was further decentralized—more so than in Van Buren's Regency. Local party organizations became schools for political leadership, and created new enduring, national identities out of grassroots organization and political mobilization. The principal mechanism that bound local partisans together was the selection of statewide officeholders. Likewise, the primary way that state partisans in one area of the country cultivated relationships with state partisans in another area was through the selection of candidates for federal office, none more important than nomination of presidential candidates every four years.

The quadrennial nomination contests hosted by each party, were, in effect, the only semblance of a national organization binding partisans together across a disparate landscape. Delegations of state officials would convene, selected by nomination processes in their respective states that stemmed from complicated organizational arrangements of various local party leaders. Implicit in the idea of the national convention was that delegates sprang directly from the rank and file, that they came as Jackson put it, "fresh from the people." State and local political leaders, with strong ties to the voters, thus became the principal intermediaries—or brokers—of presidential politics. The eventual nominee had to amass support at the convention from a set of delegations selected independently from one another and who often disagreed on fundamental political issues. Agreeable generals and "dark horse" candidates routinely captured consensus, after days—if not weeks—of arduous convention brokering and successive balloting. In some years this process led to party leaders getting it "right"—selecting a candidate who could amass a large enough national coalition to achieve victory. In other years, internal squabbles and personal politicking produced candidates whose geographic support was highly concentrated, representing one faction of the broader party, but ultimately suffering from the lack of broad support.

So, although the parties would disagree on many fundamental and deeply divisive issues—most notably on whether a national bank and system of tariffs fostered economic opportunity or a privileged elite—the general institutional structure of the system endured. Ultimately, one issue proved too polarizing for this multilevel method of brokering a national consensus: slavery. By the mid-1850s, the Whig Party collapsed over the issue while the Democratic Party was fractured between its northern and southern wings. The rise of the Republican Party, unified by its platform against the extension of slavery into the federal territories, reinvigorated party competition. But the issue of slavery so divided the country that neither the Democrats nor the Republicans could produce a viable national leader. The 1850s witnessed an increasing degree of sectionalism in presidential voting, culminating in the election of Lincoln in 1860 without a single vote below the Mason-Dixon line. Lincoln was a moderate Republican and an effective party leader; however, the outbreak of the Civil War following his election testified dramatically to how frail the system of decentralized presidential selection could be. Almost half the country rejected Lincoln and neither party produced a viable political leader who could command national unity. The Civil War put an end to the slavery issue that shattered antebellum organized party competition. Nevertheless, the existential struggle over America's original sin did not lead to a transformation of the highly decentralized yet resilient two-party system. Both Democrats and Republicans emerged from an existential struggle with their pre-war organizational structure intact, if not stronger than before. Once again, presidential candidates emerged only after painstaking party maneuvers, often appearing weak, unknown, and everybody's third or fourth choice. This was a consequence—as before—of highly fragmented authority in the selection of national delegates.

Indeed, following the Civil War and on the heels of America's industrial revolution, both the Republican and Democratic parties became more dependent on a structure of decentralized, patronage-driven electioneering.

Defying the gale force of industrialization, localized parties imposed a powerful gravitational pull on government. As Stephen Skowronek has argued: "The tenacity of this highly mobilized, highly competitive, and locally oriented democracy" routinely thwarted attempts to construct a national state on American soil.[33] In terms of party organization, there was, in effect, still little semblance of a national party. To be sure, the two major parties of the 19th century—before and after the war—competed across the nation and organized themselves in the national halls of power. But these broad coalitions were the result of decisions reached by hundreds of small, local organizations dedicated above all to maintaining their dominance of American politics and government—a "politics of organization," as Morton Keller calls it, that replaced the ideological fervor that roiled partisan conflict over slavery.[34]

The delegate selection system and the process of quadrennial nomination conventions reinforced the dispersion of governing authority in the United States throughout this period. Political leaders at the state and national level owed their political fortunes to local party officials who viewed the maintenance of party organization as an end in itself. Citizen choice or recourse to insurgent challenge was limited. Corruption, misuse of funds, and government favoritism were rampant. Appeals to higher levels of political authority routinely fell on deaf ears, even when an opposing political party possessed national power. After all, elected officials in both parties depended on this decentralized framework for their next election, and neither faced a strong imperative to disrupt the status quo that had sent them to the statehouse or Washington. Organized and administered by loyal partisans who owed their livelihoods to keeping their party in power, state and local "bosses" forged connections between the government and its citizens, many of them new immigrants from southern and eastern Europe.

Since the founding of the Democratic Party, this "spoils system" had been critical to the ability of parties to secure financial resources and to mobilize support all the way down to the local precinct. But industrialization and urbanization only raised the stakes for partisan control of governing institutions and made that system more entrenched in the country's political structure. Both parties benefited from the widespread system of patronage politics, government contracts, and institutional rules that structured the electorate in their favor. With this development, the party system, which was founded as an institution to strengthen the democratic character of the Constitution, ossified. By the end of the 19th century, both the Democrats and Republicans were engaged in hotly contested and highly mobilized campaigns, but the party system was driven by partisan maneuvers that maintained a system of graft, electoral fraud, and limited government accountability. Neither party had any real incentive to challenge the prevailing order that maintained strong party organizations and decentralized governance.[35] After the notorious "Compromise of 1877," when Democrats and Republicans struck an unsavory bargain to resolve the disputed 1876 presidential election and to end Reconstruction, neither party showed the moral fortitude to ameliorate the economic disruption of the industrial revolution or to confront the shame of Jim Crow laws in the South. Fragmented, corruption-prone, and "stunted" by comparison with the political associations of other developed nations, political parties came to be viewed as the main obstacle to strengthening national resolve in the face of massive social, economic, and international dislocations at the end of the 19th and beginning of the 20th century.

The Threat of Agrarian Protest

It was during the tumultuous post–Civil War era that another massive populist protest engulfed the country. In what was clearly the largest and most widespread populist movement to date, thousands of farmers across the Midwest and South launched a decades-long attack on the political establishment and the two-party system that nourished it. Infused with a sense of indignant furor against eastern banks, local merchants, and a corrupt political class, American agrarians organized themselves in order to take advantage of the country's growing economic prosperity, which had left their communities behind. Like the Anti-Masons before it, the Populist Movement helped to usher in a dramatic remaking of the party system, paving the way for additional reforms during the Progressive era and New Deal. Yet they were unsuccessful in enacting their most ambitious plans for economic and political equality. In response to populist unrest, both Democrats and Republicans used the built-in advantages of the late 19th-century party system to largely stifle the agrarian movement. Any gains made by the Populists—in constructing an accessible financial system, in regulating railroads, or in democratizing politics—came later, if at all.

Drawing on the language of the common man, these "plain people" of the American heartland tapped into America's egalitarian spirit, which had animated the Anti-Masons a generation earlier. That same sprit would soon embolden other populist movements at the turn of the 20th century, including organized labor and a nascent civil rights movement. Yet none were as noticeable, organized, or potentially disruptive as were the Populists. In many areas of the country, they represented the clear majority of the population, and their grievances—at the time, and in retrospect—were legitimate. The party system's negligence was a consequence of its structure; empowered local and state bosses had, as reformers argued, rigged political and governmental processes in their favor. So decentralized was the system of mass politics that the Populists struggled to make inroads into the political establishment or to launch a successful third-party insurgency, even when they had majority support in parts of the country. Election after election, in state after state, the Populists faltered.

Many students of American history credit the Populist movement as a successful revolt, but these accounts often overlook the anti-partyism that infused the Populist crusade. Nevertheless, such favorable accounts of the agrarian revolt make two analytical mistakes in explaining Populism and partisanship: first, they often neglect how the Populist Movement sought to demolish, not remake, the two-party stem. It is true that in 1896, the Democrats nominated self-styled populist William Jennings Bryan as the presidential nominee. Bryan proposed to inflate the money supply—the free coinage of silver—displayed the evangelical righteousness that had galvanized the the farmers' protest. His nomination might be seen as evidence of the decentralized party system's flexibility to take on new ideas and construct new coalitions.[36] Yet Bryan's nomination offers a low bar for evaluating the movement's success. He represented a co-optation of Populist idealism—a co-optation Populist leaders had long warned against, which is why they sought to dismantle party organization, not join it. Similarly, Bryan's loss in 1896, followed by defeats in 1900 and 1904, is often viewed as a testament to democratic politics and his inability to persuade a majority of voters that substantial reform was needed.[37] However, such accounts of the era often gloss over the illegitimate political obstacles—ballot rigging, spoils, extortion, Jim Crow—that allowed the decentralized party system to prevail even as it remained unresponsive to popular protest. The fully decentralized party system, in which nomination and governance decisions were characterized by minimal national leadership and competition, provided no incentive or organizational capacity that might have led party leaders to respond to a national movement.

The Populists recognized this extraordinary degree of party insularity, and the movement distanced itself from organized national politics from the start. The multi-regional "People's Party" that emerged in the 1890s had gone through multiple iterations over a 20-year period that pre-dated the Populist platform in 1892 and Bryan's nomination in 1896: the National Labor Union (1871), the Greenback Party (1876–84), and the Union Labor Party (1888). But none of these organizations—or even the People's Party—ever represented the full scope of agrarian insurgency. In fact, the movement often scorned electoral politics—testifying to insurgents' lack of faith in an insular party system.

At the start of the movement, the Populist assault on machine politics began as an attack on the country's banking and currency system. The Civil War and the need to finance it, spurred a revolutionary change in the way the nation's banks operated and, more generally, in the relationship between government and private financial institutions. These developments gave rise to a form of agribusiness that was heavily dependent on the politics of eastern-controlled monetary policy. Family farmers owed mortgages on new land; purchased new machinery on loans; and incurred new obligations at the start of every planting season for seed and equipment, not to mention subsistence supplies to support their families until harvest. Paid once a year, when the crops came in, famers were carefully attuned to the country's credit markets. Gone were the days of simple frontier trading: not even the most remote farmer was immune to the decisions made in the large banking houses back east. The irony, however, was that most farmers lacked access to the major networks of credit. Instead, they relied on a provincial system whereby farmers took out loans with local merchants at the beginning of the season and placed their forthcoming crop as collateral against the loan. Lack of competition, unfavorable loan terms, and high-risk market conditions produced an impossible situation. Across the country, farmers engaged in this "crop-lien" system could not sell their crop for enough money to cover what they owed back to the merchant. Another loan, with interest, was added to the ledger each year, tying indebted farmers to their unprofitable land and leaving them dependent on the vagaries of weather and crop prices for financing their enterprises.

The Populists recognized how the system of national and state party politics abetted this system of tight money and burdensome debt. The federal Homestead Act, enacted in 1862 as part of the Republican Party's program to stimulate commercial development, made land cheap and abundant, increasing production, and depressing prices on agricultural goods. It also tied land reform to the prerogatives of party elites. New railroads, subsidized by government at all levels, brought the promise of economic prosperity but, in fact, formed a national agricultural market that made small farms further susceptible to surges in supply and lower prices. Moreover, it would be a mistake to view the late 19th century as a period of "unregulated banking." The nation's banking and currency system was highly regulated, but in favor of large banks, which held the country's debt. With a growing population and with increased production on the farm, farmers and industrialists alike needed access to credit, which, by law, was influenced by the rates set by the US Congress for how its bonds could be redeemed, and at what rate.

In 1873, a little noticed provision was inserted in a large banking bill, which served as a flashpoint in the Populists' claim of elite intransigence. At the behest of large financial houses, the new law abolished all silver coinage, making the United States fully dependent on the gold standard. The bill passed the Congress with large majorities in the House and Senate after lengthy but superficial debate. Such a policy had the effect of constraining the money supply (making each dollar more valuable), which advantaged those who issued debt and raised the real costs placed on holders of debt, namely, farmers. But what made this change a full-blown scandal was its surreptitious passage; few recognized, even some who voted for the legislation, that the "Crime of 73" had taken place at all. It was only when silver miners were spurned by the mint months later that newspapers and local organizations realized the full implication of Congress's machinations. The farmers' plight was not solely attributed to the 1873 Coinage Act, but the bill became a clarion call for the fight against a corrupt political establishment that was all too willing to do the bidding of the nation's bankers, often in secret, without public accountability.

The early Populists viewed the rigged money supply as a formidable obstacle to their struggle for economic justice. Likewise, they disdained partisan politics and the corruption that fueled it. While there was a two-party system that contested elections across the nation—most notably for president—most Americans, in effect, were subject to a single party that governed their state and locality. In the South, the party of Lincoln, the Republican Party, repulsed an electorate still reeling from the emotional and physical wounds of the Civil War. The Democrats owned the region, capturing the loyalties of the former confederacy with their steadfast promise to reestablish racial hierarchies and prevent Black suffrage. The crop-lien system reinforced these developments, as the majority of Black southerners were doubly disadvantaged—first by the credit system and then by sharecropping for larger landholders. While southern Democrats restored White supremacy, the Republicans dedicated their energies to electioneering in the North and West. Reminding voters that they had saved the Union, Republicans further reinforced the geographic divisions of party competition by "waving the bloody shirt," kindling memories of a disastrous war and a contemptable former "slave power" that should be kept from public office at all cost. Where the Democrats succeeded in the North, it was because of the strength of their urban machines, which were nourished by the votes of new immigrants, many of them Roman Catholic. The Republicans excoriated the Democrats as the party of "Rum, Romanism, and Rebellion," deflecting attention from the economic issues that agitated late 19th-century American politics. Both parties mobilized support by antagonizing the ethnic, racial, and regional differences of the American electorate, and they used the spoils system and the public coffers—and sometimes outright bribes—to sustain their organizations.

Rather than challenge the two-party system, the Populists sought to alleviate their woes through economic cooperation and local organizing. In 1878, a "Grand State Farmers Alliance" formed in the booming but unjustly concentrated economy of Texas. Alliance members and the local networks of sub-alliance groups sought to use their collective purchasing power to break the hold of monopolistic creditors on the region, and use their market presence to reduce costs placed on the small farmer through railroad price gouging. Cooperative, "self-help" was the initial response to the unfair practices of the ruling establishment.

Within a single year of organizing, the Alliance's membership swelled from 10,000 to 50,000 in Texas alone; by 1888, 250,000 farmers claimed membership in the Texas Alliance.[38] Leaders in Texas deployed an army of paid lecturers throughout the South and Upper-West to educate communities about the benefits of agricultural cooperation and to urge replication of their success; an estimated 2 million famers (in a country of 63 million) in 43 states listened to an Alliance lecturer.[39] As Lawrence Goodwyn has documented, the national organizing campaign touched even the remotest communities in the country:

In what were now thousands of sub-alliances, famers learned from their business agents and their country trade committees the nature of the opposition. . . . [A]t earnest lectures on the monetary system they learned how the gold standard directly affected their lives. At other lectures they learned about the sub-treasury system and discussed it with their brethren. They became variously thoughtful, indignant, hopeful, and ready for action. In such ways—and unseen by the rest of the nation—the movement culture of Populism came to rural America.[40]

Yet the rest of the nation dismissed the growing Populist tide because of its inability or unwillingness to crack the two-party system. Ambitious Populists who tried to organize candidates for office faltered under the "tyranny" of the Democratic and Republican machinery. The Greenback Party, which grew in popularity as an economic depression wracked the country, was dealt a fatal blow in 1887 when the economy rebounded, vindicating party politics as usual, especially the Republican commitment to the gold standard. A year later, the Union Labor Party met the same fate; after its demise, one party organizer reflected:

I know that for the man who sees the evils of the time—the want, ignorance, and misery caused by injust [sic] laws—who sets himself so far as he has strength to right them, there is nothing in store but ridicule and abuse. The bitterest though, and the hardest to bear, is the hopelessness of the struggle, "the futility of the sacrifice."[41]

Unlike the previous era of party politics where competition threatened both parties with defeat in the next election if they did not respond to constituent demands—the hyper-decentralization that defined the late 19th century advantaged the status quo. For example, Alliance members in Dothan, Alabama, actually fulfilled the cooperative dream by erecting a new, collectively owned warehouse, whereby they could challenge the power of local merchants, bankers, and shippers over unfair prices. However, the Dothan Democratic Party responded by levying a tax on the new warehouse; when the Alliance moved outside of town limits, they levied another new tax on all cotton imports sold within city limits. Efforts to enforce the new ordinance resulted in a gun fight between city officials and farmers; Populists encountered the swift hand of partisan frontier justice, with two dead and another wounded. The Dothan Alliance was a microcosm of the organized political resistance Populists faced throughout the South and West.[42] Elsewhere, similar groups met a common fate. In Texas, the largest Alliance experiment in agricultural self-help was bankrupted by well-organized state officials. The Texas Alliance had devised a plan that would connect the fate of every Alliance farmer in the state to one another; collectively leveraging their land and future crop, they hoped to sell directly to the factory and evade the local merchant who dominated the crop-lien system. Recognizing the fundamental threat the Alliance posed to the economic and political hierarchy of the state, local Democratic leaders made sure that not a single bank in Texas agreed to underwrite the massive stock that the farmers had collectively pledged. The Texas Alliance barely survived the growing season.[43]

As the Populists struggled to organize, a "class-consciousness" nevertheless arose in the minds of farmers. Increasingly, the movement's leadership recognized the need to change course and directly confront powerful party bosses in order to realize their vision on behalf of the plain people. The new national Alliance president, L. L. Polk, drew from the fount of democratic enthusiasm his organization had been building for nearly a decade and began to encourage sub-alliances to run slates of candidates: "Congress could give us a bill in forty-eight hours that would relieve us," he liked to argue in one of his stump speeches, "but Wall Street says nay. . . . I believe that both parties are afraid of Wall Street. They are not afraid of the people!"[44]

Alliance members in Kansas proved especially capable in carrying forward the movement's new approach. In 1890, Kansans held "the convention of the people," and nominated Alliance leaders for office. They won five of Kansas's seven congressional districts, 96 of 125 seats in the state legislature, and narrowly lost the governorship. President Benjamin Harrison, observing from Washington, fearfully noticed his party's "election disaster": "If the Alliance can pull one-half of our Republican voters, our future is not cheerful," he told his cabinet.[45]

Kansas, however, was the exception to the Populists' disappointing electoral efforts. In neighboring Nebraska, the Alliance seemed to be successful in the 1890 elections, but electoral victory did not translate to meaningful reform. County-level party leaders—both Republican and Democrat—joined the masses of disenchanted farmers to create fusion tickets, often against the advice of Populist leaders, who foresaw how compromise on the campaign trail would beget compromise once in office.[46] Democratic fusionists had the most success, including a young William Jennings Bryan, who was elected to the House of Representatives that year. But when "Independent Party," fusion legislators arrived in Lincoln, the state capital, they were overwhelmed by politics as usual. Lincoln's notorious "oil rooms"—where corporate and railroad interests "oiled" legislators with alcohol and financial contributions—proved too alluring for delegates that lacked a formal political organization with a history of electoral success. Having defeated an insurgent challenge, Nebraska's powerful Republican governor squashed any lingering reformist sentiment by vetoing the sole reformist bill to make it to his desk that session, before his party took control once again in the next election.[47]

Lacking robust leadership to organize disparate interests across state lines, the Populists' efforts to crack the decentralized party machinery faced its largest challenge in the Deep South.[48] As in Nebraska, local and state party bosses coopted the grassroots support that the local Alliance organization had mobilized over the last decade; but they put it to use on behalf of their narrow partisan interests. In South Carolina, Ben Tillman leveraged the Populists' anti-establishment message to take hold of the state Democratic Party in 1890 and to establish himself as the de facto head of state politics for the next three decades. Tillman's success warped Populism's vision of mass democracy into a militant White supremacy, forever tarnishing the movement's appeal to Blacks living in the South. Under his command, Democratic Party bosses used a clever mix of procedure and fearmongering to crush the Alliance uprising at the state party convention that year and elected one of their own for the governorship, further limiting the movement's gains.[49] Likewise, in Georgia, party leaders paid homage to the farmers' discontent, but after the votes were tallied, Democrats quickly forgot their stump-speech promises. Most demoralizing was the Alliance performance in Texas, where the Populists could lay claim to an impressive independent organization. Even then, legislation had to go through the Democratic boss James Hogg; weighing in at around 300 pounds, "Big Jim" upbraided the railroads, banks, and robber barons pillaging his state just as vehemently as any Populist. Yet disappointed Alliance leaders would soon learn that Hogg—and other Texas Democrats—represented the worst of the Populist vision.[50] Unprincipled and opposed to the sweeping programmatic reforms laid out in the Alliance lecture series, Hogg played the race card to undermine any possibility of forging a biracial coalition of small farmers. Populist leaders came to the sad realization that the foundation of White supremacy on which Hogg and the rest of Southern Democratic Party rested would forever impede the Populists' efforts to reconstruct the crop-lien system. When so-called friends of the Populist crusade reneged on promises to reform the banking system after election day, it confirmed Alliance leaders' objections to party organization: working with a graft-ridden and impregnable party that owed its prominence to a racial and financial caste system was impossible.

In response to these early missteps, in 1892 Alliance men from around the country convened in Omaha, Nebraska, in an effort to break the movement's electoral dependence on the Democratic Party and fusion candidacies. The famed Omaha Platform spelled out a litany of radical reform proposals that would remake the American political economy and offer voters a genuine choice come election day. Only such an ambitious program, the People's Party proclaimed, could save a nation on the "verge of moral, political and material ruin." Noting that the assault on the "plain people" was occurring not just in the United States but in Europe as well, the platform warned, "A vast conspiracy against mankind has been organized on two continents, and it is rapidly taking possession of the world. If not met and overthrown at once it forebodes terrible social convulsions, the destruction of civilization, or the establishment of an absolute despotism."[51] For president, the Populists placed their faith in the former Union general, James B. Weaver. Hoping to redress the intractable sectionalism that had dominated the country since the Civil War, they selected a former Confederate major and Virginian, James G. Field, as his running mate. Weaver and Field carried four states in the general election—Nevada, Colorado, Idaho, and Kansas—but failed to win a single state from the former Confederacy. The Democratic stranglehold on the South, rooted in White supremacy, corrupt electioneering, and one-party dominance, thwarted the People's Party's efforts to launch a national offensive.

Far from representing a surging tide of Populist protest, the 1892 election marked the high-water mark for the People's Party and its assault on the traditional party system. "To break out of their electoral confinement," Kazin writes, "the Populists took a fatal leap out into compromise."[52] At the 1896 Democratic National Convention, delegates representing the reformist faction of the party wrestled control of the nominating process away from the conservative coalition that had supported President Grover Cleveland. Yet despite the high drama of his cross of gold speech that catapulted a relatively unknown thirty-six-year-old congressman to the Democratic Party's nomination for president, Bryan offered a much watered-down version of the Populist Dream.[53] In Omaha, four years earlier, the People's Party had called for government ownership of the railroads, telegraph, and telephone systems, a revamped government-controlled banking institution through the post office, the redistribution of land owned by corporate monopolies, and the imposition of a graduated income tax. Bryan offered up a solution palatable to the entrenched interests: free coinage of silver at a ratio of 16 to 1.

Of course, for most of American history, populist crusaders have had to compromise some of their most visionary objectives to influence a mainstream party. Moreover, the Populists had long viewed the restriction of the money supply and the demonetization of silver coinage as a source of their economic peril. But Bryan's exclusive focus on monetary policy, as more militant insurgents feared, appeared to condemn the broader platform of the Populist crusade to irrelevance; in fact, Bryan's cry of Free Silver was little more than a compromise within a rigged political system that was beholden to corporate interests and the Democratic bosses in the South. As the *New York Times* reported, it further aggravated the sectional lines of the Democratic Party. At the convention, delegates from "Gold States" in the North and Midwest at first refused to cast ballots, only conceding to the Great Commoner's nomination when it became clear that the enraptured delegates swayed by his emotional appeal would not be denied.[54]

The Populist Party envisioned a grassroots uprising of the producer class—farmers, laborers, and small businesses—which dotted the American landscape.[55] However, Bryan's campaign framed the 1896 contest as a decisive battle between the industrial North and rural South and West—the traditional party cleavage that the system of decentralized parties nourished. Although Bryan accepted compromise with the Democratic gatekeepers, he couched his defense of free silver with the same pietistic fervor as his more radical Populist brethren. He, therefore, failed to extend the reach of agrarian reformers to the rising class of industrial workers congregated in large metropolitan areas. As Bryan described the apocalyptic conflict between the rural and urban bastions of the country in his Cross of Gold speech: "You come to us and tell us that the great cities are in favor of the gold standard. I tell you that the great cities rest upon these broad and fertile prairies. Burn down your cities and leave our farms, and your cities will spring up again as if by magic. But destroy our farms and the grass will grow in the streets of every city in the country."[56] Such rhetoric, which infused the Great Commoner's general election campaign, alienated many Catholics and other city dwellers in the East and Midwest who usually voted Democratic.[57]

Dominated by a Jeffersonian hatred of urban elites, which the Democratic candidate expressed in evangelical terms, Bryan's campaign is better viewed as a last hurrah for the decentralized republic of the 19th century, with rhetorical flourish provided by the Populist groundswell, than as a precursor to the economic reform programs of the Progressive Era and New Deal. Bryan was accused of stoking old-world "class" resentment and threatening the surging economic progress of America's industrial revolution, an indictment that plagued him through election day. But his campaign was forward looking in one important regard. Determined to connect directly with the plain people, Bryan was the first presidential candidate to appeal directly to the voters for support. Crisscrossing the country, Bryan nursed his famed oratorical skills and riled up crowds throughout the nation, North and South. His Republican opponent, Ohio governor William McKinley, offered "a safe, traditional, solidly Midwestern contrast to the fire breathing Bryan."[58] Building on an approach that Benjamin Harrison had employed on a smaller scale in 1888, McKinley and his master political strategist, Mark Hanna, projected his stolidity and mobilized the national Republican Pary with a "front porch" campaign, which enabled McKinley to greet delegations of voters at his home in Canton, Ohio. Presenting himself as the candidate of prosperity and the "full dinner pail," McKinley attacked Bryan's platform of free silver as the southern farmers' plot to destroy the industrializing North. Inflation would hurt the laborer and wage earner in the North, he warned, and allow the South, and rural provincialism, to stifle the country's rise as a prosperous industrial nation.[59] The plain people outside the Deep South and trans-Mississipi West heard the Republican promise not to disturb the nation's growing ethnic and religious diversity and voted for McKinley. As Kazin encapsulates the ill-fated fusion of Populists and Democrats, "Bryan drew more votes than any Populist could have, but he had cast his lot on the same side of the cultural divide.[60]

The Populist crusade was thus tarnished by its organizing efforts below the Mason-Dixon line, even though it was in the South where the Populists were least influential. And Bryan did little to soften the sectional aggravations of the era as crafty agents and astute machine politicians took over and muffled Populist fervor. As Elizabeth Sanders has exhaustively detailed, "The chance for a bottom-up, farmer-labor coalition led by a sympathetic populist president was lost in 1896. Disfranchisement and industrialization would gradually undermine southern populism. And future Democratic presidents would be closer to northeastern capital, more weakly committed to labor and domestic reform, and more strongly attracted to the augmentation of national military power."[61]

Ironically, it was in the South where the Populist political dream of a pure, unmediated politics, symbolized by Bryan's barnstorming campaign, first made headway, even as their plans to combat economic privilege—the goal of Populist democratization—failed. The new crop of southern politicians who took power amid the rising tide of agrarian anger recognized the populist foundations of their support. But it was a populism distinct from the Farmer's Alliance. In South Carolina, Tillman and his organization sought to harness the people's voice and instituted the direct primary for Democratic nominations in 1896—the first in the country. One by one, other state parties in the South opened up intra-party politics, creating de facto direct elections for US senators years before passage of the 17th Amendment, and increasing turnout in an age marked by declining activism. However, while couched in the language of Populism, these reforms advanced a virulent form of grassroots politics, which further reinforced the region's racial hierarchy. The Democratic state parties of the South became the vanguards of Jim Crow, establishing literacy tests, poll taxes, and all-white primaries. Moreover, given the Democratic Party's dominance over southern politics, intra-party disputes degenerated into personal rivalries and demagogic campaigns. Far from offering southern voters a choice at the ballot box, the structure of party politics made it difficult for even well-meaning reformers to enact programmatic change once taking office.[62]

Localized party competition and decentralized governing institutions prevented the Populist movement from fulfilling its vision of American politics. Populist anger never transformed America's traditional commitment to property rights and limited government. Party leaders did respond, albeit often tepidly and sometimes oppressively. In some places, Democrats and Republicans supported legitimate citizen demands; however, in comparison to other eras, mediated party politics was exceptionally insular. In this highly decentralized form of party organization and government power, Populism was not filtered; rather a revanchist party system stifled its aspirations and exploited populist means for reactionary ends. The degree of unresponsiveness—over the course of a near half-century—so suffocated democratic change that it gave rise to another reform era committed to disentangling the party system from American political life.

The Progressive Era and Party Reform (1900–1935)

The Populist revolt marked the beginning of the end for the age of machine politics. While the state of "courts and parties" had prevented a full-scale agrarian revolt, the Populists exposed the system's fault lines. In their wake, a new crop of reformers took advantage of the sea change in national politics that came with war, industrialization, and mass migration in the early 20th century. Indeed, the Progressive Movement is distinct from previous vanguards of party reform because it envisioned a national reform movement, which would temper the sectional animosities inflamed by the 19th-century party system.[63]

The objective of transcending provincial political organizations and interests focused the attention of these new reformers on the power of the corporation and its exploitation or corruption of industrial workers, farmers, and politicians. As the pioneering progressive and pre-presidential Woodrow Wilson wrote in 1908, "The development of the last two decades, has obliterated many boundaries, made many interests national and common, which until our own day were separate and local."[64] Yet the main underlying problem Progressives identified was that government, dominated by highly decentralized party organizations, seemed powerless to control these forces. Just as Madison, Jefferson, and Van Buren had sought to promote a variant of party democracy to dismantle the centralizing policies of their opponents, so the newly disaffected and disgruntled Progressives at the turn of the 20th century focused their attention on the role political parties played in stifling purposeful national action. While the goal of the Progressive Movement was the nationalization of politics, the result of their efforts produced a fractious blend of intra-party conflict, regnant localism, and an emerging national political culture. Through new institutions such as the direct primary and citizen ballot initiative, state and local leaders at all levels of government became more responsive to the national public mood. Neither as centralized as it would become or as decentralized as it once was, this chaotic system of local parties, national electorates, and more direct forms of selecting candidates and policymaking increased citizen choice in party affairs within a still largely decentralized system of party organization.

The Progressives had disparate motivations, partisan identities, and reform objectives, but their critique of existing party government gave unity to their movement.[65] For this new crop of would-be reformers, the failure of the Populist Movement taught them that building popular support for progressive principles and programs could not be achieved with an enervating struggle to capture a deeply entrenched and localistic party system. Far from being an institution that corrected the deficiencies of the Constitution, Progressives argued, political parties had supplanted the framers' objective to provide for responsible, accountable, and active government. Many Progressives acknowledged that Jeffersonian and Jacksonian reforms were necessary in the 19th century to obstruct the "aristocratic" pretensions of the Federalists. But the problems thrown up by the industrial revolution demanded that Progressives revisit the potential for national democracy in the original Constitution. Increasingly, they united around the belief that localized, patronage-based parties had to be destroyed in order to rescue American democracy from the corrupting influence of professional politicians, vested corporate interests, and patronage-based municipal government. As the late 19th-century reformer Henry Adams wrote, "No serious impression can ever be made on [the evils of political corruption] until they are attacked at their source; not until the nation is ready to go back to the early practice of government and restore to the constitutional organs those powers which have been torn from them by the party organizations for the purposes of party aggrandizement." Above all, Adams predicted, future reform must ensure that "the relation between the party system and the constitutional framework" be "reversed."[66]

This reformist imperative—to create a new competitor within the decentralized system—gave rise to the formation of the Progressive Party in 1912, a convocation of insurgents led by the popular former president, Theodore Roosevelt. Promoting a radical reform program that promised to expand the responsibilities of the federal government and make it more responsive to popular economic, social, and political demands, Roosevelt and his political allies won 27.4% of the popular vote and 88 electoral votes. However, the Progressive Party was forlorn four years later, unable to survive its charismatic leader's return to the Republican fold. In fact, Barry Karl has observed that the Bull Moose campaign, as Roosevelt famously dubbed his crusade, with its platform of political reform—championing measures such as the primary, initiative, referendum, and recall that would advance a direct form of democracy—was as much an assault on the very idea of the party system as it was an effort to form a militant reform party that would advance a program of national reconstruction.[67]

While earlier populist movements coalesced around an anti-party disposition, progressive strains formed in both the Democratic and Republican parties whose leaders believed that parties should not be destroyed but reconstructed. One leading Progressive who held this view—and had made an academic career of thinking about such issues—was elected president in 1912. Woodrow Wilson acknowledged that the two-party system played a critical part in fostering a sense of citizenship and unity in the decentralized republic of the 19th century. Yet he argued that if a party-style democracy was to be saved, it would have to be adapted to the growing domestic and international responsibilities that the national government was assuming in the wake of the industrial revolution.

Wilson, like Madison and the other framers, understood parties to be the natural outgrowth of democratic politics. Furthermore, given the United States' complicated arrangement of power between the states and the nation and within the federal government, parties were essential in helping citizens make sense of the dozens of different elected leaders any single US citizen was bound to have represent them. Wilson's concern, however, was that the parties had become too independent of public opinion and that the fragmented arrangement of governing power made national representation and accountability to voters impractical. Wilson and other leading progressives argued that the two parties had to be recast as national and programmatic organizations to offer meaningful alternatives to voters at the polls. Indeed, Wilson was deeply influenced by the Populist uprising of the late 19th century and the fundamental threat he believed it posed to American government. As he thought (too simply, for sure) and argued in his five-volume *A History of the American People*, the agrarian revolt was evidence of the "disintegration of the Democratic party"—a situation in which politicians "allowed themselves to be attached to particular interests, put party pledges aside very lightly, acted like men who had forgot the compulsions of political principle and played each for his own benefit." Worse still, amid the disarray, the Democratic president, Grover Cleveland, faltered as a "President without a party." Such organizational weakness decimated the Democrats' position, ultimately allowing the "charlatans in the convention" of 1896 to bring Bryan to the floor. Bryan's capture of the party, Wilson lamented, weakened its position in the North and Midwest and ended the Democrats' control of the federal government. Not until Wilson was able to exploit the Republicans' own internal divisions did the Democratic Party resume command of the White House.[68]

The lesson of the Populists' demise, Wilson believed, was that only a reformed party system, composed of ideologically coherent and distinct parties freed from the gravitational pull of localized politics and spoils, could cultivate a public debate over what new responsibilities the federal government should assume. Theodore Roosevelt and his followers believed that Progressive democracy would reach its fulfillment in a direct alliance between public opinion and the autonomous executive—the "steward of the public welfare"—who might transcend the constraints of traditional party organizations and practice. Wilson recalibrated the Progressive Party's vision of democracy in joining direct appeals to the public to a new form of partisanship in which the president, rather than Congress or state and local governments, would "stand at the intersection of party organization and national public opinion"—where he might "harness each to great national effect."[69] Wilson thus envisaged an uneasy alliance between executive power and partisanship, an executive-centered party, that would preserve a measure of collective responsibility by empowering the president to give "the country at once information and statements of policy which will enable it to form its judgments alike of parties and men."[70]

Wilson's actual imprint on the two-party system, even on his own Democratic Party, was by all accounts limited. Although he promised African Americans "fair dealing" during the 1912 campaign, Wilson formed an alliance with the southern wing of his party to gain their support in his pursuit of economic reform. He brought into the executive branch White southerners who strengthened the grip of Jim Crow laws on southern Blacks and extended the doctrine of separate but equal to the federal civil service.[71]

Wilson's commitment to party reform was limited by his prejudice and his party; however, he did continue the transformation of the presidency that began during Theodore Roosevelt's time in office. He oversaw the vast expansion of the federal government's administrative responsibilities—especially during World War I. Nevertheless, his political capital had faded considerably by the end of the "Great War," which aroused strong opposition on the homefront. Wilson worked effectively with congressional Democrats during his first term to achieve industrial reforms, such as the creation of the Federal Reserve Board. In part, his failed crusade for a League of Nations in 1919, which put the idea of an executive-centered party to its first rigorous test, is a testament to the limits of his ideas and practice of party leadership. More generally, the Senate's failure to approve a new role for the United States in world affairs confirmed that although the presidency had attained considerable prominence since the turn of the century, the office was still constrained by a powerful, if no longer, dominant Congress and the vagaries of public opinion. The American people reacted to the economic and political disruption of the war and the polarizing battle over the terms of peace by electing the Republican party stalwart Warren Harding, who promised a "return to normalcy" in the landslide presidential election of 1920. Republicans assumed power in March 1921, militant in their determination to restore Congress and the party organization to their former stature. The progressive task of reforming, or reconstituting, the status of party democracy would have to wait until Franklin Roosevelt assumed power in his own landslide victory in 1932.

The Threat of Economic Nationalism

The Great Depression and FDR's presidential stewardship provided the opportunity to consolidate developments that began during the Progressive era. Perhaps only once before, during the Civil War, did the American people place so much faith in their president. The allure of FDR's first 100 days in office has captured the imagination of every subsequent president-elect, and much of our modern-day vision of the potential for presidential leadership is drawn from the extraordinary power Roosevelt commanded over national politics. Congress delegated substantial political authority and administrative power to the new president, placing the White House in the central position of American political affairs—a position it has continued to occupy as a result of Roosevelt's leadership.

To be sure, throughout FDR's unprecedented tenure—just over 12 years—critics assailed his policies and personally vilified him as a power-hungry dictator. Free elections continued to challenge his prominence and the Supreme Court struck down the administration's most transformative and inventive economic policies. But the most important check on Roosevelt's power may have been his own party. Democrats commanded large majorities in the House of Representatives and the Senate for every year that Roosevelt was in office. Yet Democrats were not a Roosevelt party. FDR's fellow partisans routinely spoke out against him, joined Republicans to block his legislative efforts, and resisted his most aggressive executive actions. Various members, particularly from the South, won reelection not as a result of the president's popularity—which was diminished after the 1937 economic downturn, and once again as war approached—but because of the strength of their own support in the states and localities. Despite the tension between them, the president and the party needed one another—a symbiotic relationship forged by a president's ambition to centralize governmental authority during domestic and international crises in a party system that remained, despite the abundance of Progressive reforms, stubbornly decentralized.

That government could concentrate power in a single institution while sustaining a relatively decentralized party system is a puzzling feature of the New Deal political order. So too is the collective fate of two of its most important political actors. On the one hand, President Roosevelt enjoyed tremendous success, even as he was routinely checked by members of his own Democratic Party—let alone a vocal opposition party, a Supreme Court dominated by appointees of the previous decade, and myriad state and local politicos. On the other hand, the nation's most popular radio person-ality, a Canadian-born priest, Father Charles Coughlin—the son of Irish immigrants who captivated a large audience with his weekly tirades against the government—failed to translate his popular power into programmatic action. Both men navigated the treacherous political waters of the 1930s, as America sank deeper into the Great Depression and populist agitation grew. FDR sought to contain its force; Coughlin sought to exploit it.

In comparison to previous eras of unrest, the populism of the 1930s was, by far, more vast and potentially disruptive. The underlying cause of the farmers' struggles continued after Bryan's ill-fated candidacy in the late 19th century. During World War I—when prices for farm goods soared—most farmers took out new mortgages to finance expansions and increase pro-duction; when prices plummeted as Europe regained its footing, American agriculturalists once again found themselves beholden to far-away creditors. Their alienation was made all the more painful by dramatic cultural changes during the Roaring Twenties when cities thrived and the rural heartland be-came more marginalized. For the first time in American history, a majority of the US population lived in urban areas; print and radio media reflected this transformation, giving greater purchase to the farmers' claims that they had been left behind by a ruling elite. The largest political fight of the decade was a fractious culture war over traditional values of individual responsi-bility and temperance, aroused by the federal government's massive efforts to enforce Prohibition.[72] Bryan rose to prominence, once again, but this time in the defense of a Tennessee law that forbade the teaching of evolution; the Scopes trial was the harbinger of a new age in American sensibilities.

Farmers were not the only group reeling from these social and economic changes. The country's industrial class—many of whom fled their small towns either in Europe or on the American frontier—continued to fight for job security, higher wages, and a permanent place in the management of their workshops. In comparison with their European brethren, American labor leaders had thus far failed to cultivate a unified movement on behalf of American workers, who were divided along sectional, ethnic, and racial lines. Earlier efforts, none more prominent than the American Federation of Labor, succeeded in providing limited benefits to only a small subset of "artisan" workers, thus leaving out the growing sector of unskilled laborers, especially women and racial minorities. The widespread persecution and deportation of communist organizers and intellectuals following World War I further stifled efforts to reform the American workplace through institutional channels. And while municipal reform and progressive settlement experiments drew much needed attention to the living conditions of the urban, industrial poor, the gains made throughout the decade were obliterated by the market crash in 1929. Thousands of veterans—many still reeling from injuries of the world's most gruesome conflict and left out of an increasingly professional workplace—descended on Washington, DC, in the summer of 1932, pleading with government officials to pay advances on their promissory notes earned after fighting overseas "to make the world safe for democracy." The army torched the tent-city these veterans pitched during their "Bonus March," just blocks away from the Capitol.

In short, the potential for a widespread populist revolt was already great by the time FDR took office, but the terrain for demagogic exploitation was made more fertile by the development of new technologies, such as the radio. In Europe, Adolph Hitler and Benito Mussolini had already demonstrated the power of mass rhetoric, allowing leaders to personally reach into the homes of millions, amplifying the voices of the dispossessed and claiming to speak for the downtrodden. Years before President Roosevelt's own "fireside chats," Father Charles Coughlin harnessed this new medium and built a loyal following from the ground up, challenging the constitutional system from the outside.

The "radio priest" had grown in popularity throughout the 1920s and early 1930s—expanding his Royal Oak, Michigan, audience into a national following. Millions of Americans tuned in every Sunday to hear his fiery and richly enunciated sermons. Coughlin's radio sermons tapped into the pervasive sense of injustice among farmers and laborers that wracked the country and directed it toward his own self-perceived enemies: the titans of high finance who perpetuated the system of "modern industrial slavery." As one Massachusetts Democrat would write to FDR, Coughlin's followers were "sullen, discontented and bitter, using any argument that they think will appeal to the hearer."[73] At his height, Coughlin's radio show, "The Golden Hour of the Little Flower," reached into the homes of nearly 40 million Americans.

Coughlin also joined his pioneering use of the radio to more personal forms of persuasion. Recognizing the power of celebrity and fanfare—he filled the pews of his church and maximized the weekly offering by inviting superstars, such as Babe Ruth, to take the collection. As the donations poured in, he built a new church to accommodate the nearly 30,000 worshiper-tourists who flooded the small town each weekend.[74] And as his popularity swelled, Coughlin extended his personal reach and crisscrossed the country, selling out convention halls, stadiums, and music venues—including Madison Square Garden—to denounce the sins of the ruling class and to give voice to his downtrodden but enraptured audiences. Editors of the major dailies repeatedly plastered the text of his speeches and sermons on the front pages of their newspapers, often alongside an alluring photograph of the humble, plainly clothed priest.

At first, Coughlin's sermons were uncontroversial; his growing audience was a testament to his marked cadence, smooth tenor, and wistful Irish brogue. He preached a traditional Catholic sermon and only ventured into overtly political topics that were not divisive: denouncing the Soviet assault on pious Christian worshippers, disapproving the spread of birth control, celebrating the declining influence of the local Ku Klux Klan organization—messages that resonated with the overflow crowds who first attended, and then moved to join Coughlin's parish.

With time, however, Coughlin began to focus more on the "unemployment situation," promising his listeners that he would figure out and address the root causes of the economic collapse and identify those accountable. Implicit in his promise to speak out for the common man was a harsh rebuke of the existing political class. Indeed, Coughlin's transition to political sermons, occurring just as his audience was expanding, made his sponsors uneasy. Officials at CBS, which had picked up his broadcast for national syndication in 1930, privately warned him to tread carefully. In promising to name names and in preaching an "inflammatory" doctrine on the government's responsibility to help the working poor, Coughlin had crossed the line of political caution that CBS had drawn. Yet, in true populist fashion, Coughlin used these warnings to his advantage. This was evidence, he shouted, of a large conspiracy against him—of his effort to preach the truth in an "unpreachable sermon." Coughlin denounced CBS's conspiracy to muffle him, lectured its executives on the values of free speech, and established his credibility as the unfiltered and fearless voice of the people. An estimated 400,000 letters flooded the local post office in support of the radio priest following his first sermon of 1931, in which he unabashedly promised to expose further truths that had so far been left untold.[75]

CBS did not renew his contract, but, relying on a network of smaller radio stations, Coughlin defiantly preached his unpreachable sermon despite being ousted from the dominant networks. In its substance, it was a standard condemnation of the "international financiers" and American "plutocracy," which had rigged the global marketplace following the Great War "in the blood bonds born of an unjust treaty [Versailles]." While he was not alone in questioning the true interest of the "billionaire secretary of the treasury"— Andrew Mellon—or in his claims to have unveiled a lurid "oil plot" that allowed American companies in Venezuela to evade import tariffs, Coughlin was an unmatched political celebrity who had gained the trust of millions.[76] He wove facts into his discourse and spewed lines of statistics that gave him the aurora of erudite legitimacy—a persuasive and sacred foundation for his belief that "rebellion to tyrants is obedience to God." As Alan Brinkley recognized, "other public figures were espousing the same sort of vague radicalism during this period without evoking a comparable response. What made Coughlin different was his medium. . . . Coughlin was exploiting a system of communication whose potential conventional politicians had not yet begun to appreciate. . . . [H]e was a man in the right place at the right time."[77]

When FDR accepted the Democratic nomination in the summer of 1932, Coughlin abandoned any semblance of political neutrality and put his listeners squarely in the camp of Roosevelt. In capturing the nomination and eventually the presidency, FDR took notice of Coughlin's power and persuasive sensibilities. As election day approached, Coughlin took direct aim at Hoover, lambasting the administration's conservative approach to economic and social issues. Roosevelt spied great potential in Coughlin's populist appeal—a charismatic messenger who might span the widening gap between the Democratic Party's rural wing in the South and its growing immigrant constituency. Throughout his administration, Roosevelt paid careful attention to the challenge and promise Coughlin posed. On the one hand, grand overtures on the scale of the little flower could create a "new stimulation of united American action"; on the other hand, too much reliance on visionary rhetoric would play into their power and turn "the eyes of the audience away from the main drama itself."[78]

The fact that Coughlin's support of the new president grew as the New Deal was launched made FDR's efforts to distance himself all the more paramount. Coughlin peppered his sermons with warnings that it was "Roosevelt or Ruin!" and that "The New Deal Is Christ's Deal"—making it appear the Roosevelt's plans were just the same as his own.[79] Moreover, Coughlin was not content to be a cheerleader; he desperately wanted to play in the game. In his mind, Roosevelt had expropriated *his* message of social and economic justice. Roosevelt's coalition was *his* audience, which he had been grooming since 1920, when James M. Cox and his running mate—an up-and-coming Franklin Roosevelt—had lost.[80] At the announcement of each new economic intervention, Coughlin sent his personal endorsement straight to the president, coupled with a few lines of recommendations for FDR to consider. Coughlin's persistence led President Roosevelt to express deep concern within the counsels of the White House that the radio priest resembled other demagogues, such as Louisiana strongman Huey Long, who aroused the public with their "haranguing method," "unscrupulous use of specious appeals," and "arousing of hate, envy, fear, and all the animal passions" during a time when the people were deluded with the "disorders of democracy."[81] Now wary of appropriating populist rhetoric, FDR ordered his advisors to "tame these fellows" by distancing themselves from Coughlin and other populist leaders clamoring for power.

Dismayed by the White House's cold shoulder, Coughlin responded by promoting his own ideas in his radio addresses, dismissing FDR's New Deal as far too tepid to treat the severe domestic crisis. When the president declared a bank holiday and federal guarantees for deposits, Coughlin argued that the country needed to abolish the Federal Reserve entirely; when FDR advocated voluntary price controls, Coughlin bespoke the old panacea of the free coinage of silver. As Brinkley summarizes, there was in Coughlin's prescriptions for recovery an alluring and deceptive simplicity characteristic of populist jeremiads—an implication that a few painless alterations in the banking-and-currency system would restore prosperity. More complicated problems of distribution and investment received no attention. What was left was, in large part, a simplistic promise of quick and easy wealth.[82]

Unlike the Populists of the late 1800s, however, Coughlin found a receptive audience in the halls of Congress and within statehouses across the country. Coughlin nourished these relationships and garnered even greater attention by holding weekly audiences with the press.[83] A highly manicured profile in the *New York Times* detailed Coughlin's daily routine: taking phone calls with governors, getting ready for conferences on Capitol Hill, conferring with farmers in Minnesota, and protesting FDR's agricultural policy.[84] On the eve of a major international conference on global finance,

85 members of Congress pleaded with Roosevelt to appoint Coughlin as a special advisor to the proceedings.[85] Coughlin's political ambitions grew as his publicity soared, and by 1934, he officially organized his own political lobby, the National Union for Social Justice. Coughlin had boasted that the president learned everything about economics from him; with his own organization in place, he set about teaching Roosevelt lessons on the art of mass politics. However, even as Coughlin entered the partisan fray, he remained, as the *New Republic* editorialized, "dangerous, not because he promises too much, but because he does not know how to fulfill his promises."[86]

Despite his growing appeal, Coughlin and other would-be leaders of the downtrodden masses had to compete with Roosevelt's own-brand of populist rhetoric. "FDR's generous manner, his grasp of the civil religion, and his use of memorable populist phrases—like 'economic royalists' and 'the forgotten man,'" Kazin has written, "framed the rhetorical limits for social movements during the 1930s and World War II."[87] Yet unlike the iconoclastic Coughlin, Roosevelt's rhetorical powers were compromised by the demands of forging a new majority coalition. Although the Democrats had been partially turned into a national programmatic organization during the Progressive Era assault on machine politics, the party system was still highly decentralized. Roosevelt was able to rise to power and capture the presidency only through the wheeling and dealing, delegate-wrangling process that left presidential nominees beholden to convention floor promises made to state and local party bosses. As president, FDR remained as dependent on his partisan brethren for their support as they did on his. While Roosevelt would launch a reformist crusade on the party system during his second term, the president's first years in power were marked by the same sort of party negotiations that had constrained presidential leadership since Andrew Jackson. In administering New Deal programs, careful attention was paid to the distribution of federal largesse in the states and cities so as to combat the administration's political adversaries and win over unlikely partisan allies.[88] Some of these bargains severely constrained the possibilities of reform, most notoriously the president's "Faustian bargain" with southern Democrats ensuring that New Deal policies would not challenge Jim Crow.[89] The White House commanded unprecedented influence on the scope and direction of federal policy, but it worked through a Congress dominated by parochial and disparate interests. Federal policy, as a result, reflected the patchwork of localized party democracy that continued to thrive well into the 1930s.[90] And while Roosevelt, from his very first days in office, sought to forge a direct connection with the American people in an effort to transcend partisan politics, come election day he depended on the long memories of party identity and local officials' command of issues affecting small, diverse communities.

In contrast, Coughlin laid claim to a hollowed out, institutionally vapid organization, which struggled to exist as anything more than an expansive mailing list for the distribution of his sermons and special messages. Years after his movement's collapse, Coughlin himself would confess that the National Union was "more notorious for its *lack* of organization than for its organization."[91] Coughlin's efforts to mobilize his impassioned audience failed largely as a result of the strict rules he imposed on the local organizations that used his name: they were not to participate in state and local politics; they had to receive his personal endorsement of any candidate they believed upheld Union values before working on the candidate's campaign; and local organizations were discouraged from attracting the attention of the press that served their communities, lest they take away from the national image of the Union's supposed political virtue.[92]

Such institutional weakness reflected Coughlin's ambition to build a national organization that would transcend parties and centralize its leadership in his own hands. Frank Kent of the *Wall Street Journal* recognized the mobilizing potential of this strategy: "Organized on a non-partisan basis along Anti-Saloon League lines, [Coughlin's] power to swing from one side to the other thousands of blindly believing voters is an immense power. The conviction is that this is the power the Father consciously seeks. In effect, it would make him a dictator."[93] However, that potential was never fulfilled. Whereas Coughlin could turn a phrase and attract a mass audience, Roosevelt could harness the public's support to implement programmatic action through the channels of party coordination. The exigencies of partisan politics required FDR to attend regularly to the potential for intra-party insurgency. The president faced challenges on his left, particularly among the bloc of representatives from the Northwest who identified themselves as the heirs of Robert La Follette's Progressive Party. On his right, recalcitrant members throughout the South drew a hard line on many of the administration's plans for strengthening organized labor. Republican party leaders in Congress eagerly awaited the splintering of the Roosevelt coalition, predicting a third party run after FDR's first term, which would catapult them into office.[94]

Yet Roosevelt had honed his skills as a broker of intra-party factionalism from the start of his career and proved to be a gifted politician. An upstate

New Yorker with an aristocratic pedigree—fifth cousin of the reformist president Theodore Roosevelt—FDR rose through the ranks of the Democratic Party by going to war with the state's Democratic machine, Tammany Hall, which had effectively monopolized party politics in New York for almost a century. As an enterprising state senator and then governor of New York, FDR had become well practiced in the art of politics that demanded, not command and control leadership, but rather the ability to build consensus among a diverse constellation of stakeholders in the New Deal reform program. Institutional structure cannot totally explain FDR's political adroitness, but it does help to account for his rise to power, his governing stratagem as president, and ultimately his ability to convert many of Coughlin's soon-to-become discontented followers. Although the Democratic Party initially ceded the initiative to govern and plan for recovery to the White House, Roosevelt was still forced to placate conservative members of his own party, even as he took measures that made more progressive Democrats appear responsive to the legitimate woes of their constituents. As Raymond Clapper editorialized in 1935, Roosevelt's deft attention to the unwieldy Democratic coalition had to be reconciled with strong presidential leadership—demonstrating that he would "stand on his beliefs, preserve his self-respect, and strengthen the confidence of the country in his willingness to do what he believes is best regardless of the political consequences."[95] In short, he had to actually govern and produce results that he and his fellow partisans could collectively celebrate come election day. This required compromise within a fractious Democratic Party, especially with the racialized politics of southern Democrats. This also meant using the stick no less than the carrot. In his first term alone, Roosevelt vetoed 220 individual bills passed by the Democratic Congress. Nevertheless, by emphasizing economic reform to ameliorate the harsh conditions of the Great Depression, Roosevelt leveraged the large, albeit fractious, majorities the Democrats won in the 1932 election.

During Roosevelt's first term, parties remained collective organizations with a shared past and a concern for a collective future—strengthened in their diversity by party loyalties. In contrast, Coughlin represented a virulent strain of populism that exploited the public's anxieties and desire for collective action but offered little purposeful leadership. With one breath, Coughlin would rebuke the president's regulatory efforts for not going far enough and then celebrate the Supreme Court's decision to strike down legislation that empowered Roosevelt's administrators to act.[96] He demanded congressional action to strengthen the federal government's ability to check corporate influence while also claiming that the New Deal "transgressed the fundamental rights of State government." The administration's compromise measure over a federal minimum wage—a "prevailing wage" agreement— was evidence of FDR's "raw deal," but other efforts to regulate private property demonstrated that the entire system had been "captured by a group of scientific social workers who preach to us that big, bad bankers and good, little laborers shall submit to a multiplicity of conventional regulations . . . as they learn to habituate themselves to a strange admixture of fascism, of capitalism, of communism, and of Americanism."[97]

During the first few years of Roosevelt's administration, Coughlin's rise in popularity was abetted by the buoying spirits of the first New Deal. Coughlin's celebration of "Roosevelt or Ruin" enhanced his popularity with the Democratic Party's ethnically diversifying coalition.[98] Roosevelt recognized Coughlin's appeal and incorporated some of the radio priest's sermons on social justice into his own rhetoric. Nevertheless, despite Coughlin's protestations otherwise, it was the president who created the coalition and mastered the compromises that allowed for programmatic reform. By 1935, the famed political commentator Walter Lippmann noticed that "there can be no test of Father Coughlin's influence until he decides to stake it on a question that is not going to be decided that way anyway."[99] Roosevelt carefully threaded the needle between Coughlin's nascent movement, supporting him in vague language, while maintaining the support of Democratic Party regulars. As James Shenton, in an early study of Coughlin's dissidence reveals, "The administration's policy toward Coughlin appears to have had a double purpose: to delay as long as possible an open break, and to make the break, when it came, the decision of Coughlin."[100]

In the summer of 1935, Coughlin mobilized his organization in a test of his influence and in direct opposition to the administration's legislative priorities. Earlier in the year Coughlin had boasted that his followers foiled the president's plans to join the World Court—a treaty vetoed by the Senate after the radio priest cautioned his listeners on the danger of foreign entanglements. Emboldened by his growing influence, Coughlin championed an ambitious reform program, promoting legislation before Congress that supported his principles of "social justice" and that went further than Roosevelt's compromise New Deal.[101] Nearest to Coughlin's heart were three bills, each of which would have the desirable effect of inflating the money supply, which he charged was kept under tight control by financiers and the ruling class. In a series of radio broadcasts and public rallies, Coughlin helped to re-inflame the debate over bonuses for soldiers and pressure the federal government to print more money to meet these extensive financial obligations. Coughlin also introduced his own bill, crafted with the support of congressional allies, which would have eliminated the Federal Reserve and placed the authority to print money in the hands of elected representatives.[102] Finally, he concocted a plan that would allow farmers to gradually liquidate their debt obligations to the big banks, financed by millions in US government bonds that the Federal Reserve would have to buy.

Even though Coughlin's efforts had come to rest on a more concrete set of government proposals, he remained as uncompromising and as sure as ever. At the core of his proposals were carefully crafted tales of conspiracy between administration officials and the "princes of Wall Street" who orchestrated a "well organized attack" on his character and ideas.[103] Determined to be the rallying force for his legislative proposals, Coughlin tightened his control over the National Union in a deliberate effort to prevent its cooptation by party officials throughout the country. Kazin notes, for instance, that Coughlin "decreed how often chapters should meet, ordered that the first and most important business was to read one of his statements, and even prohibited units from holding dances or raffles lest they be accused of encouraging sexual dalliance and greed."[104] Supporters began to refer to him simply as "Father."[105]

Roosevelt's strategy in response was cunningly partisan. His goal was to deliberately demonstrate the priest's inability to translate words into action—that while Coughlin may have laid claim to moral authority, the people should not depend on him to bring about real reform. The president, relying on an extensive network of fellow partisans, kept close tabs on Coughlin and his operation. He coordinated the Democrats' strategy—one that would delegitimate the Father's claims to popular support by preempting him on some issues while discrediting him on others. Roosevelt appointed Frank Murphy—a loyal Michigan Democrat and member of Coughlin's parish—to "devote his entire time to the Coughlin situation," by personally negotiating with the priest on some days and peeling off his key supporters in Congress on others.[106] Roosevelt brought congressional leaders to the White House behind closed doors to discuss a joint strategy on how to respond to Coughlin's legislative onslaught, without appearing to credit the Father's economic philosophy. Ironically—given the immense power historians have bestowed on Roosevelt's "Fireside Chats"—the president deliberately decided *not* to exercise his rhetorical prowess against Coughlin's plans, fearing that it would drag the White House into an unwinnable fight against a talented demagogue.[107]

Rather than engage directly with Coughlin, the president, in consultation with Murphy and party leaders, set a course to erode the priest's support while appearing responsive to the public's anxieties. On the issue of farm
mortgages, the president lent a hand to the efforts of the powerful chairman
of the House Rules Committee John O'Connor (D-NY) who was keeping the
Frazier-Lemke bill bottled up in committee against Coughlin's insistence that
it be passed immediately. The legislation would have authorized the Federal
Reserve Board to buy all farm mortgages and permit the holders to gradually liquidate them at 1.5 %. Frazier-Lemke, which would also prevent banks
from repossessing farms, had a lot of support throughout the country—33
legislatures had adopted resolutions advocating its passage—but Roosevelt
feared that involving the federal government in the farm mortgage business on such a large scale would result in rampant inflation. When Coughlin
pleaded—in private and public—with the president to whip O'Connor into
shape, the president slyly demurred that he had little understanding of the
bill's status on Capitol Hill. Tensions between Coughlin and O'Connor deteriorated into school-yard antics, with Coughlin's loyalists eventually taunting
O'Connor that the priest would come down to DC to physically fight the
Rules chairman. The heavyweight political bout never occurred, as Coughlin
never arrived in the capital. Instead, O'Connor unleashed a vocal attack on
the priest, revealing how little influence he had in politics—about "as much
to do with Congressional action . . . as any elevator operator in the Capitol."
When the popular bill was eventually defeated in the House by a substantial
margin of 234 to 142, O'Connor flipped the narrative to suggest that it was
Father Coughlin, with his incendiary attacks on him and other members of
Congress, who "killed the bill." Writing an open letter in the *New York Times*,
O'Connor argued that "he [Coughlin] is the assassin, not I. And I understand
after his slanderous attack that he was informed by supporters of the bill that
he had killed it."[108]

On the question of soldiers' bonuses, Roosevelt vetoed Coughlin's
supported measure, the Patman Bonus Bill. Yet, in an unprecedented move,
the president delivered his veto message before a joint session of Congress.
His presence before Congress made the impending vote a referendum on
his leadership; however, he gained support, not through a direct appeal to
the public, but rather, through persuasion and politics.[109] Behind the scenes,
Roosevelt brokered a deal with the chambers' leadership to sustain the veto
and bring back the issue of bonuses in the following legislative session, once
the economic conditions in the country improved.[110] Before a crowd of

23,000 at Madison Square Garden, Coughlin lashed out at Roosevelt later that week, calling the president's veto a "money changer's argument" from a man who at his inauguration had promised to "drive the money changers from the temple."[111] Encouraged by this show of public support in New York, the priest openly speculated about endorsing a third-party candidate to challenge Roosevelt in 1936. Baited into drawing the line between him and the administration, Coughlin's influence and personal relationship with FDR was irreparably damaged.

Undeterred, by the end of summer, Coughlin had unleashed his organization's wrath on the members of Congress "who have lost sight of their duty as representatives of the American people." "The hunting season for members of Congress is on," he claimed; "we are compiling the record of every Representative and Senator either to applaud him as a patriot or to lash him as a Benedict Arnold."[112] On the radio and in his weekly press meetings, the priest wove together stories of the administration's efforts to pass labor legislation and price controls, concocting rumors that it was a "sham battle to protect plutocracy at the expense of the Supreme Court's prestige."[113] He suggested that two of Roosevelt's most trusted aides, Henry Wallace and Harry Hopkins, had started shell corporations in Delaware, which, if allowed to grow with government support, would lead to "unadulterated Communism and destruction of private property." Denouncing the Roosevelt administration for having "one foot in pagan Communism and one foot in plutocracy," Coughlin unleashed rhetorical fury in an ideological neverland, where government was strong and also weak, but never for "the people."[114]

Yet the damage inflicted by the Democratic Party's 1935 offensive had already been done. Although Coughlin had grand ambitions for the National Union, he closed its Washington headquarters and further personalized the image and message of the organization. Fewer members of Congress made trips out to Royal Oak, and Roosevelt went to great lengths to deny and hide a meeting between the two, set up at Coughlin's insistence in a last-ditch effort to reconcile the two leaders.[115] The *New Republic*'s famed Washington editor, T. R. B. presciently announced the end of Coughlin's movement a full year before his ill-fated foray into presidential politics: "The process of letting the air out of Father Coughlin is already well advanced. . . . [I]t was a deliberate attempt to humiliate Father Coughlin, and show how little power he had left . . . Father Coughlin now seems to have been rubbed out by a parliamentary gang. He has had the Roosevelt finger put upon him."[116] Faced with a stark choice between Roosevelt's pragmatic reform and Coughlin's distemper, Kazin writes, "[The people] rejected the side that could offer them nothing but fury."[117]

How much of this was the result of the institutional strategies and opportunities nourished by the two-party system, and how much of this was the result of sheer political creativity and genius on the part of Roosevelt? It is impossible to distinguish between these competing factors. Some of Roosevelt's actions are conceivable under different institutional arrangements. A presidency-centered party, for example, may have offered FDR even greater support against an insurgent movement. Yet, in such circumstances, what would have prevented the president from fusing Coughlin's populist rancor with a politically empowered presidency? In the final analysis, party organization neither squelched nor inflamed Coughlin's insurgency—it mediated it, transforming legitimate public grievance over government policy into pragmatic alternatives, debated by leaders who were held to account.

Far from marking the height of his influence, Coughlin's decision to endorse a presidential candidate in 1936 demonstrated that the danger of his populist crusade had reached its lowest ebb. The summer before, Coughlin had forced loyal Democrats to choose between a popular president and an untested radio personality; as the election neared, their calculus became a simple one in favor of FDR. While Coughlin organized a mass movement, he offered supporters little opportunity to set the direction of that movement. Coughlin's unilateral decision to nominate the co-sponsor of the farmer mortgage bill, William Lemke—a Republican congressman from North Dakota—as the Union Party's presidential candidate was a crowning testament to Coughlin's insularity. Even in the heavily Catholic city of Boston, where Coughlin had successfully courted its popular former mayor and now governor, James Curly, the radio priest was repeatedly rebuffed when he attempted to use the local Democratic Party to mobilize would-be Lemke voters.[118] With Curly on the ticket for US Senate, he backed Roosevelt, as did hundreds of Democratic leaders across the country. Election laws thwarted Coughlin's efforts to get on the ballot in 12 states, including New York, California, and Louisiana, where his support was probably highest; in six other states the insurgent movement could not even use the "Union Party" label. Making matters worse, Coughlin's party did not run candidates for local office. As Charles Tull argues, "With no city-hall or statehouse patronage at its disposal, the infant party existed in many areas in name only . . . which failed to render wholehearted support."[119]

Coughlin's partisan organization was thereby relegated to the bottom shelves of presidential history, but his passion remained influential in the new Congress and on the Roosevelt administration. The Democratic Party did not simply squelch populist unrest; it channeled it into popularly accountable and institutionally vibrant organizations. During this period, Roosevelt attended to party matters carefully, going so far as to hand pick Frank Murphy—FDR's "liaison" with Coughlin—to run for governor against Coughlin's candidates in Michigan and to decimate Coughlin's claims of popular support in his home state.[120] During the 1936 election, Roosevelt was much more willing to embrace populist language in defense of the common man and to propose more interventionist reforms. It is no coincidence that two of the crowning achievements of the New Deal, the Social Security Act and the National Labor Relations Act, were passed in the shadow of Coughlin's fury.

Father Coughlin did not become a marginal figure until the eve of the Japanese attack on Pearl Harbor. With the approach of World War II, he preyed on the powerful strain of isolationism in the United States. His rhetorical fire shifted from the money changers who were exploiting the forgotten men and women of America to the domestic and international conspirators who would drag the country into an anti-fascist war, especially "Soviet-loving Jews." As Kazin notes, a kind of populism animated the retreat of Coughlin and his remaining followers to this "noxious bunker." Coughlin's demagogic appeals echoed the anti-semitism of late 19th-century populists like Tom Watson who identified Jews as greedy manipulators of "other people's money" and disseminators of radical doctrines from abroad.[121] Nevertheless, just as the radical agrarian movement should not be reduced to religious bigotry, so Coughlin should not be viewed solely through the lens of his descent into virulent anti-semitism and pro-fascism. Both represented the exalted ideals and toxic intolerance to which unfiltered democracy is prone.

Intermission

The domestic and international crisis that animated the National Union appeared to signal a rising tide of populism that posed new challenges to the American party system. FDR learned in combating Coughlin's crusade that it was becoming increasingly difficult to lead a party so disparate in its views. As we discuss in Chapter 3, FDR's 12-year command of the country would eventually renew the Progressive attack on the traditional party system. Roosevelt's presidency was deeply informed by the intellectual legacy of the Progressives and the historical lessons witnessed by Wilson and Theodore Roosevelt's "stewardship" of a nascent modern executive. Some reformers found Roosevelt's assault on Democratic regulars too limited, while others found it too destabilizing. But the perilous crisis that ushered Roosevelt into office gave the president a claim to popular leadership that no other Progressive president had enjoyed. During his second term, flush with the historic landslide he achieved in 1936, Roosevelt's leadership of the Democratic Party developed into an assault on the mediating influences of the two-party system in its effort to form a national programmatic party that could subordinate localized parties to "enlightened administration."

By the time Roosevelt took up the mantle of partisan reform, the American party system had experienced a century of populist unrest and institutional change. The history of party competition prior to the New Deal is a testament to democratic institutions at work. Leaders were responsive to populist uprisings. Their response, however, was complicated by the demands placed on them by the diverse constituencies and institutional arrangements of party organization and federalism. In this way, the party system, structured differently throughout the 19th and early 20th centuries, mediated or filtered populist protest. Protest, reform, and reconstruction of party structures have constituted the rhythm of institutional change in the United States.

Our goal has not been to evaluate the movements or the outcomes created by the intersection of populist protest and party reform. Rather, it has been to suggest that the structure of institutions makes a difference. In particular, the arrangement of power within the party system itself, coupled with the arrangement of power in the formal governing institutions, leads to distinct strategies by political elites and reformers. In the first period of populist unrest, Anti-Masons worked within a system of party competition that was highly centralized. Yet governing authority remained highly decentralized. Their successes were hard fought but tempered by the difficulties in coordinating political reform in localities and states, which is where political life remained centered. Martin Van Buren and other Democratic Party leaders, in response to the Anti-Masonic threat, reorganized party life into a highly decentralized and intensely mobilized form of politics that penetrated deeply into American society, dominating the perceptions and voting habits of individuals. Not even the Civil War could disrupt the essential characteristics of the party system in the United States. For most of the 19th century, party life was decentralized and hostile to centralized power.

The decentralized party organization, operating in a fragmented governing structure, produced a dim vision of democratic responsiveness as industrialization hit the country like a gale force. So resistant to change, the decentralized party system stifled—and sometimes corrupted—a mass agrarian protest. However, in the aftermath of the Populist Movement, reformers, as they did a century before, took aim at the party system. In particular, they centralized governing authority through a variety of Progressive reforms, culminating in the New Deal. Still, party organizations themselves remained highly decentralized, even while the locus of formal governmental power shifted toward DC. Far from ending the populists' recurrent force, the New Deal merely shifted protest to the national stage. Indeed, the centralization of governmental power made 20th-century populism especially dangerous. And yet, because parties—in particular, the Democratic Party—retained enough institutional integrity to resist Coughlin's movement, FDR was able to navigate the treacherous terrain of economic nationalism.

At the same time, the Democratic Party remained resilient because it retained some of its anti-democratic institutions and practices. It maintained—indeed, depended on—a vision of White supremacy in the South; and it continued to sustain its decentralized organization with the patronage and benefits of big government, even after Progressive reforms had reduced its command of state and local spoils. As Eric Schickler has shown, the state party activists in the North and Labor began to move the Democratic Party toward a more liberal position on racial equality in the late 1930s and 1940s.[122] But the New Deal remained constrained by the Faustian Bargain that held together its northern and southern wings. United by a fragile consensus that failed to strike directly at the stubborn tumor of Jim Crow, the New Deal is not some golden age to which the country should return.

Roosevelt himself wanted to escape the gravitational pull of New Deal party life. And, following his reelection in 1936, he undertook an ambitious plan to reform party life, much as Wilson, Van Buren, Madison, and Jefferson had done. The menacing threat of Coughlin's nationalism led him to conclude that modern democracy required a presidency-generated administrative state that could transcend party organizations. We are still living in the lengthened shadow of the New Deal's consolidation of an executive-centered democracy; however, executive-centered partisanship was roiled by the antinomian culture and party wars of the 1960s. We examine the origins of executive-centered partisanship in Chapter 3 to shed light on how Roosevelt's assault on the state of courts and parties in his second term paved the way for the joining of presidential prerogative, social activism, and partisan polarization that characterizes contemporary developments in American politics.

3

Origins of Executive-Centered Partisanship and the Quest for Responsible Party Government

In Chapter 2, we traced the century-long, rhythmic history between the forces of populist protest and the mediating institutions that buttressed the American party system. In each episode, those clamoring for an unfiltered version of "pure democracy" focused their attention on the party organizations' gatekeepers who controlled the selection of candidates and the centers of power in government. However, party organizations emerged from these confrontations disrupted rather than decimated, reformed rather than ruined. Indeed, in responding to the populist revolt against "King Caucus," the architects of the new party system leveraged the fever of insurgency to create powerful institutions, imbedded in local and state governments, that dominated American politics until the Progressive Era. This decentralized and highly mobilized system had ossified by the end of the 19th century, resisting democratic unrest that unsettled the nation when the industrial revolution transformed the political economy and providing an arena for the Compromise of 1877, an unsavory bargain that sanctioned the end of Reconstruction and the rise of Jim Crow. By the time Franklin D. Roosevelt took office amid a devastating economic crisis and growing threats abroad, Progressive era reforms, most notably civil service protections and the direct primaries, dedicated to freeing the central government and executive office from the gravitational pull of localized parties, had altered the dynamics of party competition and weakened the complex, mediating organizations that dominated partisanship in the 19th century.

Like previous clashes between populism and party, Progressive reforms did not replace parties or protest. To the contrary, the new, more national political landscape gave the contest between party regulars and insurgents a new urgency. Moreover, the political and programmatic achievements of Roosevelt's first term had begun to transform the Democratic Party, hitherto an uneasy coalition of southern conservatives and northeastern "machine" bosses dedicated to local self-government, into a national programmatic party. Yet the transition was hardly complete—it depended on a truce between the regular party organization and New Dealers that would be sorely tested and eventually broken during Roosevelt's second term. The president's political aide, Stanley High, anticipated this confrontation in a 1937 article entitled "Whose Party Is It?" in which he argued that FDR's triumphant reelection campaign was but a prelude to a forthcoming battle for control of the Democratic Party. The traditional Democratic Party, High observed, had little use for the labor unions, civil rights groups, and liberal intellectuals who advocated New Deal programs. These liberal constituencies that were forging the New Deal within the White House and newly created administrative agencies, in turn, had no particular devotion to the Democratic Party save its use as a vehicle to advance the "President's Program." The popularity of Roosevelt and his program as well as the severity of the Depression had brought these two "factions" together, a "happy union" that held through the 1936 election. However, the union was one of convenience, and it was not likely to endure. The issue, therefore, High wrote, is "to determine whether the Democratic Party [is] as it has always been or whether it is now to become a liberal party."[1]

The push for a more decidedly left of center party was galvanized by a surge of populist challenges throughout the 1930s posed by Father Coughlin and other would-be populists, such as Huey Long in Louisiana. As public expectations for national leadership swelled, the Roosevelt administration renewed the progressive assault on party organization and the institutional divisions it fomented. New Deal Democrats viewed the party system as an obstacle to bold presidential action and the expansion of national administration—that is, to the executive-centered administrative state that Roosevelt and his political allies hoped to construct. During Roosevelt's second term, New Dealers pursued an administrative reform program—the "Third New Deal"—that established the president, rather than Congress or party organizations, as the center of government activity and the repository of party responsibility.[2] As the presidency developed into a more powerful and elaborate institution, it preempted party leaders in many of their most significant duties: providing a link from government to interest groups, staffing the executive department, contributing to policy development, organizing election campaigns, and communicating with the public. Moreover, New Deal administrative reform remade the presidency as the public face of a sprawling bureaucratic apparatus tasked with discovering and fixing the country's most vexing problems.

Even as the fragmented party system resisted Roosevelt's boldest plans to strengthen national administration and discouraged New Dealers from attacking the ramparts of Jim Crow, it provided numerous opportunities for the president and party leaders to stave off populist protest that not only threatened party regulars but also antagonized New Dealers' ambition to bring about an enduring shift in governing authority. But during his second term, Roosevelt's administrative reform program undermined the traditional intermediary institutions that helped the president and his political allies withstand the populist challenges to the New Deal earlier in his administration. Party regulars fiercely resisted and circumscribed the Third New Deal. And, the battle over administrative reform thrust the president to the center of politics and government, further weakening the decentralized party system and giving rise to an embryonic form of executive-centered partisanship.

Although the consolidation of executive power under Franklin Roosevelt was contested, the rise of an executive-centered administrative state reflected a fragile consensus that for a time obscured partisan conflict over national administrative power. Following World War II, many conservatives and liberals alike celebrated Roosevelt's vision of a new American state. Partisan politics reached a low ebb as citizens held high trust in government and majorities of both parties largely agreed about the direction of domestic and foreign policy, so long as national programs did not disturb a racialized political order with partial civil rights. That limited consensus unraveled amid the upheaval of the 1960s. With government and party under a full-scale assault, the political system became ripe terrain for the populist uprisings of the 1960s we will explore in Chapters 4 and 5. Inured to America's simmering racial divisions and inequalities, the architects of the Third New Deal could not foresee the powerful social movements that would soon pressure the presidency to abandon incremental reform and throw American politics "off center." Following Roosevelt's death, New Deal partisans continued the quest for responsible party government and reified the institutional developments that structure current partisanship.

While highlighting how New Deal efforts to reconstitute American partisanship and administrative government set in motion developments that broke apart the vital center, we do not celebrate the post–World War II consensus as a golden age of American politics. Indeed, just as previous populist movements expressed legitimate grievances, so too did the movements that sought to dismantle the New Deal state a generation after it was formed. The attempt to realize the Great Society during Lyndon Johnson's presidency exposed the central fault lines of the executive-centered administrative state that anchored the New Deal political order. The 1960s left many social activists feeling alienated from the "establishment," and with violent upheaval in Vietnam and in the nation's urban core, the pragmatic center that buttressed the New Deal disintegrated. To understand the populist upheaval of the 1960s, which Chapter 4 and 5 examine in detail, we must first provide a fuller account of the system that insurgents revolted against.

The Third New Deal and the Rise of Executive-Centered Government

Confronting a populist moment that was larger and potentially more disruptive than those that had come before it, Roosevelt and his New Deal political allies emerged from the first-term fight with Coughlin ready to a pursue a program that would replace traditional intermediary institutions with a presidency-centered democracy. The Third New Deal included three provocative measures: the Executive Reorganization Act, the centerpiece of the program, announced in January 1937; the court-"packing" plan, proposed just a few weeks after the administrative reform program; and the so-called purge campaign, attempted during the 1938 congressional primary elections. These measures had the common objective of strengthening national administration and consolidating responsibility for public action in a remade institutional presidency. They marked an effort to transform a decentralized polity, dominated by localized parties and court rulings that supported property and states' rights—the "state of courts and parties"—into a more centralized, even bureaucratic form of democracy that would deliver goods championed by New Dealers.

Roosevelt made clear soon after the 1936 election that he viewed the Third New Deal as a constitutional program that would establish executive dominion not just over the governmental structure but over the party system as well. The president reflected on such an exalted task during a meeting with the President's Committee on Administrative Management, comprising three of country's foremost scholars of public administration—Louis Brownlow, Luther Gulick, and Charles Merriam—which was charged with developing a blueprint for the reconstituted executive office. As Gulick's notes of that meeting read: "[Roosevelt] said that since the election he had received a great many suggestions that he move for a constitutional convention for the United States and observed that there was no way of keeping such an affair from getting out of hand what with [Father] Coughlin and other crackpots about." "But," he said, "there is more than one way of killing a cat, just [like] the job I assigned you."[3]

Progressives prescribed keeping politics and administration in their separate spheres. They championed independent regulatory commissions, such as the Interstate Commerce Commission and the Federal Trade Commission, which were governed by officials with fixed and overlapping terms. These agencies, the influential Progressive reformer Herbert Croly exalted, freed experts in various policy spheres "to do right."[4] Roosevelt and the Brownlow Committee dissented from this view, arguing that independent agencies defied public accountability and were all too susceptible to special interests that would obstruct the development of a modern state.

In joining presidential ambition to the newly remade powers of the central government, Roosevelt's plan was a response to populist demand as well as an effort to reduce its significance in the future. Roosevelt and his New Deal political allies had benefited from the Democratic Party organization in fending off the most dangerous tendencies of Coughlin's populist insurgency; but consolidating the institutional foundation of the New Deal political order required a program that would diminish the mediating role that parties played. Thereafter, the responsibility for responding to the influence of more extreme political actors—"crackpots"—would fall on an executive-centered administrative state. Most important, the Third New Deal created the "modern" presidential institution. Formed pursuant to the 1939 Executive Reorganization Act, the Executive Office of the President allowed subsequent presidents to realize the New Dealers' objective of an executive-centered party. The reconstituted executive office enabled presidents to form alliances with activists and outside groups who disdained the party "establishment," thus subordinating decentralized and pluralistic party coalitions to more national and programmatic networks that shape contemporary party politics.

The fusing of partisanship and presidential prerogative fueled the rise of the New Deal state. Bureaucratic government dates back to the late 19th century, but the American administrative state became a permanent fixture of politics and government during Franklin Roosevelt's protracted presidency. The New

Deal not only brought about policy change but also consolidated developments that bestowed legitimacy on a modern state, which gradually diminished the influence of the decentralizing—provincial—institutions, especially Congress and the states, which had dominated American politics since the Jacksonian period.[5] World War II further strengthened the fiscal and administrative capacity of the New Deal state, as agencies took unprecedented steps to build, reform, and regulate the largest sectors of the American economy.[6]

In overcoming the traditional restraints that party competition had previously placed on national leadership, Roosevelt envisioned a new age of presidential administration. Yet, it is a mistake to view him as naïve or insensitive to the ancient tribulations of democratic-populism. During his first term in office, Roosevelt had experienced populist thunder firsthand and had deftly navigated the system of decentralized parties to squelch one of the most significant challenges to constitutional government that had emerged up to that point in the country's history. In reconstituting the American political system, the president sought to establish a democratically accountable, or "responsible" form of partisanship—one that would achieve both the gains from administrative policy solutions and an invigorated form of publicly accountable national leadership.

Programmatic Liberalism and the American Party System

The decentralized party system endured through the first few years of Roosevelt's tenure, helping the president respond to the economic nationalism of Charles Coughlin and other populist insurgents who sought to capitalize on the public's fears during a time of global unrest. Nevertheless, FDR emerged from these struggles with a new desire to remake that party system. While strong party organization contributed to Roosevelt's success—providing him resources, structuring the incentives of other powerful leaders, and imposing discipline on elected representatives—localized parties were still a principal constraint on presidential leadership. No president had enjoyed as much discretion and deference as FDR had during the country's initial response to the Great Depression. And yet, he was not unchallenged or all-powerful. Moreover, as the country clawed its way back from the brink in the middle of the 1930s, the president's fellow partisans were eager to reestablish the constraining influence of the Democratic Party's old ways, especially in returning decision-making power to the states and Congress.

In response, Roosevelt and other ardent New Dealers echoed the Progressive Era's earlier call for party reform; they defined their task as overcoming the state and local orientation of the party system, which was poorly organized for the daunting challenges of 20th-century America, and establishing a national executive-oriented party, which would be better equipped for the expression of national purposes. Reflecting on his second term "purge" campaign against conservative Democrats, FDR wrote in 1941:

> There have been many periods in American history, unfortunately, when one major political party was no different than the other major party—except only in name. In a system of party government such as ours, however, elections become meaningless when the two major parties have no differences other than their labels. For such elections do not give the people of the United States an opportunity to decide upon the type of government which they prefer for the next two or the next four years as the case may be. . . . Generally speaking, in a representative form of government, there are generally two schools of political belief—liberal and conservative. The system of party responsibility in American politics requires that one of its parties be the liberal party and the other the conservative party.[7]

A revamped Democratic Party, dedicated to a national welfare state and liberal internationalism, would be the vanguard of this reconstituted partisanship. The effort to establish it would consume the Roosevelt administration after its fight with Coughlin and after the American people vindicated the president's leadership with his triumphant reelection in 1936. FDR won every state except Maine and Vermont and captured over 60% of all votes cast—to that point the greatest popular vote landslide in American history. Democrats in the House strengthened their already historic supermajority over Republicans, 334 to 88, and the Democratic coalition in the Senate maintained its filibuster-proof majority, 74–22—the most lop-sided Senate since after the Civil War.

However, those Democratic congressmen and senators did not set off for Washington eager to rubber stamp FDR's grand designs. While it is common to interpret the 1936 elections as a "realigning" force in American politics—one of those rare moments when the American people spoke with a singular voice and moved the nation in a new direction—it is also true that the 75th Congress challenged Roosevelt's stewardship of the country in ways that would have been unthinkable during the president's first four years in office.[8] Indeed, the Democratic Party's historic majorities owed as much to the party's vast diversity of opinion as it did to Roosevelt's popularity or any sense of a unified agenda. Democrats, representing the country's growing urban core and new ethnic minorities, uneasily sat alongside an unchallenged southern wing—the traditional bastion of the Democratic Party. Nor did the political conflict that threatened the pursuit of a transformed liberalism stop at the water's edge; regional and ideological differences splintered the party's response to the growing crisis in Europe and East Asia. And, while 1936 is often viewed as cementing the bond between organized labor and the Democratic Party, the incorporation of labor into the fragile Democratic coalition was not without disruption. Labor unions overwhelmingly supported the party that, in the previous year, had secured collective bargaining rights for the American worker; Labor's Magna Carta, as the National Labor Relations Act was celebrated. Yet the incorporation of Labor into the Democratic Party aroused deep concern among the unions' loudest opponents—most of them southern Democrats—who by dint of their seniority had powerful positions in the House and Senate. And, as organized labor formed an uneasy alliance with a nascent civil rights movement— which heralded, for a time, a White-Black alliance of unskilled workers—an unbridgeable gulf emerged within the party. To ease this split, party stalwarts pressured Roosevelt to oppose the radical remaking of the American workplace and its racial order. Nevertheless, the federal nature of the two-party system aided labor and civil rights groups in the North and Midwest, especially the Congress of Industrial Organizations (CIO) and the NAACP, in securing political support at the state and local level, in opposition to national leadership—a struggle between Democratic Party regulars and social activists that would reverberate through the 1960s.[9]

Indeed, it was not a foregone conclusion that the Democratic Party would become the home of progressive reform in the new party system. The Progressive wing of the Republican Party, represented by Theodore Roosevelt and Robert LaFollette, remained an important presence through the first two decades in the 20th century. It was not Wilson, but Roosevelt— especially during the Progressive Party campaign of 1912—the celebrated public intellectual Herbert Croly claimed, who advocated "the substitution of frank social policy for the individualism of the past."[10] Not until the 1920s did the Republican Party turn decidedly against government regulation of the economy and society (unless, like protective tariffs, government policies protected American industry). In fact, when the Depression hit and

Hoover's "cooperatist" solution—stressing better economic coordination and enhanced economic opportunities through voluntary action of the business sector—failed to ameliorate the harsh conditions of the Depression, few remember that an important issue of Hoover's routing and FDR's ascendance was the repeal of prohibition.

Once in the White House, Roosevelt began to embrace programmatic liberalism, which would distinguish the new Democratic coalition. But recognizing the deeply ingrained antipathy in American political culture to a national state, Roosevelt pronounced a public philosophy that he claimed comported with the Democratic Party's roots in Jeffersonian and Jacksonian democracy. The New Deal embodied a new idea of individualism, he argued, dedicated to protecting individual men and women from the abuses of big business and the uncertainties of the marketplace. Liberalism had always been associated with Jeffersonian principles and the natural rights tradition of limited government drawn from John Locke's *Second Treatise* and the Declaration of Independence. Roosevelt pronounced a new liberalism in which constitutional government and the natural rights tradition were not abandoned but were linked to programmatic expansion, an activist national government, and energetic national leadership, institutionalized in a remade presidency.

As the public philosophy of the New Deal, this new liberalism, in its programmatic form, required a rethinking of the idea of natural rights in American politics. FDR's most important rhetorical accomplishment was to defend the burgeoning American state in terms that made it seem compatible with America's rights-based culture—to redefine a social contract that privileged limited constitutional government. He pronounced a new definition of the social contract, envisioning a government that should "assist the development of an economic declaration of rights, an economic constitutional order."[11] Gone were the days of traditional self-reliance—the "rugged individualism" that Hoover praised in his 1928 presidential campaign. Recognizing that "necessitous men were not free men" in an economy remade by the industrial revolution, Roosevelt and his political allies argued that government had to combat the debilitating insecurities of a "free" market dominated by large corporations.

Roosevelt's New Deal, presupposing a departure from the "natural rights tradition" that sustained the decentralized republic, was met with fierce resistance. Many Democrats still viewed Thomas Jefferson as the patron saint of their party and jealously guarded the constitutional prerogatives of

Congress and the states. Roosevelt, therefore, not only challenged the venerable tradition of limited constitutional government but also a deep-rooted form of party politics that, even in the midst of a great economic crisis, proved to be a formidable obstacle to national reform. The origins and organizing principles of the decentralized party system had established it as a political force against the creation of the modern state. The New Deal commitment to building such a state meant that the existing party system had to be reconstituted or marginalized.

Under the leadership of Roosevelt, the reformist faction of the Democratic Party became the instrument of great national purpose and the vanguard of the party system's demise. Ultimately, this purpose was directed to the creation of an administrative state that would subordinate party politics to administration. As FDR famously declared in the 1932 campaign address at the Commonwealth Club, "the day of enlightened administration has come."[12] Viewing traditional partisanship as vested parochial interests, the Roosevelt administration pursued personnel and policy practices that weakened the grip of party leaders on the government. During his first term, as we note in the previous chapter, Roosevelt worked cooperatively with the party. He allowed the Democratic National Committee Chairman, James Farley, to coordinate appointments in response to local organizations and Democratic senators; but the recommendations of organization people were not followed so closely after 1936. Beginning especially in 1938, as Roosevelt pursued the Third New Deal, his assault on the traditional party apparatus became more aggressive, and patronage practices began to circumvent the traditional organization altogether. White House aides, notably the militant New Dealer Thomas Corcoran, became more influential in dispensing patronage. Ed Flynn, who became Democratic Party chairman in 1940 recalled the growing tension between Farley and Roosevelt:

> By reason of the coolness between the two, the President turned more and more frequently to the so-called New Dealers who were then surrounding him. Under the leadership of Corcoran, these people became more and more pressing in their urging of appointments. In a sense, this short-circuited the National Committee over which Farley presided. As a result, many of the appointments in Washington went to men who were supporters of the President and believed in what he was trying to do, but who were not Democrats in many instances, and in all instances were not organization Democrats.[13]

From a political point of view, this departure from conventional patronage practices resulted, as the distinguished scholar of public administration Paul Van Riper noted, "in the development of another kind of patronage, a sort of intellectual and ideological patronage rather than the more traditional partisan type." The decentralized party system existed for and because of the traditional spoils system, but this new form of ideological patronage would revamp the executive branch so that its personnel would support the transformation of America's liberal tradition.[14]

In addition to reforming the patronage system, the reform of governmental administration helped New Dealers refashion the very idea of the welfare state. Parties had once been key to the delivery of public goods and in providing a basic level of economic security. In redefining the social contract, which had long emphasized individual privacy and limited constitutional government, into a new understanding of programmatic rights, the economic security of the American people became a new obligation of experts and administrators who served under the presidency. This idea is embodied by the Social Security program, enacted by Congress in 1935, but which was framed as a guarantee to the American people—not something that could be taken away depending on which party was in office, or which faction controlled the new Social Security Administration. This feature of New Deal style, executive-centered democracy is seen vividly in how most citizens— even in the wake of the Reagan "Revolution"—refer to Social Security: it is a programmatic right that, as FDR foretold, "no damn politician can scrap."[15]

For New Dealers, the idea of the welfare state was not a partisan issue. It was a "constitutional" matter that required eliminating partisanship about the national government's obligation to provide a safety net for the American people. Nevertheless, this displacement of partisan politics required in the short run a major partisan effort to generate popular support for the new economic constitutional order. To a point, this made partisanship an integral part of New Deal politics, for it was necessary to remake the Democratic Party as an instrument to free the councils of government, particularly the president and bureaucracy, from the restraints of traditional party politics and constitutional understandings. In the aftermath of Congress's enactment of New Deal programs, "new policies made new politics." Partisanship came full circle, centering greater responsibility on executive administration and the new beneficiaries of the law who had a direct connection to the government's largesse, to the detriment of Congress and other establishment figures who helped design and champion the law's passage in the first place.

Purging and Packing: The Aftermath of the 1936 Election

With the development of the Social Security program and the National Labor Relations Act, and in the aftermath of his own reelection landslide, Roosevelt took even more aggressive action to forge an executive-centered New Deal Democratic Party. The fragile party coalition summoned during Roosevelt's first term remained central to the New Deal political order: labor unions, ethnic and racial minorities, and southerners secured the Democratic Party's stronghold over a majority of state governments and the federal government for almost two decades. Yet the New Deal Democratic Party was tied to a presidency-centered partisanship where fellow partisans relied on the White House to raise funds, mobilize base supporters, convey a message, and advance programs.

Roosevelt's ambition to reconstitute his party became clear at the 1936 Democratic Convention. There, he and his political allies succeeded in abolishing the party's two-thirds rule, which since 1832 had given southern delegations to the presidential nominating conventions security against candidates who might take a strong stance against racial injustice. Elimination of the rule weakened southern Democrats and removed an important obstacle to the transformation of a decentralized party responsible only to a local electorate into an organization more responsive to the will of a national party leader—the president—and the interests of that leader's personal constituency.

The most dramatic moment in Roosevelt's challenge to traditional party practices came two years later, during the "purge campaign" of 1938. During the party's nomination season, FDR took the rare step of directly intervening in one gubernatorial and several congressional primary campaigns in a bold effort to replace conservative Democrats with candidates who were "100 percent New Dealers." Roosevelt did not confine his efforts to the South during the 1938 purge attempt, but his most outspoken opposition was directed toward his party brethren below the Mason-Dixon line. Historically a multifactional party dominated by sectional interests, the Democrats after 1936 became a bi-factional party with durable ideological and policy divisions. If the Democrats were to become a national liberal party, conservative southern Democrats would have to be defeated.

The purge is noteworthy, too, for cementing the alliance between organized labor and the New Deal. John Lewis, leader of the CIO, met with the president during the purge campaign to coordinate the administration's tactics with his own organization. Not only did the CIO fully back the president's electioneering efforts, but Lewis also embraced the campaign's ideological significance for American politics: "President Roosevelt's pioneering program of social legislation must not be allowed to lapse or become ineffective through the failure of the legislative branch. . . . [The CIO's endorsements have] sought to draw the line between 'campaign liberals' and those who will be trustworthy after election."[16]

For a time, Roosevelt was hopeful that his efforts would not isolate the southern wing of the party but would bring them into a liberalized Democratic coalition. Claiming Warm Springs, Georgia, as his second home and showing reluctance to intervene in race relations, Roosevelt and his New Deal programs were very popular throughout the South—none more admired than the Tennessee Valley Authority, which brought electricity to thousands in one of the most impoverished regions of the country. Roosevelt believed that conservative democracy in that section of the country was not really an economic conservatism; rather, it was firmly established in reaction to the Populist movement at the end of the 19th century by the exploitation of racial issues. The president's silence on anti-lynching legislation and his emphasis on building an *economic* constitutional order that improved the material well-being of most Whites and Blacks represented his hope that the South could be allied to a new liberal coalition, albeit one that would be tainted by his giving tacit consent to the maintenance of racial segregation and terror.[17]

After the 1938 purge attempt, columnist Raymond Clapper observed, "No president has ever gone as far as Mr. Roosevelt in striving to stamp his policies upon his party."[18] Early in the 20th century, William Howard Taft and Woodrow Wilson used the presidency's growing prominence to insert themselves into divisive intra-party disputes. But with Franklin D. Roosevelt's interference in the 1938 primary elections, presidents had solid precedent to become more active in shaping partisan politics. Most of Roosevelt's anointed candidates were defeated and his hope that the South could be reconstructed on the basis of a national program of economic reform was disappointed. Nevertheless, this massive partisan effort clarified the factional disputes in the Democratic Party and set the course for its development as a national programmatic party. Moreover, Roosevelt's unprecedented assault on the regular party organization presupposed that the sheltering of New Deal liberalism required executive-centered partisanship. Going so far as to claim that he would prefer to have liberal Republicans than conservative Democrats elected to Congress, the president's purge campaign was a dramatic testament to the ideal that, as one Roosevelt aide put it, "the President, and not either party, was now the instrument of the people as a whole."[19]

Concurrent to his attack on the traditional party organization, Roosevelt took aim at the last remaining vestige of the "state of courts and parties," the Supreme Court. The court-packing plan sought to eliminate the final constitutional barrier to a vast expansion of government activity and a strengthened presidency. Shortly after re-inauguration, Roosevelt's allies introduced a bill that would grant the president permission to appoint a new justice for every justice who failed to retire within six months of reaching the age of 70. Six of the nine justices on the Supreme Court were already 70 or older, which meant that Roosevelt would be able to enlarge the Court from nine to 15 members by making new appointments.

Supporters defended the bill as a necessary reform to a backlogged judicial system. Yet it was clear that any newly appointed justices would help the president overcome the Court's documented resistance to the New Deal. Significantly, the two Supreme Court decisions that enraged FDR the most were *Humphrey's Executor v. United States* and *Schechter Poultry Corp. v. United States*, both of which imposed constraints on the president's personal authority.[20] The decisions were handed down on May 27, 1935, soon known to New Dealers as "Black Monday." In different ways, both decisions threatened to derail the institutional changes that Roosevelt believed were necessary to solve the underlying problems of the Depression. The Court's ruling in *Humphrey's Executor* denied the president the right to remove appointees from the independent regulatory commissions, a legal power that Roosevelt and his advisors thought had been established by tradition and affirmed by precedent in *Myers v. United States* nine years earlier. The *Schechter* ruling was a direct challenge to the modern administrative state. It declared that the discretionary authority Congress had granted at Roosevelt's request to the National Recovery Administration, the leading economic agency of the early New Deal, was an unconstitutional delegation of legislative power to the executive. Both decisions galvanized the president's efforts to make the American courts a partner of a new executive-centered democracy, not a conservator of the old order.

Like the purge campaign, Roosevelt's attempt to pack the Court ostensibly failed when Congress defeated the 1937 bill. Still, Roosevelt was not deluded in suggesting that in losing the battle, he won the war. Beginning in March

1937, Justice Owen Roberts switched from the conservative to the liberal wing of the Court, and in rapid succession the justices found constitutional a minimum wage law in Washington state, which was similar to the New York statute they had found unconstitutional just a year earlier and, more significantly, they upheld both the National Labor Relations Act and the Social Security Act. The "constitutional revolution of 1937" was cemented after a wave of deaths and retirements allowed Roosevelt to appoint a majority of justices by the end of his second term.[21] The Court never again struck down a New Deal law. In fact, since 1937 the Supreme Court has not invalidated any significant federal statute to regulate the economy, nor has the Court judged any law (with the exception of the Line Item Veto Act of 1996) to be an unconstitutional delegation of congressional authority to the president.[22] Most of the judicial barriers to presidential power have fallen as the New Deal state ratcheted up in the aftermath of a brow-beaten judiciary.

Administrative Reform and the Consolidation of Executive-Centered Partisanship

While the purge campaign and court-packing plan went far to secure the domestic legacies of the New Deal era, the core program of the Third New Deal was dedicated to establishing a strengthened institutional presidency. The 1939 Executive Reorganization Act is, in effect, the organic statute of the modern presidency. It allowed Roosevelt to fill the political vacuum created by the attack on party stalwarts and judicial conservatives with an empowered presidential office. As the *New York Times* reported in August 1938—while the campaign for the new legislation raged—this Third New Deal program above all revealed the connection between Roosevelt's party leadership and the objective of forging an executive-centered administrative state. No measure "was closer to the President's heart," and none aroused "more determination to force it through Congress than the Reorganization Bill."[23] Indeed, the administrative reform program became, at FDR's urging, a party program. Thus, ironically, a policy aimed at making party politics less important became a major focus of party responsibility. So strongly did Roosevelt favor this legislation that House Majority Leader Sam Rayburn appealed for party unity before the critical vote on the executive reorganization bill, arguing that the defeat of this legislation would amount to a "vote of no confidence" in the president.[24]

The enactment of the executive reorganization bill only came after a highly contentious two-year battle between New Dealers and a conservative coalition of southern Democrats and Republicans, which began to organize aggressively against Liberal programs in 1937. The consequences of the reorganization bill for party loyalty were not lost on fellow partisans. The fight over reorganization came after the bitter struggle over Roosevelt's effort to "pack" the Court, making the political atmosphere ripe for controversy over any increase in executive power, let alone one that would transform the presidential office into a full-blown institution. The initial reorganization bill proposed in 1937 would create the Executive Office of the President (EOP). The EOP included the Bureau of the Budget, which had been housed in the Treasury Department since its birth in 1921, and a new White House Office, to be staffed by loyal and energetic presidential aides whose importance would be constrained by their "passion for anonymity." In contrast to the cabinet departments and independent agencies, which were extensively influenced by Congress, the EOP was designed as a presidential institution, responsible for tasks closely linked to the president's personal priorities and staffed by individuals who shared the president's political and policy objectives.[25] Most of those named by the president to fill important positions in the EOP did not require Senate confirmation.

The Executive Reorganization bill also sought to enhance the president's control of the expanding executive branch. Throughout the 1800s, national administrative authority emerged from congressional action, and as the powers of the national bureaucracy grew in the late 19th century, it was the Congress that sought to exert its constitutional right of administrative oversight in reorganizing the national bureaucracy.[26] As the administrative capacity of the federal government grew alongside rising expectations for national authority during the New Deal, however, Roosevelt made the administration and requisite reorganization of bureaucratic agencies a priority. During his first term Roosevelt insisted that virtually every new program be administered by a new agency created for that purpose lest they get buried in the bureaucratic routines of the existing departments. The resulting "alphabet soup" of dozens of new agencies—NRA (National Recovery Administration), WPA (Works Progress Administration), PWA (Public Works Administration), CCC (Civilian Conservation Corps), and so on—gave the image of a forceful government response to economic collapse. But by 1937 the president confronted a bewildering array of new and sometimes autonomous government agencies whose number and independence had come to offend his vision of a unified and energetic executive. Roosevelt, in fact, remarked shortly after the 1936 election that administrative management was the least successful aspect of his first term and professed relief that the Republicans had not concentrated their fire on this weakness during the campaign.[27] The administrative reform legislation called for an overhaul of the executive branch, recommending that all of the more than 100 agencies then in existence, including the independent regulatory commissions, be integrated into 12 major departments, each controlled by the president. As the report of the President's Committee on Administrative Management exuded, with the augmentation of executive administration, "our national will must be expressed not merely in a brief, exultant moment of electoral decision, but in a persistent, determined, competent day-by-day administration of what the nation has decided to do."[28]

The presentation of the administrative reform program left Congress "dazed," according to the New York Times. "The plan," reported Turner Catledge, "was the most daring, and certainly the most far reaching, proposal for change in administrative mechanism ever made to the American Congress." Although Catledge predicted the bill would pass because of the huge majorities commanded by the administration in both Houses, he foresaw an intense battle emerging, since "no bill of this nature and magnitude," touching as it did "so many vital spots of individual political organization and Congressional 'sacred cows' had ever been "seriously pressed before."[29]

To Roosevelt's dismay, Father Coughlin played a major part in arousing dissent. The radio priest delivered an impassioned speech on March 31, 1938, just prior to the vote on the legislation, arguing that administrative reform would bestow dictatorial powers on the president. The address elicited nearly 200,000 telegrams to congressional representatives. Ten thousand alone went to New York Senator Robert Wagner—the foremost champion of the National Labor Relations Act—a staunch New Dealer, albeit one who was suspicious of executive power; Wagner voted against the executive reorganization plan. The campaign against administrative reform reached a climax when, just prior to the vote on the legislation in the House, 150 self-proclaimed and appropriately dressed Paul Reveres from Chicago, New York, and New England journeyed to Washington to demonstrate against reorganization in person.[30]

So heated did the campaign against the executive reorganization bill become that Roosevelt felt compelled to issue a public letter to an unnamed respondent denying that the reorganization bill would make the president a dictator. The objective of the legislation, he insisted, was only to make the executive branch more "business-like and more efficient."[31] Planning would not be directed at efficiency for its own sake; rather, the goal was to make American democracy responsive to the developing interest in government-provided social services—to a burgeoning welfare state, which a great majority of voters seemed to approve in the 1936 election. To opponents of the reorganization bill, however, the push for a more efficient government in the meaning of the New Deal constituted a reckless experiment that would place so much power in the hands of the president as to render any meaningful sense of party responsibility a chimera.

What gave the battle over executive reorganization special intensity was that it occurred just as the administration of government programs was becoming an important arena of public policy. As Gulick reported approvingly, the expansion of welfare and regulatory programs during the New Deal meant that the complex responsibilities of government increasingly were set forth in loosely written statutes, each little more than "a declaration of war [on a problem], so that the essence of the program is in reality in the gradual unfolding of the plan in actual administration."[32] The struggle between the president and Congress for control of the departments and agencies was no longer a simple squabble over patronage and power. The right to shape the direction and character of American society was also at stake. Consequently, the ardent New Deal opponent, Georgia senator Carter Glass, was not merely giving expression to the irrational fear that Father Coughlin stirred up when he wrote in August 1937, "As matters are now, Congress is practically a rubber stamp for the executive, and under the proposed reorganization scheme the President would have no use even for a rubber stamp, he could do his own rubber stamping."[33]

Facing a sharply divided party—widened by the populist campaign that accused him of seeking dictatorial power—FDR lost the vote of confidence on administrative reform. The 1937 Executive Reorganization bill was defeated in the House, with nearly one-third—108 of 331—of the Democrats voting against it. Yet Roosevelt persisted, making opposition to the legislation a major issue in the purge campaign. Although the purge failed at the polls, it scared recalcitrant Democrats, who became more conciliatory toward the president on a few matters after the 1938 election. Administrative reform was one of these, and in 1939 a compromise bill passed the Congress. The 1939 Executive Reorganization Act placed a two-year limit on FDR's authority to reorganize the bureaucracy and exempted 21 important government agencies. Nevertheless, Roosevelt's implementation of the 1939 statute by Executive Order 8248 achieved many of the Brownlow Committee's recommendations. The order created the EOP and moved several existing agencies under its umbrella. In addition to the White House Office (the West Wing) and the refurbished and strengthened Bureau of the Budget, which was moved from the Treasury Department, the new EOP included the National Resources Planning Board, a long-term planning agency. The transplanted Budget Bureau began to acquire much greater power, eventually assuming responsibility to oversee the formation of the president's domestic program. By the end of Roosevelt's tenure as president, the bureau had grown from fewer than 50 employees to more than 500.

Because the creation of the EOP enhanced the president's capacity to manage the expanding activities of the executive branch, it was an "epoch making event in the history of American institutions," wrote Gulick, and "perhaps the most important single step in the institutionalization of the presidency."[34] Most significant, the 1939 reforms hastened the development of the "administrative presidency," in which domestic and foreign policy is shaped on the president's behalf through executive orders, personal diplomacy, rule-making by executive departments and agencies, financial oversight, and discretion in implementation.[35] Moreover, the refurbished Executive Office was adopted and enlarged by FDR's successors, Republicans and Democrats alike. For a time, the modern presidency achieved a status above party conflict; its cachet was non-partisan leadership. Politics was now a search for pragmatic solutions to the challenging responsibilities that America had to assume, at home and abroad, in the wake of the Great Depression and World War II.[36]

Indeed, Roosevelt's commitment to executive-centered democracy was expanded and given more elaborate institutional form during World War II. In Roosevelt's 1941 State of the Union address, he stated his support for the Lend Lease Act, which for all intents and purposes ended America's neutrality in the global conflict, and pronounced the four freedoms that became a charter for the New Deal. To the traditional freedoms of speech and religion, he added the "freedom from fear," to derive from "a world-wide reduction of armaments to such a point and in such a fashion that no nation will be in a position to commit an act of physical aggression against any neighbor," and the "freedom from want," requiring a commitment "to economic understandings which will secure to every nation a healthy peace-time life for its inhabitants." These new freedoms justified changes that intensified the concentration of power in the national government, its administrative apparatus, and the president. By the end of his long tenure in the White House, Roosevelt and the New Deal thus brought about two seemingly contradictory developments that continue to shape partisanship in the United States. On the one hand, Democrats became more unified around a liberal program dedicated to greater federal intervention in domestic politics, including policies to promote ethnic and racial equality, and, in the aftermath of World War II, a greater role for the United States in world affairs. On the other hand, the programmatic and national objectives of the Democratic platform gave rise to an executive-centered administrative state, which subordinated partisanship to the political and programmatic ambitions of the White House.

The Four Freedoms ushered in a new understanding of rights, sanctified by the Constitutional Revolution of 1937, under which domestic programs like Social Security and international causes like the Cold War called not for partisanship but for "enlightened administration" (as Roosevelt had described his New Deal aspiration in his 1932 speech at the Commonwealth Club). Freedom from fear and freedom from want, representing for all intents and purposes the charter of the modern American state, were given institutional form by the welfare and national security states. To be sure, the defense of national administration infused reform during the Progressive era. But as Daniel Carpenter has shown, the early architects of the administrative state, celebrating expertise and "independent" regulatory commissions, emphasized "bureaucratic autonomy."[37] With the Third New Deal, FDR and his political allies sought to strengthen the president's influence over the departments and agencies that sprawled during his first term, a consolidation of executive power that he insisted was necessary to secure the programmatic and human rights he championed in the Four Freedoms address. Indeed, FDR exalted New Deal policies, most notably Social Security, as the cornerstone of a second "Bill of Rights"—including the right to employment, healthcare, and education, the core commitments of an executive-centered New Deal Democratic Party.[38]

From the end of the Second World War to the late 1960s, party politics was subordinated to a policymaking state, where partisan conflict and resolution were largely displaced by a new understanding of rights and the delivery of services associated with those rights.[39] With the expansion of executive authority to secure those rights, traditional decentralized party organizations lost influence. Gradually, the president became the depository of party responsibility, depriving leaders at the state and local level the power to choose candidates, whip their party's membership into line, and control the policy agenda. The executive-centered nature of the new party system appeared to reverse Van Buren's formula for collective action: it substituted the personal preference of presidential candidates and presidents for the collective responsibility of diverse, decentralized party leadership. Personal leadership can provide a rallying force during elections and offer a clear statement of principles for citizens to assess. But such a reliance on presidential leadership also threatens to weaken parties as responsible collective organizations.[40] In the aftermath of this transformation, party organizations lost their influence to moderate—or broker—elections and government action. The New Deal state was better equipped to provide domestic and international security—to uphold freedom from want and freedom from fear. At the same time, it weakened those organizations that moderated political ambition and constrained party conflict.

Consequently, the New Deal state was exposed not only to unmediated interest group demands, as Theodore Lowi charged in his celebrated critique of liberalism, but also to unfiltered populist discontent, which rejected the idea that political conflicts could be reduced to administration and policy incrementalism.[41] Although the New Deal restructured America's governing commitments and established a more active national government as a core feature of a new national consensus, the political conditions that sustained the new vital center should not obscure the deep disagreement it aroused on the left and on the right. In truth, New Deal Liberalism rested on a fragile sense of national community, one that lacked effective means of public debate and resolution, the pillars of a civic culture. Of course, the ends of community and individualism are inherently in tension with one another—a tension that sits at the heart of the country's republican experiment. Throughout the 19th century, the party system negotiated this tension by resting citizenship in localized organizations and "spoils" that appealed to individual self-interest; the New Deal attempted to elide the dilemma of republican government by grafting a national administrative apparatus and activist public philosophy onto a rights-based constitutional system and a political culture.

As such, the New Deal state posed hard challenges to the ideals of any American vital center—especially those concerned with maintaining the citizenry's moral vigor and a competitive economy.[42] Liberal efforts to remake the party system—largely in response to the expansion of executive authority and decline of congressional responsibility—never grappled with that tension. Indeed, until Richard Nixon demonstrated that the modern executive might become, ideologically, a double-edged sword that could cut in a conservative as well as a liberal direction, most liberals remained largely uncritical of the executive-centered nature of the New Deal state. Arthur Schlesinger Jr. was an eloquent defender of the changes that trended toward a presidency-centered democracy, helping to establish the myth of a presidency-savior, or liberal hero, before the election of John F. Kennedy.[43] To shed light on the dismantling of the pragmatic center, therefore, we turn our attention to the critiques of the party system offered in the post–World War II era. It is only from such a critical understanding of the New Deal party system that we can begin to ascertain how things fell apart and how a vital center might be restored in American politics.

The Responsible Party Doctrine and Executive-Centered Partisanship

Since the New Deal, several developments have brought to fruition an executive-centered politics: the emergence of new partisan media, the development of a plebiscitary presidential primary system, the enactment of campaign finance reforms that shifted funding of campaigns to "outside" groups that disdain the establishment, and major demographic shifts in the population. Each has contributed, independently and interactively, to increase demands on the presidency, heighten polarization, and raise the partisan stakes in fights over domestic and foreign policy. Five years after Roosevelt's long presidency came to an end, a group of political scientists led by E. E. Schattschneider arranged a conference to study and comment on these emerging developments in the country's two-party system. The highly influential American Political Science Association Committee (APSA) on Political Parties surely did not predict such developments leaking out of the New Deal order, but their initial diagnosis of the New Deal party system suggests that the embryonic tendencies of executive-centered partisanship were already well on display in the years immediately following executive reorganization and the centralization of party leadership.

So far, we have emphasized the development of an executive-centered administrative state—a necessary ingredient for the presidential partisanship that roils contemporary American politics. The APSA committee's judgments and proposed reforms point to the second developmental logic we emphasize in this book—a road not taken, if you will—the creation of more programmatic, national, and participatory party organizations, or, as they claimed, more "responsible" partisanship. While no team of political scientists can outright change the institutions they study, the report nevertheless left an important imprint on subsequent generations of political leadership and reformers, especially in the 1960s and beyond. It is also the case that many contemporary scholars have sought to anchor current partisan rancor in the report's recommendations—warning that even erudite scholars should be "carful what [they] wish for."[44] However, it is wrong to equate the APSA committee with Roosevelt-style partisanship. And if, as we argue, our current dilemmas are reinforced by the institutional dynamics of executive-centered partisanship, it would be unwise to discard what should be read as an overarching critique of that New Deal order—one that anticipates, not prescribes, many of the pathologies plaguing contemporary partisanship.

In short, the growth of the federal government's programmatic commitments had convinced Schattschneider and the APSA governing board that the constitutional balance between Congress and the presidency was threatened. As Schattschneider wrote shortly after Roosevelt died, "For the successful execution of the complex and delicate policies by which it is hoped a new depression may be avoided, political means must be found to bring about unaccustomed teamwork of Congress and the President and all agencies and branches of government in order to integrate closely a great variety of public activities."[45] Schattschneider was a strong defender of the New Deal. However, the rise of the bipartisan conservative coalition in Congress to block Roosevelt's initiatives in the late 1930s had underscored the inability of the president to expand further New Deal programs and pointed to the need for majorities in Congress who shared the president's goals. The institutional paradox boiled down to this: if the American people could so clearly give direction to national policy by selecting a candidate of their own choosing, why was it that Congress remained immune to these popular impulses? Moreover, Schattschneider and the APSA governing board were concerned that a greatly strengthened presidency might undermine the division and separation of powers that was a cornerstone of constitutional government in the United States. Only a more "responsible" party system could once again bind the newly empowered presidency to an accountable Congress and thereby restrain further attempts to strengthen the independence of the executive branch.

The APSA report *Towards a More Responsible Two Party System*, published in 1950, called for a party system comprising national policy-oriented organizations capable of carrying out platforms or proposals presented to the people during the course of an election. In some respects, the report echoed the New Deal critique of the decentralized American party system, lamenting that parties continued to operate much as they had before the Civil War. The expansion and growing complexity of public problems during the New Deal, most notably the emergence of the welfare and national security states, rendered the traditional party system all the more antediluvian. It was "no longer safe for the nation to deal piecemeal with issues that can be disposed only on the basis of a coherent program," the report read.[46]

Roosevelt's assault on the lingering state of courts and parties thus anticipated the APSA Committee's critique of the American tradition of party politics. Indeed, Schattschneider noted in his seminal *Party Government*, published eight years earlier, that Roosevelt's attempt to reform the Democratic Party, particularly the purge campaign of 1938, "represented one of the greatest experimental tests of the nature of the American party system ever made."[47] Yet Schattschneider and his colleagues renewed the idea of Woodrow Wilson that political parties in the United States should not be transcended by an empowered, independent executive, as the New Dealers argued; they should, the APSA report argued, be made more responsible. They should remain central mediating institutions, not hollowed-out repositories for the president's loyal followers.

As such, the APSA committee took up the arduous and imaginative task of building national institutions that could enable the party system to better coordinate political action by the president, Congress, and various party leaders. Ultimately, they would, in a sense, design an American version of the British parliamentary system, which had clear lines of authority centered in the presidency (much like a prime minister) but also maintained important constraining impulses on that centralized leadership (akin to cabinet meetings, votes of no confidence, and clear ramifications for declining public approval). It was imperative, the report insisted, to create an "effective" party system, meaning, first, that the parties be able to create national programs to which they commit themselves and, second, that they possess sufficient internal cohesion to carry out those programs. In the absence of a link between party program and public policy, they argued, party responsibility at the polls tended to vanish—and representative democracy became an illusion.[48]

Often overlooked is that internal party cohesion was to be brought about by a reconstructed institutional logic that empowered different elements of the traditional party system and encouraged collaboration among them: congressional leaders, state and local party officials, the president, and other party officials. Party unity was not to be achieved by a dominant and dominating executive who would come in with each new nomination cycle and impose a new, personalized brand on the party. The renewal of institutional partnerships was thus the overarching goal of the APSA Committee on Political Parties. And yet, the inherent tension in the New Deal order between executive dominion and collective responsibility made the task of achieving "responsible" political parties a very tall order. In fact, the Brownlow Committee, in consultation with the White House, fully considered the doctrine of responsible party government while preparing the report of the President's Committee on Administrative Management; however, they viewed party government as an impractical solution to the ills that plagued American democracy and deliberately chose instead an alternative road to a stronger national government. Brownlow reiterated the New Deal dedication to concentrating policy responsibility in a revamped executive in a 1943 memorandum to Roosevelt: "We must reconsider critically the scholarly assumption, which has almost become a popular assumption, that the way to produce unity between the legislature and executive is to take steps toward merging the two." Commenting on Harvard government professor William Y. Elliott's proposal that the United States abandon its presidential system in favor of a parliamentary system, Brownlow added:

> In view of the extreme improbability that such a measure would receive organized support, it is worth considering only because it carries to a logical conclusion the common proposals (1) to have the Congress establish by statute a cabinet or administrative council for the president; (2) to give department heads or "Cabinet" members seats in Congress, the right to take part in Congressional discussions, or the duty to defend their administration before the Congress; (3) to set up a joint executive-legislative committee, or committees, to plan policy or supervise administration; (4) to create a committee of congressional leaders to advise the President. . . . *In direct opposition to this assumption and these proposals, it may be suggested that the objective to be sought is not to unify executive and legislature, but to unify governmental policy and administration.*[49]

Roosevelt and his political aides believed that the overall failure of the purge campaign, which was successful in only two of the 12 states targeted, made clear that resistance to party government was not merely built into government and laws but also deeply rooted in a political culture that gave preference to a different way of governing. Schattschneider drew a different conclusion. Taking account of the fact that the purge campaign involved Roosevelt's making a direct appeal to public opinion rather than trying to reform the Democratic Party organization, Schattschneider asserted in a 1948 lecture that its failure did not render the struggle for party government over. "The outcome of the purge of 1938," he argued, "does not prove that a more serious attempt supported by the whole body of national leaders could not bring overwhelming pressure to bear on the local party leaders who control congressional nominations."[50]

In fact, Schattschneider and colleagues endorsed several reforms that would further isolate the president from the now weakened, institutionally dependent party organizations. Committee members called for an "honestly prepared," politically achievable party platform to be written at national conventions—a process, which even by 1950 had become dominated by the presidential nominee taking center stage every four years. The committee also suggested that state delegations within the convention be proportioned by the party's share of the presidential vote within each state—a principle that would strengthen the national character of the parties and its dependence on presidential elections. And the report emphasized the mischievousness of the committee system in Congress, where "party campaign promises are kept or broken," but mostly broken. To the extent that committee strength and committee independence are the life blood of an effective modern Congress—and especially important in overseeing the executive branch—this recommendation likewise undermined the goal of constitutional balance between the president and Congress.[51]

These developments were unanticipated, suggesting the Committee's failure to understand just how deeply ingrained executive-centered partisanship had become as a result of New Deal institutional reforms. More to the point, far from endorsing the ambitions of Roosevelt's executive-centered democracy, the committee issued a dire warning of an outsized executive, less constrained by constitutional checks and balances, threatening the fabric of the nation's civic culture. Some of the most prescient passages in the committee report—especially in the aftermath of Vietnam, Watergate, and the culmination of the White House's dominance of the party councils during

Donald Trump's first term in the White House—are those that voice appre-
hension about a presidency grown too powerful and independent.[52]

To be sure, the Committee granted that presidential party leadership was
necessarily a principal ingredient of forging a party government. The New
Deal had established presidential domination in policy formulation: the
White House had become the first mover in budgetary, economic, and especially foreign affairs. Moreover, this growth of executive power was joined to
a greater emphasis on national politics, firmly establishing the president as
"the only politically responsible organ of government." However, the committee warned, "the President has no magic wand." A strong national party
organization could provide the White House with opportunities for institutional collaboration with Congress and the states—as well as a stable basis of
popular support. Lacking party backing for a broad program, the president
could attempt, as New Deal partisanship prescribed, "to fill the void caused
by the absence of an effective party program by working up a broad political
program of his own." But the ultimate implications of such a course of action
would be grave. As though in dialogue with the Brownlow Committee, the
APSA report echoed Van Buren's fears of an executive unhinged:

> There are people who say that [executive-centered partisanship] is a real-
> istic way of getting somewhere with good political ideas, especially ideas
> bound to leave cool both Congress and the larger part of the President's
> party. Some others say that the scheme is not the happiest thing but the
> only one practically available under presidential-congressional govern-
> ment. . . . *Yet can there be much doubt about the ultimate implications? When
> the President's program actually is the sole program in this sense, either his
> party becomes a flock of sheep or the party falls apart. In effect this concept
> of the presidency disposes of the party system by making the President reach
> directly for the support of a majority of the voters. It favors a President who
> exploits skillfully the arts of demagoguery, who uses the whole country as his
> political backyard, and who does not mind turning into the embodiment of
> personal government.*[53]

Fearing that the absence of party reform would lead to a level of executive aggrandizement that would render the party system obsolete, the
APSA Committee rejected many of the reform possibilities long touted by
Progressives who championed the president as the steward of the people—
reforms that reemerged and took hold in the 1970s and 1980s. For example,

the committee rejected a proposal first floated by Woodrow Wilson, to turn the presidential nomination contest—anchored by the national conventions—into a plebiscitary national primary. Although the report did not condemn the expansion of primaries, it prescribed that elected delegates and party leaders do more than register the verdict of a national primary system. As a traditional "party agency," the Convention should be augmented rather than relegated to the task of coronating presidential candidates. "With certain modifications," such as reducing the number of delegates to a more manageable size of 500–600 members, the convention could "quite satisfactorily attend to its customary functions. These are to nominate presidential candidates (or, should the presidential primary be established on a national scale, to declare the results); to adopt or approve the party platform; to adopt rules and regulations governing the party; and in general, to act as the supreme organ of the party." To assume these additional responsibilities, the Report added, it should meet biannually to afford party members the opportunity to express and harmonize their views between presidential elections.[54] The committee also warned against further regulating campaign finance, writing that "existing statutory limitations work toward a scattering of responsibility for the collecting of funds among a large number of independent party and nonparty committees."[55]

Moreover, despite recent suggestions to the contrary, the report did not recommend that party leaders in Congress be able to remove at will committee chairmen who did not toe the party line: "we are not arguing here or elsewhere for parties made up of yes-men," the report read. "Dissent is not undesirable in itself. It can be wholesome and constructive when it operates on a common basis. We are arguing the need for that common basis."[56] Most significantly, the objective of reform was designed to moderate presidential domination by providing more opportunities for collaboration between the White House, elected officials, national and state party leaders, and constituency groups. With this in mind, the report suggested that the Democrats and Republicans both establish a 50-member Party Council made up of members from the national party committee, members of Congress, a regionally balanced selection of state parties, several governors, and other party-aligned organizations. "Ideally," the report read, "the council would be the most important link between the party of the President and his Administration. . . . There must be sensible give-and-take between both, on the basis of a party program which will have to be implemented *by the Administration, Congress, and the council.*"[57]

The leaders of the country's two-party system did not embrace the APSA Report's recommendations to enhance collective party responsibility and rein in presidential domination of the party system; for the most part, the New Deal push for the centralization of party leadership within the White House remained unchallenged.[58] In truth, the APSA report remains historically significant because it reflects the widespread consensus of the era that a return to the decentralized and chaotic structure of the pre–New Deal party system would be a mistake—that the chaotic politicking of the state of courts and parties was incompatible with administrative action. Indeed, there are elements of the report that seem to be taken right from the pages of FDR's speeches. "Historical and other factors," the report reads, "have caused the American two-party system to operate as two loose associations of state and local organizations, with very little national machinery and very little national cohesion. As a result, either major party, when in power, is ill-equipped to organize its members in the legislative and the executive branches into a government held together and guided by the party program. . . . This is a very serious matter, for it affects the very heartbeat of American democracy. It also poses grave problems of domestic and foreign policy in an era when it is no longer safe for the nation to deal piecemeal with issues that can be disposed of only on the basis of coherent programs."[59]

As a matter of institutional reform, Schattschneider and his colleagues also recognized how central the two-party system had been in safeguarding certain features of American federalism. Consequently, in addition to the Party Council and midterm convention recommendations, the report prescribed that the strengthened national party organization should take greater control for expelling state and local officials who displayed "conspicuous or continued disloyalty" to the national organization.[60] In writing platforms, the Committee bemoaned, "The fact that the national and state platforms are separately framed and adopted makes possible the sharp divergencies that may appear within the same party."[61] Like New Dealers, the Committee indicted decentralized parties for emphasizing provincial interests and local representation at the cost of dimming political debate and resolution over the high-stakes domestic and international challenges national leaders faced in post-war America. Its members hoped that national programmatic parties would nationalize politics integrating state and local organizations into a programmatic party.

Existing primary laws of most states define party membership in terms
of support of party candidates rather than allegiance to a common program. . . . The development of a more program-conscious party membership may attract into party activity many who formerly stayed away,
including public-spirited citizens with great experience and knowledge. It
will thus be a factor in giving the parties a greater measure of intellectual
leadership. Concerted action in the name of the party cannot and should
not eliminate the intransigence of the rebel who goes his own way, but it can
and should avoid both casual challenge to an accepted line of action and the
waste of bloated dissent.[62]

All of this is to suggest that the dangerous tendencies of executive-centered
partisanship were recognized almost as soon as it formed; however, given
the bipartisan support for the New Deal state, the political scientists who
warned of the dangers it posed to stable government and deliberative, open
politics appeared to be calling into the wind. Most New Dealers either were
indifferent to or condemned the report. Among the sharpest critics was
Schlesinger, who questioned the practicality of forging a British-style party
government on American soil. Even if it was feasible, he feared that party
government in the American context might arouse raw and disruptive conflict over race or religion that would fracture the nation: "If the party division
were strictly ideological, each presidential election would subject national
unity to a fearful test," he warned. "We must remember that the one election
when our parties stood irrevocably on questions of principle was the election
of 1860."[63] For all its flaws, Schlesinger counseled, the prevailing American
party system might be "better suited to the genius of a country considerably
more far flung, diverse and heterogeneous than Britain."[64]

Such a view likely underestimated the hollowing out of traditional parties
at that point in time and the need to build collective national, if not centralized, party organizations to hold the New Deal state accountable, especially
with a revamped administrative presidency (something Schlesinger and
other New Dealers would grapple with once Richard Nixon took office). The
authors of *Toward a More Responsible Two-Party System* understood that the
development of a more purposeful national government meant loosening
the hold of traditional parties on the loyalties and voting habits of citizens.
But they failed to appreciate the purpose these parties served as channels for
democratic participation and platforms for building a national consensus. In
the APSA Committee's view, no less than New Dealers, party politics should

no longer mediate a plurality of interests; it must serve one national interest. By default, that important task fell to the national representative, the president. Yet the 1960s would show all too clearly that the modern executive, even with the tools of mass communication, cannot truly embody the national interest. By then, politics was no longer an enterprise to mold a majority coalition in a large and diverse society; it was expected to carry out a platform mandated by a national election.

Even recent scholarship, which has questioned the emphasis that the APSA report places on nationalizing partisan politics, continues to discount how the decentralized and institutionally robust form of state and local party contestation helped to create national consensus.[65] Moreover, as we will detail in later chapters, the disabling effects of presidency-centered democracy, unencumbered by strong party organizations, have been aggravated since the 1960s by the tendency of liberals and conservatives to deploy the president's administrative powers, forged on the New Deal political order, for their own objectives. In this sense, party politics has been displaced by partisan administration.

Conclusion: 1960s Civics and the Cosmic Crack-Up of the Vital Center

The relationship between partisanship and populism has endured throughout American political history, manifesting itself differently in a variety of institutional contexts. The development of those institutional arrangements were responses to periodic moments of populist protest. And yet, with the major exception of the Civil War, the mediating institutions built into the Constitution and the extra-constitutional protections afforded by party organizations ultimately channeled democratic unrest and popular disagreement into more structured and less destabilizing forms of political engagement. These mediating institutions and organizations emerged from each episode not so much stronger or weaker, as transformed—responsive to the new politics of the age. And yet, as we will see in Chapters 4 and 5, executive-centered partisanship metastasized in an institutional context ripe for ideological polarization, presidential overreach, and few limits on national power. Contemporary executive-centered partisanship is not a direct lineal descendant of the New Deal and the consolidation of presidential power; it is a product of how the Great Society and '60s-era populism responded to New Deal institutional reforms. Contemporary partisanship combines the New Deal's embrace of presidential leadership with a widespread faith in an unfiltered national, majoritarian democracy that arose amid the populist upheavals of the 1960s.

The proliferation of social movements of that decade accelerated the demise of traditional party organizations, which were roiled by populist pressures. Seeking to tap into the surge of movement politics, Lyndon Johnson deployed the powers of the modern presidency in the service of these electorally vulnerable and highly mobilized constituencies: women, racial minorities, and immigrants. Richard Nixon, too, saw the potential to bring in a new field of Republican voters disgruntled with the liberalization of sexual, racial, and patriotic mores. Both presidents established new agencies within the Executive Office for the explicit purpose of managing the president's political affairs. In the aftermath of Watergate, Congress attempted to re-exert its authority over the "Imperial Presidency"; however, although legislators gained more authority and resources to scrutinize executive action, they never challenged the president's primacy in regulatory policy, budget authority, or personnel management.

Presidents Johnson and Nixon demonstrated the mobilizing potential of the modern presidency. Since then, parties have relied on presidents to advance programmatic objectives and mobilize the base. Notwithstanding the usual objections raised by the party out of office, both Republicans and Democrats have a debilitating dependency on the instruments of executive governance. And with the development of an independent and expansive White House Office, presidential candidates have been able to monopolize the party's programmatic ambitions while running for office, and to dominate the governing process once inaugurated.

The combustible mixture of executive aggrandizement and movement politics has undermined the New Deal faith in enlightened administration. Both liberals and conservatives have frequently denigrated government institutions since the 1960s even as they have demanded more from them. In Hugh Heclo's account, even as they distrust and weaken the authority of government, Republicans and Democrats, liberals and conservatives, have become "policy-minded." Fear of centralized power is deeply ingrained in American political culture; but Heclo argues that the fierce, enduring battles over civil rights and the Vietnam War gave rise to a novel antinomianism. During the 1960s, "the emphasis shifted from traditional suspicion of power" to a defiance of all authority. The coexistence of distrust in institutions and a willingness to use institutional power has led each side to clash, not only on principle but also by denying the legitimacy of the opposition.[66]

Although most critics of contemporary partisan rancor blame the Republicans for fracturing America, it was leftists, especially the leaders of the civil rights and anti-war movements, who first rejected the working arrangements of the New Deal state for its compromises with racism, corporate greed, and the imperialism it pursued under the banner of protecting global freedom. This ideal manifested itself most fully in the social causes championed by Johnson's Great Society. The partisan rancor that roils contemporary politics, for all its ugliness, had its origins in the idealistic, insurgent assaults from the left against a New Deal state that appeared to insulate American government from public accountability and to encourage massive indifference in the face of festering problems that perpetuated gross injustice.

The 1960s left many social and anti-war activists feeling alienated from the "establishment"; but they remained active in government during the 1970s through "public interest" groups, dedicated to remaking rather than dismantling administrative politics. Celebrating "participatory democracy," these public lobbyists gained access to the regulatory process, opened up the courts to further litigation, and democratized congressional procedures, with the consequence that programmatic liberalism was extended to affirmative action, environmental and consumer protection, and education.[67] As Paul Pierson argues, these policies gave rise to an activist and polarized state centered on "a range of profoundly contentious issues. . . . The character of these issues made compromise difficult, and created incentives for polarizing forms of mobilization."[68] The "new" liberals also transformed the presidential selection process, affirming Schattschneider's insight that "new policies create new politics."[69] As the APSA Committee feared, between the late 1960s and early 1970s, in the absence of responsible national party organizations, the old local and state party-based convention system of presidential nomination was upended by a system of direct primaries and open caucuses. Although liberal activists initiated the changes in party rules that established the system of direct primaries and open caucuses, the Republicans also accepted them. The bipartisan commitment to a media-churning, plebiscitary presidential selection process gave institutional form to campaigns that encouraged presidential candidates to denounce Washington, and promise, if elected, to seize the powers of the modern executive in the service of the policies that their most loyal supporters demanded.

Can collective and restraining organizations be restored in a form that might contribute to the forging of a new "vital center"? Even our brief history of the two-party system suggests that collective partisan engagement has been joined to ambitions to remake American democracy: Jefferson saw it as the young nation's best hope to promote an agrarian republic of small, independent farm-based communities; Van Buren saw it as a system dedicated to the country's tradition of decentralized self-governance, but with a restrained, nationalizing spirit; Franklin Roosevelt recognized that the forging of an executive-centered party, not "neutral competence," was necessary to redefine the nation's rights-based tradition that limited the national state's responsibilities.

The rancorous politics of the post–New Deal era, we believe, cries out for such imaginative institutional thinking.[70] Party organizations can be collective repositories of political ambition and disagreement, can restrain obstructionism, and can promote, in the end, affirmative agendas of cooperation. But while moderating political hubris and the dangers of popular leadership, party government need not remain insensitive to the problem of leadership in democratic communities. Parties require strong voices and popular figures, but they encourage them to emerge responsibly—as the steward of a coalition of interests that must be convinced of a presidential candidate's ability to advance principles and programs they share. Successful democratic leadership in a party system, therefore, is always temporary, flexible, and pragmatic.[71]

Paradoxically, the partisan conflict that emerged from the turmoil of the '60s is less responsive and responsible than that occurring in previous eras, even as more people have become involved in the selection of party nominees. The proponents of more democracy did not realize that the newly empowered voices, such as party activists, would undermine efforts to build majority coalitions that represented a national consensus and would weaken constitutional norms and institutions. Both traditional party leaders and partisan activists relish power. But when authority is fragmented and no one leader can exercise monopolistic control over the governing coalition, contenders for the party leadership might agree to keep authority divided, decision making dispersed, and nationalist outcomes respectful of the autonomy exercised within the constituent parts. When authority is centralized and a single coalition of like-minded individuals can dominate the selection process and form alliances with presidents who use unilateral power to advance their causes, they may achieve fleeting political success, but at the cost of enduring achievement. This creates leaders who form strong bonds with a personal base of support but fail to fulfill the promise of vital collective action.

The paradox of greater participation and diminished government account-ability was deepened by the dissatisfaction with Franklin Roosevelt's redefini-tion of rights. During the 1960s and 1970s, liberal programmatic rights were extended beyond economic security to encompass social causes such as a free and appropriate education, equal access to public transportation, racial and sexual injustice, and environmental and consumer protection. This "rights revolution" and the evolution of a liberal judiciary combined by the 1970s to pull the courts into the vortex of partisan combat—the "storm center" of American life, as David O'Brien argues.[72] The expansion of programmatic rights, which conservatives embraced with support for commitments such as "the rights of the unborn" and new rights to protect religious communities against civil rights enforcement, secures national partisanship from the in-fluence of localism as represented by Congress, the states, and the traditional party system. It does so, however, by narrowing further the idea of democ-racy and party politics. As we argue in chapters below, both Democrats and Republicans have become obsessed with controlling the levers of adminis-trative power rather than reimagining them in line with citizen needs; such administrative aggrandizement makes likely that those who currently "have" will keep on getting, while those left behind will become ever more hopeless about the promise of republican self-government.[73]

Indeed, the failure to build a national party system has resulted in primary elections that too often reduce nomination contests to a plebiscitary form of politics—to the celebration of a cult of personality. Presidential candidates capitalize on the candidate-centered, media-driven primary system to cap-ture the nomination with a coalition of their own making. In order to dis-tinguish themselves in a crowded field of fellow partisans, candidates tout their individual accomplishments and personal approaches to governance. They must demonstrate their independence from the stifling "establish-ment" in Washington that finds too much comfort in the status quo. These atomized appeals arouse the passionate few but denigrate the party organi-zation as an independent entity that is capable of raising funds, mobilizing support, or collectively solving problems without a charismatic leader. And, as a result of delegate allocation rules in the states, aspiring contenders can sometimes earn the nomination without a majority of partisan support. New selection rules have intensified the plebiscitary character of presidential aspirants' campaigns. Presidential contenders now claim not only the mantle of party leadership but also the responsibility to wage an intense war for America's soul. Partisan support has become less wavering as the presidential campaigns are more likely to be waged in such apocalyptic terms. Even when party members dislike or are highly skeptical of their candidate, the winner of the plebiscitary nomination contest forms direct, personalized ties with supporters. The party thus becomes the party of a single individual, dependent on the successes of each new fleeting candidacy.

Executive-centered partisanship has not made the president all-powerful. The federal courts, the states, and even Congress are still constitutionally equipped to challenge presidential prerogative and limit executive overreach in many cases. Yet these bulwarks against presidential power have eroded as the collective fate of party members has increasingly come to depend on the president's personal successes once in office.[74] And since changes in American partisanship have made it more difficult to pursue programmatic governance through the legislature or piecemeal through the states, White House leadership has become all the more indispensable for the attainment of party goals. The new style of campaigning gives presidential contenders the authority to command the party; administrative government is what gives them the power.

Although bitter political conflict and constitutional struggle are as old as the country itself, there is no guarantee that the current spell of mischievous factionalism can be resolved. This is where history can help. By understanding how changes and challenges to the party system—inflicted from outside and within—emerged in the 1960s, it might be possible to trace a path forward. Perhaps then we can try to recover parts of a tradition that made essential, necessary correctives to the constitutional order that had failed to provide for a vital civic culture.

4

Liberalism Transformed

The Democratic Party Since 1960

We have argued that executive-centered partisanship resulted from two related developments that played out over the course of the 20th and 21st centuries: the rise of executive administration as the linchpin of national politics and policymaking in the 1930s and the emergence of a populist mode of movement-driven and anti-institutional politics starting in the 1960s. As we discussed in Chapter 3, the 1939 Executive Reorganization Act was the organic statute of the "modern" executive office consolidated during the New Deal era, which greatly expanded opportunities for presidents to carry out policies unilaterally. This gave the presidency the power to govern on behalf of its partisan coalition, especially during the protracted emergencies of the Great Depression and World War II. The exercise of presidential partisanship during Roosevelt's tenure continued a process, originating during the Progressive era, that led to a slow decline in the organization and operation of the decentralized party system. Beginning in the 1960s and culminating with the McGovern-Fraser reforms, an antinomian movement politics came into its own that sapped local and state parties of vitality and organizational relevance. By the end of Richard Nixon's presidency, the two underlying causes of executive-centered partisanship converged. Presidency-centered partisanship was joined to a movement politics practiced by donors, interest groups, and social activists who scorned the pragmatic politics and compromises hitherto credited with forging majority coalitions.

Chapters 2 and 3 traced the rise of an executive-centered state that subordinated parties as collective organizations with a past and future to the ambitions of a reconstituted executive office; this chapter and Chapter 5 emphasize the changes in American partisanship, often galvanized by calls for bold presidential action, which accelerated the demise of parties as mediating institutions. We first turn our attention to momentous developments in the Democratic Party that begin with the stewardship of the New Deal coalition by John F. Kennedy and Lyndon Johnson. Their efforts to come to terms with a surging civil rights movement advanced a tense but potentially fruitful relationship between the White House and social activists, an uneasy alliance that energized demands for a direct, unmediated relationship between presidents and social activists. By the time Barack Obama ran for office, the interplay between presidents and movements had become so ritualized that executive-centered partisanship came into full view. A self-styled movement president, Obama built his own, parallel organization—Organizing for Action—that struggled to meet the demands of social activists whose expectations were heightened by the election of America's first African American president.

Democratic Liberalism's Reckoning

The election of John F. Kennedy in 1960 trumpeted a new beginning for the American left and the Democratic Party. In our collective memory, American democracy itself never looked so bright. The electorate ushered in a charming, youthful, and energetic new personality whose optimism in politics was matched only by the grace of his family's deep roots in the nation's cultural and political elite. Nearly 63% of eligible citizens turned out to vote that year—the highest percentage since William Howard Taft was elected in 1908 and a number that stood as the post–World War II record until the 2020 presidential election. The outcome of the election delivered an urgent message: the Democratic Party had returned to power after eight years of Eisenhower's restrained leadership to reenergize a restless nation. With a sluggish economy, a simmering civil rights movement, and the threat of Soviet aggression creating doubts about America's future, the time had come, Kennedy proclaimed, to "get this country moving again."[1]

The excitement stirred by the 1960 election deflected attention from the profound injustices that ravaged the country and besieged the Democratic Party's ability to manage the coalition FDR had cobbled together 30 years earlier. Black and Latino citizens still had no right to vote in many parts of the United States; fewer than 20% of the nation's African American citizens were registered to vote, let alone felt safe enough to travel to the polls to cast their ballot.[2] The new Democratic majorities that Kennedy's election celebrated were predicated on the fact that since 1876, an entire region was, through a combination of poll taxes, literacy tests, and virulent intimidation, guaranteed to support his party, but only so long as it did not confront Jim Crow and violate the Democrats' "Faustian bargain" with the South.[3] Kennedy talked about racial injustice during his campaign for the White House—and he worked to release Martin Luther King, Jr. from a Birmingham jail during the latter months of his campaign. But he would not have been elected had he taken a harder line against the Jim Crow South and not won a majority of the former Confederate states.

Overlooked, too, is what really distinguished the young senator's campaign: his fervent commitment to fighting the Cold War. Denouncing Eisenhower's inattention to what he falsely claimed was a glaring "missile gap" between the United States and the Soviet Union, Kennedy's inaugural address called on a "new generation" of Americans to "pay any price, bear any burden, meet any hardship, support any friend, oppose any foe to assure the survival of liberty."[4] But this celebration of the fight for freedom abroad only highlighted the hypocrisy of a party returning to power that tolerated the denial of basic freedoms to a large number of its own people. Tellingly, Kennedy's iconic inaugural did not even mention civil rights.

Indeed, the election of 1960 encapsulates much of the liberal dilemma that has tormented the Democratic Party since the New Deal. While the memory of Kennedy lives on in many sections of the American left, the contradictions sewn into the very fabric of the New Deal order were exposed during his presidency and spurred one of the most tumultuous decades in American history. It was the first of many moments that would reveal the frail foundation of executive-centered partisanship as liberal leaders struggled to simultaneously fulfill the promise of a technocratic manager, consensus-builder, and the nation's preacher, all while anointed as leader of the free world. Roosevelt and his New Deal allies—pressured by the emerging labor and civil rights movements—sought to construct a more inclusive coalition that included African Americans, ethnic whites, and labor unions.[5] However, the expansion of democracy that defined New Deal liberalism undercut the Progressive claim to expertise and pragmatism that also were hallmarks of the New Deal State.

Every Democratic president since Kennedy has sought to emulate, if not out-do, the transformative leadership of Franklin Roosevelt. But in their obsession to out-Roosevelt Roosevelt, they weakened core institutional features of the New Deal order that once sustained the "vital center." To be sure, the full pathologies of executive-centered partisanship on display 60 years after Kennedy's inauguration were embryonic during this turbulent decade. Yet, in promising to expand the programmatic commitments of the New Deal

State, the American left invested extraordinary power in the presidential office, whose occupants soon laid claim to a hollowed-out party organization, a bureaucracy ripe for politicization, and a federal government in which Congress delegated a significant measure of its powers over the purse and national security to the White House.

Kennedy attempted to overcome the emerging tensions of New Deal liberalism by translating its competing principles and arresting self-doubt into the single, axiomatic idea of the 1960 campaign: "get the country moving again." Far from just being another substance-less campaign slogan, this nostrum reflected Kennedy's commitment to reinvigorating liberal activism. When the USSR succeeded in launching the satellite *Sputnik* into outer space, it gave resonance to Kennedy's message that the time had come to lift the United States out of the complacency that seemed to have settled on it during the Eisenhower years. Instead, invoking Schlesinger's idea of a re-energized liberal consensus, Kennedy proclaimed that the nation "needs a Chief Executive who is the vital center of action in our whole scheme of government," one who is "willing and able to summon his national constituency to its finest hour—to alert people to our dangers and opportunities—to demand of them the sacrifices that will be necessary."[6] When Kennedy asked Americans, in the most famous line of his inaugural address—"Ask not what your country could do for you, but what you can do for your country"—he was urging them to sacrifice self-interested politics and to enlist in the fight against communism.

But then Vietnam emerged as a nettlesome proxy of the Cold War; the civil rights movement dismantled the ramparts of Jim Crow; and the New Deal coalition faced the double strain of Saigon *and* Birmingham. The country was moving, but at the cost of disrupting the New Deal political order. The transformation, or "unraveling,"[7] of American liberalism after 1960 was spearheaded by social activists who rejected the working arrangements of the New Deal state because of its compromises with racism and corporate greed.[8] In suggesting that liberal activists of the civil rights and anti-war movements helped to throw America off center, we are not questioning the moral purpose of their causes. Civil rights activists are rightfully renowned for their contribution to American justice; few developments are more widely celebrated than the groundbreaking legislation that advanced the cause of civil rights, in combating public discrimination (1964), voting restrictions (1965), and segregated housing practices (1968). When Vietnam became a quagmire that overwhelmed the Johnson administration and fractured the nation, the idealistic, all-consuming Cold War that Kennedy exalted in his inaugural address was called to account by liberal activists as imperialism disguised as "man's noblest cause." Our concern is with the institutional developments wrought by "Sixties Civics"—the combustible combination of demands for more government and distrust of governing authority. Those who march against systemic racism and imperialism today must contend with the way reforms changed the country's governing institutions, especially in the way those developments might stifle reform.[9]

Each one of the challenges liberalism confronted—economic, social, global—brought about a deep wariness if not downright disillusionment with the institutions that contained liberal commitments. None of these institutions were as severely challenged as the modern presidency—the anchor of the liberal state. So long as liberal pragmatism, buttressed by an executive-centered administrative state, was viewed as a strategy to retain the Democratic Party's fragile North-South alliance and an activist foreign policy, the champions of forging a more inclusive, national community strongly condemned it. As a result, activists renewed reform efforts that began at the dawn of the 20th century to make the office a more responsive and democratic institution. With new demands for public engagement and openness in the election process, presidents invested new capacities in the White House Office, which, in turn ratcheted up expectations for partisan administration.

While Kennedy's presidency further opened the rift growing inside American liberalism, the tension between presidential prerogative and partisanship came into even fuller view during Lyndon Johnson's momentous and troubled five years in the White House. The Roosevelt "revolution" dedicated itself to tangible government entitlements, thereby forging a coalition of African Americans, liberal intellectuals and professionals, labor union members, and white ethnic groups who looked to the modern presidency and the "liberal establishment" for leadership and programmatic benefits. Johnson's Great Society summoned policy advocates, representing broad causes and movements, who resisted "presidential management"—and were less willing to delegate political responsibility to administrative agencies. The movements and groups that FDR, Truman, and Kennedy had kept at a distance—those representing minorities, women, environmentalists, and consumers—Johnson hoped to incorporate into a new liberal coalition. Johnson thus revitalized the moral purpose of executive-centered partisanship; at the same time, his monumental achievements forged a more direct and combustible relationship between executive power and movement politics that challenged and sharply divided the country.

The trajectory of liberal disillusionment and distrust of governing institutions escalated throughout the following decades until another young senator—this time from Illinois—promised to fulfill the promises so bitterly disappointed in the social and political upheaval of the 1960s. However, as with every liberal president since FDR, Obama's ascent did not result in the revitalization or reform of the party system; rather, he pioneered new forms of executive-centered partisanship that further diminished the role of party organizations in politics and government. By the end of his two terms as president, the rearguard of the Democratic establishment appeared to have given way to an unfiltered strain of populism that nearly catapulted a self-proclaimed democratic socialist, Vermont senator Bernie Sanders, to the 2016 Democratic nomination; indeed, they rocked the foundation of what had become a weathered and fatigued Democratic establishment. A 74-year-old Vermont senator, a self-proclaimed "democratic socialist" no less, who denigrated the rearguard of the party "establishment," almost captured the party he had joined just weeks before announcing his candidacy. Even though his "revolution" fell short, Sanders's remarkable campaign made its impact on the election: Hillary Clinton and the Democrats were pushed far more to the left than would have been the case in the absence of Sanders's campaign and suffered the slings and arrows of disaffected insurgents throughout the campaign.

It is unlikely that any of these insurgent pressures will subside; indeed, as the 2020 election approached, Sanders and other self-styled populists such as Massachusetts senator Elizabeth Warren argued that the scorched earth politics of Trump's presidency made clear that the Democrats must fight fire with fire—that there is no return to normalcy. The rallying of Democratic primary voters around the candidacy of former vice president Joseph Biden, who has promised to restore civility to American politics and celebrated his ability to broker legislative compromises with Congress, revealed that the Democratic Party had resisted the populist impulses of its progressive wing more effectively than the "Never Trumpers" were able to withstand right-wing insurgency. Nevertheless, Biden's support appeared to have more to do with the deeply felt imperative of defeating Trump—Biden's "electability"—than with the resilience of the the Democratic establishment. For better and worse, the reverberation of 1960s civics through the tumultuous 2020 campaign portended the final demise of the New Deal state that had anchored the vital center of American political life since the Second World War.

The War on Poverty

The historically unparalleled stretch of economic prosperity lasting from the end of World War II to the late 1950s was a boon to the Democratic Party and the New Deal order. Years of depression and war rationing left Americans with a hunger for economic life—new toasters, a home in the suburbs, that new 1951 Studebaker two-door sedan. Millions of veterans came home to government subsidized home loans, four years of paid college, and guaranteed unemployment.[10] The joining of government and civil society during the Great Depression and World War II was loosened with the transition to a peacetime economy, but government remained an important presence in American life. In fact, with the signing of the 1946 Employment Act, the American people were assured that it was now the government's permanent responsibility to guarantee full employment and a path toward the middle class.[11]

The expansion of the federal government in mobilizing for war and in taking charge of its new economic responsibilities privileged technocratic expertise, economic growth, and national security. But in empowering administrative agencies and economists, the modernization of the Executive Office muffled public debate and often bypassed legislative processes—the pillars of civil society in a representative constitutional government. After years of economic desperation and sacrifice, most Americans were willing to assume that such a transformation was necessary to control the vicissitudes of a market economy. As the *New York Times* opined, "The day has been brought nearer when the specter of mass unemployment and catastrophic losses in a major depression will no longer haunt American workers."[12]

In retrospect, such glowing optimism over the government's control of the American economy seems naïve. But by the 1960s, a bipartisan consensus had formed in support of the New Deal political economy, guided by the tools of the modern presidency. Using the methods of modern economic theory, known then as Neo-Keynesian economics, liberals promised to meet, if not exceed, the citizenry's growing expectations that government simultaneously curb inflation, promote full employment, and expand the economy's overall capacity. Such faith in the promise of government spending had spread so by 1965 that the prominent conservative economist, Milton Friedman, would confess, "We are all Keynesians now."[13]

Keynesian economics dovetailed with the expansive New Deal state that embodied Franklin Roosevelt's promise to alleviate the American people's "freedom from want." But Keynesianism also embraced public-private partnerships, mass consumption, and technological development that advantaged large private corporations. Rather than opposing big business, Keynesian economics depended on corporate America in practice. So long as a "countervailing power" in the form of labor unions and administrative agencies existed to effectively check corporate greed, liberal thinkers believed that Keynesianism was compatible with the privileged position of big business.[14] As such, with the triumph of a Keynesian political economy, much of the New Deal left abandoned the idea of a more radical reformist political economy. The Democratic Party, especially, coalesced around the idea that it was no longer necessary to fundamentally alter the partnership between government and private enterprise.

Most New Dealers never defended, as conservatives charged, an anti-capitalistic, top-down redistributive, or perpetually invasive regulatory state. As Allen Matusow notes, "Political liberals assumed corporate hegemony and pursued policies to strengthen it. . . . [W]hat was good for the corporate system would be good for the country."[15] Franklin Roosevelt—even when denouncing "economic royalists"—believed this to be true, as did Harry Truman, as did Kennedy, and as did his successor Lyndon Johnson.[16] Consequently, the New Deal Democratic Party was the party of free trade, tax reform, and benign anti-trust enforcement, so much so that in the lead up to 1964 elections, the New York Times reported that "support for President Johnson is particularly marked in 'big' business circles—the nation's major corporations and banking houses—that have traditionally backed Republican politicians and policies."[17] Few things are better for big business than government-guranteed stability.

Of course, some post-war Democrats called for a more "humane" political economy. There was a widespread and growing concern on the left that the traditional Keynesian focus on expansionary economic policies—material prosperity for the sake of material prosperity—threatened to mute the chords of civic virtue that animated the spirit of participatory politics. Fearing that an obsession with "quantitative" liberalism would detract from more "qualitative" concerns, liberals such as John Kenneth Galbraith joined Schlesinger in his disillusionment with the pragmatic commitment to economic stability and business friendly policies.[18]

Yet these critiques were not so much condemnations of the post–New Deal Democratic Party as they were calls to modestly reorient its focus and capture what Schlesinger, in The Vital Center, called the "radical nerve" of the

American left. In a way, the yearning for a more qualitative liberalism fit into the Democratic Party's attempt to "get America moving again" by engaging the nation in a Manichean struggle against communism and demonstrating the superiority of the American system to the world through unbridled economic prosperity, buttressed by new cultural achievements and civic commitments, including civil rights. FDR galvanized the country with its two-front war—at home and aboard—in bringing America into the modern age. So too did Kennedy seek to use the powers of the executive office to project a New Frontier—to engage labor and business in economic policy, enlist experts in solving economic and social problems, and, most alluringly, launch a project to put a man on the moon.[19]

But even Kennedy's New Frontier could not restore the luster of the New Deal and work out this debate within the American left. The president's domestic agenda, subdued by an unwavering commitment to what Bruce Miroff has called the "pragmatic illusion," could not silence the voices in the early 1960s of an emerging "new left," whose advocates derided the Democratic Party's economic platform for its deference to corporations and materialism.[20] Kennedy's economic policies gave them plenty to condemn. It was during Kennedy's administration, for example, that the Democratic Party sought to revamp the nation's tax code. Although it did not abandon the progressive system of income tax redistribution, the Kennedy administration slashed the crippling high rates at the top income bracket (from 91% to 70%). Michael Harrington, the author of the highly influential *The Other America*, lambasted the benefits Democrats had given to "the rich and the corporations." "We . . . should not lose sight of the homely, old-fashioned, and sectarian truth," he wrote, "that the efficient operation of a capitalist economy disproportionately and unjustly rewards capitalists, ignores urgent social priorities and maldistributes wealth, unless there are strong countermeasures which substitute political decisions for economic 'laws.'"[21] Perhaps no critique cut as deeply or spread as rapidly as that offered by Tom Hayden and the newly formed Students for a Democratic Society (SDS), which published the resonant Port Huron Statement. Arguing that America's economic might was nothing more than "a glaze above deeply felt anxieties," the SDS sought to rally a new generation to embrace an alternative, participatory political economy: the new guiding principle should be "that the economy itself is of such social importance that its major resources and means of production should be open to democratic participation and subject to democratic social regulation."[22]

These appraisals from the "new left" represented the first sustained attack on the economic lifeblood of the New Deal Democratic Party. When Lyndon Johnson became president, aides like Bill Moyers and Richard Goodwin urged him to listen to these voices. Johnson was an ambitious politician who achieved success through the pragmatic wielding of institutional power.[23] However, speaking at the University of Michigan, the home of Tom Hayden and the SDS, less than six months after taking office, Johnson gave a commencement address, drafted by Goodwin, that, far from recommitting his administration to the technocratic, elite-dominated, corporate liberalism of his predecessors, echoed the criticisms boiling up on the left, especially those expressed in the Port Huron Statement. " In your time," he told the graduating students, "we have the opportunity to move not only toward the rich society and the powerful society, but upward to the Great Society."

> The Great Society rests on abundance and liberty for all. It demands an end to poverty and racial injustice, to which we are totally committed in our time. But that is just the beginning. The Great Society is a place where every child can find knowledge to enrich his mind and to enlarge his talents. It is a place where leisure is a welcome chance to build and reflect, not a feared cause of boredom and restlessness. It is a place where the city of man serves not only the needs of the body and the demands of commerce but the desire for beauty and the hunger for community. It is a place where man can renew contact with nature. It is a place which honors creation for its own sake and for what it adds to the understanding of the race. It is a place where men are more concerned with the quality of their goals than the quantity of their goods. But most of all, the Great Society is not a safe harbor, a resting place, a final objective, a finished work. It is a challenge constantly renewed, beckoning us toward a destiny where the meaning of our lives matches the marvelous products of our labor.[24]

The Great Society testified to Johnson's outsized ambition—his desire to tap into the radical liberal ferment of the 1960s, presupposing a departure from rather than embellishment of the New Deal political order. Whereas Franklin Roosevelt and his New Deal allies had advanced reforms to bring about the day of "enlightened administration," the Great Society launched a new phase in the development of American liberalism that would imbue the national state with moral fervor. Yet in seeking to satisfy the New Left's "hunger for community," Johnson seemed to disregard how a newly empowered executive office was in tension, if not incompatible, with the new left's reform aspirations. In placing the presidency at the vanguard of a massive reform to the American economy, Johnson further shifted the locus of collective responsibility for domestic affairs inside the White House and outside the traditional bastions of fiscal governance, especially the Congress.[25]

This tension between executive administration and movement politics would play out most dramatically in the signature Great Society policy: the War on Poverty's Community Action Programs (CAPs). Codified by the 1964 Economic Opportunity Act, Johnson and political aides like Goodwin and Sargent Shriver, who headed the War on Poverty, envisioned CAPs as a new type of government agency that would respond to the new left's pervasive condemnation of New Deal–style bureaucratic politics. In empowering local communities to develop and deliver social welfare programs, the Great Society reimagined the meaning of effective governance: it would amend the sprawling machinery of federal bureaucracy that had, as the SDS charged, "developed indifference to human affairs."[26] By creating new avenues of political participation and neighborhood advocacy, community action programs sought to reinvigorate the grass roots institutions between the people and their government—to ameliorate, in particular, the declining sense of civic responsibility and governmental efficacy that plagued impoverished homes. CAPs were therefore to be an important intervention in addressing the "quest for community," as the renowned conservative sociologist, Robert A. Nisbet phrased it.[27] Johnson's hope, however, was not to diminish the national state, as Nisbet prescribed, but rather to pioneer a new form of top-down, bottom-up politics that would ameliorate the torpor of the New Deal Party system. Indeed, by federal law, community action programs had to be organized by a public or private non-profit agency, *not* a political party or elected official.[28]

In simplest terms, the 1964 Economic Opportunity Act injected funds into communities reeling from a vicious cycle of systemic poverty. The federal government piloted new programs and initiatives for this task including the Jobs Corps to provide basic education and vocational training for young men and women. Yet the real thrust of the Economic Opportunity Act was to reinvent *how* the government at all levels, including states and localities, spent money to aid the poor.[29] At first glance, CAPs seemed to honor America's historical commitment to local problem solving and an appreciation for the limits of federal interventionism. But Johnson and the architects of the War on Poverty were also deeply critical of local self-government as it had traditionally worked in the United States.

Splitting the difference, federal guidelines required CAPs to promote the "maximum feasible participation of residents of the areas of the groups served." This pledge to inspire "participatory democracy" was a deliberate move to loosen the power that existing local and state governments had over federal dollars pouring into their communities. The ideals of local community and political participation had to be redefined to address the underlying problems of America's poor.

The Johnson administration was especially determined to probe the deep roots of racial injustice. As Frances Fox Piven, who played an active role in the development of poverty programs, has observed: "Some deference to 'citizen participation' has always been important in legitimizing governmental action in America. But the Great Society programs went beyond token representation. They gave money to ghetto organizations that then used that money to harass city agencies. Community workers were hired to badger housing inspectors and to try to pry loose federal welfare payments. Later the new community agencies began to organize power to picket the welfare department or to boycott the school system."[30]

CAPs thus sought broad-based participation, but in doing so, the poverty programs inspired highly emotional, radically inspired condemnation of existing institutions: attacks on the schools for failing to educate; derision of the police departments for racial biases and militant violence; blaming the local party machine for years of political neglect; liberation from the paternalistic welfare counselors who presumed to impose "middle class" values on their clients. Such a response, far from being unwarranted, accurately expressed the frustration felt by many of these communities at the seeming indifference of political elites to the immense problems they faced. Schools were not performing adequately; cops were biased; local social welfare officials were rigid and formulaic. What matters for the politics of the vital center is not only the accuracy of these claims but also the political consequences of the institutional arrangements meant to address and respond to those discontents. As Matusow notes,

> Community action was supposed both to elicit the cooperation of local institutions and reform them—to promote community consensus and to risk conflict. Naïvely, the planners hoped for a creative synthesis in which the institutions would respond positively to protest, and the protesting poor would accept the necessity of compromise. These hopes were soon blasted.[31]

Rather than reform local institutions, CAPs fostered a deepening distrust of them—a federally sponsored attack on the "establishment" that discouraged vested interests in the communities (local political leaders, more established reformers, middle-class neighbors) from enlisting in the War on Poverty. When these tensions hampered the success of the Johnson administration's plans to remake social welfare policy, civil rights and other new left activists only became more disillusioned with liberal reform. Almost a billion dollars per year was funneled through CAPs between 1964 and the early 1970s— money that did a lot of good for a lot of communities. But at what political cost? Johnson seethed privately about the "revolutionary" activity that some CAPs were fomenting. Nonetheless, encouraged by White House aides' reports of their valuable work in ameliorating the alienation of ghetto dwellers from American society and government, he never repudiated them publicly and continued to support federal funds for neighborhood organizations.[32] As Sargent Shriver, director of the Office of Economic Opportunity, which oversaw the CAP, testified to Congress, "Nobody would be yelling if nothing was happening. This is like going back to the old New England town meeting concept of getting things done."[33] But others, such as Daniel Patrick Moynihan, a former Kennedy and Johnson aide who became disillusioned with the Great Society and joined the Nixon administration as a domestic policy advisor, lamented that CAPs' "tactics, when they became disruptive, were presumably seen by the rest of the urban population as signs of the *further* deterioration of the community as a whole. What may or may not have been therapeutic for the poor was evidence to the non-poor that the community was sicker than ever."[34]

Johnson never fully appreciated the tension between executive management, local government, and the empowerment of marginalized communities. Democratic mayors—the linchpin in local party organization—revolted against the president's grand designs. When they were not openly condemning the president's handling of the grant-making process, they worked behind the scenes to stifle specific CAPs that threatened their hold on power.[35] Without backing from the nation's mayors, especially from his own party, the president was left with little option than to consolidate central features of the program, to the dismay of community activists.[36] Eventually, fellow congressional Democrats became so disenchanted with CAPs that they shifted its funding and program responsibility into a new cabinet-level department, Housing and Urban Development (HUD), whose success was directly tied to presidential oversight and management. And yet, HUD, even though it was designed to institutionalize the demands of the urban poor, never fulfilled the promise of remaking America's cities. Instead, it became another bureaucratic responsibility foisted upon the presidency—a source of power, but also a window for activist demands.[37]

Nor did Johnson sufficiently appreciate that the civil rights movement was a catalyst for a form of populist politics that was inherently suspicious of presidential leadership. The community action agencies took on the energy and aspirations of the civil rights movement and refocused it, thus giving a new generation of Black leader's entrée into local and administrative politics. As a 1967 Senate investigation of the War on Poverty put it: "The Office of Opportunity policies and programs have produced a cadre of citizen leadership, heretofore neither seen nor heard in the community arena." They have brought "to the fore a sizeable cadre, for the first time in the Negro community, especially, of young energetic and striving leadership."[38] That "cadre of striving leaders," instrumental both in the increasing election of Black mayors in American cities and the growing influence of civil rights groups on social policy during the late 1960s and 1970s, developed political bases that were not tied directly to the Democratic Party or the White House. Nonetheless, having invested his immense ambition in the Great Society and having staked his political fortunes in the social movements that it empowered, Johnson had little choice but to support the Office of Economic Opportunity and the community organizations it spawned, even as he grew increasingly aware that it aroused leadership and populist forces that he could not control and which directly undermined his claim to progressive leadership.

These populist forces played out dramatically through the final two years of the Johnson presidency, roiling race relations and fracturing the liberal coalition. Decades later, these rifts were still on display as protestors, employing a remade populist trope—"We are the 99%"—rejected the Democratic Party's "neo-liberal" policies that supposedly worked only for the economic elite.[39] Like Johnson, President Obama found the prospect of tapping into movement politics compelling, even as he recognized the potential hazards of identifying too closely with a populist uprising. Although Obama, speaking as a former community organizer, sought to channel their grievances, proclaiming that he too stood against the rapaciousness of the 1%, members of the Occupy Wall Street movement protested what they perceived as the administration's complicity with banks and financiers in its response to the Great Recession: "Shame, Shame"! they shouted as they marched past the White House gates in the fall of 2011.[40] There is a real sense in which these activists were the latest incarnation of the Democrat's ongoing struggle to craft a truly progressive economic policy—an open sore that has disrupted the party and its presidential leaders since the late 1960s.

Paying the Debts of the Faustian Bargain

To fully understand how economic discontent has fueled the rise of presidential partisanship since the 1960s, it is also necessary to more deliberately explore how those inequities are layered on top of a racist political and social order. Race and racism are inextricable parts of the American experience. The division and discord it bred and continues to arouse is deeply engrained in American political life. The triumph of the "long civil rights movement" in the 1960s, the decades of changing demographics in the United States since then, and the rise of a new class of civil rights leaders that followed all contributed to the fracturing of the New Deal political order.[41] With the transformation of liberalism, civil rights organizations replaced labor as the core constituency of Democratic partisanship, establishing issues related to racial, gender, and ethnic discrimination as central to the party's political campaigns and policy commitments. Statistics dramatically testify to this change. No Democratic presidential candidate since Lyndon Johnson has won a plurality of White, non-Hispanic voters, a trend that played large in the 2012, 2016, and 2020 elections. Running against the first African American president, Mitt Romney won White, non-Hispanic voters by 20 percentage points in 2012 (59% to 39%). In the racially charged election of 2016, White voters preferred Donald Trump over Hillary Clinton by 21 percentage points (58% to 37%). Meanwhile, African American voters preferred Barack Obama by an 87-point edge in 2012 (93% to 6%); although Clinton did not do quite as well with voters of color, her margin over Trump was still a substantial 80 points (88% to 8%).[42] In 2020, despite the chaos and discord of the Trump administration's response to COVID-19, the racial patterns were largely the same: Trump secured a 17-point advantage among Whites, while the Democrat, Joe Biden secured a 75-point margin among Black Americans and a 33-point margin for Latino Americans.[43]

Any attempt to consider how the Democratic Party might recover its vital center must atone for the fact that New Deal political consensus was dependent on a pragmatic politics that did not directly assault the ramparts of Jim Crow.[44] Although the current racial divide between the two parties had its origins in the politics of the 1960s, the Democratic Party had been sharply divided over the status of African Americans decades prior to the more visible and widely studied civil rights movement. A critical moment in this intramural conflict was the 1948 Democratic National Convention, when a young mayor from Minneapolis, Hubert Humphrey, along with Illinois Senator Paul Douglas, advocated a plank declaring the party's commitment to civil rights. They succeeded in adding the first civil rights plank to a Democratic platform, albeit with just 52.7% of the delegates' votes. The adopted proposal referenced executive actions that the Roosevelt and Truman administrations had taken in response to relentless pressure by the March on Washington Movement and other pioneering social movement organizations, led by the civil rights and labor activist, A. Philip Randolph, to ameliorate racial discrimination in the defense industry, armed services and federal workforce. It then pledged the Democratic Party to continue its efforts "to eradicate" all forms of racial discrimination.

> We again state our belief that racial and religious minorities must have the right to live, the right to work, the right to vote, the full and equal protection of the laws, on a basis of equality with all citizens as guaranteed by the Constitution.[45]

After the party adopted this plank, all the delegates from Mississippi and about half of those from Alabama stormed out of the Convention hall in protest. When an effort to include a "states' rights" plank alongside the new civil rights plank failed, the remaining southern delegations voted for a protest candidate instead of Truman—Senator Richard Russell of Georgia. It is not always the case that history leaves such vivid signposts of change. But as Humphrey declared, the triumph of civil rights liberals in the party trumpeted a "new emancipation proclamation" for the country. "We are 172 years late in acting," Humphrey proclaimed. "It is now time for the Democratic Party to get out of the shadow of states' rights and walk forthrightly in the bright sunshine of human rights, [and] march down the high road of progressive democracy."[46]

About 1.1 million voters in the South chose not to join Humphrey or the Democratic Party on that high road. They chose instead to cast ballots for the newly established "Dixiecrat" Party and its candidate, South Carolina Governor Strom Thurmond.[47] Four years later, those protesting states returned to the Democratic fold, but a majority of voters in Virginia, Tennessee, Texas, Oklahoma, and Florida voted for Eisenhower over the

Democrat Adlai Stevenson in the general election, marking the first major inroads of the "Party of Lincoln" into the South. Those same states, with the exception of Texas, chose Nixon over Kennedy in 1960 and have remained staunchly Republican for the rest of the 20th century.[48] As noted, Kennedy needed the remaining southern States and their 76 electoral votes to become president. Thereafter, however, the Democratic Party's adoption of a civil rights program incited the South's massive defection from its traditional party and advanced a major regional realignment.

The passage of the 1964 Civil Rights legislation and the 1965 Voting Rights Act followed years of intense mobilization against forced segregation in the South and the gradual acknowledgment by both Republican and Democratic partisans of activists' demands—demands not to be violently beaten for riding a bus, demands not to be blocked by an angry mob from attending the school of their choice, demands not to be lynched for registering neighbors to vote. Federal action came slowly, and as civil rights leaders were to learn, it was often badly compromised. "If tokenism was our goal," Martin Luther King Jr. mocked after Kennedy issued a tepid executive order to prevent discrimination in federally funded housing, "the administration moves us adroitly toward it."[49] Yet, when Lyndon Johnson assumed the presidency, an unlikely confluence of events, personages, and institutional developments merged in the enactment of landmark civil rights reform: the South was no longer a lock for the Democrats and the political calculus of the party lay in courting Black voters in the North; the nation mourned a charismatic young president who months earlier had finally publicly supported the cause of civil rights; years of agitation had exposed the brutality of Jim Crow and the mockery of incremental, piecemeal reform; and the presidency had achieved its pinnacle status as the rallying force for progressive reform.

The momentous civil rights reform, Reverend King exclaimed, was a "brief shining moment on the conscience of man."[50] But battles would continue over the meaning of racial justice and the public actions that were required to achieve it. The Civil Rights Act of 1964 prohibited discrimination in schools, employment, and public accommodations; the Voting Rights Act of 1965 prohibited discrimination in the act of voting; the 1968 Fair Housing Act, the overlooked third and final victory of the decade, prohibited discrimination in the act of selling or renting homes. However, ensuing battles would reveal a painful, obvious reality: prohibiting forced segregation, although a great achievement, does not immediately redress existing inequities; and forbidding discriminatory actions does not compensate for the social and economic deprivations that taint the country's history.

Just five days after Johnson signed the Voting Rights Act, 21-year-old Marquette Frye was pulled over near his home in the Watts neighborhood of Los Angeles for suspicion of drunk driving. Frye was Black, the arresting office, Lee Minikus, was White. It was an unexceptional, all too usual interaction between the cops and a poor, Black resident—until Frye's neighbors came to the intersection to observe the contingent of police officers who had become involved. A shoving match began, and then more police arrived, shotguns at the ready. Rumors spread door-to-door about the police's actions and then taunts followed. One member of the crowd allegedly spat on an officer—flying chunks of sidewalk came soon after. Within hours, thousands of Black residents had come outside, armed with bottles and rocks, chanting the slogan of a local radio personality, "Burn, Baby, Burn!"[51] Throughout the night the crowds refused to disband as more police flooded the nearby streets. Soon, the National Guard poured in, but the crowds grew in kind. Before order was restored, 34 had died, 1,032 had suffered injuries, 3,438 adults had been arrested, and 600 buildings—most of them White-owned stores—went up in flames.

The Governor's Commission on the Watts Riots, or the McCone Report, described the situation in Los Angeles as a "dull devastating spiral of failure." Commenting on the thousands of Black residents who had recently migrated to the burgeoning West, the report recognized that "equality of opportunity, a privilege [they] sought and expected, proved more an illusion than a fact . . . a crisis in our country." All this from a city that the Urban League—a prominent civil rights group—ranked as first among 68 large American cities for housing, economic opportunity, and education for Black residents.[52]

The Watts riot was but the beginning of the long hot summers that churned American cities for the final four years of Johnson's presidency. The post mortem on these shattering episodes of violent civil disobedience, issued by President Johnson's "Advisory Commission on Civil Disorders" (or the Kerner Commission), echoed the McCone Report's earlier evaluation. In what remains one of the leading accounts of urban unrest, the Kerner Commission was unequivocal in its assessment: "Segregation and poverty have created in the racial ghetto a destructive environment totally unknown to most white Americans. What white Americans have never fully understood—but what the Negro can never forget—is that white society is deeply implicated in the ghetto. White institutions created it, white institutions maintain it, and white society condones it."[53] Put more poignantly, Ernest Boynon, columnist for the African American newspaper *Chicago Defender*, wrote, "the greatest losers were all of us, but particularly White America which appeared to be missing the lesson that Black people were trying at such awful cost to say: that no society, no matter how rich, can afford to throw away the talents and the lives of part of its members."[54]

Crippled by the quagmire of Vietnam, the Johnson administration failed to reclaim the mantle of moral leadership it had achieved during the struggle for civil rights legislation. Lacking the necessary political capital (and budgetary resources) for the sort of massive social welfare actions the Kerner Commission prescribed, the president was unable to convince African American leaders that the administration grasped the cause of urban conflagration. The fact-finding missions and task forces that Johnson ultimately employed—from White House aides' "ghetto visits" to blue-ribbon commissions—provided some of the most detailed and penetrating analyses of urban unrest and systemic poverty, but it was too little too late. Indeed, even the more established leaders of the civil rights movement, including King, now struggled to convince poor African Americans in urban ghettos that they understood their problems. As the civil rights movement moved into urban America following its victory over Jim Crow in the South, millions of still disenfranchised Blacks embraced a new political approach, captured by the powerful rhetoric and charismatic personalities of Stokely Carmichael, Huey Newton, Malcom X, and Floyd McKissick. As James H. Cone—an African American theologian—described the turning of the tide:

> During the first ten years of the civil rights movement, Martin King and others had assumed that the blacks of the North would benefit indirectly but significantly from the victories gained in the South. The Watts riot and the dramatic rise in the popularity of the black nationalist philosophy of Malcolm X showed that Martin overestimated the self-esteem that northern blacks would receive from the "straightened up backs" of their southern brothers and sisters. While surveying the devastation of Watts, he was surprised that many blacks there had never heard of him. When he gave a talk to a crowd of three hundred blacks at Westminster Community Center and counseled nonviolence, a man shouted, "Get out of here Dr. King! We don't want you!" Martin was particularly troubled when he heard a group of young blacks boasting, "We won." "How can you say you won," Martin retorted, "when thirty-four Negroes are dead, your community is destroyed, and whites are using the riots as an excuse for inaction?" "We won because we made them pay attention to us," they shouted at him.[55]

As his carefully planned incursions in Birmingham and Selma made clear, King did not shy away from confrontation; but the fiery denunciations of the American system by "Black Power" advocates like Carmichael and McKissick were more than just impatience with the slow work of non-violent protest. Instead, they scorned and abandoned the principal objective of King and other civil rights leaders: full racial integration. In their view, the moral authority of King and other more established leaders was marred by the compromises they struck with Johnson, most notably the compromise to resolve the conflict over the seating of the Mississippi delegation at the 1964 Democratic Convention in Atlantic City. At issue was the challenge that the Mississippi Freedom Democratic Party (MFDP) lodged against the seating of the lily-white delegation that the regular Mississippi Democratic Party selected to represent the state at the national convention. The grassroots activists' spiritual leader was the civil rights heroine Fannie Lou Hamer, former sharecropper and vice chairman of the delegation, who argued with great effect in the televised hearings of the Credentials Committee that she and the MFDP viewed the delegate fight as part of a broader battle for the right to register to vote—to "become first class citizens."[56]

Yet fearful that seating the MFDP would lead to a fractured party and contentious convention, Johnson, with the help of Hubert Humphrey and labor leader Walter Reuther, worked out, or more accurately, forced a compromise on the MFDP delegation.[57] The compromise plan included the seating of the regular Mississippi delegation, provided its members signed a loyalty oath that pledged them to support the presidential ticket; the symbolic gesture of making MFDP delegates honored guests at the convention, with two of its members seated as special delegates at large; and a prohibition of racial discrimination in delegate selection at the 1968 convention, to be enforced by a special committee to assist state parties in complying with this expectation.

King and his moderate allies in the movement accepted the concession, albeit not without a great "sense of distress."[58] Not only were southern states threatening to walk out of the convention if the regular Mississippi delegation was purged, but Johnson and Democratic leaders also warned civil rights leaders that an unruly convention would cost the party the support of several border states and deprive Democrats of a chance to win a historic landslide—and a mandate for further reform.[59] Johnson kept his part of the bargain, forming an alliance with civil rights leaders after his great election victory that resulted in the enactment of the 1965 voting rights legislation. Nevertheless, the MFDP controversy divided civil rights activists, portending a fundamental rift that eventually would result in a full-blown crisis for Johnson and the modern presidency. The MFDP compromise proved to be a formative experience for many grassroots activists who became disillusioned with formal party politics, and the type of convention-style wheeling and dealing that kept true reform always at arm's length. As the Student Nonviolent Coordinating Committee's Cleveland Sellers described this transformation, "Never again were we lulled into believing our task was exposing injustices so that the 'good people' of America could eliminate them. We left Atlantic City with the knowledge that the movement had turned into something else. After Atlantic City, our struggle was not for civil rights, but for liberation."[60]

As Carmichael and political scientist Charles Hamilton wrote in *Black Power*, a manifesto for the ascending militancy of the civil rights movement, the MFDP compromise that Johnson and established civil rights leaders struck "clearly said betrayal and clearly symbolized the bankruptcy of the establishment." "The goal of the Black people must *not* be to assimilate into middle class America," they argued, "for that class—as a whole—is without a viable conscience as regards humanity. The values of the middle class are based on material aggrandizement, not the expansion of humanity. The values of that class do not lead to the creation of an open society. That class *mouths* its preference for a free, competitive society, while at the same time forcefully and even viciously denying the Black people as a group the opportunity to compete."[61] In his autobiography, Carmichael added that "the underlying and fundamental notion [of Black Power] was that black folks needed to begin openly, and had the right and the duty, to define for ourselves, *in our own terms*, our real circumstances, possibilities, and interests relative to white America."[62]

In truth, Carmichael and other Black Power advocates often vacillated between pluralistic conceptions of race relations in America and a more radical variant of Black separatism. In either case, their voices posed a powerful challenge to moderate civil rights advocates and liberal reformers who had sought to remake the Democratic Party into the party of civil rights. Whatever form it took, Black nationalism heralded a "movement politics"—an unfiltered populist insurgency—that scorned institutional arrangements, including the remnants of traditional party politics that relied on compromise and incremental adjustment to sustain a Democratic majority. Responding to the riots in the summer of 1966, Johnson lectured urban Blacks whose behavior supposedly threatened the gains of the past, and the potential for future reform.

"Equality must be given," he tried to convince them, but it was only given to those who "cooperate with constituted authority." Yet as the journalist Tom Wicker countered:

"Constituted authority" is not performing well enough; the thought pro-cesses, the innate reactions, the interests of white moderation were born and nourished in a racially different environment from those of the rioters and the looters and the parents whose children's toes are nibbled by rats. To the one the established order is a friend; to the other it is oppression.[63]

With the backlash aroused by Watts and Johnson's preoccupation with the Vietnam War, the energy and resources committed to the Great Society, es-pecially its anti-poverty measures, began to suffer. African Americans were among the first to sense this change, and even Dr. King, who had formed a successful working arrangement with the president, became a visible partic-ipant in the anti-war movement. King, who first publicly expressed his op-position to the Vietnam conflict in September 1965, saw the war not only as morally questionable but also as a growing commitment that would di-vert resources needed to address problems at home. As he told a rally of the National Conference for New Politics in Chicago, the president had deferred "the dreams of American Negroes and shipwrecked them off the coast of Asia in the Vietnam struggle."[64]

Earlier civil rights leaders often saw war as an opportunity for Black Americans to prove their legitimate claim to equality. From Frederick Douglass advocating on behalf of Black regiments to fight for the Union to A. Phillip Randolph who used World War II to expose the injustices of American democracy, war had been a catalyst for African Americans' quest for justice. In contrast, King believed that the Vietnam War was an unjust intrusion in a foreign nation's quest for independence, a futile exercise that brought an abrupt end to the "shining moment" of fundamental reform embodied by the civil rights acts of 1964 ànd 1965. Indeed, his signature anti-war speech delivered at the Riverside Church in New York spoke of how Vietnam not only stalled progress on civil rights but also cut off the promise of the Great Society: "A few years ago . . . [it] seemed as if there was a real promise of hope for the poor, both Black and White, through the poverty program. There were experiments, hopes, new beginnings. Then came the buildup in Vietnam, and I watched this program broken and eviscerated as if it were some idle political plaything on a society gone mad on war. And

I knew that America would never invest the necessary funds or energies in re-habilitation of its poor so long as adventures like Vietnam continued to draw men and skills and money like some demonic, destructive suction tube."[65] In the final analysis, civil rights leaders who joined the anti-war movement were most disheartened—and ultimately enraged—by the cold truth that a dis-proportionate number of young soldiers killed in the Vietnam jungles were Black men.[66]

The Democratic Party clearly did not become the party of civil rights as a result of the landmark legislation enacted on Lyndon Johnson's watch. Deep ideological disagreements over the means *and* ends of racial justice ensured that the politics of the 1960s would continue well into the future. Racial prog-ress of the type that marked Johnson's approach to reform celebrated the essential "Americanness" of individual men and women. But the abandon-ment of integrationist ideals—what Harold Cruse celebrated as a transfor-mation of the "politics of civil rights" to a "politics of black ethnicity"—posed a more perplexing problem for party leaders and presidential aspirants, who had to win a majority of votes to make good on their promises.[67] In retro-spect this is hardly surprising. When one considers the underlying problems identified by the reports of the McCone and Kerner commissions—police brutality, restricted access to affordable housing, employment and consumer discrimination, the absence of quality pre-K education, higher rates of un-employment—it is easy to understand why these issues remain central to contemporary American politics; why no president, even when aligned with formative social movements, could dismantle the institutions of systemic racism; and why the vital center could not hold.

Throughout the 1970s and the 1980s, Democratic Party leaders strug-gled to come to grips with the aftermath of these polarizing issues. No doubt much of this internal strife was spurred by an attempt to respond to the effec-tive politicking of the Republican Party and backlash of many White voters, a subject to which we will turn in subsequent chapters. But the national con-servative offensive against a spiraling civil rights movement was effective, in part, because it exposed internal conflicts that had hobbled the Democratic Party's reform program since the New Deal. Moreover, when so much of the civil rights "debate" was delegated to the courts and bureaucratic agencies, the party never fully came to grips with an important tension sewn into the fabric of its broader constituency. Policies of corrective redress—affirmative action, public housing, supplementary funds for education—however nec-essary or good incur costs. And those programs were particularly taxing on other members of the New Deal coalition—especially White, middle class union workers.

Beyond policy trade-offs, the new configuration of groups and interests that roiled the liberal consensus led to an irreconcilable identity crisis in the Democratic Party. Less than 20 years after the 1965 Voting Rights Act, millions of Democrats could celebrate the candidacy and viability (within the party) of its most accomplished African American leader, Jesse Jackson. Jackson, who competed for the presidential nomination in 1984 and 1988, symbolized the dawn of a new era in American race relations—the promise of what Jackson celebrated as a "Rainbow Coalition," which might summon a new form of partisanship that would bring marginalized issues and actors to the center of Democratic politics. However, millions of other Democrats felt detached from a campaign that remained largely at that symbolic level, elevating Jackson the person over Jackson's ideas. As Elizabeth Drew commented following his 1988 second-place finish (with 29.4% of the Democratic primary vote),

> For a large portion of Jackson's supporters and would-be supporters, whether his proposals stand up to scrutiny is irrelevant. Their support for him is in a different category—as the leader of a movement. Jackson has become the vehicle for their discontent—with current policies, with the other candidates. He stands in bold, interesting contrast to some fairly dull candidates. He is the anti-politics candidate. Measuring his program is linear, rational, while most of the support for him is based on emotion.[68]

Jackson's candidacy was thus a harbinger of a new stage of executive-centered partisanship, combining the persona of the presidency with energetic movement politics. The emotion of Jackson's followers was fueled by an anti-establishment populism—a claim that the partisan politics had stifled the voices of dissent for too long had to give way to a new grassroots movement and leaders who cut their teeth on the streets during the 1960s. After two unsuccessful bids for the presidency, which made racial issues the central focus of heated primary contests, Jackson threatened to bolt the party entirely. Echoing the lament of the APSA Committee on Political Parties that the New Deal had failed to strengthen the Democratic Party—or give rise to a responsible party system—Jackson wrote in an op-ed for the *Washington Post*: "If an issue is morally wrong, it can never be politically right. We must never let ourselves be pulled from the high plane of morality and legality into the valley of expedient politics and race consciousness. . . . We cannot win by offering a pale imitation of the Republican Party, staging elections in which there are two names for one party, with one set of assumptions and one set of solutions."[69] Jackson's diagnosis of the Democratic Party's malaise called for the fulfillment of the Great Society's lost promise—a completion of liberalism's transformation.

This critique was given more than a little credence when Massachusetts governor Michael Dukakis suffered a disappointing loss in the 1988 presidential election. As Jackson argued one week before election day, "Some want us to spend our time and efforts pursuing Democrats who've defected, but I think our future is pursuing the vast number of people who feel they've been left out—blacks, Hispanics, women. We should enlarge the franchise, not change it."[70] Jackson was expressing the culmination of a long process of social reform and party change—a development that President Johnson's aides who made ghetto visits recognized as early as 1967, when they feared that civil rights advocates increasingly identified Johnson "as part of the white apparatus which created and fostered the perpetuation" of racial injustice—not as a powerful ally who could remake the system from within.[71]

Jackson's strategy also exposed another Democratic frailty. While race and the partisan realignment of the South surely contributed to the decline of the liberal consensus, it is also important to note that a civil rights "debt" was incurred not only to racial minorities and indigenous populations but also to women. To the extent that much of the economic thinking that lay at the heart of liberal interventions—from the New Deal union protections to the Great Society's Job Corps—were often predicated on preexisting family archetypes (i.e., a single male wage-earner), the feminist movement also struggled against traditional Democrat orthodoxy. Nor did advocacy groups confine their insurgency to this, pejoratively labeled, "breadwinner liberalism." Challenging an array of assumptions about the traditional nuclear family, gay and lesbian rights advocates joined the clarion call to make those who held office under the banner of the Democratic Party more representative of ascending liberal constituencies.[72] Consequently, the liberal activists who rose to prominence during the 1960s and 1970s sought to displace the traditional pragmatic character of Democratic politics with a partisanship more attuned to social movement organizations and their causes.

Jackson lost the battle for the Democratic nomination but appears to have won the war for the soul of the Democratic Party. Between the dawning of Jackson's "Rainbow Coalition" and Barack Obama's "coalition of the ascendant," as Ronald Brownstein calls it, Democrats succeeded in capturing the presidency only by twice electing a moderate governor from Arkansas dubbed—despite going to Georgetown, Oxford, and Yale—"Bubba." Yet the playing out of civil rights reform combined with massive demographic shifts led to the maturing of the new Progressive coalition during the administration of America's first African American president. Obama's two terms as president, however, left many activists disappointed. Although he achieved important healthcare reform—the party's holy grail since the New Deal— and advanced social policy in support of the rights of African Americans, the LGBTQ community and Latinos—his compromises in domestic and international politics drew the ire of left-wing Democrats who heaped scorn and derision on Obama's hand-picked successor, Hillary, the heir apparent of the Clinton dynasty.

It is revealing that Bernie Sanders, the personification of the "cantankerous left wing," also struggled to maintain cordial relations with many civil rights groups, including Black Lives Matter (BLM) during the 2016 and 2020 nomination contests. By design, protest movements—as illustrated by their interruption of Sanders's campaign rallies—are meant to disrupt and antagonize. To the extent that such actions help elevate an agenda and get more mainstream candidates like Hillary Clinton to "protect her flank" as *Slate*'s Jamelle Bouie described it, then the tactics work.[73] It has and will remain part and parcel of democratic politics. To the extent that in a system of competitive elections based on persuasion, such tactics have not succeeded in building winning majorities, Democrats remain at the frontline of a raw and disruptive partisanship that makes forging an enduring political consensus unlikely.[74] As we consider in Chapter 6, the massive shift in public attitudes toward the Black Lives Matter movement following mass demonstrations in the spring of 2020 might suggest an inflection point in this strategy; however, only time will tell whether responses to a pollster will translate to a new party realignment, let alone institutional change.[75] This political agitation is not only fueled by domestic struggles; no less pivotal in the breaking apart of the vital center has been the decline of liberal internationalism.

Shutting Down the "Arsenal of Democracy"

As his inaugural address trumpeted, John F. Kennedy was an avowed Cold Warrior. Speaking to the American Legion Convention weeks before the

1960 election in Miami Beach—90 miles away from the newest communist country on the globe, Cuba—Kennedy drew the starkest line between him and his opponent, not over economic policy or civil rights but military spending. "I have never believed in retreating under any kind of fire," Kennedy declared to rapturous applause. "I want Mr. Khrushchev and anyone else to understand that if the Democratic Party wins this election, he will confront in the 1960s an America which is not only militarily strong, but which is waging the offensive for freedom all over the globe."[76]

This struggle against communism was to take many forms—from an expanded arsenal of conventional and nuclear weapons to an increase in foreign aid to newly independent countries. The United States needed to do whatever was necessary, Kennedy argued, to regain and demonstrate "the nerve, the will, and the determination for a long, long hard fight" with the Soviet Union. Such rhetoric was not unusual for Democrats. Kennedy, after all, was the standard-bearer for the party of FDR—the leader of American forces in the fight against another variant of totalitarianism. Even prior to World War II, Roosevelt spoke with the vigor and moral certitude that Kennedy echoed. In a December 1940 fireside chat—as Nazi bombs rained down on London—President Roosevelt told the American people that "we must be the great arsenal of democracy. . . . We must apply ourselves to our task with the same resolution, the same sense of urgency, the same spirit of patriotism and sacrifice as we would show were we at war."[77]

Kennedy and his predecessors Roosevelt and Truman were not hawks, if hawkishness refers to a type of glorification of war. But each president spoke about and articulated a vision of America's central place in a tumultuous, ever-changing state of global affairs. Truman urged a nation still skeptical of "entangling alliances" to embrace the new post-war global institutions and to "support free peoples who are resisting subjugation by armed minorities or by outside pressures." The Cold War that Truman heralded proved to be the crossing of the Rubicon, for the view that the United States had a critical, enduring place to play in the world was embodied in the development of the national security state. Established by the aptly titled National Security Act of 1947, this large military establishment included the National Security Council, the Central Intelligence Agency, and the Department of Defense. The development of a large, powerful and permanent military establishment was unprecedented in America; indeed opposition to it was deeply rooted in the country's history.[78] Some of the framers of the Constitution, including James Madison, feared that a "standing army" would extend the powers of the executive beyond its proper bounds while their formidable opponents—the Antifederalists—were united above all by the dread of a military dictatorship, voices of dissent that echoed through World War II. As Truman's travails in Korea and Johnson's nightmare in Vietnam dramatically revealed, the forging of a national security state in the post-war years did not snuff out the dread of an imperial executive. The all-consuming struggle against the Soviet empire spawned enervating campaigns against communist "proxies," with the United States becoming involved in quagmires that cost presidents popular support and threatened national resolve. And just as the civil rights movement scorned the vital center, so the anti-war movement, which grew directly out of the struggle for racial justice, excoriated the Arsenal of Democracy.

Although the United States was rattled by Korea, it was the Vietnam War that undermined liberalism's commitment to the national security state. War in Southeast Asia and its ever-expanding domain of military activity brought down the Democratic President Lyndon Johnson, galvanized a new cohort of activists who sought to transform the party, and exposed a deep rift in the cultural outlook between those on the left and "middle America." To suggest as much is not to make a judgment about the struggle—to argue that the war was a "success" or a "disaster," "honorable" or "fought in vain." However one judges the necessity of the Vietnam War, this battle against what the country's leaders viewed as a proxy for communism was a critical chapter in American political development, and its wounds are still being felt in the Democratic Party.

As early as February 1965, less than one year into the war's "official" beginning, liberals foresaw a moral implosion as a result of America's growing involvement. Daniel Ford was a freelance journalist who embedded himself in an American platoon for two months as they trekked through the South Vietnamese mountains. On his return, he published his account in *The New Republic*—a story that foreshadowed the deep skepticism that liberals would soon come to hold against any American interventionism overseas. As Ford concluded,

> Our last day's objective was a town recorded on the map as Tan Hoa. We could not find it. There was nothing where Tan Hoa should have been, except a road, a river and a grassy field where we spent the night. Next morning, as we were waiting for the helicopters which would take us out, we found some ancient fighting holes and a graveyard with fine granite

tombstones, Gallic in design. That was all that remained of Tan Hoa—foxholes dating back to the Indochina War, a few French graves, and a name on a French-made map. All the rest had moldered in the 10 rainy seasons, and turned to dust in the 10 dry seasons, which separated their war from ours.[79]

For Ford and other embedded reporters, now capable of sending back day-of footage to the evening news broadcasts, the war took on an intimate, tragic quality. American military and political leadership spoke of the war's necessity—a crucial sacrifice in the effort to stave off communism's spread. But the obligation was indefinite and the resolution hard to envision. Later that year, in another *New Republic* exposé, a reporter illustrated that despite the clear presence of American military might and firepower, they brought little clarity to the political situation in Vietnam. After American "victory," Bernard Fall wondered, "a prostrate South Vietnam, plowed under by bombers and artillery and still in the hands of a politically irrelevant regime, may become the victim of aroused social and political forces for which no aircraft carrier and eight-jet bomber can provide a ready answer in the long run."[80] Such a perspective suggested that victory was largely unachievable, regardless of how much blood or treasure was spilt in pursuit of military dominance.

Johnson's political stature deteriorated further as doubts grew about whether any kind of victory was possible. Both presidents Eisenhower and Kennedy sent military "advisors" to Vietnam to support the fledging regime of Ngo Dinh Diem against communist insurgencies. When Diem's government lost popular support—and he, with the complicity of the Kennedy administration, was assassinated by his own generals on November 2, 1963—US military advisors grew more determined in their belief that direct American intervention was necessary. An excuse to expand the war and protect the nearly 20,000 American troops already stationed in the country came on August 2, 1964. Two ships in the Gulf of Tonkin off the coast of northern Vietnam reportedly engaged with vessels carrying torpedoes. Five days later, after a unanimous House vote and a near-unanimous Senate vote (two senators voted nay), Johnson received broad authority and virtually unlimited financial resources to conduct full-scale military operations in the region.

The Vietnam War thus became, in an unprecedented way, the president's war. Truman had at least been able to claim that the United States was "carrying out an obligation for the United Nations" when he sent troops to fight in South Korea. But in Vietnam, as the political scientist Richard Pious has noted, "no treaty obligations or other commitments required the United States to intervene." Nor did the Gulf of Tonkin Resolution declare war; rather, its sweeping language delegated to the president the authority to decide when and how to use military force in Vietnam.[81] The Resolution stated that Congress "approves and supports the determination of the President, a Commander-in-Chief, to take all necessary measures to repel any armed attack against the forces of the United States and to prevent further aggression." Johnson welcomed this legislative blank check; but he and the State Department insisted on an even broader grant of war-making authority, arguing that Article II in the Constitution granted all the authority the president needed to deploy troops in Vietnam.[82]

Johnson's personalization of the war in Southeast Asia assured that he would be blamed if the consensus at home crumbled. Beyond the effect on his political support, Vietnam demonstrated the more troubling aspects of the modern executive and subjected the national security state to the scrutiny of Congress, and, ultimately, the movement politics that fractured the Democratic Party. As over a million tons of bombs and missiles hammered the Vietnamese countryside in operation "Rolling Thunder," doubts grew about whether the Gulf of Tonkin incident had actually taken place. In December 1967, Senator J. William Fulbright, a Democrat from Arkansas, announced that he had already begun an inquiry into what the president and US military actually knew prior to seeking the Gulf of Tonkin resolution.[83] At the same time, reporters began to express doubts that the official military statistics fed to the papers regarding combat operations and the Department of Defense's new metric for quantifying battlefield success—the "body count"—were accurate.[84] And then, on January 31, 1968, communist fighters captured over 100 small towns and cities in South Vietnam on the lunar new year holiday Tet, weeks after the president claimed that American troops were finalizing their offensive. Johnson's secretary of defense, Robert McNamara, was brought before a Senate committee inquiry and received a cold reception from his fellow Democrats. As chairman Fulbright later said, the whole purpose of the investigation was to interrogate the idea "that the Government has a right to lie to the people of this country."[85] Joining Fulbright on the committee investigation was another skeptical Democrat from Minnesota, Eugene McCarthy.[86]

Several months earlier, McCarthy had revealed his intention to undertake what seemed like a quixotic campaign to challenge the formidable incumbent of his own party for the 1968 nomination. Announcing his candidacy on November 30, 1967, McCarthy pledged to "alleviate the sense of political helplessness and restore to many people a belief in the processes of American politics and American government." For McCarthy and the thousands of college student activists who rallied to his cause, such disillusionment was the result of an administration that seemed "to have set no limits on the price that it will pay for military victory."[87]

When McCarthy, shocking the press and Democratic Party regulars, received 42% of the vote in the New Hampshire primary (to Johnson's 49%), his insurgent campaign suddenly posed a serious challenge to the party "establishment." His strong showing exposed Johnson's vulnerability; most significantly, it encouraged Robert Kennedy, who many liberals considered the rightful heir of Camelot, to enter the fray against a sitting president. But it would be a mistake to conflate the anti-Johnson sentiment with anti-war sentiment in the Democratic Party. Political scientist Philip Converse and his colleagues, relying on survey data of New Hampshire voters, noticed soon after the 1968 election that much of McCarthy's support in the primary challenge had less to do with American intervention in Vietnam than with Johnson's personal handling of Vietnam.

> Surprisingly, in view of McCarthy's clear and dissenting "dove" position on Vietnam, the vote he drew in New Hampshire could scarcely be labelled a "peace vote." . . . There was, of course, some hard-core peace sentiment among New Hampshire Democrats that was drawn quite naturally to McCarthy. Among his supporters in the primary, however, those who were unhappy with the Johnson administration for not pursuing a *harder* line against Hanoi outnumbered those advocating a withdrawal from Vietnam by nearly a three to two margin!"

Moreover, as the election neared, Converse asked a representative sample of Democrats who opposed the war what they thought about the "peace dissenters," the youthful, activist contingent most associated with McCarthy; a majority disapproved of the protesters, and a full quarter of these supposed doves were "extremely hostile" toward them.[88]

In truth, McCarthy and the student activists supporting him were just a small note in a cacophonous protest whose participants disagreed over what to do about Vietnam: how to win, how to preserve American dignity, and how to make amends for a generation now scarred by conflict. One clear consequence resulted from these competing attitudes toward the war: the president was the single greatest casualty. But when Johnson announced on March 31, 1968, that he would not seek or accept the Democratic nomination, the scapegoat unifying a fractured party disappeared. And while Johnson's departure placated some in the party, the nomination of Vice President Hubert Humphrey at the disastrous Democratic National Convention in Chicago later that year reignited the fractious contest over the meaning of liberalism. The anti-war protesters marching down Michigan Avenue in front of the convention hall were themselves not clearly united on a new understanding of Democratic principles; however, their antinomian struggle testified to a full-scale assault on the party establishment. The renowned American author, Norman Mailer, who was watching the scene unfold from his hotel room, illustrated a domestic war zone:

> The National Guard was out in force. On the side streets of the hotel, two-and-a-half-ton Army trucks were parked, jamming every space. Traffic was cut off. The Daley-dozers, named yesterday by a newspaper man, those Jeeps with barbed-wire grids in front of their bumpers, were lined in file across Michigan Avenue just south of the Hilton. . . . The huge searchlights near the Hilton were shining from a height of ten or fifteen feet, from a balcony or a truck. . . . For some reason or other, a hydrant had been opened on Michigan Avenue in the hollow square formed by lines of National Guard and police barriers before the Hilton, and the lights of the searchlight reflecting from the wet street gave that dazzle of light an urgency and glamour unique to a movie company shooting in a city late at night, crowds dazzled themselves by their own good luck in being present.[89]

Mailer's literary embellishment foretold the collapse of the Democratic establishment. With the rise of the anti-war movement, LBJ saw his leadership of the new liberal coalition pass to Eugene McCarthy and then to the likes of South Dakota senator George McGovern, the anti-war Democratic presidential candidate in 1972. When Nixon beat Humphrey in 1968, he escalated the conflict in Southeast Asia with a massive bombing campaign in Vietnam and then neighboring Laos and Cambodia. Anti-war activists remained committed to ending the war by bringing down both Nixon's presidency and the Democratic leadership that they believed made it possible. McGovern's acceptance speech at the 1972 Democratic Convention laid out the vision for a new liberal order—one that challenged the venerable idea that America was an exceptional nation, a "city on a hill." "It is the time for this land to be-come again a witness to the world for what is just and noble in human affairs," he announced. "It is time to live more with faith and less with fear, with an abiding confidence that can sweep away the strongest barriers between us and teach us that we are truly brothers and sisters."[90]

Senator McGovern lost a landslide election to the incumbent Nixon, winning only Massachusetts and Washington, DC. But rather than return to normality in the face of this electoral debacle, party leaders remained plagued by the "Vietnam Syndrome"—a pervasive reluctance to continue Cold War policy as usual and a deepening distrust of the American political institutions, especially the presidency. Arthur Schlesinger Jr., once a strong defender of the modern executive born of the New Deal political realign-ment as the "vital center" of the liberal state, now embraced the anti-estab-lishment sentiment among liberals—a sentiment that had spread beyond the peace-niks and the college students taking over administrative halls on their campuses. The progressive faith in strong presidential leadership had gone too far, Schlesinger acknowledged in *The Imperial Presidency*. "The presumed requirements of a global and messianic foreign policy," he wrote, "had thus begun to swallow up the congressional power. . . . As the American Presidency came to conceive itself the appointed savior of a world whose interests and dangers demanded rapid and incessant deployment of men, arms, and decisions, new power, reverence and awe flowed into the White House." To our collective chagrin, Schlesinger concluded, "The image of the President acting by himself in foreign affairs, imposing his own sense of re-ality and necessity on a waiting government and people, became the new orthodoxy."[91]

When the North Vietnamese Army and the Viet Cong stormed the American embassy in Saigon on April 30, 1975, the war in Vietnam finally ended. But for American foreign policy makers and the rest of the political establishment, the war had sacked the credibility of Cold War orthodoxy: the United States was the sentinel for free society. In the days leading up to the city's capture (or liberation), images poured into Americans' living rooms where they had watched the war in living color for the past decade. There they now saw US diplomats and South Vietnamese fleeing by helicopter evacuation. At the same time, a select committee in the US Senate, chaired by Frank Church (D-ID) had begun its investigation into the American in-telligence community.[92] Its task was direct and ominous—to interrogate and address the "massive wrong-doing" of secrecy and foreign interventionism endemic to the system of national intelligence that was built to further the objectives of three post–World War II Democratic administrations.[93]

To a point, Jimmy Carter's nomination in 1976 represented the Democratic Party's renunciation of the Cold Warriors who had failed to fulfill the New Deal promise of an American-led international order. At the same time, Carter epitomized the danger that a weak presidency posed to the Democratic Party's political fortunes. Just four years after witnessing evacuation in Saigon, Americans were forced to flee an Iranian regime that collapsed in February 1979. Iran was another US-backed government—a tributary that had become even more important as oil prices skyrocketed. But, as the Iranian monarchy collapsed, 52 Americans remained trapped inside the American embassy, where they were held hostage for 444 days. Unable to project American might—in the most pathetic of circumstances— Carter failed to straddle the dueling objectives of a presidency that was bound to peace, but not so tightly that it would not be able to protect American interests when attacked.

It is no wonder, therefore, that 12 years after the Democrats lost the presidency due in large measure to the fractious 1968 primaries, Carter too almost suffered defeat in a bitter challenge from within his party. At the end of a drawn-out primary contest, Carter pulled ahead, winning just over 51% of all primary votes cast. However, Carter's challenger, Ted Kennedy—the "liberal lion of the Senate"—won the states that would increasingly come to dominate the Democratic Party: California, New York, Massachusetts, Connecticut, and New Jersey. Carter's most notable actions in foreign policy that year were the refusal to attend the Moscow Olympic games—in response to the Soviet invation of Afghanistan—and a failed helicopter rescue of the Iranian-held hostages. Despite Carter's muted response to Soviet aggression and the Iranian-hostage crisis, Kennedy fueled his campaign on the anti-war, anti-imperialistic strain that continued to rouse the left.[94] Kennedy opposed economic sanctions and Carter's proposal to reinstate the draft as provocative, derided the "overreaction" to the Russian invasion in Afghanistan, and warned of an over-extension of America's military presence. For him, the potential pathway to the Democratic nomination lay in denigrating the country's faltering foreign policy establishment: "We should not be moving toward the brink of sending another generation of the young to die for failures of the old in foreign policy. Exaggerated dangers and empty symbols will not resolve a foreign crisis. . . . [S]ometimes a party must sail against the wind."[95]

Carter's landslide defeat to Ronald Reagan after the divisive nomination battle appeared to concede the issue of patriotism to the Republicans. Twelve years later, Republicans laid claim to the collapse of the Soviet Union, the institution of new democracies on every continent, and the demonstrable truth that the Cold War was in no small part won by the United States' persistent engagement in securing international cooperation. Republicans did not deserve all the credit (Democrats still controlled Congress for most of that period), but Democrats, nevertheless, failed to redeem themselves as a party of foreign affairs. With the collapse of the Soviet Union, domestic issues— namely, taxes, budgets, and financial crises—framed the 1992 elections, leading to the elevation of Bill Clinton to the White House.

Bill Clinton's foreign policy sought to restore a measure of resolve to Democratic foreign policy commitments. His administration's tepid engagement in Somalia and Rwanda were strongly criticized, but its intervention in Kosovo was largely praised for confirming the effectiveness of bipartisan, multi-lateral foreign policy. Moreover, a series of terrorist attacks—the World Trade Center in 1993, the 1996 barracks bombings in Saudi Arabia, the bombing of the Kenyan and Tanzanian embassies and the USS *Cole* off the coast of Yemen in 1998—were not so consequential as to arouse a conservative backlash. Indeed, the only significant challenge against Clinton's foreign policy came from the nascent anarchist movement whose leaders focused their energy on protesting meetings of the World Trade Organization, the International Monetary Fund, and the World Bank. Each of those three international organizations were pillars of the New Deal global order that Democrats and Republicans were struggling to preserve. But the challenge failed to take off and seriously disrupt Clinton's presidency.[96]

Nevertheless, Vietnam had an enduring effect on the progressive wing of the Democratic Party—and the reverberations have aroused a new generation of activists with a set of concerns that echo the anti-war protesters of the 1960s and 1970s. As important as economic issues were to the insurgent candidate of 2008, Barack Obama, the ongoing wars in Iraq and Afghanistan dominated the debate prior to the full-scale collapse of the American economy. As a junior, first-term senator, nothing was perhaps more essential for Obama than securing a seat on the respected Senate Foreign Relations committee—a position that allowed him to travel to Iraq in 2006 and showcase his diplomatic acumen. By the time Obama and his senatorial colleague, Hillary Clinton, were fighting each other in the primaries, many Americans, especially Democrats, had turned against the global War on Terror, and progressive activists were searching for a candidate who had taken a clear moral stand against it. Clinton voted for the Iraq war—an unforgivable sin in the eyes of liberal activists; Obama opposed it from the start. As Michael Crowly described the former First Lady's dilemma in 2007, "Hillary Clinton's entire political identity has become defined by that vote and her subsequent refusal to apologize for it."[97] Of course, Obama, then serving in the Illinois state legislature, had no opportunity to vote for the war, as did a majority of Democratic senators. But that did not matter; Clinton's vote for the Iraq Resolution, which like the Gulf of Tonkin Resolution gave the president a blank check to decide when and where to go to war, and Obama's criticism of it drove the wedge that helped cede the Democratic nomination to the self-styled outsider.

Eight years later, the concerns about Secretary Clinton's original sin endured, even as President Obama, who had taken steps to remake American foreign policy during his second term, sought to anoint her his heir apparent. Bernie Sanders tapped into the widespread suspicion of Clinton to fuel his insurgent candidacy. To be sure, Sanders's commitment to democratic socialism made an appeal to a number of constituencies, especially unions, whose political influence on the Democratic Party had declined since the 1960s.[98] But his core supporters were the millennials, who were drawn to his 1960s-like assault on corporate capitalism and American imperialism. Attending the Democratic National Convention in Philadelphia in July 2016, we can report that the loudest chants to be heard from the Sanders supporters were echoes of the rage of the 1960s: "No More War!"

The Anti-Institutionalism of the Democratic Party

Presumably, it is possible to imagine a situation where Democratic Party leaders wound down the war in Vietnam; secured a more responsible role for America's military might; championed the civil and economic opportunities of Black, Latino, female, LGBTQ, and poor Americans; and remained committed to a politics of increasing economic growth and opportunity. That would have been some feat, to be sure, but parties as collective organizations are responsive to popular pressure. Leaders, after all, want to get elected and stay in power. Yet the history of the Democratic Party does not just involve a trail of broken promises and competing policy demands. To understand the particularly difficult dilemma the modern Democratic Party faces today, it is also necessary to understand how activists sought to restructure the party organization and its relationship to the modern executive.

In the final analysis, party and administrative reform that remade liberalism had a common objective: the empowering of "the people," that is, the social movement organizations that transformed the meaning of partisanship during the late 1960s and 1970s. In the time of what some historians call the "long Sixties," the convention system, which empowered local and state party leaders and national public officials to nominate presidential candidates, was supplanted by a candidate-centered, media-driven primary system. The Sanders insurgency—indeed, even Barack Obama's victory in 2008—is inconceivable without the demise of the national party convention and the party leaders who ran it. Likewise, the campaign finance system—for as much scorn as it received from liberals after the 2010 decision *Citizens United*—is still more reflective of a "reformed," candidate-centered, activism-promoting system than it is a party-oriented one. In remaking institutions and setting new rules, the Democratic Party is beholden to social causes and programs in the areas of civil rights, immigration reform, environmental and consumer protection, and education.

The rise of movement politics began with Lyndon Johnson's Great Society. Johnson allied himself to reformers who championed "participatory democracy" and, at times, viewed the very concept of national governmental authority with deep suspicion. But as Hugh Heclo explains, during the 1960s a new movement politics emerged that combined a deep distrust of government with a demand for a more moral and ambitious form of public authority. "From right to left across the political spectrum, activists translated policy problems and disagreements into a denial of rights-demanding compensatory public-policy actions to put things 'right.' . . . The search was on for a higher public order in a policy culture denying there could be any such thing. Here was a situation ripe for demagoguery and for citizens' mounting disgust with the politics to which they were onlookers."[99] Consequently, the reforms of this era constrained presidential power and opened up new avenues of power for self-styled public lobbyists and social movement organizations, with the paradoxical effect of weakening the link between average citizens and their government. Yet the riots that engulfed America's urban core, the police beatings of young activists, the deepening discontent over the Vietnam War, the defeat of Hubert Humphrey in 1968 by the left's arch-nemesis Richard Nixon—none of these signs that the vital center had given way completely snuffed out the liberal idealism that had glowed so brightly during the previous decade. Indeed, amid liberalism's travails, activists on the left, far from playing it safe, succeeded in nominating George McGovern for president in 1972—the political insurgency that the political scientist Bruce Miroff describes as the "last true liberal moment" in presidential politics.[100]

McGovern's improbable capture of the Democratic nomination heralded the high tide of grassroots activism—the anti-party and anti-war mentality that had galvanized the left during the Kennedy and Johnson years. As Miroff aptly characterizes this crusade, McGovern's was "a sixties campaign in." Even though he suffered a terrible defeat in the general election (the worst defeat ever dealt a Democratic presidential candidate), McGovern's ascendance as the party favorite marked progressive reformers' final triumph over the traditional semblance of decentralized party organization. McGovern's insurgent campaign—building on the strategies and experiences of Eugene McCarthy's challenge four years earlier—suggested that a new politics had replaced the old—that partisanship was now driven by a new cadre of leaders who were beholden to the ideas born of the 1960s rebellion.

In fact, McGovern's nomination was the phoenix that emerged from the ashes of the 1968 Convention. As McGovern charged, the selection of Hubert Humphrey at the 1968 Democratic National Convention in Chicago, even though he did not enter a single primary during the emotional Democratic contest, made clear that for all the disruption of the civil rights and anti-war movements, the rearguard of New Deal politics was still in charge. "The Democratic presidential nominating process," he and his political allies protested, was still "dominated . . . by party wheel horses, entrenched office holders, and local bosses" who thwarted the will of "the people."[101]

Yet the challenge to the party brokers' influence were incubated amid the chaos of the 1968 convention. In spite of the establishment's control of the nomination, the Democrats undertook measures, spearheaded by civil rights and anti-war activists, that would eventually lead to the triumph of populist politics over the regular party machinery. One measure put state parties on notice that they would henceforth be admitted only if they "assured" that voters participated fully in party affairs without racial or ethnic discrimination. To monitor the integration efforts, the convention created a special committee on equal rights headed by Governor Richard J. Hughes of New Jersey. The committee on equal rights completed its work just prior to the opening of the 1972 convention, which also convened in Chicago; Governor Hughes then assumed the responsibilities of the full Credentials Committee.

This reform effort was a sequel to the bitter struggle over seating the Mississippi delegation at the 1964 Democratic Convention. Often lost in the heat of the betrayal felt by the MFDP activists was that Johnson sought to defuse the Mississippi controversy by championing a fundamental reform of convention rules that would have enormous long-term consequences for the Democratic Party. Having found no evidence that the Mississippi Democratic Party had "complied either with the spirit or letter" of the conventional call prohibiting racial discrimination, the Credentials Committee voted overwhelmingly to bar the Mississippi regular delegation from its seats. A biracial delegation, including Fannie Lou Hamer and many other members of the 1964 MFDP was seated in its place. The regular Mississippi Democrats, supported by southern delegates, as well as the Democratic National Committee chairman, John Bailey, sought to save their seats with an 11th-hour offer of another compromise. Bailey's support for a deal apparently followed from the warnings of other southern delegates that they would not be able to carry their states for Vice President Humphrey or any other northerner if the Mississippi regulars were not admitted. But this time, with both Humphrey and McCarthy supporting the insurgents, the offer of compromise was rejected. Hamer, an official delegate at last, received a standing ovation from the convention as she took her seat.

The action taken in the Mississippi case was, according to many civil rights activists, a "monumental victory in the fights against the lingering effects of Jim Crow." As the *Chicago Daily Defender* editorialized, the Mississippi activists' challenge to the regular state delegation rested not just on their adherence to the 1964 mandate but also was a "determinative test of the depth to which the national Democratic Party [was] willing to commit itself on the question of racial integration in the rank and file."[102] The Democrats had given at least one demonstration that their national party had a basic belief in racial equality, and if an existing state party was not willing to abide by that belief, the convention was prepared to grant official status to a new state party that would live by it. Before the end of the Chicago meeting, the convention gave one more demonstration of this maxim. Pushed by the McCarthy supporters, the convention agreed to share the Georgia vote between rival groups led by Atlanta State Representative Julian Bond and the segregationist forces of Governor Lester G. Maddox, although most of the "regulars" rejected the settlement and walked out—another sign of the ongoing transformation of partisanship instigated by the civil rights revolution of the 1960s.

The Democratic National Convention's seating of two integrated southern delegations appeared to vindicate the politically oriented and non-violent approach that characterized the initial alliance between the Johnson White House and civil rights leaders. Yet the triumph of the insurgents in Mississippi and Georgia was part of a larger national offensive against the regular party organizations and the modern executive office. Building on the momentum of their victory in the contests over the Mississippi and Georgia delegations, insurgents, championing the New Left cause of "participatory democracy," broke through the surface and demanded immediate attention to their cause. Besides supporting the integration drives in still disputed delegations, the McCarthy forces used the same convention call for full participation to charge unfairness and undemocratic procedures in many states, including New York, Pennsylvania, Connecticut, Minnesota, and Washington, DC. With respect to northern delegations, the charge was not confined to the question of race but extended to the entire system of delegate selection, particularly the dominance of local and state party organizations in this process. The central question was whether Humphrey's advantage at the convention was achieved by methods that allowed party professionals in the various states to unfairly impose their choices on the district and state conventions and caucuses.

McCarthy's challenge of those delegates who owed their presence at the convention to state and local party leaders became a cause célèbre for progressive reformers. It culminated in the Commission of the Democratic Selection of Presidential Nominees, headed by Iowa governor Harold E. Hughes. The Hughes commission was set up initially on "private" initiative, but its report was presented to the 1968 rules committee of the Democratic Convention. Denying it had any interest in a specific candidate, the Commission on Democratic Selection of the Presidential Nominees contended that the convention system was on trial. "To an extent not matched since the turn of the twentieth century, events in 1968 have called into question the integrity of the convention for nominating presidential candidates," the report read. "Recent developments have put the future of the two-party system itself into serious jeopardy."[103]

The McCarthy forces and the band of reformers led by Governor Hughes, well known for his interest in remaking the party system, did not wield enough influence to deny Hubert Humphrey the nomination in 1968. McCarthy did not get the seats he wanted; however, the reform principles he espoused with the support of the Hughes Commission were well on the way to becoming official party doctrine. Following the recommendation of the Hughes Commission report, the delegates voted to abolish the unit rule as binding on the delegates for the 1968 convention. For 1972, it would no longer be valid at the precinct level, either. The unit rule bound individual delegates to vote in accordance with the preferences of majority of the state delegation. As such, it was used by party leaders to strengthen their positions at national conventions, even if there was disagreement in the local ranks; moreover, by using the unit rule on local levels at caucuses that sent delegates to state conventions, party moguls were able to diminish the power of insurgent groups seeking to affect the delegate selection process. Even more significant for the future of the party system were decisions to establish two commissions, one to deal with party structure and delegate selection and another to take up convention rules that would consider structural reform to guide future conventions.

The fractious 1968 convention thus prepared the way for the sweeping changes made between 1968 and 1972 by the national committee and the McGovern-Fraser commission. In 1969, the committee, acting under the mandate from the Chicago convention, established the Commission on Party Structure and Delegate Selection. Under the chairmanship first of McGovern, who had put himself forward in Chicago as the dovish alternative to McCarthy, and after 1971, of Representative Donald Fraser, the commission developed a set of 18 guidelines governing the state parties' procedures for selecting their delegates for the national conventions. The Hughes Commission report offered elaborate documentation of the procedures then in use and its recommendations as to what was wrong with them; then it provided the basis for the guidelines. Their purpose, therefore, especially with respect to the demand for the expansion of the direct primary, supported the Hughes Commission's praise of "direct democracy." In effect, the 1968 Convention's adoption of the Hughes Commission's proposals to guide future conventions sounded the death knell of the traditional party structure. The objective of weakening the prevailing party organization in the name of "meaningful and timely opportunities" for participation, adopted in the form of a mandate by the Chicago convention, was clearly spelled out in the Hughes Commission report.[104]

The DNC accepted all the guidelines of the McGovern-Fraser Commission. It declared in the call for the 1972 convention that the guidelines constituted "the standards that State Democratic Parties, in qualifying and certifying delegates to the 1972 National Democratic Convention, must make all efforts to comply with." And, "[the DNC] made it stick," said Austin Ranney, himself a member of the McGovern-Fraser Commission.[105] Most states were in full compliance with the guidelines by convention time; those not in compliance risked not being seated. The most dramatic evidence that the new rules were fully operational was the rejection of the Chicago delegation slated by Mayor Richard Daley, the symbol of fierce old guard resistance at the 1968 convention. The Credentials Committee, dominated by McGovern supporters, refused to seat Daley and 58 other Chicago delegates to the 1972 Democratic National Convention because the procedures by which they had been selected for the Illinois primary violated the new party rules. By a vote of 71 to 61, the committee awarded the places to a slate of challengers, dominated by McGovern backers, in large part because it was much more representative of women, Blacks, Latino Americans, and young people.[106] "Boss control" of the presidential nominating machinery had come to an end.

Given the results of the 1972 election, scholars have debated the extent to which these reforms truly represented a populist movement. Assuming the leadership of a fractured Democratic Party, McGovern's insurgent presidential campaign was an electoral disaster. Nevertheless, there is no doubt that the reforms emerging from the 1971–1972 McGovern-Fraser Commission amounted to a "quiet revolution" in American politics.[107] The Commission extended, and ultimately codified, two somewhat competing objectives of liberal activism that continued into the 1970s: "participatory democracy" as expressed in popular primaries or caucuses; and the inclusion of groups previously denied access to the political process, namely, minorities, women, and the young. The enactment of these reforms deprived party leaders of the power they had exercised since the early part of the 19th century to select delegates to the national convention, to determine the place and time when the party—in its traditional form—would engage in the important work of writing a platform and selecting candidates for office, and to maintain a sense of collective responsibility.

The McGovern-Fraser reforms are not as memorable as civil rights legislation, and the Commission report lacks the rhetorical lift of the Port Huron Statement and Johnson's Great Society speech. But these procedural changes remade American democracy. Reflecting on the importance of this transformation, the distinguished political scientist David Truman credited the implementation of the reforms with bringing to a culmination developments that began during the Progressive era: the expansion of the national government's responsibility for managing the economy and society (or, the end of "dual federalism"), and the rise of a media-driven plebiscitary nomination process. With the triumph of party reform, he concluded, "the nominating function of the national convention was reduced to no more than a ratifying action. By imposing these changes on the state Democratic parties, the McGovern-Fraser 'reforms' destroyed almost all semblance of a federal national party. . . . This was institutional upheaval and displacement of one set of elites by another set on an impressive scale."[108]

Rather than seeking to strengthen the party against the excesses of executive aggrandizement—one of the concerns of the 1950 APSA Committee report that prescribed a more "responsible" two-party system—the goal was to fundamentally transform the very nature of partisanship itself. It was, as James Ceaser has written, "a major attack on the entire principle of representation . . . made in the name of direct democracy . . . undertaken with an underlying confidence in the efficacy of institutional change."[109] The consequence of this party reform was to accelerate a process that resulted in weak parties and heightened partisanship. In 1976, the Democrats nominated Jimmy Carter, the ultimate Washington outsider who so disdained the Washington establishment and bonhomie of professional politicians that one of his first actions once ascending to the White House was to sell the presidential yacht—a symbolic act to scourge the modern executive of its imperialist trappings.[110] Yet the regnant national state—rooted in the elusive progressive ideal of "enlightened administration"—made it difficult for Democrats to reconcile their promise of insurgency and the growing commitments of the liberal state, which demanded a different type of presidential stewardship. Viewing the president as the agent rather than the steward of the public welfare, the new liberals embraced the general ideas current in the late 1960s that presidential politics and governance should be directed by social movements.[111] Carter's failure to straddle insurgency and managerial imperatives, inciting the hostility of liberal activists and the strong primary challenge by their champion—Ted Kennedy—ended in the landslide defeat to Ronald Reagan in 1980.

Changes to campaign finance law in 1974 and again in 2002 further pushed partisanship beyond the party. Such "reform" ostensibly sought to make the quid pro quo relationship incurred by financial transactions less likely. Under the 1974 Federal Elections Campaign Act, a Democratic Congress sought to limit both campaign donations and expenditures—in effect, making it more difficult to raise and spend money in each campaign cycle. As a result, a new core campaign institution arose from this framework, political action committees (PACs), codifying a place for "independent" groups, which prior to reform had little choice but to work through the party for electioneering purposes. When the Supreme Court struck down limitations on campaign expenditures in *Buckley v. Valeo* (1976), candidates were now free to spend unlimited amounts of money, albeit under a set of rules that made it more difficult for them to raise funds from individuals. PACs stepped in and filled the place of the traditional donor who tended to have close ties to the party. Then, under the 2002 Bipartisan Campaign Finance Reform Act, Congress sought to limit direct contributions to parties, thereby further advancing the candidate-centered nature of elections. No longer dependent on parties for their contributions, candidates became more beholden to those groups and individuals outside the parties who could raise the massive funds necessary to run increasingly expensive campaigns.[112]

The beneficiaries of the reforms, its supporters claimed, would be the common citizen who felt disenfranchised. Yet, as Morton Keller suggests, "the voices of newly empowered groups turned out to be not vox populi but activists whose claims as spokesmen lacked verification by elections and opinion polls." And, as a result, "the policy agenda came to be defined less by the parties, with the moderating effect they usually brought, and more by leading voices of the new regime: the media, advocacy groups, judges, lawyers and law professors, academic experts and foundations, bureaucrats, presidential and congressional staffers."[113] In other words, diminishing the influence of traditional party organizations and leaders did not level the playing field. As Byron Shafer claims, it simply brought "the *next* most extensive and next best organized groups and individuals" into the political system.[114]

The "next best organized groups" that replaced organized labor as the core of the liberal coalition were environmentalists, feminists, civil rights leaders, and LGBTQ activists. Over the next several decades, these groups transformed the very idea of what it meant to be a Democrat and used the remade institutional processes to give form to that image. Election after election, convention after convention, their voices grew as the party became mired in the difficult challenge of harmonizing their demands.[115] As Thomas and Mary Edsall recognized, such procedural changes disadvantaged those "white voters who were on the frontlines of urban housing integration, who were the subjects of busing orders, who were competitors for jobs as policemen, firemen, and union craftsmen governed by affirmative action consent decrees, and who found the liberal Supreme Court rules on criminal rights, abortion, school prayer, busing, and obscenity incomprehensible." As a result, there was a "refusal to address conflicting evidence—of policy failure as well as policy success—[which] permitted the political right to capture the debate."[116] Unsurprisingly, the political right also captured many disaffected Democrats' votes.

Leftist critics of the post–New Deal Democratic Party deny that such a conversion ever took place. Liberalism, they insist, did not become more demanding; rather, under the pressure of big business and imperialism, it gave way to a "neoliberalism" that sacrificed the idealism of social activism to large campaign contributions and compromised programmatic ambition to appease powerful lobbyists. The advent of neoliberalism was confirmed, they argue, by the "Third Way" politics of faux populist Bill Clinton and the thwarting of the 2016 "democratic socialist" campaign of Bernie Sanders by the rearguard of the Democratic establishment, determined to elect Hillary Clinton and to continue the Clinton dynasty.[117]

Yet the emergence of the "New Democrats" who boosted Bill and Hillary Clinton, and the Democratic Leadership Council (DLC) that spearheaded the Third Way represented a more politically savvy effort to resolve the same tension between insurgency and the managerial demands of the modern executive that afflicted previous Democratic presidencies. The DLC and the New Democrats' critique of the liberal wing, as articulated in 1989, was prescient: activist demands did not speak to many Americans' economic concerns; indeed, they often appeared hostile to the variegated moral landscape of the electorate; and national movement organizations often threatened to undermine local and state bases of partisan support.[118] Yet the DLC did not prescribe a strengthening of traditional party organizations. Rather, its formula for success was to create a strong base of support among disaffected "middle America"—outside the party establishment and centered on the broad appeal of a single charismatic individual. Theirs was an insurgency to fight insurgency.

Prior to developing a blueprint to elect Clinton, the DLC had sought to work inside the party—to reform nominating rules and create more opportunities for elected officeholders to create party doctrine. For example, they lobbied effectively to establish the "Super Tuesday" primary, which gave southern voters greater say in the selection of the Democratic candidate. But, when Al Gore lost the nomination to Michael Dukakis in the 1988 nomination contest, the DLC shifted their approach and sought to advance the

Third Way through the same sort of "extra-party" organizations they had earlier derided but which nevertheless enjoyed great success. In choosing to embrace "post-reform" politics, the DLC accelerated the decline of the Democratic establishment by using the same movement-oriented approach, but from the center.[119]

Consequently, the DLC's "success" did not provide a formula for rebinding the vital center. The DLC won office only when it abandoned its institutional focus on the Democratic National Committee, attempting instead to win the presidency using the reformed nomination process its leaders had earlier vilified. Bill Clinton's 1992 campaign, therefore, gave him the opportunity to obviate the opposition of liberal activists during the nominating campaign, but it failed to provide the means to transform the party when he took office. Clinton thus followed an activist liberal course during his first two years, most notably in seeking to enact comprehensive health insurance, a cause he scarcely mentioned during his campaign. Sobered by the disastrous 1994 midterms, which saw Republicans assume control of both congressional chambers for the first time since 1954, he veered to the center as the 1996 election approached, a retreat that included a rapprochement with Republicans on welfare "reform." As a consequence, Clinton became the first Democratic president to be elected to a second term since FDR; but his candidate-centered campaign did little to create an enduring pragmatic center or to help elect Democrats down ballot. Indeed, those Clinton staffers who joined the next Democratic administration in 2008 took lessons from opportunities squandered decades earlier. Barack Obama benefited from their experience in pushing through the Affordable Care Act, the signature policy achievement of his administration and the first major social welfare program to be enacted without a single Republican vote. The president embraced the title his fierce political opponents gave to this measure—"Obamacare"—signaling that the first African American to occupy the White House fully accepted the executive-centered partisanship his predecessors had refined over the previous 50 years.

Conclusion

New Deal liberalism is a celebration of reason, modernity, and the individual right to basic economic security within the structure of free-market capitalism. "Post-modern" liberalism defends a far more expansive program of rights and entitlements—especially for disadvantaged constituencies—and demands that presidents embrace movement-style politics in seeking government redress for past injustices. It is skeptical of government authority and pragmatism, especially the sorts of bargains that might ease the partisan gridlock that hamstrings the contemporary Congress. More dependent on administrative agencies and the courtroom than the legislature to advance their causes, contemporary liberals see little need for strong parties, favoring social movement organizations and advocacy groups that will not readily sacrifice their causes on the altar of political expediency. The expansion of rights during the 1960s and 1970s sought redress to fundamental injustices that demanded government action. But vital parties require some compromise between a deep and abiding commitment to rights and a due attention to common deliberation and choice—some decisions must be left to the messy business of legislating and logrolling. The organization that is the Democratic Party today is not congenial to such partisan responsibility because the party is, in effect, a coalition of disparate rent-seekers, policy advocates, interest groups, and particularized constituencies. Candidates can create a broad menu of policy options that give these constituencies causes to celebrate free college, Medicare for all, fair trade deals, and a $15 minimum wage. But any discussion of costs, trade-offs, or unintended consequences—in a word, compromise—is suppressed. As Wilson Carey McWilliams once noted, such cross-purposes "amount to a long-term prescription for frustration and failure."[120]

The transformation of Democratic partisanship, as we will discuss in Chapter 5, agitated the emergence of a post-modern form of Republican conservatism. This fundamental partisan transformation has been abetted by a full-scale assault on the modern executive office that anchored the liberal state. The modern presidency currently operates in a political arena that is seldom congenial to meaningful political debate and which all too often is guilty of deflecting attention from the painful struggles about the relative merits of contemporary progressivism and conservatism (or, for that matter, classical liberalism). Instead, with the liberation of the executive from the many constraints of party leadership and the rise of mass media, presidents have resorted to rhetoric and administration, tools with which they have sought to forge new, more personal ties with the public. But as the nation has witnessed all too clearly during the past 50 years, this form of "populist" presidential politics can all too readily degenerate into rank opportunism. Moreover, it risks exposing the people to the kinds of public figures who will exploit citizens' impatience with the difficult tasks involved in sustaining a healthy constitutional democracy.

This chapter began by reflecting on the inaugural words of John F. Kennedy's presidency: a plea for communal obligation, individual sacrifice, and, ultimately, a recognition of the free society's moral superiority. There is a glimmer of the hope to "Get America Moving Again" today. Barack Obama's invocation of "Yes, We Can"—that summoned millions of new voters and activists to participate in politics—echoed the energy and movement of Kennedy's clarion call. And Joe Biden's inaugural similarly spoke to the need for, above all, "that most elusive of things in a democracy: unity, unity."

Yet Kennedy was a confident Cold Warrior, who stood in defiance of a nascent new left that challenged the notion that the "American way of life" was worth fighting for. What made Kennedy and his magnetism so powerful was that he could confront the problems of New Deal liberalism while simultaneously projecting an air of optimism in its future. When President Obama attempted to do the same thing in 2008, the beam on which to balance such a precarious position was simply too narrow. Speaking in Berlin in 2008—the Cold War battleground in Europe over which Kennedy ordered supplies to be flown—Obama echoed the call for a renewed national spirt. "Now is the time to join together, through constant cooperation, strong institutions, shared sacrifice, and a global commitment to progress, to meet the challenges of the 21st century," he urged. "It was this spirit that led airlift planes to appear in the sky above our heads, and people to assemble where we stand today. And this is the moment when our nations—and all nations—must summon that spirit anew." It was glowing rhetoric, filled with the can-do American spirit. But it never answered the essential question the left has provoked since the 1960s: how can we succeed as a nation so flawed—in an America that is no longer a city on a hill?

5

Conservatism Transformed

The Republican Party Since 1960

Lyndon Johnson's historic landslide victory over Barry Goldwater in 1964 announced the end of an old division in American politics and a day of reckoning for the Republican Party. Americans seemed united in their support for the transformed liberalism that was taking shape in the 1960s. Months after the assassination of their president, John F. Kennedy, the electorate appeared to affirm his successor's pursuit of a Great Society—to fighting a war on poverty, rebuilding the nation's decaying cities, extending full citizenship to African Americans, and continuing the all-consuming fight against communism abroad. Johnson swept 44 states and the District of Columbia with 61.1% of the popular vote—the highest percentage of the modern era, outpacing even FDR's reelection rout in 1936. And, just as Roosevelt's momentous victory ratified an enduring expansion in governing authority, so too did Johnson's great triumph push the bounds of American liberalism—a new liberalism, dedicated not just to the old guarantees of economic security but one that would "advance the quality of American civilization." Goldwater promised to return the country to its former self, a land where individual liberty and self-reliance flourished—what Herbert Hoover declared to be America's spirit of "rugged individualism." But the American electorate overwhelmingly rejected Goldwater's promise "to return to proven ways" and, as many post-mortems suggested, relegated conservatism's ancient truths to the dustbin of history.[1] America's exceptional embrace of limited government was over.

With the benefit of hindsight, we know that the reports of conservativism's death were greatly exaggerated. Liberty, self-reliance, individualism—these values are still woven into the fabric of American political discourse. Conservatism is not a bygone dogma, and the Republican Party has proven remarkably successful in the 50-plus years after Goldwater's defeat. Since its devastating loss in 1964, the Republican candidate for president has captured the office in eight of the last 14 elections. In 1994 Republicans took control of the House of Representatives for the first time since 1952 and have maintained a hold on that chamber ever since with the exception of a four-year hiatus (2007–2011) and the Democrats' recent reoccupation in 2019. A plurality, nearly two in five, of Americans label themselves "conservative."[2] And the United States remains an outlier in the group of industrialized nations for what it lacks—no guaranteed, paid maternity or paternity leave; no widespread right to collective bargaining; no national healthcare system; no free college or universal access to Pre-K education. It is no wonder that scholars and pundits routinely characterize the United States as an inherently conservative or right-leaning nation.[3]

Nevertheless, the election of 1964 did present a dilemma for the Republican Party. On the one hand, Goldwater's loss came with a populist upwelling of conservative enthusiasm and a pointed challenge to the principles of New Deal liberalism. The message was clear and it enthralled a burgeoning conservative movement. Goldwater crusaders rejected the liberal state as an insidious form of despotism that would destroy rugged individualism at home and America's "exceptional" global place abroad. Indeed, Goldwater was the first Republican presidential candidate to frame the stakes in the battle between liberalism and conservatism in apocalyptic terms. "I would remind you that extremism in the defense of liberty is no vice," he told the GOP national convention in 1964. "And let me remind you also," Goldwater continued, "that moderation in the pursuit of justice is no virtue."[4]

On the other hand, the expansion of the conservative movement undercut the Republican Party's traditional claims of good governance, fiscal responsibility, and constitutional restraint, especially the use of executive power. So messianic were conservative leaders in their assault on the liberal state that they too sought to fuse populist presidential leadership with social activism. Just as the "New" Left populist uprising scorned party organizations, bureaucratic autonomy and a pragmatic approach to public policy, so the New Right, summoned by Goldwater's candidacy, sought to use power to weaken the guardrails that moderated representative constitutional government in the 20th century. No less than liberals, conservatives sought to dismantle the norms and institutions that buttressed America's "vital center."

In many ways, modern conservatism's strategy to dismantle the liberal welfare state is taken right from Goldwater's playbook. When Goldwater spoke of making Social Security "voluntary," he foreshadowed a decades-long battle waged by the right, culminating in President George W. Bush's calls to "privatize" the program. When Tea Party patriots waved their signs lambasting Obamacare as socialism, they drew on Goldwater's conviction that Medicare was the vanguard of a radical egalitarianism. "Having given our pensioners their medical care in kind," he said, "why not food baskets, why not public housing accommodations, why not vacation resorts, why not a ration of cigarettes for those who smoke and of beer for those who drink?"[5] In 1964, Goldwater blamed policymakers' blind faith in the promise of global governance and multi-lateral organizations like NATO and the United Nations for imposing "slavery" on the United States; in 2016, Donald Trump fueled his campaign, in part, by castigating decades-old commitments to these institutions, especially those devoted to extending free trade—what the president would later describe in a series of tweets as "fool trade."[6]

Although it is possible to draw many comparisons between Goldwater's presidential campaign and the leading voices on the contemporary American right, no less telling are the differences. Drawing a straight line between Goldwater and modern conservatism is quite problematic because doing so risks neglecting the particular political circumstances of the Goldwater campaign: its place in the broader Republican Party, the relationship between Goldwater's style and the substance of his message, the fact that Goldwater was so badly beaten in 1964. In truth, in the wake of the 1964 electoral disaster, Goldwater's movement operated at the margins of a still resilient Republican establishment. Few Republicans agreed with his no-holds-bar, anti-establishment rhetoric. Leading Republican officials refused to endorse him after he secured the party's nomination. The night after his rousing Republican National Convention speech, former president and party elder Dwight Eisenhower hinted that he wished he had done more to prevent Goldwater's nomination; during the campaign, the popular Ike refused to aid the presidential hopeful in crafting a more moderate foreign policy.[7] Party leaders, following Goldwater's humiliating defeat, tried to understand how to prevent another embarrassment four years later. They did not buy into the conventional ploy, fabricated by Goldwater's allies after the fact and still peddled today, that Americans voted for Johnson solely because he adroitly tied his political fortunes to a young and popular leader whose promise was cut short by a tragic death. In reality, a historic majority of Americans voted for Johnson because they did not trust Goldwater, whose militant opposition to civil rights and contemplation of the use of nuclear weapons in Vietnam placed him very far outside the mainstream.[8]

Yet the shadow of Goldwater remained when Republicans regrouped in 1968 behind Richard Nixon, whose campaign sought to strike a balance between the populism that Goldwater unleashed and the "Modern Republicanism" that he and Eisenhower preached during the 1950s. The conservative insurgents who Goldwater summoned thus found themselves in an unusual predicament. Nixon took conservatives into the mainstream; however, he sought to master rather than roll back the modern executive that anchored the liberal state. Nixon, in fact, faced political circumstances that encouraged him to rely more on executive power than had his Democratic predecessors. When Nixon entered the White House, he became the first president in the modern era to do so without the aid and support of unified government. Democrats still controlled the House and the Senate. The new president also faced demands from an aroused activist base, a circumstance that encouraged Nixon to seek many of his objectives unilaterally—to strengthen what Richard Nathan dubbed the "administrative presidency."[9] Nixon, therefore, sought to demonstrate that the vast powers of the modern presidency—built originally for progressive governance—were, ideologically, a double-edged sword that could cut in a conservative as well as a liberal direction. Although Nixon was far more pragmatic than Goldwater, many of his executive actions, most notably his efforts to end the War on Poverty and shape a more conservative court, drew inspiration from and began to give effect to the populism stirred by Goldwater conservatism.

There is a real sense, in fact, that Nixon's vision for America was cast in the same set of transformative principles that Goldwater expounded—a strong sense of individual rights, faith in entrepreneurship, liberty before equality—and to which conservatives had always subscribed. Yet conservatives traditionally believed that this version of America was achieved only in a system of resilient restraining institutions and a respect for constitutional norms. Congress, in particular the Senate, was designed as a conserving institution that would limit the scope of national power. The courts, a long-standing vanguard of precedent and restraint, were supposed to protect personal property and set strict demarcations on national authority. And federalism would bring individuals into civic life and nourish the necessary habits of civic virtue. Together these institutional forms restrained a powerful presidency that threatened to mobilize mass support with false promises of more efficient and beneficent government. In contrast, beginning with his 1968 presidential campaign, Nixon and the former acolytes of Goldwater's ill-fated revolution, redefined conservatism and wedded it to the idea of a powerful presidency. An "institutional" conservativism, dedicated to limited constitutional government, that once joined the disparate voices on the

American right faltered alongside the illusory gleam of a more ideological and presidency-centered movement.

With Richard Nixon's election, the Republican Party seemed to have redeemed itself from the embarrassment of Goldwater's campaign, but Nixon's appropriation of presidential power in defense of conservatism's traditional causes is a testament to the establishment's beleaguered state. The Democratic Party was torn asunder by a movement-style politics oriented toward reforming the New Deal state's compromises with racism, imperialism, and corporate liberalism. The Republican Party was besieged by conservative insurgents who feared that the Great Society and the social activists it unleashed had so denigrated "traditional values" that it was no longer possible to forbear from statism. In response to claims that civil rights had gone too far and threatened ordered liberty, the GOP deployed national administrative power in defense of "law and order"; and responsive to the resentment the anti-war movement set off in middle-class Americans and neoconservative intellectuals, Republicans greatly expanded the country's military capabilities. Chapter 4 revealed how social, economic, and global challenges pushed the Democratic Party to enact procedural reforms in the name of "the people"; this chapter reveals how Republicans developed their own blueprint to remake American democracy. The "New Right" presumed to be the servants of the "silent" majority who venerated God, country, and family. Consequently, by the turn of the century, the vital center had not only undergone a decade-long assault led by progressive insurgents; its right flank also was attacked by self-styled conservative populists who captured a party that once stood for preserving limited constitutional government.

Law, Order, and the Southern Strategy

Seven months before the 1968 presidential election, the nation's capital city was burning. Martin Luther King Jr. was dead—assassinated by an avowed white supremacist James Earl Ray on Thursday, April 4. Four thousand armed troops poured into the city, setting up barricades on the lawn of the White House and Capitol building. "So many fires were burning," the *Washington Post* reported—at least 100—"that the city's Fire Department could not tabulate the number. A wide pall of smoke hung over the inner city."[10] Parents and wives from adjacent neighborhoods overwhelmed the telephone lines looking for missing husbands and children; a massive traffic jam spawned by the federal government's early closure prevented thousands from leaving downtown. The 14th Street bridge—a gateway into the heart of the city—shut down. The stores along the U-street corridor, the symbol of Black culture and sophistication—once known as "Black Broadway"—crumbled.

Over 100 other US cities convulsed that week, but the discord just steps away from the White House and Capitol building were most shocking. The newspapers did not have to describe the scene as a war zone; pictures of troops standing in front of iconic American landmarks said it all. Former representative and long-time champion of civil rights Adam Clayton Powell predicted the worst: "It was going to be a long hot summer anyway. Now the problem is that nonviolence has been struck down by violence. Disillusioned young people in the King camp are going to ally themselves with the black militants. It's going to be a tremendous army."[11]

In truth, the race riots that had engulfed urban America since 1964 affected the livelihoods of most White Americans very tangentially. White flight into the suburbs not only continued but intensified the segregation between Whites and Blacks in modern America. As President Johnson's National Commission on Civil Disorders—the Kerner Commission—summarized, "Our nation is moving toward two societies, one black, one white—separate and unequal."[12]

Yet perceptions are what count in politics. And the riots mattered in a country that aspired to be a Great Society. Johnson had announced just days prior to King's assassination that he would not seek the Democratic nomination at his party's convention. The eventual Democratic candidate, Vice President Hubert Humphrey, did not fare as poorly as one might have thought given the fractious state of the party—its own war scene erupting at the Chicago convention (see Chapter 4). However, Humphrey did poorly in the South, foreshadowing a massive political realignment that would dramatically change American politics. George Wallace, running as a third-party candidate on a platform of avowed racial segregation, won five Deep South states: Alabama, Arkansas, Georgia, Louisiana, and Mississippi. Nixon added to the conservative incursion below the Mason-Dixon line, capturing the border states of North and South Carolina, Florida, Virginia, and Tennessee. As important as these states and the South more generally would become to the prospects of the Republican Party, Nixon did not become president solely because of those electoral votes. Rather, the enduring legacy of Nixon's campaign is that he demonstrated a viable strategy to appeal to voters in traditional Democratic strongholds—the Midwest, and, most important, the fastest growing region of the United States, the Sunbelt. Nixon aide Kevin Phillips—one of the principal strategists behind the Republican Party's ascendency in the late 1960s and early 1970s—recognized that the

> Democratic "Great Society" programs aligned that party with many Negro demands, but the party was unable to defuse the racial tension sundering the nation. The South, the West, and the Catholic sidewalks of New York were the focal points of conservative opposition to the welfare liberalism of the federal government; however, the general opposition which deposed the Democratic Party came in large part from prospering Democrats who objected to Washington dissipating their tax dollars on programs which did them no good.[13]

Nixon capitalized on this pervasive anxiety. Or, as Robert Novak's pithy retrospective summarized, Nixon's was a campaign that promised to welcome those disillusioned with the Democratic Party, which had become the party of "abortion, amnesty, and acid."[14]

The "Sunbelt," coined by Phillips, grew as a distinct political region in the 1950s and 1960s. And, as a testament to Phillips's analysis and politicians' responses to it, the Sunbelt remains a distinct area of political and cultural life. After Johnson and the Democratic Congress enacted the Immigration and Nationality Act of 1965—replacing the 1920s quota-based system that awarded preferential treatment to immigrants of northern and western Europe—the Sunbelt, where there was an influx of Latino immigrants, outpaced the rest of the country in its ethnic diversity.[15] This region had always been more racially and ethnically diverse than the rest of the country, so these changes provided fertile ground for Republicans to supplement the Southern Strategy, fueled by racial resentment, with a "suburban strategy" driven by color-blind arguments, individualism, and free-market consumerism.

Although troubled by school and housing desegregation efforts, White suburbanites sought to evade rather than resist segregation by settling in "island" communities protected by de facto rather than de jure segregation. Nixon promised security for these enclaves of traditional privilege. As Matthew Lassiter has argued, these middle-class neighborhoods rejected overt appeals to racism and legal segregation, arguing instead for open schools and freedom of choice within residential areas.[16] This strategy ameliorated the worst elements of the southern racist legacy and enabled Republicans to forge a center-right coalition, allowing them to evade more direct confrontation with the economic and racial injustices of de facto discrimination. In the pursuit of "free choice," Republicans learned how to use federal, state, and local power to craft policies essential to the creation of a majority party in the Sunbelt. They changed federal housing policy and captured supportive state and local zoning boards to make massive internal migration financially viable for White, middle-class Americans. Consequently, what was once a predominantly rural landscape, transformed into a sprawling suburban scene, dotted with low-density metropolises like Charlotte, Jacksonville, Houston, and Phoenix. Burgeoning tourism economies were further buttressed by direct federal subsidies in space and engineering facilities and large military complexes.[17] By 2018, five of the eight fastest-growing states were in the Sunbelt: Utah, Nevada, Florida, Colorado, and Arizona. Their explosive growth stands in sharp contrast to the states that were once the centers of political power but were now losing population or growing very slowly: Illinois, Connecticut, Pennsylvania, and New York.[18]

The 1964 election—a contest between two sunbelt candidates—revealed that President Johnson and the Democratic Party did not forsake this rapidly growing part of the country. After all, the Sunbelt was a political construction, and politicians fought over its largesse: voters. Johnson was a native Texan, and federal programs supported by liberals poured billions of new dollars into this region. The Great Society included a host of programs for rural redevelopment; the expansive suburbs of the South needed the federal funds made available by LBJ's administration for new infrastructure; and the leading proponents of federal research funds—those monies that fueled America's mission to the moon and effectively subsidized new industries in the region—were outgrowths of President Kennedy's New Frontier. However, when the beneficiaries of these new programs went to the polls, they repudiated the presidential administrations that had launched them.

The Sunbelt's embrace of the new Republicanism was not just a matter of the laissez-faire myth that offered a warped image of suburban success. It also testified to the pervasive fear during the late 1960s, stoked by the Nixon administration, that '60s liberalism had little regard for the rule of law. Many Americans did not see progress; they saw lawlessness and decay. Nixon and other influential Republican politicians in the Sunbelt, such as Ronald Reagan—who was elected governor of California in 1966—promised them law and order. "Concern over law and order plainly embraces a wide variety of national afflictions," the *Wall Street Journal* editorialized in September 1968, "—muggings in the streets, racial riots, the continued rise in recorded crimes, inroads by the Mafia, police-demonstrator battles in Chicago. . . . It is hard to articulate, but we suspect what bothers most citizens is the cumulative effect. There are too many people resorting to violence for too many reasons, and together the outbursts amount to an assault on the decent and civilized values by which most Americans have always lived."[19]

Liberals countered that law and order was a codeword—a dog whistle—used to animate a subliminal view that rioting Blacks were ungrateful and impatient and that anti-war protestors were naïve and utopian. Civil rights leader Whitney Young wrote in 1968, "The people who are loudest in shouting for law and order don't seem to mind that federal laws against discrimination are not enforced, that the nation's highest court is slandered, or that the black ghetto gets inferior police protection. This indicates they don't care about law, order, or justice except as it applies to them."[20]

As is often the case when trying to make sense of partisan rhetoric, the truth lies somewhere in the middle. In this case, it is not as if both perspectives are entirely incommensurate with one another. Many White Americans did harbor deep animosities, no doubt, when for five consecutive years race riots broke out in the cities. Did they fail to appreciate the deep and systematic influence the cycle of inner-city poverty had on those who took to the streets to finally make their voices heard? Yes. Did they view para-military groups in the cities as an illegitimate challenge to local police rather than as a response to years of brutality and racial harassment from those meant to serve and protect? Yes. Had they been led to believe that expert administrators, armed with the latest tools of social science and public policy, were going to completely eradicate it, and fast? Yes. Did they therefore grow weary as leaders came back year after year with requests for more money? Yes.

Still, Nixon won the 1968 election with 2 million fewer votes than he earned in his 1960 defeat. And the Republican Party did not have the sole claim to either the law and order issue or its rhetoric. Incidentally, some of the first occurrences of that phrase in American political discourse emerged from civil rights leaders in their opposition to more antagonistic tactics in the name of racial justice. "The very last ones to renounce law and order," the African American newspaper *New Journal and Guide* argued in 1964, "as a means to their end should be Negro Americans. . . . The apologists may attempt to excuse the rioting and disorder. The sociologists may contrive rational explanations for them. But stripped of the high sounding verbiage, these outbreaks are little more than desecrations of the society of which the Negro strives so mightily to be a full-fledged part."[21]

Indeed, the Johnson administration voiced similar concerns about how the civil rights movement seemed to be spiraling out of control. In 1965, President Johnson announced a new federally sponsored "war on crime," and signed the Law Enforcement Assistance Act (LEAA) on September 22. In providing millions of dollars in funding, imposing professionalization requirements, and arming local police with more sophisticated weaponry, the LEAA moved the federal government into issue areas long dominated by local and state control. The upshot, as Elizabeth Hinton convincingly argues, is that "in deciding to bring punitive measures into urban policy . . . the Johnson administration helped to lay the groundwork for subsequent federal action generally associated with conservatism."[22] Indeed, in the spring of 1967, the Democratic Party feted Chicago Mayor Richard Daley as the "Best Democrat of 1967" for his commitment to law and order. Standing alongside President Johnson, Daley foretold the dividing wedge among the center left that Republicans would exploit for the next half century: "I believe in civil rights," Daley said, "but with law and order in our streets, and not disorder. Today we have many faint hearts in our party. We never had faint hearts before. We have always had the courage to stand up and speak out for what is right."[23] Floyd McKissick, a prominent civil rights activist and columnist for the *New York Amsterdam News*, summarized it best: "The trend, obviously, is bi-partisan in nature and national in scope. . . . The actions of opportunist politicians are nothing new, but in the conditions of today, they are more dangerous than ever."[24]

In a sense, Nixon poached the issue of crime from the Democratic establishment who foresaw the issue's mobilizing potential. But he did not embrace this cause in a bipartisan spirit. After all, Johnson viewed the riots as a symptom of deep-rooted racial injustice that showed the need for the expansion, rather than the rolling back, of Great Society programs. Nixon exploited the sense of lawlessness in the country to transform law and order into a core Republican issue, indeed a program that gave rise to the carceral state—a "front lash," as Vesla Weaver describes it, which transposed the country's commitment to social justice into an obsession with crime and punishment.[25]

Law and order was a clear rallying point that not only unified a disparate set of voices, but also spurred new voters to join the Republican cause. As Byron Shafer and Richard Johnston explain, law and order "found resonance . . . with resentful voters who in 1968 would vote for George Wallace and then vote Republican from there on out. It also resonated with the suburban voter, who, because of government policy, was overwhelmingly white, middle-class, and drawn to a particular set of economic arguments that pitted city against the suburb, white against black."[26]

Law and order became an enduring a part of the conservative lexicon, even if it morphed for a time into softer rhetorical nods to safe streets, broken-windows policing, and homeland security. It also uniquely contributed to the conservative embrace of a powerful, more forceful presidency. Nixon followed up on his campaign rhetoric by developing plans and securing from Congress the necessary funds to build a massive network of federal prisons while reducing the national government's control over federally sponsored welfare programs. Ronald Reagan continued the Republican effort to transfer government resources to an all-out "war on drugs." More committed to reknitting the social fabric of American society, however, Reagan also preached the importance of community volunteering, modeling responsible behaviors for America's youth, gainful and stable employment, and quality of life in reducing crime. But crime became a national campaign issue, and the politics of the executive centered partisanship did not reward forbearance or measured solutions. Aggressive prosecutions, tougher and mandatory sentencing, empowered tactical policing, and criminalizing minor drug offenses, Reagan stated in language freighted with racist overtones, would reinforce "the thin blue line that holds back a jungle which threatens to reclaim this clearing we call civilization."[27]

A little more than a decade after Reagan left office, George W. Bush echoed his message that individual responsibility had to be nurtured by a stronger sense of community. However, Bush's "compassionate conservatism" also gave way to the harsher tones of crime and punishment. As governor of Texas, Bush promised to crack down on juvenile delinquents, trying as adults youth as young as 14, and working with federal officials to deport the thousands of "criminals" coming over the Mexican border.[28] As president, Bush's commitment to law and order infused his administration's approach to border control, homeland security, and criminal justice. Under the administration's directive, billions were funneled to local police departments in the name of homeland security. The stage was thus set for a recrudescence of the chronic struggle between law enforcement officers and African Americans—dramatized by the massive numbers of African Americans who had been incarcerated as well as the disturbing images of unarmed Black men killed by police that were projected across social media and cable news.

The battle over the "carceral state"—forged in the aftermath of the 1960s riots—was graphically depicted in in the summer of 2014 with the killing of Michael Brown by a White police officer in Ferguson, Missouri, a flash point for the emergence of the Black Lives Matter movement. Brown's shooting prompted Darrel Moore, a writer and activist based in Brooklyn to coordinate "freedom rides" to Missouri from New York, Chicago, Portland, Los Angeles, Philadelphia, and Boston. Just as this campaign and the protests that followed recalled the grass roots activism in Mississippi and Alabama at the height of the civil rights movement, so the image of police officers in riot gear carrying M-4 military assault rifles who faced down the demonstrators was a telling reminder of the bitter harvest of a law and order campaign that Michelle Alexander has indicted as the "new Jim Crow."[29]

As Desmond King and Rogers Smith have argued, the Republicans' embrace of policies like law and order has made race and identity politics the major fault line of a sharply divided nation.[30] Prior to Nixon, Republicans drew considerable support from minority communities; in 1956 Eisenhower made the Black vote an essential part of his electoral strategy.[31] Ike secured the endorsement of every leading Black newspaper with the exception of the *Chicago Defender*, and opinion polls that year all speculated that the Republican Party—the party of Lincoln—would regain its position within the Black community.[32] The president did not exercise any strong rhetorical leadership on the issue of civil rights, but neither did Kennedy until the Freedom Rides forced his hand, and Attorney General Robert F. Kennedy promised federal protection in the name of safeguarding interstate travel. The 1964 Civil Rights Act would not have passed in a Democratic Congress unless a majority of Republicans voted for it; indeed, as a percentage of the party caucus, a larger percentage of Republicans voted for the bill than did Democrats.

Armed with the tools of an empowered administrative presidency and the rhetoric of law and order, Nixon spearheaded a racial realignment. Although Goldwater summoned a more aggressive assault on the liberal order, it was Nixon who welded the promise of law and order to state power. Goldwater viewed domestic unrest as a disease of heighted expectations; the welfare state denigrated the human spirit and created a legacy of government dependence inimical to a free society. In contrast, Nixon prescribed conservative management of social welfare policy. As he remarked on a radio broadcast in early September, "The next President must unite America. He must calm its angers, ease its terrible frictions, and bring its people together once again in peace and mutual respect. . . . This requires leadership that believes in law, and has the courage to enforce it."[33] Nixon had more clearly imprinted the "law and order" brand on his party a month earlier in his address before the 1968 Republican convention in Miami, Florida. "Yes," Norman Mailer opined, "in San Francisco in '64 [Republicans] had been able to be insane for a little while, but now they were subdued, now they were modest, now they were looking for a leader to bring America back to them, their lost America, Jesusland."[34] Strong presidential leadership, Nixon surmised, could bring America back to the GOP: "Let those who have the responsibility to enforce our laws and our judges who have the responsibility to interpret them be dedicated to the great principles of civil rights," he adumbrated before a party whose 1964 presidential candidate had voted against the 1964 civil rights bill. "But let them also recognize," he continued, "that the first civil right of every American is to be free from domestic violence, and that right must be guaranteed by this country."[35]

The transformation of the Democratic South into a Republican stronghold and the increasing centrality of Sunbelt politics were complicated developments that elude simple explanation. Yet it seems improbable that the partisan realignment in American politics would have been so consequential if not for the changing relationship between the modern presidency and the parties. In order to build a winnable electoral college coalition, Nixon and his strategists pushed issues that would mobilize anxious voters where it counted. But it was the increasing centrality of presidential politics that made other Republicans fall in line. Liberal Republicans from the North and Midwest, such as Nelson Rockefeller, Wendell Willkie, Thomas Dewey, and Jacob Javits at one point found common cause in a party dedicated to good management of government programs, cordial relations with big business, and federally sponsored prohibitions on racial discrimination and segregation. And yet, as the tenor of presidential rhetoric and policies increasingly isolated their more moderate and diverse constituencies, Republican gains in the South were offset by Democratic monopolization of eastern, more heavily urbanized states.[36]

Moreover, Nixon and Reagan formed direct ties with an ascending conservative base that weakened the Republican Party organization that traditionally had arbitrated party factions. Consequently, Democrats and Republicans became sharply divided over cultural issues—the very meaning of American identity—an emerging dimension of conflict that gradually displaced traditional disagreements that turned on the tension between personal responsibility and governmental obligations.[37] Gone are the "catch all" and regionally diverse parties of the New Deal era; they have been replaced by ideologically unified partisan organizations that have fractured the country so severely that scholars and pundits warn we are now embroiled in a "Cold Civil War." Exacerbating the divide is the fact that the cultural wars that have torn America apart since the late 1960s are fueled by a nationalized mass media landscape that further elevates presidential politics. In this era, few Republicans dare to rebuke the divisive language of their party's leadership; and seldom can you find a Democrat who raises legitimate political concern over crime, security, and redistributive measures.

The result has been a raw and disruptive partisanship that sows sectional, racial, and religious conflicts. As Kevin Phillips foretold in a 1970 *New York Times* interview, "From now on, the Republicans are never going to get more than 10 to 20 percent of the Negro vote and they don't need any more than that . . . but Republicans would be shortsighted if they weakened enforcement of the Voting Rights Act. The more Negroes who register as Democrats in the South, the sooner the Negrophobe whites will quit the Democrats and become Republicans. That's where the votes are."[38]

In 2016, only 8% of African Americans voted for Trump, just two points better than Goldwater's 6 points with all non-white voters. Fewer than 23% of White men without a college degree supported his Democratic opponent, Hillary Clinton. As we discuss in Chapter 6, the cultural divide that emerged from the 1960s was further exacerbated by the disruptions of Trump's four years in the White House. The confrontational 1964 election was thought to be largely an aberration, fueled by the Republican presidential candidate's iconoclastic opposition to civil rights legislation; yet Trump captured a Republican Party that had been remade into a more racially homogenous organization defined largely by its opposition to civil rights and immigration reform.[39] The Southern Strategy did its work.

From Anti-Communism to Neo-Conservatism

By the end of the Johnson era, the liberal state and its institutional anchor, the modern presidency, were beleaguered establishments. Even many of those who once celebrated the exercise of presidential power, none more confidently, as we discussed in Chapter 4, than Arthur Schlesinger Jr., soon came to the conclusion that the office had exceeded its constitutional authority – become an "imperial presidency"—especially as it pertained to foreign affairs. Schlesinger spoke for the new skeptics on the left; Nixon spoke for those who remained committed to the idea of strong presidential leadership in foreign affairs—those who, in the words of the former New Dealer Irving Kristol, had been "mugged by reality" and believed that the United States must remain vigilant in a cruel and chaotic world that harbored hostile states targeting American freedom. As post–New Deal liberals chastised the imperialist pretentions of America's "arsenal of democracy" and the executive aggrandizement it nurtured, unrepentant anti-communists were in search of a new home. They found one in the Republican Party remade by conservative politicians determined to uphold the idea of patriotism that "neo-isolationist" liberals scorned in the wake of the Vietnam War—a sentiment, neo-conservatives were certain, that still inspired most Americans to see their country as an exceptional nation and a beacon of freedom for those trapped in immoral regimes.[40]

Neo-conservatives did not seek to restore the vision of Pax Americana. Franklin Roosevelt believed that American participation in multi-lateral institutions could provide stability in a world wracked by chaos and uncertainty. For a time, conservatives defended many of those institutions and pursued alliances, treaties, and free trade in support of an anti-communist crusade. But these new conservatives elevated anxieties about American engagements in the institutions of global liberalism; they argued that liberal internationalism was giving way to the "spirit of nationalism" that had come to imbue Europe and the United States. NATO, for example, placed European nations in a position of dependency with the United States that prevented either from serving their own interests. Only if the United States left NATO to the Europeans, Kristol and other neo-cons argued, could the nations of Europe serve their own interests. More to the point, the United States' foreign policy had to place America First.[41]

Like law and order, the spirit of a more nationalistic foreign policy committed conservatives to a strong executive. The end of World War II left the global stage with two clear superpowers: the United States and the Soviet Union. After the first Great War and throughout the 1930s, conservatives remained the bulwark of what was once a domineering isolationist perspective on foreign affairs. When Woodrow Wilson first declared the need to make the world safe for democracy, he ushered in a new age of global internationalism.[42] Institutions like the ill-fated League of Nations, and international agreements like the rosy-eyed Kellogg-Briand Pact were supposed to ensure that no great war would erupt again. When those institutions failed to prevent another world war, many conservatives questioned whether the time had really come for the United States to dispel its long-standing reluctance to enter foreign entanglements. The League of Nations had failed; so would the United Nations (UN). Likewise, they argued that foreign nations had discrete financial interests in protecting their own goods and industries, so global intermediaries like the World Bank and International Monetary Fund would, in the end, hurt American businesses.

With his call for a more militant conservatism during the 1964 campaign, Goldwater did not abandon the post-war conservative skepticism that rejected new international engagements. Goldwater argued that communism had to be defeated by recovering a sense of American exceptionalism. Excessive entanglements with NATO and the UN drained American resources. And both those international organizations abetted presidential unilateralism—an institution mollified by its ambitions to seek "peace" and "negotiate" with the "Soviet menace."[43] Regarding financial institutions, the United States had to "look out for our own economic interest, because no one will do so for us." In the event that the country had to deploy its great military might, leaders needed to follow a "policy of the free hand" and allow the generals to fight the war they wanted to fight; senseless concern over the diplomatic fallout or America's "image" on the world stage was a sign of weakness.

While his rhetoric pertaining to the necessities of war projected the use of America's powerful arsenal, Goldwater nevertheless echoed an enduring conservative argument that associated presidentialism with the diminishment of liberty. In a speech titled the "Return to Liberty," given several months after World War II, Senator Robert Taft—"Mr. Republican"—upbraided the complacency of a Congress—including Republicans—who had given the president carte blanche authority to negotiate tariffs, control the State Department, and confer with other countries through the UN's Security Council. "Almost the only restraint upon him today is the power of the purse," Taft remarked in 1946. "Unlimited delegation of discretion to the President," he warned, "in all foreign affairs can easily lead to a complete absence of freedom at home."[44] Increased international commitments necessarily increased federal spending, and a "garrison state" at home represented just as fundamental a threat to the American creed as did massive government welfare programs.

As with domestic politics, Nixon harnessed the raw enthusiasm of Goldwater's condemnation of the liberal state and joined it to a defense of energetic presidential leadership. During the 1968 campaign, invoking the distinguished scholar who coined the phrase "constitutional dictatorship," Nixon dismissed the traditional conservative view that foreign policy, no less than domestic affairs, should be constrained by constitutional forms. "The tasks confronting the next President abroad are among the most complex and difficult ever faced," he argued in a 1968 radio address, "And, as Professor Clinton Rossiter has observed, 'Leadership in foreign affairs flows today from the President—or it does not flow at all.'"[45] On entering office, Nixon redirected rather than curtained the executive aggrandizement of the Johnson years.[46] He further centralized foreign policymaking in the National Security Council and ordered covert bombing raids in Cambodia and Laos. Nixon thus expanded the institutions and prerogatives of the presidency-centered national security state. Lyndon Johnson bore his personal responsibility for Vietnam like a crown of thorns; Nixon embraced the burdens of what had become the president's war with alacrity. Foreign policy was presidential policy; American greatness abroad was presidential greatness at home; and disagreement with American policy was an attack, not only on the president but the nation.

As in his crusade for law and order, Nixon stoked concerns over America's declining role in the world to mobilize the conservative base that Goldwater summoned. The Vietnam War crippled Lyndon Johnson's presidency and the support of his most progressive allies; yet Nixon believed that the war provided an opportunity to remake the modern presidency, forged by liberal presidents, into the leading edge of a revitalized conservatism. Ten months after becoming president, Nixon sat behind the Resolute Desk to announce a new policy in the war—a plan to ensure "peace with honor," but one with indefinite timetables and a recommittal of American resolve. At the end of the address, after giving token acknowledgment to the students and anti-war demonstrators—the idealists—the president stared straight into the camera and called out to those who did not join the growing anti-war demonstrations:

> If a vocal minority, however fervent its cause, prevails over reason and the will of the majority, this Nation has no future as a free society. . . . And so tonight—to you, the great silent majority of my fellow Americans—I ask for your support.[47]

The following spring, Nixon's "silent majority" did more than speak up; defenders of the president and his Vietnam policy engaged in angry and violent assaults on those protesting against the incursion into Cambodia. On May 4, 1970, 13 students were shot at Kent State University by National Guardsman during a protest of the Vietnam War; four of them died. Four days later, in New York City, over 1,000 anti-war demonstrators, hoping to shut down Wall Street, marched through the Financial District and convened at Federal Hall to protest. Mayor Lindsay called for the flag at City Hall to be lowered to half-mast in honor of the fallen Kent State students. About 200 outraged construction workers, some of whom had buried their own sons or neighbors' sons in flag-draped caskets, stormed City Hall and forced city workers to raise the flag back up. They then surrounded the students and beat them with hard hats, construction tools, and their fists. Rather than protecting demonstrators from this blue-collar fit of brutishness, the New York "thin blue line" egged the construction workers on. When a group of hard hats moved menacingly toward a Wall Street plaza, a patrolman shouted: "Give 'em hell, boys. Give 'em one for me!" Neither the hard hats nor their legal guardians were ever held accountable for the breakdown of civilization in the commercial center of New York City.[48]

For the next two weeks, impromptu demonstrations broke out throughout downtown Manhattan, culminating in a massive rally of over 150,000 pro-war, pro-Nixon demonstrators (the New York *Daily News* called it a "Parade for Nixon").[49] As they climbed lampposts to wave American flags, ticker tape showered down on the protestors from supportive office workers. For blocks the marchers chanted "Stop leftwing TV," "Impeach the Red mayor" (in protest of Mayor Lindsay—a liberal Republican, who had declared May 8 a "day of reflection"), and "Spiro is my hero" (in support of Nixon's polarizing vice president). "History is being made here today," one of the organizers proclaimed, "because we are supporting the boys in Vietnam and President Nixon." Marchers echoed similar sentiments:

> "I'm backing the President all the way. . . . [Vietnam is] small compared with 100,000 a year like we did in World War II. It has to be paid. It's a sad thing, but it has to be realize [*sic*], or else we'll be by ourselves in this whole world and we can't stand up."
>
> "I'm very proud to be an American, and I know my boy that was killed in Vietnam would be here today if he was alive, marching with us."
>
> "I feel they [college students] have been with the silver spoon in their mouth too long and somebody has to take a hand in this to stop them, because if not, the country will come to ruins."

"I'm for this country. These are my people right here."

"We're part of the silent majority that's finally speaking—and in answer to the creeps and the bums that have been hollering and marching against the president."[50]

Nixon invited the march's leaders to the White House, where they gave the president hard hats as a gift. Styling himself the steward of patriotism that Democrats had forsaken, he had become a hero of white working-class men and women, many of whom left the Democratic Party for a Republican Party newly infused with populist enthusiasm.[51] As Pat Buchannan—working then as an aide to Nixon—wrote the president in a memo, "These, quite candidly, are our people now."[52]

Goldwater sought to give voice to those who knew in their "hearts that he was right"; so, Nixon sought to deploy executive power to arouse that newly awakened "silent majority." The 1960s and 1970s are remembered as a period of social turmoil on the left—Students for a Democratic Society, civil rights, environmentalists, and feminists—but movements of the right were also active. There was "the other side of the sixties," as John Andrew has documented. Student groups like Young Americans for Freedom (YAF) emerged alongside liberal student organizations and rebelled against the consensus liberalism of their parents.[53] Vietnam proved so cataclysmic that the bedrock of New Deal liberalism, organized labor, even wavered. Dismayed by draft dodgers and student deferments, blue-collar workers resented protestors who stayed behind as their sons were shipped overseas. In the aftermath of the "hard hat riots," George Meany, president of the AFL-CIO, publicly declared his strongest support for Nixon and his policy in Vietnam. Meany never endorsed GOP positions on the economy, but distrustful of the Democrats' acquiescence to students and other anti-war groups, he did not shy away from blending pro-union policies with appeals to traditional American values of patriotism, hard work, and a blue-collar version of rugged individualism.[54]

The Vietnam War and the surge of campus discontent challenged the vitality of the conservative youth movement, but waiting in the wings was Ronald Reagan, the former actor whose charisma and rhetorical gifts were especially well suited to the message of transcendent values and American exceptionalism. His frequent invocations of America as a "shining city on a hill"—a reference to John Winthrop and the early Puritan settlers of Massachusetts—sought to recover the idea of America as a beacon of liberty and hope in the world. In challenging President Gerald Ford for the Republican Party's nomination in 1976, Reagan harnessed the Goldwater passion of the prior decade and tied it to a polished, viable campaign message that strong leadership—not Ford's conciliatory politics—could resurrect American greatness. As Ford later remarked, while he and moderate Republicans "had most of the generals on [their] side . . . Reagan had most of the troops."[55] Running against the "Washington buddy system," Reagan's campaign in 1976 and then again in 1980 proved how committed the former California governor was to conservative principles in comparison to other GOP leaders who sought to patiently chip away at the margins of the New Deal State.

In fact, ever since his iconic October 27, 1964, address in support of Barry Goldwater—"The Speech"—Reagan and his admirers put forward a single message: policy experts, social welfare workers, party leaders, however well-intentioned, had sapped the country of its energy and had failed to protect American interests overseas:

> Those who would trade our freedom for the soup kitchen of the welfare state have told us they have a utopian solution of peace without victory. They call their policy "accommodation." And they say if we'll only avoid any direct confrontation with the enemy, he'll forget his evil ways and learn to love us. All who oppose them are indicted as warmongers. They say we offer simple answers to complex problems. Well, perhaps there is a simple answer—not an easy answer—but simple: If you and I have the courage to tell our elected officials that we want our national policy based on what we know in our hearts is morally right.[56]

Seventeen years later, in accepting his party's nomination, Reagan delivered the same message in proclaiming that "adversaries large and small test our will and seek to confound our resolve," and in promising that "it is the responsibility of the President of the United States, in working for peace, to ensure that the safety of our people cannot successfully be threatened by a hostile foreign power. As President, fulfilling that responsibility will be my Number One priority."[57]

Foreign policy analysts differ over whether Reagan's interpretation of the Soviet "menace" was accurate or whether his policies did, in fact, contribute to the toppling of the communist bloc. There is no question, however, that Reagan contributed significantly to the formulation and empowerment of the new form of conservatism that arose in the 1960s, not only in domestic matters but also—perhaps to an even greater extent—in world politics. He went further than Nixon in fusing presidential power, party doctrine, and conservative cultural values, completing a fundamental shift in the Republican position on foreign affairs. Decades earlier, in debating Truman's plea to enter NATO, Arthur Vandenberg, a Republican, persuaded his members to back the Democratic president, memorializing the phrase that American "politics stops at the water's edge."[58] In contrast, Reagan gave clear voice to the "silent majority" in defense of the Republicans' post-Vietnam commitment to recapture the idea of patriotism that liberals had forsaken. For the first time since the start of the Cold War, a president and his followers viewed foreign affairs as a partisan issue—one that would mobilize support at the polls.

Tapping into the populism that reverberated in the anti-student protests, Reagan made patriotism and military pride a pillar of the modern right. Speaking before the Veterans of Foreign Wars weeks after his nomination, and just five years after the fall of Saigon, Reagan delivered his sermon on the Vietnam malaise to an organization that had never before endorsed a presidential candidate. More important perhaps than any policy statement was a message of American resolve—a message he claimed liberals had clearly abandoned. "For too long," he insisted,

> we have lived with the Vietnam Syndrome.... It is time we recognized that ours was, in truth, a noble cause.... We dishonor the memory of 50,000 young Americans who died in that cause when we give way to feelings of guilt as if we were doing something shameful, and we have been shabby in our treatment of those who returned. They fought as well and as bravely as any Americans have ever fought in any war. They deserve our gratitude, our respect, and our continuing concern. There is a lesson for all of us in Vietnam. If we are forced to fight, we must have the means and the determination to prevail or we will not have what it takes to secure the peace. And while we are at it, let us tell those who fought in that war that we will never again ask young men to fight and possibly die in a war our government is afraid to let them win.[59]

Reagan's accusation against the establishment politicians who were "afraid to let them win," reopened wounds that had festered since the 1960s—with rhetoric that was more militantly partisan than Nixon's promise to pursue "peace with honor." Reagan had been making this argument since 1964, but his words were especially poignant after the fall of Saigon, on Ford's watch, seemed to desecrate the ultimate price paid by so many American soldiers. Over 58,000 soldiers died in action or in prisoner of war camps; over 150,000 suffered injuries they would bear for the rest of their lives. As the country struggled to figure out how to honor those lost in such a highly controversial engagement, the political battles that defined the 1960s reemerged in a fight over the Vietnam War memorial, completed in 1982.

It is a testament to the grief and guilt felt by Americans that Congress agreed to memorialize those killed in Southeast Asia so quickly after combat ended; the World War II national memorial, in contrast, was not completed until 2004, 59 years after V-J Day. Winning out over 1,400 other submissions, the selection committee chose to commission a young 21-year-old Asian American, Maya Lin to memorialize those who gave their lives in Southeast Asia. Lin's submerged wall of black-granite with the names of the dead etched over the facade symbolized the irredeemable sacrifice of a scarred generation. Leading conservative figures were horrified, labeling the memorial a "black gash of shame" and a "nihilistic slab of stone." As Jan Scruggs, a wounded veteran who had led the campaign for a national monument, recalled, "This is what killed us: Why is it that every other monument in Washington is white, but this one is black?"[60]

The memorial set off a firestorm of debate, fueled by the cultural and political criticism of leading conservative thinkers. Charles Krauthammer—still writing for the liberal *New Republic*—launched a devasting salvo that resonated widely. "To treat the Vietnam dead," he wrote, "like the victims of some monstrous traffic accident is more than a disservice to history. . . . It is an act of arrogance for us to assign them the status of victims, and nothing but victims. These people saw themselves if not as patriots at least as soldiers. . . . it is surely an excess of revisionist zeal to deny the dignity and nobility of dying in the service of one's country, something many of these soldiers believed in."[61] Meanwhile, the conservative *National Review* spearheaded an effort to "stop that monument," telling readers that "it will be a perpetual disgrace" and "if the current model has to be built, stick it off some tidal flat, and let it memorialize Jane Fonda's contribution to ensuring that our soldiers died in vain."[62] After Lin's name was revealed, the attacks became personal and directed at her own opposition to the war and her Asian-ethnicity. Patrick Buchanan stirred up the old trope that she was a communist; Ross Perot labeled her an "egg roll."

To his credit, President Reagan persisted with the memorial's construction in opposition to his party and his interior secretary, who had refused to issue the building permits. And, after the monument opened—after people could experience the "considerable power and even eloquence" of the memorial—even the *National Review* confessed that "Miss Linn . . . has created something unusual and beautiful."[63]

Nevertheless, Reagan's defense of the Vietnam Memorial did not prevent the populist denouncement that fired up the conservative base. Indeed, Reagan tapped into the ideological fervor of the Cold War and the sharply divided American foreign policy community to make patriotism a partisan issue. The Republican Party, he argued, stood for American interests and pride while the liberal party stood for weakness and accommodation, if not outright guilt. This was not merely rhetorical flourish. Compromising with congressional Democrats over welfare spending, Reagan managed to rapidly increase the budget for conventional and nuclear weapons in the hope that it would bring the Soviet economy to a breaking point. More controversially, the White House secretly built an alternative intelligence network within the staff of the National Security Council (NSC), which funneled money from arms sales with Iran to support the anti-communist Nicaraguan contras— in direct violation of congressional prohibition. Although the Iran-Contra scandal cost the Reagan administration dearly in the coin of public support, he regained command with a deft, idealistic approach to the Cold War. In 1987, the president stood at the Brandenburg Gate and demanded that the Soviet chairman Mikhail Gorbachev tear down the Berlin Wall. Four years later, the Soviet Union collapsed, consecrating the idea that strong presidents, conservative politics, and ardent belief in American exceptionalism combined to create a formula for an effective foreign policy.

By the 1980s, therefore, the politics of foreign policy had become so bound to competing conceptions of American identity, patriotism, and civic duty that a core principle of the vital center was greatly diminished: politics, clearly, no longer stopped at the water's edge. As Nathan Glazer, a prominent neo-conservative later recalled, "As the antiwar movement itself began to conceive of American power in the most Manichean and moralistic terms, it became easier for a new generation of conservatives to subordinate discrete arguments about Vietnam to a broader cultural counterattack."[64] The anti-war movement's derision of America's imperialist past lingered well past the war's ignominious conclusion, so that Vietnam and then the debate over how it should be memorialized became a seminal moment in the polarization of the country. The meaning of patriotism itself drove a wedge between conservatives "proud" of their country and those post–New Deal liberals who denied that America was truly a "shining city on a hill."

The joining of domestic and foreign responsibilities within an administrative presidency—abetted by the conservative braiding of law and order and patriotism—reached a new level during George W. Bush's tenure. On September 11, 2001, two hijacked planes tore into the World Trade Center and another flew into the west side of the Pentagon; a fourth plane on its way to the US Capitol building crashed in southwest Pennsylvania. With enthusiastic support from both parties, the United States invaded Afghanistan alongside an international coalition. Two years later, the administration warned that the Iraqi regime had developed weapons of mass destruction (WMD). Such a possibility was well within reason; Hussein had used chemical weapons against dissident Kurdish people in 1988, killing up to 5,000 in Northern Iraq. Within weeks of taking the Iraqi capital and with few American casualties, the president declared victory. In July 2004, a congressionally mandated 9-11 Commission report revealed that no credible evidence existed to prove that Iraq had aided Osama bin Laden in carrying out the attacks. Months later, in September, a Pentagon-led "Iraq Survey Group" released its findings that cast considerable doubt on the administration's previous claims that Hussein's regime was well equipped to develop WMD.[65]

Politics submerged facts and reason. Another presidential election was under way and the decision was framed not in terms of accountability or programmatic action—but of personality. Who had the resolve to make the tough decisions to keep Americans safe from harm: George W. Bush, the incumbent Republican who once stood triumphantly next to first responders on the smoldering ashes of the Twin Towers, or John F. Kerry, who "flip-flopped" on funding that supported American troops in Afghanistan?

The backgrounds of representatives to the US Congress reveal the lengthening shadow of 1960s politics. In 1959, 191 of 295, or 71%, of Democrats in the House of Representatives were veterans; 90 of 140, or 64%, of Republican representatives had served in the armed forces. In 2016, 19 of 194 Democrats, barely 10%, were veterans; 62 of the 239 Republican representatives, about 26%, had served.[66] The 1959 numbers might be inflated due to World War II and the Korean War, as well as the draft, but changes in partisanship—and the development of a professional military—account for the significant changes that had occurred by 2016. Moreover, survey evidence has confirmed a

changing relationship between active military duty and party loyalty, especially since the Iraq War shattered the national unity that briefly prevailed
after the attacks on the Twin Towers and the Pentagon. A 2009 survey from
Georgetown University suggested that in 1976, just one-third of senior military officers identified with the Republican Party; in 1996, that number had
jumped to two-thirds.[67] And a 2011 Pew Research Center poll suggests that
while all veterans are more likely to identify with the Republican Party (by
almost ten points), post-9/11 veterans are especially prone to identify as
Republicans.[68]

Building a Conservative State

Given Republicans' rhetorical attack on government, it is not surprising
that scholars and public commentators tend to equate conservatism and
anti-statism. "In this present crisis, government is not the solution to our
problem," Reagan famously declaimed in his first inaugural address; "government is the problem."[69] And yet, animated by the causes of law and order and
patriotism, conservatives have relied on presidential prerogative and administrative power to uphold private property, protect "middle-class" values, and
fight foreign threats by building up the nation's military. Moreover, rather
than rolling back the government to unleash the power of the free market,
conservatives have devised novel policies that subsidize private interests and
inject business practices into social welfare programs. In fact, Republicans
have surpassed Democrats in fusing executive prerogative and partisanship—accelerating the declining influence of party organizations that might
moderate the most dangerous populist tendencies of the new right.

By exploiting the issue of law and order, Richard Nixon tied his presidential fortunes to the new politics of the Sunbelt—and demonstrated to
the Republican Party how they could crack the Democratic Party's hold on
the vote-rich states of the South. Goldwater, as he enjoyed pointing out, ran
on FDR's 1932 policy platform of sound currency, balanced budgets, and a
reduced federal payroll. Nixon would take America off the gold standard, use
federal fiscal policy to impose price controls, expand the federal bureaucracy,
and repurpose, not cut, federal programs.

Nixon was not a liberal in sheep's clothing. He was a strategic conservative
who fulfilled his campaign promises through aggressive administrative tactics to remake inherited domestic commitments. To the surprise of many, he

did not immediately dispense with LBJ's signature Model Cities program but rather reconstituted it to give business interests greater influence over the deployment of federal funds while diminishing the role of poverty advocates in urban planning. Moreover, he transformed the Budget Bureau into the new Office of Management and Budget (OMB), adding a cadre of presidentially appointed assistant directors of policy who stood between the OMB director and the bureau's civil servants. Consequently, the budget office became one of the presidency's most important instruments for planning new programs, administering old ones, and setting the public agenda. Finally, mirroring his empowerment of the National Security Council, Nixon established a new Domestic Council to further centralize policymaking in the White House. Nixon's commitment to politicizing the executive branch resulted in a doubling of the size of the White House, which swelled from a full-time staff of 203 under Johnson to 522 comparable employees by the end of Nixon's first term.[70] Although Nixon's efforts to further consolidate presidential power by overhauling executive departments and agencies during his second term were thwarted by a Democratic Congress and Watergate, his deployment of conservative administrators in a revamped structure that would be more responsive to the expanded White House Office paved the way for Reagan's conservative administrative presidency. As Bert Rockman has observed, "It was the Nixon presidency, particularly in the aborted second term, that became celebrated for its deployment of the [administrative presidency]," but "the Reagan Presidency intended to perfect the strategy and to do it from the beginning."[71]

Goldwater's rhetoric and Nixon's instrumentality thus laid the groundwork for a conservative state—a bastion of institutions, norms, policies, and relations that promoted a new conservative worldview. As Goldwater's nomination and campaign showed, conservative activists scorned the social welfare policies of the liberal state. Yet viewing populist insurgency as a force that could disrupt the liberal political order, conservatives sought to install policies that would mobilize support for the Republican Party. Hardhat wearing, pro-war demonstrators were not the only activists to respond to the social movement forces dominating leftist politics. Conservative social movements also developed, and these pressured Republican leaders to use state power in the service of their objectives. Conservativism thus evolved from an attack on the administrative state to a strategy that involved the creation of parallel organizations to *redeploy*, rather than dismantle, the levers of national power.[72]

The development of a redeployment strategy required grassroots as well as formal institutional support. Leading that charge was the "Sweetheart of the Silent Majority," as she was later anointed, Phyllis Schlafly, a crusader for government support of "traditional values."[73] Schlafly burst on to the scene in 1964 with a powerful tract denouncing Eastern establishment "kingmakers" who sought to prevent Goldwater's nomination.[74] Her book, *A Choice Not an Echo* sold over 3 million copies that year, and Schlafly came to embody a living refutation of liberals' claim that conservative women were powerless in the Republican Party. Schlafly was a successful lawyer, prolific writer, and mother of six, who was ensconced in the halls of power.

When congressional Democrats sent the Equal Rights Amendment to the states for ratification in 1972, Schlafly organized thousands of women in successful opposition—the first true demonstration of modern conservative social movement politics.[75] Schlafly and her newly established "Eagle Forum" collected donations from around the country to organize women in defense of "pro-family" government policies. Schlafly argued that the ERA would require women to register for the draft, that single-sex bathrooms would be eliminated, and that same-sex couples would be allowed to marry.[76]

The ERA was just one of many issues conservative activists viewed as evidence of America's crumbling moral order and erosion of traditional values.[77] Schlafly demonstrated the power of anti-liberal movement politics and tied it to Republican electioneering. Her anti-feminism and sermonizing on moral decay resonated with religious conservatives, particularly evangelical conservatives who became the core constituency of the New Right.[78] As with the civil rights movement, the rise of a conservative countermovement has roots that extend further back than the 1960s.[79] But the '60s produced a litany of causes that galvanized conservative Christians: mandatory sex education, court rulings prohibiting school prayer, and the inclusion of controversial authors like Malcom X and Allen Ginsberg in public school reading curricula. The increased presence of gay rights advocacy and a general liberalization of sexual mores on television and film further evidenced the conservative claim that, in the words of the Moral Majority leader Jerry Falwell, "America, our beloved country, is sick," and under "concerted attack by ultraliberals."[80] Parochial school attendance increased throughout the decade, as those "in search of another country" fought to establish separate institutions outside the federal government's new civil rights regime.[81]

In the South, white evangelical conservatives resisted the dismantling of Jim Crow, denounced the "trouble-making" of African American preachers like Martin Luther King Jr. and his followers, and established private religious schools that critics called "segregation academies" because they excluded non-white students. Conservative evangelical leaders suggested that private evangelical schools held special appeal to parents who wanted their children "to study under born-again teachers in a Christian environment with academic excellence."[82] Critics, by contrast, charged that many of these private institutions were formed primarily as "white-flight schools" to enable white parents to have their kids instructed apart from African American children at precisely the same time that federal and state governments mandated desegregation of public schools.[83]

Tellingly, Thomas Road Baptist Church established its Lynchburg Christian Academy only a few months after Virginia's commissioner of education ordered all public schools in 1966 to implement far-reaching integration plans. Billed in the local news as "a private school for white students," Lynchburg's African American clergy protested "the use of the word 'Christian' in the title of a school that excludes Negroes and other non-white people."[84] Proponents of racial justice and school desegregation pressed the federal government to challenge and sanction this proliferation of segregation academies. Christian school officials responded that they were not trying to thwart racial desegregation; instead, they explained, they were resisting government efforts to regulate licensure, hiring practices, admissions, and curriculum standards that they considered intrusive. During the 1970s, regulations of the Internal Revenue Service (IRS) governing tax-exempt status for private schools became the focal point of this conflict.[85]

The rise of conservative social activism was thus directly associated with the strong cultural reaction to the 1960s liberalism; yet the different strains of the religious right eventually found common purpose in fighting for the "rights of the unborn." A year after Schlafly's anti-ERA crusade began, the Supreme Court ruled that the US Constitution guaranteed women the right to an abortion through the second trimester. Roe v. Wade unleashed a firestorm of protest and conservatives who had taken notice of the ERA fight turned to similar tactics.[86] Roe proved to conservative leaders how important it was to transform American political institutions, and their eyes fixated on the presidency as the wellspring of institutional reform. Tolerating the onslaught of changes was a moral crime, and politics offered a venue for the country's redemption. Evangelicals joined with other causes such as the anti-tax crusades in the West, neo-conservative intellectuals in the East, and Schlafly's Eagle Forum to establish the New Right movement in American politics.

In response to the mobilization of Christian conservatives, President Nixon spied an opportunity to make partisan use of a reconstituted executive office. The modern presidency, he believed, could harness the energy of conservative activists to strengthen the party's collective position. "The days of a passive presidency belong to a simpler past," he foretold. "Let me be very clear about this: The next president must take an activist view of his office. He must articulate the nation's values, define its goals and marshal its will. Under a Nixon Administration, the presidency will be deeply involved in the entire sweep of America's public concerns."[87]

Richard Nixon's pledge to restore law and order not only implicated the politics of race and war; it was also a direct attack on what many on the New Right perceived to be a radical judiciary, more committed to a liberal agenda than to convicting criminals. Throughout the 1960s, the federal courts had gradually expanded the rights of criminals and transformed local police department procedures. At the start of the decade, the Supreme Court, led by Chief Justice Earl Warren, ruled in favor of Dollree Mapp, whose home had been raided by police in search of a fugitive. There police discovered certain "lewd and lascivious books, pictures, and photographs." Rather than ruling on whether such materials were obscene or whether they were protected on First Amendment grounds, the court ruled that any evidence gathered without a specific warrant was inadmissible in court.[88] In the 1963 case *Gideon v. Wainwright,* the court ruled that Florida, and all states thereafter, must provide public defenders for those accused of capital cases.[89] And, most famously, in 1966, the court mandated that it was incumbent upon police officers to make sure that criminals are aware of their right to remain silent to avoid self-incrimination and of their right to public counsel if they cannot afford an attorney—their *Miranda* rights.[90]

Conservatives drew a direct line between a judiciary, stacked with appointees from Kennedy and Johnson (never mind that Warren was an Eisenhower appointee), and post–New Deal Liberalism, which was weak on crime and permitted the lawlessness that preyed on the central city.[91] In May 1969, less than four months after his inauguration, Nixon had his opportunity to make good on his law and order pledge. The appointment of Warren Burger to serve as chief justice was an unambiguous message from the White House. As an appellate judge, Burger promoted positions on crime that paralleled Nixon's, echoing the candidate's declaration that the Warren Court had strayed too far, excusing criminals from any responsibility by neglecting the "moral basis of the criminal law."[92] In a dissenting opinion issued two months before the announcement of his appointment, Burger, in what has always been a common tactic of marginalized jurists, directly struck at the Court's *Miranda* decision. "The seeming anxiety of judges to protect every accused person from every consequence of his voluntary utterances," he wrote,

> is giving rise to myriad rules, sub-rules, variations and exceptions which even the most alert and sophisticated lawyers and judges are taxed to follow. Each time judges add nuances to these "rules" we make it less likely that any police officer will be able to follow the guidelines we lay down. We are approaching the predicament of the centipede on the flypaper—each time one leg is placed to give support for relief of a leg already "stuck," another becomes captive and soon all are securely immobilized. Like the hapless centipede on the flypaper, our efforts to extricate ourselves from this self-imposed dilemma will, if we keep it up, soon have all of us immobilized. We are well on our way to forbidding any utterance of an accused to be used against him unless it is made in open court. Guilt or innocence becomes irrelevant in the criminal trial as we flounder in a morass of artificial rules poorly conceived and often impossible of application.[93]

Nixon openly celebrated Burger's insights on the "anxiety of judges" and coupled it to the larger argument for conservative presidential leadership. Ironically, Burger would write the opinion ruling against Nixon's claim of "executive privilege," thereby requiring the president to turn over the secret White House tapes concerning the Watergate scandal, which led to the impeachment proceedings that forced him from office. Burger, too, would oversee the Court's most contentious cases of the decade, further welding the future of conservatism to control of the White House and its powers of judicial appointment: *Roe v. Wade* (abortion rights), *Lemon v. Kurtzman* (proscribing reimbursement for parochial schools), *Swann v. Charlotte-Mecklenburg* (constitutionality of busing). Burger thus helped to construct court majorities in opposition to the conservatives who celebrated his appointment. Yet, far from discouraging activists, these cases spurred conservatives to dedicate themselves to forming entirely new organizations such as the *Federalist Society* that could counter liberal hegemony in law schools and on the courts.[94]

For a time, Watergate torpedoed the burgeoning connection between the Republican presidency of Richard Nixon and the New Right. In 1980, however, the movement found its prophet. While running for president, Reagan ensured that his conservative bona fides were clear and that the GOP's platform was compatible with the New Right's message: the GOP no longer would support the ERA; the party platform added planks calling for constitutional amendments to protect "unborn children" and to appoint judges "who respect traditional family values"; and under a Reagan presidency, Christians could be guaranteed that the IRS would stop its investigation of private schools for civil rights offenses.[95] Reagan's harsh rhetoric denouncing communism for its godlessness and lack of spiritual foundation made the New Right an ardent supporter of the GOP's foreign policy in Central America and Eastern Europe.

The cultural conflicts spurned by the conservative counterrevolution embraced the political strategy of presidential management. Regulation writing, grant administration, budget planning, personnel selection, and rhetorical prowess are consequential forms of power in the modern American state. As former Nixon aide Richard Nathan, recognized, "Operations is policy."[96] Nixon and Reagan laid the groundwork for using presidential power in the service of movement objectives. Instead of cutting spending, the federal government increasingly relied on contractors to rapidly build up the nation's armaments, further extending the Sunbelt's reliance on America's military industrial complex.[97] Goldwater had once proposed doing away with the New Deal edifice by automatically cutting taxes every five years, starving the beast, and fully privatizing popular agencies like the Tennessee Valley Authority. Under Nixon and Reagan, conservative policy came to embody the principle of devolution and decentralized administration.[98] Instead of grants for purposes deemed worthy in Washington, states, armed with federal waivers that encouraged a repurposing of social welfare programs, would decide how best to spend federal tax dollars. As the budgets busted, Republicans abandoned their centuries-long opposition to deficit spending and followed their president's lead in enacting supply-side tax cuts, redistributing the nation's economic largesse to the top-earners in the hope of encouraging more investment (Reagan's vice president George H. W. Bush labeled this conservative adventure in fiscal policy "voodoo economics" during the 1980 Republican primaries).[99] Decades of congressional acquiescence or "delegation" to the executive branch abetted the president's reach in unilaterally advancing conservative policies, often through innovative administrative changes that evaded congressional control.[100]

The growth of national administrative power under Nixon, Reagan, and Bush bestowed bipartisan legitimacy on executive-centered partisanship. Put simply, liberals and conservatives fought for the soul of the New Deal state that Franklin Roosevelt anointed in his Four Freedoms address: conservatives embraced the national security state —freedom from fear—while liberals devoted more attention to the welfare state—freedom from want. Yet the events of 9/11 and the subsequent "War on Terror" brought the foreign and domestic executive closer than they had ever been before, blurring the line between the two. Creating a permanent condition of crisis that posed novel threats to civil liberties and the rule of law made the need for "homeland security" paramount.[101] Republicans have accepted this state of perpetual war and George W. Bush exploited his party's ideology and organization to extend the conservative administrative state into a preventative war against terrorist states, or the "axis of evil." Obama's adoption of a "surge" strategy in Afghanistan in 2009 and use of covert drone strikes reveals resemblance rather than contrast with his predecessor. However, the partisan rancor over Obama's refusal to define his objectives as a War on Terror and the enemy as "Radical Islamic Terrorism" indicates that the Democrats took a different approach to national and homeland security—an approach defined by multinational rather than unilateral action, surgical strikes rather than massive troop deployments, and diplomacy rather than brinksmanship.

In the wake of 9/11, George W. Bush built on his conservative predecessors' legacies to further enshrine the new presidency-centered orthodoxy of the GOP. With his party in control of both the House and the Senate, Bush simultaneously pursued an aggressive supply-side economics—passing the largest tax cuts in history in 2001 and 2003—and an increase in the national government's programmatic responsibilities: the expansion of Medicare in a way that attended to conservative objectives; the creation of a new department of government, Homeland Security, which Republicans sought to make their signature commitment; and consistent with this ambition, the launching of wars in Afghanistan and Iraq.

The Bush administration viewed the Medicare drug benefit, which cost more than $50 billion annually, as a first step in generating public support for the further diversion of Medicare services to the private sector in the future.[102] It delegated delivery of the program to competing, private insurance companies to enhance their power. The policy was designed this way to give a conservative cast to national government activism. Delegation to private actors subtly redeploys state power to recast rather than dismantle this particular social program. Bush's effort to "reform" Social Security during his second term had a similar aim. This reform, the president claimed, would yield beneficiaries a better rate of return on their contributions, but the federal government would still force people to save, restrict the investment choices they would make, and regulate the pace at which they could withdraw their money at retirement. While Congress ultimately balked at the president's proposal, Bush relied on a series of unilateral orders to strengthen state control in making decisions over abortion access, stem-cell research, and LGBTQ rights. In doing so, the president capitalized on a decades-in-the-making ideological transformation in which conservatives grew comfortable with the idea of "big government" so long as it was *their* version of big government.

The mobilization of the Christian Right as a core Republican constituency joined evangelical fervor to conservative statism. During his 1988 campaign for the presidency, Pat Robinson motivated millions of evangelicals to embrace national administration, telling them that "Christians should not hesitate to use the lawful power at their disposal."[103] And at the same time, a new generation of conservative lawyers were constructing a novel doctrine in defense of state power. As a young lawyer working for the American Enterprise Institute, eventual Supreme Court justice, Antonin Scalia, would write, "The . . . basic goal of the Republican Party is . . . making vigorous use of the legitimate machinery of government to achieve their goals."[104] Fred Barnes, executive editor of the conservative *Weekly Standard*, took this position in defending President Bush to fellow Republicans. "The real gripe, he noted, "is that Bush isn't their kind of conventional conservative. Rather, he's a big government conservative. This isn't a description he or other prominent conservatives willingly embrace. It makes them sound as if they aren't conservatives at all. But they are. They simply believe in using what would normally be seen as liberal means—activist government—for conservative ends. And they're willing to spend more and increase the size of government in the process."[105]

The liberal vision of freedom from want made the American state hospitable to the claims of marginalized groups. Even with liberalism's transformation, however, progressives maintained a lingering commitment to the executive as the "steward of public welfare," which presumed non-partisan leadership of public opinion and management of the bureaucracy as the essential means for enhancing economic and social reform. However, as we noted in Chapter 4, Democratic presidents since the 1960s have found it difficult to balance the idea of enlightened administration with the demands of the advocacy groups and social movement organizations that yearn for a more aggressive brand of partisan administration.

Republican presidents have been less reluctant partisans. Nixon championed the New Deal orthodoxy of presidential governance, at home and abroad, but he used the institution's powers to form a different vision of the state—what Nixon speech writer Pat Buchannan later called a "counterreformation"—to secure Americans freedom from fear: "This is not a conservative trend of the kind that will produce a sudden run on the works of Edmund Burke, or double the newsstand sales of the *National Review*. It is indeed as much a counter-reformation as a conservative movement."[106] As Republican presidents proved effective in wielding the powers of the institutional presidency to mobilize the base and turn out the vote, conservatives embraced the progressive notion of a powerful, unilateral presidency.[107]

At the end of Bush's second term, Democrats and Republicans no longer fought over whether there should be a large national government, tasked with extensive responsibilities. The struggle that had dominated the Roosevelt years had been replaced by a battle for the services flowing from national administration. Conservatives, no less than liberals, as the political scientist Hugh Heclo puts it, became "policy minded," and so they have remained. The waning of the traditional decentralized party system brought on by the merging of grassroots mobilization and executive prerogative has had the two-fold effect of nationalizing policy debate and centering that debate on the ends the newly empowered national state should serve. During the 1960s and early 1970s, the locus of party politics shifted from the cities, counties, states, and Congress to the presidency. Tip O'Neill, the ebullient Democratic Speaker of the House during the Reagan era, famously declared, "All politics is local"; but in fact, by the beginning of Ronald Reagan's two terms, that refrain was vacuous. Democrats and Republicans came to depend on presidents and presidential candidates to raise funds, mobilize grassroots support, articulate the party's message, and advance party programs.[108]

The Anti-Institutionalism of the Republican Party

The conservative counterrevolution involved more than a set of policy prescriptions and conservative state-building. Supply-side economics, "law and order," and "traditional values" provide talking points that infuse modern-day Republican partisanship. However, it is also necessary to understand how activists and their leaders sought to restructure party and governmental organizations to fulfill those promises. Democrats, to be sure, pioneered the transformation of the party's relationship to the chief executive by reforming the nominating process and strengthening the president's institutional capacity to set party priorities and advance partisan causes administratively. Republicans readily adopted like changes in the presidential selection process, and in many ways surpassed liberal activists in creating new avenues for an activist insurgency within the party. Although Republicans played catch up in challenging the party establishment, they more rapidly harnessed the reformist impulse to reconstitute other institutions, particularly Congress.

Goldwater's ability to capture the Republican nomination in 1964 signifies that the Republican Party was just as, if not more, susceptible to a grassroots revolt by the 1960s. The increasing importance of primaries in the selection of party nominees might have originated with progressive reform, but the Republican Party gradually became more open throughout the 20th century as many of these changes were mandated by new state laws. Just as Johnson's excesses and the disastrous 1968 convention motivated Democratic Party leaders to "democratize" the selection system, so too did Nixon's crimes and the Watergate scandal lead Republicans to create a more candidate-centered, media-driven primary system. Following the Democratic Party's McGovern-Fraser reforms, Republicans revised their own nomination procedures, making conventions celebratory confirmations of state primaries and caucus results.

The impetus for additional Republican Party reform followed from a 1972 court challenge by the liberal faction within the Republican Party, represented by the Ripon Society, which followed the McGovern-Fraser playbook. The Ripon Society's legal challenge was both ideological and pragmatic: the traditional allocation rules, which, in the words of a Mississippi party chair, were originally designed to "punish" the South for their Democratic loyalties, now worked in favor of the smaller, Republican-leaning states in the

South and West. Coupled with the customary "unit-rule," which bound all delegates to the winner of a state's at-large and congressional district contests, the influence of liberal Republicans diminished whenever a Democratic presidential candidate captured a northern state—a more likely occurrence in the aftermath of the New Deal. Prior to the 1972 Republican convention, the federal courts ruled that those states received an unconstitutional and outsized proportion of delegates, relative to their population. The party was thereby forced to rewrite the party's delegate allocation rules that awarded "bonus" seats to states that traditionally voted Republican. Indeed, at the 1972 convention, the Republican Party's own lawyer pleaded with the party's rules committee to change the allocation formula so that he could actually have "a case that I can win," as the court challenge worked its way through the judiciary.[109] The party worked out a compromise position that the courts eventually found satisfactory; ironically, however, the concessions that liberal Republicans won to expand the number of delegates and make the Convention proceedings more transparent made other marginalized factions more prominent with time. One of these concessions gave bonus delegates to states that elected Republican governors and members of Congress. Four years after the rule changes, Ronald Reagan launched a debilitating primary challenge against Gerald Ford, which was only made possible by the Ripon Society's challenges to the allocation rules that nearly doubled the size of California's delegation.

At the time, the reallocation compromise—Rule 29—was viewed as a boon for northern states that were trending Democratic. But as the South and Sunbelt grew in population, the allocation formulas tilted the Republican Party further toward the big-state conservativism of the Sunbelt.[110] At least one "old guard" Republican saw the handwriting on the wall. Chilton Williamson observed in the *National Review* that while the party's appeal to these "Country and Western Marxists" might "elect conservative candidates in the short run, there is nevertheless a great risk that populism, having entered conservative politics, might proceed to digest them and go on to minister to the quasi-proletarian constituency that is its sociological base."[111] The Watergate scandal that embroiled the entire party apparatus placed further pressure on the Republican Party to appear more transparent and less beholden to the establishment. And, in at least one way, their selection procedures were riper for populist exploitation than those of their opponents: Democrats restored a role for party elites in the role of "super-delegates" in the aftermath of the perceived failure of Jimmy

Carter's "outsider" presidency; Republicans, whose political fortunes soared on the wings of Reagan's insurgency, did not establish a similar mediating institution.

Reagan's 1976 primary challenge and his nomination in 1980 would have been less likely without the Republican Party's adaptation of progressive nominating reforms. Coupled with campaign finance reforms that privileged "independent" organizations and individual donors, this media-driven, plebiscitary system had advanced so far by 2016 that an iconoclastic businessman and reality television star was able to commandeer the Republican Party label, establish a campaign largely independent of the formal party, and use a personal base to win a majority of delegates without winning a majority of primary votes. In some ways, Trump poses a novel and imposing challenge to the vital center. However, his governing strategy and capture of the party establishment following his inauguration must be understood in light of Republican-led reforms dedicated to empowering "the people" in the Republican Party, the Congress, the courts, and the presidency.

The institutional reformers on the right emerged in response to liberals' transformation of the American state in the aftermath of the Great Society. Since liberals were the first to challenge the vital center and denigrate the institutional supports that buttressed it, Republicans have more often than not been in the defensive posture of adapting these institutional measures to serve their own objectives. As liberals turned on the presidency in the aftermath of Watergate and Vietnam, Republicans rallied around their partisan brethren in the White House and legitimated new forms of administrative power. When Reagan was elected, Democrats renewed their commitment to congressional deliberation and committee oversight, only to encourage Republicans to concoct new arguments about the president's executive privilege and extra-constitutional powers. The Iran-Contra scandal followed in no small measure from the way the Reagan administration joined executive prerogative to a messianic anti-communism. Locked out of the White House in 1992, Republicans then captured Congress two years later. Using the powers that they had derided a few years earlier, they now turned on the modern presidency, and impeached Bill Clinton—only the second president at the time, and the only elected one—to suffer such an indignity.

The six years of unified government under George W. Bush renewed the Republicans' commitment to executive aggrandizement—indeed, boosted it to new levels, as partisans defended the "unitary executive doctrine" while further reforming Congress to make it less responsible to collective party control. By the time President Obama took office, Republicans were just as responsible as the Democrats in setting the stage for a widespread assault on the country's governing elite. Perhaps it is just by chance that the financial bubble burst right as a Democratic president was taking the helm. A committed pragmatist at the outset of his presidency, Obama continued the policies of his Republican predecessor, even retaining the chairman of the Federal Reserve.[112] As a result, when the political reaction boiled over, Republicans found themselves once again in the position of exploiting populist outrage and distrust of government officials. The Tea Party was just another chapter in a decades-long story of rightist anti-establishment furor; but by the end of Obama's two terms, institutions were at their breaking point, clearing the ground for the election and tempestuous presidency of the ultimate outsider, Donald Trump.

Few would have predicted such a trajectory when Congress confronted the excesses of the Nixon presidency. Nixon's embellishment of the executive administration provided an opportune moment for collectively minded members of Congress to recommit themselves to the hard but necessary work of institutional maintenance. Faced with a hostile president who sought to enact change primarily through unilateral power, Congressional Democrats attempted to reinvigorate the system of checks and balances by altering chamber procedures and reorganizing the committee structure. To be sure, much of the incentive for legislative reorganization, which strengthened the legislative and oversight capacity of subcommittees, was the result of the lingering animosity liberal members felt toward seniority norms for ceding too much power to southern members of the Democratic caucus, who year after year returned to office from their safe districts.

Democrats, nevertheless, also set their sights on the "imperial" presidency in several consequential ways. First, as the White House reorganized the Budget Bureau into the modern-day Office of Management and Budget, Congress reorganized so as to more efficiently divide the workload and oversight functions of its several standing committees. Significantly, the decision to devolve more power to subcommittees also came with congressionally authorized spending increases for committee staff and research services.[113] With the war in Vietnam dragging on, Congress passed the War Powers Resolution in 1973, which required presidents to notify and seek approval from Congress in order to commit troops to combat for a prolonged engagement. Finally, in response to Nixon's decision to impound, or not spend, congressionally appropriated funds for several liberal programs, Congress passed the 1974 Budget and Impoundment Control Act. This presidency-curbing legislation not only stripped the president of a self-declared prerogative to restrict spending (upheld one year later by the Supreme Court), but it also strengthened Congress's role in preparing a budget and evaluating policy alternatives by establishing standing budgetary committees and the Congressional Budget Office.

These three reforms equipped Congress during the 1970s and 1980s to challenge the modern president's preeminence in legislative affairs. As R. Shep Melick has written,

> Using subcommittee resources, members initiated new programs and revised old ones, challenging the president for the title of "Chief Legislator." No longer would Congress respond to calls for action by passing vague legislation telling the executive to do something. Now Congress was writing detailed statutes, which not infrequently deviated from the president's program. Subcommittees were also using oversight hearings to make sure that administrators paid heed not just to the letter of legislation, but to its spirit as well.[114]

However, this assault on the modern presidency did not really restore checks and balances; rather, it revamped the Madisonian system for partisan confrontation. When new Democratic members—the "Watergate Babies"—entered Congress in 1975, they used the new rules to challenge the party's leadership and strengthen the caucus's commitment to the causes and policies of post–New Deal liberalism.[115] The imperial presidency had hardly become imperiled, as some critics of the Democratic Congress claimed; but it was caught in the crosshairs of growing partisan confrontation.

Republicans responded by redoubling their commitment to executive-centered partisanship. They defended Nixon and his aggressive use of the administrative presidency to further conservative objectives. When the president's office took its electioneering and partisan mobilization strategy too far—ordering the break-in of the Democratic National Committee's offices at the Watergate Complex—Republicans did not challenge the premises of the prerogatives that had accrued to the modern executive office. In a now familiar refrain, Gerald Ford, when serving in the House, denounced Representative Wright Patman's (D-TX) Committee to investigate Watergate as a "political witch hunt."[116] As newspaper reports dug deeper, Senator Robert Dole picked up on the White House's frequent attacks on the media and claimed that the entire Republican Party had been "the victim of a barrage of unfounded and unsubstantial allegations by George McGovern and his partner in mud-slinging the *Washington Post*."[117] A majority of Republicans on the House Judiciary Committee voted against recommending the several articles of impeachment to the full House, citing insufficient evidence. Only when the White House tapes proved otherwise did Nixon's partisan allies jump ship.

Watergate was not an isolated event. Just over 12 years later, news broke that the Reagan White House had knowingly funneled money to support the anti-communist Contras, thus violating the Boland Amendment that proscribed such aid. While less narrowly political in nature than the robbery ordered by the White House-run Committee to Re-Elect the President (CREEP), the Iran-Contra affair nevertheless placed Republicans in a similar predicament of having to defend an administration that willfully violated congressional law. In the middle of the Reagan presidency, Theodore Lowi offered a prescient analysis of the dilemmas of modern presidential governance that would routinely lead Republicans to denigrate constitutional restraint in a partisan defense of a constitutional office: an institution firmly attached to a party that staked all hopes of future victory on the legacy of a single man with an impossible job. "Deceit is inherent in the present structure," Lowi argued. "Since more is demanded than can ever be delivered . . . deceit will always be used to save the president as well as to defend the fundamental interests of the state."[118]

Politics makes strange bedfellows, and political reforms provide alluring opportunities for former opponents. In 1979, a young college professor from Macon, Georgia, finally won election to the US House of Representatives on his third try. Quickly thereafter, Newt Gingrich climbed the ranks of the Republican Party taking advantage of the Democratic-led caucus reforms enacted a decade earlier. After he led the fight for an ethics investigation that ultimately led to Democratic Speaker Jim Wright's resignation from Congress, conservative Republicans propelled Gingrich into the formal party leadership. While the party's Southern Strategy had proven successful in winning several presidential elections, congressional Republicans still found themselves in the minority year after year. Through sheer personal force, ideological commitment, and political genius, Gingrich made congressional races an intractable feature of the party's grand strategy and convinced caucus members that strong, more militantly partisan congressional leadership was a viable strategy for securing majority status.[119] He developed strong ties with the growing network of conservative policy advocacy groups like the Heritage Foundation and Grover Norquist's Americans for Tax Reform. These organizations provided necessary research services and organizational support to a long-suffering minority party. In 1994, Gingrich put forward the "Contract with America," which pledged specific legislative policies that a Republican Congress would enact. Elevating local races into a national referendum on the Clinton administration, Gingrich achieved something that no Republican leader or advocate had done since 1952: secured a House majority.

Gingrich launched his revolt from the adversarial, movement-based politics of the previous decades. The Contract with America put forward a host of specific policies, but its real purpose was the same sort of self-effacing critique of governmental institutions that Reagan so brilliantly capitalized on. On the first day of the new Republican rule, the House enacted a wide-ranging series of reforms aimed at its own institution: cutting committee staff, term-limiting committee chairmanships, and making committee meetings open to the public. Shortly thereafter, Republicans introduced a constitutional amendment to term limit all members of Congress; it fell short by 63 votes.

These reforms had the effect of further strengthening the role that partisan insurgents played in setting the legislative agenda and creating national campaign issues. Coupled with party and campaign finance reforms that gave greater sway to activists and primary voters in determining the outcome of party nomination contests, congressional leaders faced greater incentives to play to the base and galvanize their most enthusiastic supporters, who happened to hold the most extreme, or off-center, policy positions.[120] The substance of proposed bills changed as an increasing number became symbolic or "message votes," used to motivate party activists during elections.[121] Likewise, the role of the individual members of Congress transformed from one in which they had a relatively small but meaningful role in drafting bills, channeling constituent interests and gaining policy expertise, to one in which they were ever more beholden to militantly partisan members and advocacy groups.[122]

Congressional Republicans now found themselves in a position to torment a popular Democratic president. On the other side of the institutional combat that had roiled party politics since Nixon, Gingrich and his top-brass wasted little time in capitalizing on President Clinton's numerous scandals: Whitewater, Travelgate, the death of Vince Foster, numerous accusations of sexual misconduct. During the Reagan and George H. W. Bush presidencies, Republicans had strongly criticized the 1978 Ethics in Government Act, enacted as part of the post-Watergate effort to curb the "imperial" presidency, which contained provisions for the appointment of independent counsels to investigate charges of presidential misconduct. Yet they changed their tune once a Democrat was in the White House; throughout his two terms, Clinton was plagued by such investigations. Goaded by congressional Republicans in 1998, Special Prosecutor Kenneth Starr's team followed up on rumors that the White House had used its resources to cover up a sexual affair with a young intern, Monica Lewinsky. In a deposition for a different sexual harassment lawsuit, the president testified that he did not have "sexual relations" with Lewinsky, thereby setting off alarms on Capitol Hill that Clinton was guilty of obstruction of justice and perjury.

The congressional response was symptomatic of Gingrich's reliance on partisan warfare to shore up his personal support. Never did a majority of the American people support the impeachment investigations. Yet, pressured by howls of conservative talk radio and the newly established partisan cable network, Fox News, Republicans leaders stifled the efforts of their more moderate members to forgo impeachment proceedings by slapping the president on the wrist with a censure vote. Harsh partisan tactics faltered as the president, benefiting from a robust economy and a near 70% approval rating, survived the Senate trial. Nevertheless, the Clinton impeachment spectacle left deep scars on the polity. As Andrew Rudalevige has observed, "The American political system did not bounce back fast from the impeachment process, and surely was not stronger at its broken places. Contemporary polarized dysfunction mirrors the snarling politics that took root in the 1990s. Far from repairing the breach, Clinton and his enemies made it deeper."[123]

The Republican Congress and the George W. Bush administration combined harsh legislative partisanship and executive aggrandizement. The new Speaker, Dennis Hastert, adopted an informal rule, thereafter followed by each of his Republican successors, that no bill would go up for a vote unless a majority of the majority party supported its passage. Bipartisanship, even if it did exist, was procedurally blocked out of the legislative process. In the White House, the president and his staff used the prestige and institutional capacity of the executive office to rally Republicans around a War on Terror that mobilized the conservative base.[124]

Undoubtedly, there were many within Congress who opposed the leadership's embrace of big government conservatism and executive-centered partisanship. Foreshadowing the rise of another insurgent force on the right, a second-term congressman from Indiana, Mike Pence, led a small group of House Republicans to oppose the president's plans for Hurricane Katrina relief.[125] Demanding budget cuts to offset the new spending, the fiscal hawkishness of "small government" types would resurface following Bush's $700-billion Troubled Asset Relief Program (TARP) and Obama's $831-billion stimulus package. "Obamacare," as it was first dubbed by the president's political enemies, with its requirement of an individual mandate to purchase health insurance and a variety of new taxes, was the breaking point for the Tea Party patriots.

Few would have predicted such a trajectory when Congress confronted the excesses of the Nixon presidency. The key elements of Nixon's health-care proposal—an employer mandate to purchase health insurance and expanded coverage for the poor to "assure every American financial access to high quality health care"—continued to shape subsequent proposals by both Democrats and Republicans. However, signifying the rise of the "new right," opposition to Obamacare became the rallying cry of grass roots activists as the GOP swept to power in the 2010 midterm elections. Tellingly, Tea Party activists supported "middle class" class entitlements. In the early days of the movement an iconic and ironic image of DC hating Tea Partiers was a sign reading: "Keep your government hands off my Medicare."[126]

Still, more principled conservatives celebrated the Tea Party as a movement to capture the hearts and minds of those Americans who understood and opposed the bank bailout's upwards distributive effects, who revered the Founding Fathers, and who carried their pocket Constitutions with the 10th Amendment dogeared and underlined. They were anti-establishment, but not anti-elitist; theirs was an insurgency against the current rulers in an effort to create a new meritocracy.[127] The erstwhile champions of "big-government conservatism" found a new charismatic leader to respond to the demands of the disaffected: Sarah Palin. In the Alaskan governor and former running mate of John McCain, conservative leaders such as William Kristol, the editor of the conservative magazine, the *Weekly Standard*, saw someone who could harness the grassroots energy of "Hockey Moms" and "Joe Six Pack"—a new Andrew Jackson, or even Reagan, to fight in the new era of crony capitalism.[128]

And yet, the congressional Republican leadership, which rose to power as part of a populist assault on the Old Guard, was not able to withstand the disruption brought about by the Tea Party movement.[129] The Speaker of

the House and former vice-presidential candidate, Paul Ryan, once a darling of the Tea Party, announced in early 2018 that he would resign his office following the midterm elections—no doubt a reflection of the fact that
Republicans, even with unified government, failed to make good on their
loudest and most enduring promise to "repeal" Obamacare. Lest it be forgotten, Ryan's departure came on the heels of his predecessor, John Boehner's,
resignation—a decision precipitated by near constant threats from fellow
Republicans to oust him.

These are not personal failings but institutional ones. Congress still suffers
from a lack of staff; staffers themselves report that they do not have the time
to become experts on public policy; the institutional resources of the CBO
and Congressional Research Services are strained as a result of Gingrich's
"good government" reforms; and stifled by partisan gridlock, members remain beholden to executive action in setting the priorities for bureaucratic
agencies.[130] As Christopher Demuth has aptly summarized, "Single-member
activism has replaced the committee hierarchies and autocratic chairmen
of times past. Members do not need to bow to the leadership or patiently
master the arts of legislative negotiation and coalition building. They advance their careers by demonstrating fidelity to the principles of general affinity groups and coaxing the executive agencies on behalf of discrete affinity
groups."[131] Compromise is a dirty word for the members of this conservative
partisan network, who exploit the primary system to challenge more cen-
trist conservatives. Leaving all too little room to register dissent or channel
alternatives, the populist reforms within Congress set the stage for a factional
movement to hijack a party, and then hijack an institution.

Many on the right have sought to renew the party's strength by invoking
the more uplifting leadership of Reagan, the prophet of a conservatism that
insisted—in opposition to the globalism of the McGovern Democrats—
that America still was a "city on a hill," a message that Reagan heir-apparent
George W. Bush projected in the wake of the attacks of 9/11. Consider that
the first sentence of the 2016 Republican platform reads: "We believe in
American exceptionalism," an uplifting sentiment that Donald Trump virtually ignored. Yet this nostalgia for the Reagan "Revolution" overlooks how,
under these kinder and gentler partisans, the Republican Party built a conservative base whose foot soldiers rallied to their cause because they believed
that liberalism had so corrupted the country that the national government
had the responsibility to support "family values"—a view that permeates
proposals to restrict abortion and same-sex marriage; to require work for

social welfare programs; and to impose standards on secondary and elementary schools.

Most relevant to contemporary partisan combat, in the wake of the 9/11 attacks and the Great Recession of late 2007 to 2009, the main targets of conservative statism became radical Islamic terrorism and illegal immigration. Appealing to the angry Republican base, the 2012 Republican candidate, Mitt Romney, who was to disdain Trump's provocations four years later, embraced an immigration policy—calling on undocumented immigrants to "self-deport"—that was hardly less harsh than Trump's would prove to be. Romney and the other Republican contenders for the nomination who took hawkish position on immigration sought to harness the outrage of Tea Party activists, who, for all their rhetoric about rolling back government, tended to take a stronger stand against immigration than establishment Republicans. For example, a 2014 PRRI/Brookings poll revealed that 63% of Tea Party Republicans believed that the growing number of newcomers to the country threatened "American customs and values." Republicans who did not identify with the Tea Party were divided, with 48% saying immigrants threated traditional values while 45% said they strengthened American customs.[132]

In truth, the Tea Party was less a new, independent movement than a reinvigoration, and further incursion, of the conservative assault on the halls of power spearheaded by the partisan offensive of the Christian Right. The principal conservative social movements, in fact, have collaborated on issue advocacy and electoral campaigns. The alliance between Tea Party and Christian Right activists formed the foundation of the Faith and Freedom Coalition, organized by Ralph Reed, which has been very active in primary and general elections as well as policy campaigns since 2012. The followers of this new conservative insurgency have been determined to hold the GOP accountable to the same principles—tax relief, family values and patriotism—that Reagan and his Christian Right allies trumpeted.[133]

Trump, therefore, is more than a cult of personality. His political success must also be attributable to his giving unfiltered expression to a Republican coalition that is more than five decades in the making. Obama saw himself as the leader of a new "coalition of the ascendant," the legatees of the Great Society: young people, minorities, the LGBTQ community and educated white people, especially single women. Trump and his strategists view him as the steward of a "coalition of restoration"—comprised of blue-collar, religiously devout, and non-urban whites who are exceedingly anxious about social change that is turning the United States into a country to which they no longer feel an allegiance.[134] These populist forces were unleashed in the early 1970s and helped Republicans succeed at the ballot box. Insurgents also spawned institutional change that weakened mediating institutions like formal party organizations that restrained rancorous partisanship. As George Hawley—in his exhaustive study of "right-wing" thought—recognizes, "In the years ahead . . . the conservative intellectual movement may lose its ability to determine the boundaries of acceptable right-wing thought. Furthermore, thanks to the Internet, dissident right-wing voices are now able to spread their message on a once-unthinkable scale."[135]

Conclusion

Modern-day Republican Party politics is the outgrowth of institutional and cultural developments on the right since the 1960s. Law and order was an effective clarion call for a distraught generation who either felt left out of the Great Society or for whom the Great Society went too far. Donald Trump's law and order spoke to an older generation weary of the country's dramatic demographic change and society's preoccupation with political correctness. Nixon, Reagan, and the Bushes all championed America as an exceptional, honorable, proud place, whose foreign policy commitments followed from its strength and resolve. Trump's "America First," reminiscent of traditional isolationist strains on the right, has aroused a yearning among his base for a past that belies the transformation of conservatism since the late 1960s. Adapting the progressive ideal of a strong president, conservatives became the loudest proponents of executive-centered government—at home and abroad—and presidency-centered parties. Trump is a symptom of, not a departure from this development. Accepting the Republican nomination in July 2016, Trump depicted a once proud nation in a spiral of decline, bereft of leadership capable of guiding it back to its former greatness. Standing before a rapturous assembly of delegates in Cleveland—many of them first-time attendees to a national convention—Trump voiced an unabashed message of executive aggrandizement. Having convinced the Republican Party that only an outsider who had long jousted with the "establishment" could truly reform a "rigged system," he boasted, "Nobody knows the system better than me, which is why I alone can fix it."[136]

The last two chapters make clear that both Democrats and Republicans contributed to the falling apart of America's vital center. This account of polarization differs in some respects from two influential scholarly perspectives that also seek to explain the transformation of conservative partisanship. First, we seek to distinguish ourselves here from a common—perhaps the most common—interpretation of 1960s reactionary politics on the right as a reflection of voter backlash.[137] Many scholars seeking to understand the lingering effects of the Great Society, Vietnam, and Johnson's fall from grace have labeled the period spanning Nixon and George W. Bush as the "conservative turn" in American political development. The American people simply became weary of big government, susceptible to the allure of lower taxes, local control, and "color-blind" policy, and voted Republican. As a result, the Republican Party cast aside its pragmatic sensibilities that defined it in the post-war era and became a decidedly oppositional party that denigrated government, indeed, outside of the military, the very idea of public service.

Public opinion and changes in the mind of the average voter certainly were important for the type of politics we have just traced. And yet, something was going on that was more than just a "conservative turn" in American politics. Indeed, analyzing the growth of conservative politics as a consequence of the rise of conservative sentiment verges on tautology; and such an explanation deflects attention from the very deliberate decisions made that helped to redefine American conservatism by tapping into the populist currents the 1960s unleashed. Moreover, we believe that the framing of contemporary American politics as a struggle between champions and enemies of government fails to account for the rise of a new right that seeks to redeploy rather than roll back the national state forged by progressive reformers. This is a hallmark of populist politics and a direct challenge to the vital center. Such a development might make possible a fresh bracing debate over what objectives the government should serve. Our concern is that such a partisan contest is unlikely to occur without effective party organizations that can both mediate and enlarge disagreements between liberals and conservatives. These institutions have been weakened by the unleashing of populist forces that abjure appeals to the "median voter" in favor of efforts to mobilize liberal and conservative partisans.

Second, our account of the long durée of the vital center's demise departs somewhat from the highly influential position among political scientists who place primary blame for the erosion of institutional norms and constitutional constraint on the Republican Party. Claims of "asymmetric" polarization are replete in the discipline purporting that radical conservatism has taken over the Republican Party, rendering the possibility of restoring a vital center a chimera. The Democrats, they argue, remain a pragmatic party, on some accounts a "neo-liberal" reactionary force in American politics. The most prominent analysis of how militant Republican partisans have hijacked the polity is provided by Jacob Hacker and Paul Pierson, who credit Gingrich, the Tea Party, and powerful interest groups for throwing politics "off center."[138]

We agree that the 1994 Contract with America represented a watershed moment in the development of a more ideologically cohesive and polarizing Republican Party. We disagree that it began with Gingrich and that it was a phenomenon contained on the right. For most scholars, the centralization of party leadership and the imposition of homogenous party orthodoxy is the problem. But the "success" of the Republican Party under Gingrich proved to be a temporary condition. In other words, centralized leadership at one point in time did not beget effective leadership in the long run.[139] Ideological homogeneity within the party does not seem to be the source of America's present discontents; rather, the lack of collective responsibility and partisan constraint stand out.

In contrast to the received wisdom, we argue that both Democrats and Republicans have been complicit in forging a direct, combustible connection between populism and partisanship, stoking the passions of their most loyal supporters but undermining the public's trust in representative government. This is not to claim that liberal and conservative activism is the same. As we will discuss in Chapter 6, which analyzes the culmination of executive-centered partisanship during the Obama and Trump administrations, populism on the left and right is animated by entirely different worldviews; and the Democratic Party, composed of a more diverse coalition, is more resistant to populist demands. Yet the shortened time horizon in much of the asymmetric polarization literature fails to recognize that many of the Republican reforms built on precedents and procedural changes in the presidential selection process and the structure of Congress that were instigated by post–New Deal Democrats intent on transforming liberalism. Indeed, the last three chapters have shown that executive-centered partisanship—the joining of executive prerogative and movement politics—has been advanced by important actors on both sides of the ideological spectrum. Roosevelt, Johnson, Nixon, and Reagan all contributed to the decline of party organization and the heightening of partisan rancor. And all presidents since Johnson have sought to come to terms with and capitalize on populist energies within the electorate that were aroused by the culture wars of the 1960s. They did, perhaps, what we would expect any politician to do in order to build winnable coalitions and secure office; after all, populism is an inextricable feature of a free society.

Nevertheless, it is in neither party's best interest to routinely exploit voter disgust, anxiety, or resentment in pursuit of short-term electoral victory and partisan causes. The temptation will always remain, but strong institutions can make it a less enticing prospect. There is no prospect of returning to a golden past era; to yearn for the past is to ignore how the pragmatic center that aroused insurgent assaults from the left and the right bred apathy and allowed deep-seated problems to fester. The novel and pressing challenge for those who would take the idea of party renewal seriously is to reimagine intermediary institutions that will allow for a clash of liberal and conservative ambitions but discourage the sort of existential struggle that defies common ground and rattles the national resolve. However, as the next chapter of our story makes all too clear, current developments make the path forward a treacherous one.

6

Culminating Developments

Presidential Power, Liberalism, and
Conservatism in the 21st Century

Twin Diseases

Amid the fear that partisan polarization was tearing apart the fabric of constitutional norms and institutions—at a time when scholars and pundits anxiously contemplated that American democracy might even die—the country was hit in the winter of 2020 by a global pandemic that had claimed over 100,000 lives by the end of May, shuttered the economy, and confined the vast majority of Americans to their homes. As the coronavirus wrought carnage that Donald Trump's apocalyptic inaugural address could not have anticipated, the nation was further disrupted in the spring by the death of George Floyd at the hands of four Minneapolis policemen—the latest of many high-profile cases of police brutality against Black Americans to come to light in recent years. As a video went viral and cable television endlessly repeated it, the world watched a horrific act of murder that exposed the American state in its rawest form. Defying the social distancing recommendations that public health officials had for months urged them to follow, thousands of Americans, with pent-up frustration from isolation and a cratering economy, took to the streets in cities and towns all over the United States and marched in the most widespread demonstrations the country had witnessed since the late 1960s.

Faced with the twin diseases of the coronavirus and police brutality, hopes were expressed in the media and other public forums that the country might come together and that the rancorous partisanship in Washington, DC, and many state capitals might ease. All levels of government were struggling to come to terms with the worst pandemic since the "Spanish flu" of 1918 and the massive protests against the systemic racial injustice of America's carceral state. As we have demonstrated in this book, American democracy has rarely been harmonious; even during crises like the Great Depression, party conflict, aggravated by populist uprisings, has aroused fundamental debates and bitter resolutions about who "We, the People" are, and how the challenges of economic, racial, and religious conflict can be met in a way that fulfills the rights promised by the Declaration of Independence and the Constitution. It is not surprising, then, that passionate political conflicts over American identity, already aroused by the Trump presidency, shattered any illusions of harmony as fears of an insidious virus and anger over the stubborn tumor of racial injustice agitated a divided nation. Republicans and Democrats disagreed vehemently over how serious a threat the pandemic posed to the country and when the economy could safely be reopened. And although public opinion, on average, moved dramatically to favor police reform, partisan differences engulfed the supposed harmony soon thereafter. Republicans and Democrats could not agree on whether the demonstrations in solidarity with their Black and Brown neighbors were a landmark moment in the country's long march toward equal justice or a sign that radical forces were ravaging private homes and businesses. The fact that the coronavirus hit African Americans and Latinos especially hard, exposing invidious inequalities in the healthcare system and workplace, made the partisan responses to the twin diseases especially volatile.

Although harsh party conflict in the United States is not new, the momentous and polarizing events of 2020 were mired in an all-consuming partisanship that the country had not witnessed since the Civil War. Many commentators nervously dubbed contemporary developments in American politics the "Cold Civil War." As we have argued, contemporary partisanship is especially combustible because it takes place in the absence of vital party organizations that historically have channeled democratic unrest and popular disagreement into more structured and less militant forms of political engagement. In the past, these mediating institutions emerged from each populist challenge not so much stronger or weaker, as transformed—responsive to the new politics of the age.

If the past were prologue, stronger party organizations might have encouraged more Republican senators to join Mitt Romney in the streets, willing to say three simple words that their party's presidential candidate refused to utter: "Black Lives Matter." More vital organization might have enabled Democrats in Congress to seize the moment offered by dramatic shifts in public attitudes on police reform, and work with the states and cities to demilitarize local police and end well-known discriminatory practices. Democrats actually might have been in a position to pursue criminal justice reform in the states if their support "down ballot" had not been severely weakened over the past decade—subordinated to the presidency-centered politics of the Obama administration. Most urgently, we are left to wonder whether the concluding weeks of Donald Trump's presidency might have been different had the Republican Party not been captured by a cult of personality. The lame duck president might have left office peacefully, instead of stoking an armed insurrection at the Capitol building. And if President Trump persisted in his efforts to resist a peaceful transfer of power in opposition to a Republican Party buttressed by a stronger sense of collective partisan responsibility, he might have left office disgraced instead of retaining the overwhelming support of his party—a party with few remaining members who are willing to openly acknowledge the danger of a populist demagogue.

We are not claiming that vital party organizations would necessarily have forged a consensus that unified the country in the face of a global pandemic; nor would strong party organizations readily have allowed for a bipartisan resolution of the racial injustice that has long tarnished American society. However, we do believe that the disruptive events of 2020 exposed the weakness of American institutions in a way that we feared when we began writing this book in the aftermath of the 2016 election. The results of that election seemed to reveal the cumulative impact of a developmental path driven by two factors: the consolidation of the modern presidency during the New Deal, which accelerated the crumbling of traditional party organization that had begun during the turn of the 20th century; and the rise of movement politics loosed by the culture wars of the 1960s, which pulled the modern presidency into the vortex of fierce partisan conflict. Executive-centered partisanship as it first emerged during the New Deal weakened party organizations and centered partisan responsibility on the modern executive with the expectation that the conflict between liberalism and conservatism would now be mediated by administration—a policy state better suited to managing the expanded government responsibilities at home and abroad than could be expected from a decentralized party system rooted in state and local governments and provincial interests. As Chapters 4 and 5 document, the idea that the New Deal state would subordinate party conflict and populist uprising to the pragmatic pursuit of domestic and international security came under full-scale attack from the left and the right during the 1960s. This insurgency did not dispel executive aggrandizement; rather, it produced a combustible mixture of presidential power and all-consuming partisanship.

The merging of executive aggrandizement and movement politics that resulted from the populist uprising of the 1960s reached a fateful reckoning in 2020—a country mired in a concoction of public health, economic, and civil rights crises remained intractably divided by the cultural clashes and antinomian surges that fractured the country a half century before. The upshot—a self-styled movement president following a playbook that Steven Levitsky and Daniel Ziblatt characterized as an existential threat to American democracy—testifies dramatically to how the norms and institutions that had constrained demagogues in our past have badly deteriorated. Trump's total domination of the Republican Party, they warned, was especially foreboding. "The real protection against would-be authoritarians," Levtiky and Ziblatt write, "has not been Americans' firm commitment to democracy but, rather, the gatekeepers—our political parties."[1]

The developmental track we identify has dramatically reshaped American politics. On the left, activists pushed for civil rights, women's rights, and an anti-war agenda in the 1960s and 1970s, shifting power further away from party bosses and elites. During the 1980s and 1990s, conservative evangelicals and other right-wing activists transformed the GOP into a movement party that focused on the party's most fervent base supporters rather than the mythical median voter. In the years since, both progressive and conservative movement activists have pulled the parties away from the center, energizing grassroots bases, shattering areas of postwar consensus, and fueling ideological polarization and legislative stalemate. In this context, political moderation and compromise win few, if any, rewards. Like new partisan openings, the expansion and concentration of power in the hands of modern presidents also created more political traction for both liberal and conservative movements. The enlargement of unilateral executive power provided opportunities for privledged social movements to secure support and action from the nation's top leader. The emergent power and visibility of the White House made it a focal point for varied movements in the Progressive and New Deal period; but president-movement relations became more significant and regularized from the Great Society years onward.

The development of executive-centered partisanship thus reveals how the idea of a "state" cuts more deeply than suggested by Max Weber's definition of "a human community that (successfully) claims the monopoly of the legitimate use of physical force within a given territory." Beyond the powers of government, the state represents a centralizing ambition to cultivate, or impose, a vision of citizenship. In Randolph Bourne's words, the state is a "concept of power" that comes alive in defense of or in conflict with an ideal of how such foundational values of Americanism as "free and enlightened" are to be interpreted and enforced. The ideal is symbolized not by the Declaration and the Constitution but rather in rallying emblems such as the flag and Uncle Sam. A key mobilizing force is patriotism, a concept at once centralizing and conflictual.[2]

The battle over patriotism—what it means to be a proud American—has been at the very core of the struggles over American identity since the 1960s. For anti-war protestors, burning a draft card was no different from throwing tea into Boston Harbor—an act against tyranny. For construction workers and union members who took to the streets in response, Americanism was about service overseas, if that was what the president demanded. The Vietnam travail was not just a struggle over foreign policy; it was a contest to determine whether America was still a city on a hill, as conservatives insisted, or an imperialistic power that deprived developing nations of their right of self-determination, as the Antiwar Movement contended. The emblem of American pride, the flag also became a fraught symbol on the home front, as it came to represent a mark of whether the American experiment in self-rule was the pursuit of liberation, which the civil rights movement championed, or a laboratory to nurture Judeo-Christian values, as the Religious Right proclaimed. When, as president, Donald Trump took to the stage of the annual Conservative Political Action Committee (CPAC) convention, and hugged and kissed the American flag to rapturous applause, he was exploiting the festering wounds of an American civic culture long tormented by partisan agitation.

Donald Trump may have represented the apotheosis of executive-centered partisanship, but he exploited developments set in motion by his predecessor. Barack Obama, although he was a reluctant partisan warrior, was forced to navigate the tensions between the modern presidency and emerging social movements that championed the rights of immigrants, the LGBTQ community, and criminal justice. In a new liberal era, these movements braided their narratives to a vision of Americanism born of '60s protest and decades of failed idealism. Combining top-down and bottom-up politics, supported by a pioneering information-age grassroots organization, Obama deftly played the role of a movement leader, relying on partisan administration, especially after the Democrats lost control of the House in the 2010 midterm elections. The election and presidency of

Donald Trump confirmed that executive power had become the vanguard of an enervating contest between liberal and conservative policy demands, which weakens the system of checks and balances, diminishes the integrity of decentralizing constitutional institutions like Congress and the states, and erodes citizens' trust in the competence and fairness of the national government.

Because his administration used executive power so aggressively, most scholars and pundits place Trump outside the tradition of American conservative thought, and many regard him as a disruptive force inside conservatism's institutional vessel, the Republican Party. The story we have told thus far shows this to be a dubious proposition. The association of conservative Republicanism and retrenchment elides a critical change in the relationship between party politics and executive power that has taken place over the last six decades and which Donald Trump determinedly nurtured: the rise of executive-centered partisanship characterized by presidential unilateralism, social activism, and polarizing struggles over questions of national identity that sharply divide the nation by race, ethnicity, and religion.[3]

This is not to say that we should "normalize" Donald Trump's disruptive four-year reign, but it is incumbent on us to use the normal tools of political science to understand the unique threat he poses as an individual, within a system that is likely to outlive his presidency. The imminent threat of Trump's populism was a problem that could only be solved at the ballot box; but the transformation of partisanship and the enduring shift in governing authority that brought him to power is a task for institutionally minded reformers. As the impeachment inquiry, pandemic crisis, and Black Lives Matter demonstrations highlight, the Trump presidency represents a novel challenge to American constitutional government, in the sense that long-standing rules and norms are belittled and circumnavigated. Moreover, although both Democratic and Republican presidents have centralized power in the White House since the Nixon years, attenuating protocols and institutions that maintain departments and agencies as independent sites of public policy, the Trump administration represents a new, more extreme assault on "bureaucratic autonomy."[4] Current developments make the path forward a treacherous one. After reviewing the culmination of executive-centered partisanship during the Obama and Trump presidencies, our task in the concluding chapter is to look for some light at the end of this dark passage.

Obama, Trump, and the Politics of Personality

Obama's partisanship was a critical prelude to Trump's tactics and policies. While they presented starkly different visions of a remade American society, it is impossible to understand the momentum and force of Trump's presidency without taking account of Obama's sustained reliance on partisan administration. Scholars and pundits have usually depicted Obama as a prisoner of partisan rancor in Congress, which was especially fierce and obstructive on the Republican side of the aisle during his two terms in office. Indeed, many young activists, especially those who were central to the Black Lives Matter movement, criticized Obama for being too pragmatic and failing to meet the ferocious resistance of the Tea Party and the Republican Party with sufficient partisan fervor.

Nevertheless, Obama actively if sometimes reluctantly embraced the role of party leader, even in the management of the bureaucracy, the arena in which the modern presidency's claim to transcend partisanship was nurtured.[5] During the final six years of this presidency, when Obama faced a Congress with at least one chamber controlled by Republicans, he surpassed the institutional strategies of the Bush administration in combining programmatic achievement and partisan calculation. Most of his executive actions were directed to strengthening a widely scattered but potentially powerful coalition that had been forming since the Great Society: minorities, youth, the LGBTQ community, and educated White voters, especially single women. Many of Obama's administrative actions in the service of environmental protection, women's rights, and criminal justice reform appealed to those constituencies. Similarly, the administration's direction to the Justice Department in February 2011 to stop defending the Defense of Marriage Act (DOMA), which barred federal recognition of same sex marriage, against constitutional challenges sealed the White House's partnership with the LGBTQ movement.

Perhaps the most significant and polarizing action the Obama administration took to strengthen support of this coalition was in the controversial matter of immigration. Failing to reach an agreement with the Republican Congress on comprehensive immigration reform, Obama took strong administrative action that provided deportation relief and work authorizations to more than 5 million undocumented immigrants. These administrative initiatives in support of the "Dreamers" (DACA) and parents of permanent residents and citizens (DAPA) greatly strengthened Obama's often fraught relationship with the immigration rights movement. As Marielena Hincapie of the National Immigration Law Center announced, this meeting of the minds between the Obama administration and social movements organizations was "one of the rare times in history when the White House and activists are completely in agreement."[6] It is not coincidental, therefore, that Obama's immigration initiatives defined the lines of rancorous partisan conflict in Congress, the courts, and the 2016 election campaign.

Although the political philosophies and policy objectives of Obama and Trump could not be more antithetical, the style of politics they practice reflects two key areas of common ground: a detachment from party organization and a vision of the White House as the vanguard of a movement. Obama planned his administration as a progressive crusade that marked a new stage in the fusion of executive power and partisan politics. He coupled his ambitious administrative strategy alongside an innovative political organization that was dedicated to linking him directly with potential supporters. Born during the 2008 campaign as "Obama for America," this mass mobilization effort was incorporated into the Democratic National Committee as "Organizing for America" during Obama's first term in the White House; after 2012, the group was spun off as a non-profit social welfare agency called "Organizing for Action" (OFA). Obama's information age, grassroots tool was critical not only to his two presidential campaigns but also to the enactment of major legislative reform including his signature policy achievement, the 2010 Affordable Care Act. Obama further solidified an executive-centered Democratic Party when he removed OFA from the Democratic National Committee, with the promise that such a change would strengthen the organziation's potential as a grassroots movement. Candidate-centered organizations had been a staple of American politics since the Kennedy administration, but Obama was the first president to keep his electoral machine intact as the vanguard of a movement that would free him from the constraints of the Democratic "establishment" and connect him directly to a new progressive coalition. Significantly, just as Obama's attention shifted to executive action in 2011, OFA redeployed its staff and volunteers to defend the president's administrative initiatives, touting with special urgency the unilateralism that would advance climate change policy, LGBTQ rights and immigration reform.[7]

Yet, as much as Obama paid tribute to the civil rights activists of a previous generation who made his political ascendance possible, and as much as he hoped to channel the popular energies of his 2008 campaign into a formidable movement of his own, the imperatives of his administration and of social movements remained at odds. Black Lives Matter advocates were especially critical of the president's seeming lack of partisan fire on their behalf. Emblematic of the Democratic Party's regnant allegiance to non-partisan administration, Obama accommodated his message of change to persistent efforts to reprise the policy state. He issued an executive order that would phase out the incarceration of federal prisoners in private facilities; barred the military from transferring certain types of equipment to police or sheriffs' departments, including tracked armored vehicles, armed aircraft or vehicles of any kind, .50-caliber firearms and ammunition, grenade launchers, bayonets, and camouflage uniforms; issued clemency to over 1,000 inmates, many of them long-serving non-violent drug offenders—more than his three predecessors combined; and authorized the Department of Justice to impose federal oversight on eight large police departments over his two terms (in their sixteen years combined, Clinton and George W. Bush oversaw just six).[8]

According to one of his aides, Van Jones, despite these administrative measures, the president's support of Black Lives Matter was muted by his hope that he could "build bridges across race and party under his presidency."[9] "Obama himself was an activist and a community organizer . . . but he is not, by temperament, a protester," noted Ta-Nehisi Coates after a series of interviews with the president. "He is a consensus builder; consensus, he believes, ultimately drives what gets done. He understands the emotional power of protest, the need to vent before authority—but that kind of approach does not come naturally to him. . . . The notion that a president would attempt to achieve change within the boundaries of the accepted consensus is appropriate. But Obama is almost constitutionally skeptical of those who seek to achieve change outside the consensus."[10] These critiques from the left underscore the pressure Obama felt but also acted on. Indeed, even though his base often fretted his consensus-posture early in his administration, Obama saw himself as the leader of a new "coalition of the ascendant," one who could corral a movement into the mainstream of American political life.[11]

Trump's odds-defying ascendance to the presidency in 2016 appeared to complete the fusion of centralized administration and partisanship. As president, Trump surpassed Obama in attending to his base. As we noted in Chapter 5, just as Obama styled himself as leader of a coalition of the ascendance, so Trump and his strategists positioned him as the steward of a "coalition of restoration" made up of blue-collar, religiously devout, and non-urban Whites who feel that traditional Republican politicians have forsaken their needs and demands.[12] Trump lacked an independent grassroots machine as organized or as institutionally sophisticated as Obama's. However, Trump's reliance on variegated media platforms (social and traditional) and raucous mass rallies galvanized his supporters with even more fervor and passion than the liberal advocates under OFA. Trump did not disband his movement at the end of the campaign; rather, the president-elect took off on a "thank you tour" during the transition period, revealing his determination to continue to hold mass rallies after he entered the White House.[13] Until the pandemic shut the country down in mid-March, these rallies, sustaining a direct, unmediated relationship between the president and his base supporters, continued regularly, averaging two a month, energizing his supporters, and renewing their faith that the president spoke for them.

With the approach of the 2020 election, Trump rallies, which resumed in the middle of the pandemic, became more meticulously produced than the spontaneous and thinly staffed events of his first presidential campaign. Although no longer covered by cable networks, the campaign turned them into "giant, roving field offices that vacuum up personal data from rallygoers, register new voters and sign up his most enthusiastic supporters as volunteers."[14] And lest anyone believe that such a direct, personable technique is fruitless in a country as vast as the United States, Trump's 2016 campaign manager Kellyanne Conway recalled that their first campaign "mastered the art of putting Donald Trump where he was best, which was in these big rallies, these huge settings in swing states, in front of the people. . . . Donald Trump does best when he's with the people. He can take his message directly to the American people and cut through the noise or through the silence, whatever the case may be. It was a masterful way of doing it . . . because it was low-cost; it was high-energy."[15]

In contrast to Obama's persistent, albeit frustrated, efforts to transcend partisanship, Trump's efforts to mobilize support for his controversial plans to "Make America Great Again" entailed unrelenting appeals to core supporters. Despite pleas among fellow Republicans to act "more presidential," Trump relished his administration's unapologetic support for, as one White House aide put it, the former businessman's most "loyal customers."[16] The diminishing but still spirited band of Never-Trump conservatives bewailed Trump's war cry that America is no longer a great nation but the stooge of its international trading partners and the victim of predatory immigrants. Such a dire message, they lamented, abandoned the more up-lifting conservatism that Ronald Reagan expressed—a conservatism that insisted, in opposition to '60s liberals, that America still was a "city on a hill." This message of resilience and religious tolerance inspired the position that Reagan heir-apparent George W. Bush projected in the wake of the attacks of September 11, 2001. Nevertheless, as we chronicled earlier, this nostalgia for the Reagan "Revolution" overlooks how Trump forged ties with a Republican base, most notably the Christian Right (which Reagan enlisted in his administration's conservative crusade) and the Obama-era Tea Party, which Republican presidential candidates had been courting since its inception. The unyielding opposition of the Christian Right and the Tea Party to Obama's efforts was rooted in deep cultural issues that 1960s-era protests and counterprotests spawned.

Significantly, Trump, a thrice-married and one-time New York liberal, received strong support not only from Tea Party activists but also from conservative evangelical leaders. One of his strongest champions was Ralph Reed, chairman of the Faith and Reform Coalition. Recounting the Christian Right's long march toward a leading place in the conservative coalition, Reed expressed appreciation for Trump's strong pledge to make appointments to the administration and the Supreme Court who would oppose abortion, stand up for the traditional family, and protect Christian schools from the Department of Education.[17] Other crucial defenders included Liberty University President Jerry Falwell Jr., Focus on the Family's James Dobson, and the Family Research Council's Tony Perkins. "We're not electing a pastor-in-chief," Falwell explained to Fox News, echoing the expediency his father expressed in championing the candidacy of Ronald Reagan. "Sometimes you have to be pragmatic. You have to choose the one with the best chance of winning and who is closest to your views."[18]

Trump's ascendance was not only due to his unique demagogic, anti-immigrant appeals. As Douglas McAdams and Karina Kloos argue, conservative activists were ensconced in the Republican Party well before the 2016 election.[19] But it is not surprising that his partisan fury focused most directly on undocumented immigrants. Foreign-born individuals now make up about 14% of the US population, historically the same levels as in the late 19th and early 20th centuries, which, as Nolan McCarty has pointed out, is the other period in American history roiled by ritualized partisan combat.[20] Since 2012, we have noted, Republican presidential candidates as well as GOP state officials and congressional members embraced harsh crackdowns on unauthorized immigration and demonized undocumented immigrants. To a point, Trump's appeal to the Republican base has been fueled by the economic despair of a declining working class. Yet the major factor in his elevation to the White House was an appeal to fear, often racialized, and to the feeling felt by a large number of Americans that immigrants are responsible not only for the country's economic problems but also for the terrible threat that "radical Islamic terrorism" and undocumented immigrants pose to the security of the homeland.

Donald Trump and the Administrative State

As a candidate, Trump denounced the Obama administration's "major power grabs of authority." But as president, he not only rescinded Obama-era actions, but he also redeployed administrative power to serve conservative objectives. Moreover, Trump appointed three Supreme Court justices—Neil Gorsuch, Brett Kavanaugh, and Amy Coney Barrett, whose appointment was rushed through during the final months of the 2020 campaign after the death of liberal icon, Justice Ruth Bader Ginsburg. Trump and the Republican Senate also ensconced in the judiciary a record-breaking number of district and appellate judges, who will likely shift the balance on the court toward greater acceptance of public action that advances conservative policies in national security, protection of the homeland, policing, and civil rights. Trump's imprint on the judiciary loomed large in the sharply divided Supreme Court's approval of a Muslim ban, albeit a modified version of the original order that was blocked by the lower courts, and the emergency decree to build the Wall.

Trump's partisanship did not abrogate the administrative state, as many critics allege. Rather, shifting resources between departments and agencies, inserting policy activists in key administrative positions, and repurposing policies, he redeployed administrative power to serve a racialized politics of fear. For example, Trump's substantial cuts to the Departments of State, Labor, and Education were more than offset by his administration's expansion of personnel in the Departments of Veteran Affairs, Defense, and Homeland Security. Far from destroying the administrative state, the Trump White House's partisan strategy marked a concerted effort to protect favored constituencies by recasting social welfare policies as conservative programs and by redistributing resources throughout the federal government.

Protecting the Homeland

Trump's partisan administration on immigration was especially polarizing. For decades, no Republican candidate had been able to unite the party behind a comprehensive immigration plan. Reflecting this ambivalence, the Republican National Committee's "autopsy report" following Romney's 2012 defeat urged GOP leaders to reach out to minority voters—especially Hispanic voters who have contributed significantly to the transformation of the country's population.[21] Emblematic of executive-centered partisanship, Trump defied the RNC's importunities. By constantly stoking his base, the president rallied partisan support for his immigration policies. Trump galvanized rather than created party differences. Republican voters had been trending toward nativist positions before Trump's candidacy. But Trump made undocumented immigration his signature issue and a core commitment of Republican partisanship: just 10% of Americans in February 2016 believed immigration to be the primary problem facing the country; by July 2019, immigration had risen to the top of the list of the most important issues in the country, with 22% of Americans—and 35% of Republicans—citing it as the major problem facing the nation.[22]

Given the way he centered Republican partisanship on immigration, Trump's decision in early 2019 to declare a national emergency and redirect nearly $3.6 billion in military construction appropriations for a border wall was neither a show of force nor a sign of institutional weakness.[23] It was a rational strategy for an institution that derives its power from exacerbating partisan divisions, energizing its most ardent supporters, and flouting constitutional restraints in the name of "the people." By the time Congress exercised its statutory obligation, according to the terms established by the National Emergency Act of 1976, to approve or reject the president's emergency declaration, esoteric constitutional deliberation gave way completely to visceral presidential partisanship. As Trump threatened in an interview with Fox News several weeks before the vote, "I really think that Republicans that vote against border security and the wall . . . put themselves at great jeopardy."[24] Not surprisingly, few Republicans challenged the president, and those who did risked the ire of his fiercely loyal supporters. Senator Thom Tillis (R-NC) witnessed the specter of a potential primary challenge after he disavowed the president's emergency declaration; so credible was the threat that even after Tillis authored a widely publicized op-ed against Trump, he switched his position and voted for the president's declaration.[25] In the House of Representatives, just 13 Republicans voted to overturn the president's declaration. In the Senate, a significantly higher proportion of the caucus—12 members—broke party ranks. Noticeably, just one of those senators—Susan Collins of Maine—was up for reelection in 2020.

Trump's eager deployment of executive power also reflected a strategy to obviate divisions within his party over the pillars of America First conservatism - immigration and trade. Indeed, Trump's estrangement from the GOP establishment over the tenets and policies of conservative nationalism resulted in some striking evidence of how presidents now dominate their party's "brand"—how they can denigrate parties as collective organizations with a past and a future. Trump's harsh positions on immigration and trade did not win over the Washington establishment; however, he forged strong ties with the GOP's base through tweets, mass rallies, and administrative action—dramatically transforming GOP loyalists' views on issues such as the "Wall" and tariffs.[26] These defining issues of Trump conservatism were joined in the president's threat in June 2019 to deploy tariffs as a surrogate barrier to the surge of Central American migrants coming to the United States through Mexico. Threatening to slap tariffs as high as 25% on all goods from Mexico unless it thwarted the transit of undocumented immigrants and refugees to the United States, Trump adumbrated America First policies that mobilized his base. The threat to deploy tariffs to stem the flow of immigrants to the United States, which risked harming the economy and undermining a trade deal to replace NAFTA as a potential legislative achievement under divided government, testified dramatically to how struggles over national identity have become all-consuming, sharply dividing the country and weakening the national resolve.[27]

The all-out fight of the Trump White House to add a citizenship question to census forms is another example of how policy battles have become red meat for the president's base. The White House lost this fight in the Supreme Court, when Chief Justice Roberts, who sided with the Trump administration in the cases pertaining to the Muslim ban and declaration of an emergency to build the Wall, ruled against its effort to weaponize the census. Nonetheless, the contretemps over the citizenship question allowed the president to cast himself as a strong leader, willing to shake things up in defense of the "silent majority."[28] Indeed, it was more fodder in his claim that a true conservative was needed in the White House to remake the nation's judiciary (his appointees voted "right"). And, true to the dynamics of executive-centered partisanship, Trump responded by placing two new political appointees at the head of the Census Bureau, just as operations resumed from the COVID-19 pandemic.[29]

Having reinforced the agency with political allies, the president signed a memo, issued in July 2020, stating that it would be the "policy of the United States to exclude from the apportionment base aliens who are not in a lawful immigration status under the Immigration and Nationality Act." This provocative move to exclude undocumented immigrants from the census was unprecedented and it seemed to contradict the Constitution's directive that the decennial exercise count all "persons" living in the United States.[30] Like Trump's effort to include a citizenship question on census forms, this order was challenged by a flurry of lawsuits. This time, however, the administration won a reprieve. The Supreme Court, now fortified by six conservative justices, chose not to rule on the order, arguing that it was "premature" to resolve a case that "was riddled with contingencies and speculation." As the unsigned opinion, which legal experts speculated was authored by Chief Justice Roberts, concluded, "Right now . . . we don't know what the president is going to do. We don't know how many aliens will be excluded. We don't know what the effect will be on apportionment," so why, he asked, aren't we "better advised" to wait until we have that information.[31]

Just as the judiciary acted with forbearance in response to the White House's campaign to weaponize the census in its war on undocumented immigrants, so the Supreme Court's decision to "overturn" the president's repeal of Obama's Deferred Action for Childhood Arrivals (DACA) policy did not impose a major constraint on presidential authority to remake immigration policy unilaterally. In fact, even though it labeled the president's administrative action's "arbitrary and capricious," the court tacitly recognized the president's authority to unilaterally terminate the policy so long as, in the future, it provided the rationale to do so at the time of repeal.[32] In effect, the justices offered the administration—or future administrations—a legal roadmap for repealing DACA, which the Trump administration soon embraced in the middle of his reelection campaign.[33]

Although battles over controversial measures to control the border and the rescission of DACA were divisive measures that garnered extraordinary media coverage, the contours of the modern administrative state also created multiple, subtler avenues for the exercise of presidential power. Seemingly benign changes add up and seep through departments and agencies that hold secondary, and even tertiary responsibility for policy change. Collaborating with anti-immigration activists who have staffed positions throughout the federal bureaucracy, Trump has deployed the full force of the executive branch to implement his desired policies, from revising the rules that the Department of Housing and Urban Development uses to curtail rental assistance to unauthorized migrants; to delaying and often suspending the enlistment of foreign-national military recruits; to Homeland Security's expansion of the "Public Charge" rule to prevent less fortunate migrants from coming to America and to deter legal and undocumented immigrants from accessing health, housing, and food assistance benefits; to establishing a new form of information sharing between the Office of Refugee Resettlement, which sits within Health and Human Services (HHS), and Immigration and Customs Enforcement (ICE), housed in the Department of Homeland Security, that puts those who seek to take custody of migrant children at risk of deportation.[34] The White House also instructed ICE officials to arrest unauthorized immigrants deep in the US interior, even targeting sensitive sites long viewed as off limits to immigration enforcement, such as courthouses and churches.[35]

Remaking the Welfare State

In addition to redeploying national state power to serve the president's pet causes in the name of fear, the Trump administration sought to recast social welfare policies to serve his base's conservative objectives. Trump's Department of Education (ED) Secretary Betsy DeVos had long championed local control of public schools, but once in power, she did not hesitate to take administrative measures that encouraged market-driven education reforms such as charter schools and vouchers.[36] DeVos thus weakened the authority of some department divisions while retooling and empowering others. Not surprisingly, ED's Office of Civil Rights lost much of the independent regulatory authority it built for itself over the previous decade. Trump issued an executive order in April 2017 that called for a review of the department's regulations and guidance documents;[37] four months later, DeVos rescinded the Obama-era "Dear Colleague letter" that universities and colleges used to adjudicate Title IX complaints.[38] In May 2020, while most schools were struggling mightily to come to terms with the coronavirus, ED issued a new rule that defined sexual assault more narrowly and enhanced procedural rights for accused students.[39] Just as DeVos repurposed the authority of the Office of Civil Rights, she also creatively used the department's student loan division to support for-profit colleges and universities and to protect student loan providers. By rewriting the gainful employment regulations and contracting with private collection agencies to more aggressively recoup student loan debt, the Department of Education was not weakened; rather, it was retooled to provide state support for for-profit education providers.[40]

Similarly, the Trump Justice Department sought to redefine decades of civil rights enforcement and to reshape the notion of whose rights the federal government should protect. Since its founding six decades ago, the Justice Department's civil rights division (CRD) had used the Constitution and federal law to expand protections of African Americans, gays, lesbians and transgender people, immigrants, and other minorities—efforts that have extended the government's reach from polling stations to police stations. During Republican administrations, the division has been restrained, particularly during the Reagan and George W. Bush presidencies. But civil rights enforcement was not curbed under Trump's attorneys general Jeff Sessions and William Barr; instead, it shifted to people of faith, police officers, and local government officials who maintained they had been treated with contempt by the federal government. The department supported state laws that could remove thousands of people from voter rolls; pulled back on the Obama administration's administrative oversight of police departments found to have violated the rights of citizens in their jurisdictions; supported religious conservatives in business and local government who resisted the advance of LBGTQ rights; and sided with plaintiffs challenging affirmative action plans in higher education.[41]

In redefining the mission of civil rights enforcement, the Trump administration did not gut the CRD; rather, it sought to repurpose it. In one telling example, the Trump White House started a new project to spearhead the redeployment of federal civil rights enforcement in higher education, which enlisted lawyers who were interested in working on "investigations and possible litigation related to intentional race-based discrimination in college and university admissions." The project did not operate out of the civil rights division's Educational Opportunities Section, where career Justice Department attorneys oversee cases on universities, but instead in the front office of the more politicized division.[42]

Perhaps the most telling example of the Trump administration's commitment to repurposing social welfare policies was its plan to reconstitute the Affordable Care Act (ACA), or Obamacare. After the Republican Congress failed to overturn Obamacare, largely because any conceivable plan violated the president's easy-to-digest campaign slogan, "repeal and replace," Trump's appointees to Health and Human Services resorted to an administrative approach to recast a centerpiece of the ACA: the extension of Medicaid benefits to those with annual incomes below 138% of the federal poverty level. Almost one year after taking office, the Trump administration informed each state's Medicaid office of a new demonstration project, encouraged by Republican governors' demands. With the permission of the Centers for Medicare and Medicaid (CMS), housed in HHS, states could rescind the Medicaid benefits of able-bodied adults if they were not seeking work or demonstrating active "community engagement." Amid legal battles that set aside work requirements in four states, six states received approval and 10 more states had waiver applications pending when Trump left office.[43] These administrative changes to the Affordable Care Act encouraged Republicans in the 17 states that had previously opposed Medicaid expansion to do so. But signaling the Trump administration's commitment to remake health benefits for the working poor, CMS director, Seema Verma, who worked with then governor Mike Pence to impose premiums on Medicaid recipients in Indiana, wanted to alert state leaders across the nation that a new era was dawning: some people would be required to work in exchange for Medicaid benefits.

The press and pundits viewed the Republicans' inability to repeal and replace Obamacare as a great failure. But with a waiver from CMS, state officials tried to remake healthcare for the poor into a more conservative program—to redeploy the most redistributive features of "Obamacare" through administrative fiat. In fact, because of the incentives these waivers provide for red states, Medicaid was projected to expand as a result of this policy—but only for individuals who live up to the conservative credo of the "deserving poor."[44]

In other areas of healthcare reform, the administration tied federal welfare benefits—an administrative decision—to the toxic politics of America's culture wars. Given the Trump administration's close ties with the Christian Right, it is not surprising that political appointees in HHS sought to reduce health benefits for the LGBTQ community and women seeking reproductive health services. In January 2018, HHS established a new division in its Office for Civil Rights (OCR), which was headed by Roger Severino: the Conscience and Religious Freedom Division (CRFD). According to HHS, CRFD was established to "more vigorously and effectively enforce existing laws protecting the rights of conscience and religious freedom." Prior to joining the Trump administration, Severino used his platform at the conservative think tank, the Heritage Foundation, to oppose the rule implementing the non-discrimination provision of the Affordable Care Act—Section 1557—since it agreed with a growing number of federal courts that interpreted gender identity discrimination as prohibiting sex discrimination. As director of the OCR, he was tasked with enforcing this rule. In a request for information titled "Removing Barriers for Religious and Faith-Based Organizations to Participate in HHS Programs and Receive Public Funding," Severino sought public comments from healthcare providers on potential changes to regulations or guidance. Some of the comments submitted—expressing the opposition of conservative healthcare providers to LGBTQ rights—seemed to foreshadow how his office's prioritization of and funding for the promotion of expansive religious exemptions would permit discrimination against transgender patients to go unchecked. More broadly, Severino issued a rule that radically redefined federal laws to expand religious, moral, and conscience exemptions that might reverse decades of case law expanding what constitutes discrimination on the basis of sex.[45]

The fractious state of American politics and the vast network of progressive social movements and advocacy groups that had formed during the Obama presidency ensured that Trump's executive actions in the service of conservatives would arouse ferocious opposition from the Democratic Party's base. Mounting a "Trump Resistance Movement," Progressive activists employed grassroots protest, social media, and legal action to protect the hard-won programmatic achievements in healthcare, immigration, climate change, and civil rights. Moreover, Black Lives Matter formed an aspirational coalition that championed comprehensive criminal justice reform, the rights of the LGBTQ community, and the protection of immigrants laboring under the heightened scrutiny of social and economic equality.[46] From the first day of his presidency, therefore, the Trump administration found itself governing in a political war zone, which grew all the more combative after Democrats took control of the House in the 2018 elections. Given the president' truculent temperament, it is hardly surprising that he responded in kind, using Twitter and mass rallies in small towns and non-urban areas to attack, indeed declare illegitimate, the insurgent opposition to his program.

Although the relationship between presidents and social movement organizations had become commonplace since the 1960s, Trump appeared to become especially dependent on conservative activists. As the president's poll numbers dropped to historically low numbers during the first year of his presidency and the administration became embroiled in a scandal that risked exposing collusion between his campaign and the Russian government and obstructive tactics to hinder Special Prosecutor Robert Mueller's investigation of potential high crimes and misdemeanors, Trump maintained the close ties to the leaders of the conservative movement that he had cultivated during the general election. Trump's efforts to take credit for a robust economy were at risk of being overshadowed by his championing of the issues that had become the template of movement conservatives over the past four decades: "traditional" family values, law and order, enhanced border security, opposition to affirmative civil rights policy, and the war against "radical Islamic terrorism." Relentlessly emphasizing these issues in the 2018 elections and his 2020 reelection effort, Trump doubled down on the politics of fear—conservative statism—gambling that the mobilization of a passionate base can substitute for the cultivation of a majority coalition.[47]

The 2018 midterms, which saw the Republicans lose 40 seats and control of the House, further revealed that Trump's partisan administration put moderate Republicans at risk. In effect, Trump's rancorous politics and the prerogatives of the modern presidency combined to forge a leaner and more united Republican Party. The Republican Party's support was increasingly confined to those places—rural and outer ring suburban areas—where Trump performed well in 2016. Of the 170 contested races that a Republican won in the 2018 midterms, the president's 2016 numbers outperformed the Republican candidate in 94 districts, or 55.3%. Trump won those districts with an average 58.8% of the vote while Republican congressional candidates averaged 59.1% of the vote. Trump thus tied the fate of Republican candidates to his political fortunes.[48]

Even in those many instances where Trump did not achieve policy successes, such as adding a citizenship question to the census form, the president further aroused his movement by blaming the "deep state" and "radical" Democrats. Trump was thus an instrumental figure in buttressing a highly personalized constituency, and through aggressive administrative action and a determined political strategy to remake the Republican Party, he further embittered partisan conflict. Joining executive prerogative, grassroots mobilization, and high stakes battles over domestic and foreign policy, executive-centered partisanship provided the Trump White House with a range of administrative and political powers to promote his agenda and to forge a visceral connection with his base of supporters who disdain the virtues of deliberation, compromise, and pragmatic governance.

Just how deeply ingrained partisan administration had become in American politics was dramatically on display when Trump became the third president of the United States to be impeached. The president's interference with independent counsel investigations, his refusal to comply with congressional subpoenas, and the condemnation of the press as "the enemy of the people" posed unprecedented dangers to the norms and institutions of liberal democracy. Yet the raw factionalism of Trump's impeachment revealed that the transformation of the party system has severely weakened the ability of Congress to hold the president accountable for abuses of power. Although the Mueller report did not directly accuse Trump of collusion to influence the 2016 election outcome, it was highly critical of his behavior. The report's criticisms, emphasizing the president's efforts to obstruct the independent counsel's investigation, were not sufficiently exculpatory to incite an impeachment inquiry. But revelations in the fall of 2019 concerning his attempts to pressure Ukraine to investigate the "corruption" of then leading Democratic candidate former vice president Joe Biden and his son Hunter, led to the eruption of a full-blown impeachment inquiry.

As news broke that the president had withheld much needed military assistance to Ukraine and made its release contingent upon a politically motivated investigation that would target his potential Democratic Party opponent in 2020, the extraordinary events fit a predictable pattern. The president and his allies denounced the proceedings as a partisan "witch hunt"; Democrats closed ranks and relentlessly pursued the impeachment and trial of the president with virtually no support from Republicans. Many hoped that the calm presentation of facts and hours of deposition by respected foreign service officers might have persuaded at least a few minds. But, as it turned out, the drama peaked during a show-down vote in the Senate on whether to permit witnesses. Just two Republicans broke party lines: Susan Collins and Mitt Romney. Romney then became the first senator in history to vote to convict a president of his or her own party. The vote to remove Trump from office on February 5, 2020, fell fourteen votes shy of the constitutionally required two-thirds majority.

The partisan fury of the Trump impeachment was not in itself unexpected. As Alexander Hamilton wrote in *Federalist 65*, "[Impeachment] will seldom fail to agitate the passions of the whole community. . . . [It] will enlist all their animosities, partialities, influence and interest on one side or on the other; and in such cases there will always be the greatest danger that the decision will be regulated more by the comparative strength of parties, than by the real demonstrations of innocence or guilt." The impeachment of Andrew Johnson and Bill Clinton seriously agitated the nation. Even Nixon's reckoning was a highly partisan affair until a "smoking gun" was discovered. Yet Hamilton could not have envisioned how the fusion of presidential power and ritualized partisan combat, which reached a dangerous culmination during the Trump presidency, made the public and its representatives recklessly coarse to constitutional norms.

Indeed, the president's actions were a direct consequence of the political developments that have given rise to executive-centered partisanship. Trump and his Republican allies defended his actions by invoking the progressive conceit—embraced by conservatives in the wake of the polarizing conflicts of the 1960s—that the president embodies the national interest. The mystique of presidentialism led Congress to delegate immense power to the executive, with little oversight, further conflating the president's personal or partisan goals with the nation's foreign policy. Trump deployed the powers of the modern executive office with more impunity than his predecessors. Yet his indiscretions exploited the precedents set by Congress and the courts, which have emboldened presidents to carry out a vast array of policies unilaterally, to withhold appropriated funds, to undertake major foreign policy initiatives secretly, and to direct intelligence and law enforcement agencies to do the president's bidding. Few defenders of the separation of powers will find consolation in the fact that the public, let alone members of Congress, were only aware of Trump's Ukrainian machinations because documents were illegally leaked.

Trump's usurpations were abetted by the subordination of institutional to partisan loyalties. In a political context where the political fate of Democrats and Republicans depends on the fortunes of their respective party's president, achieving bipartisan support for holding the White House accountable is highly unlikely. Given how deeply executive-centered partisanship is now rooted in American democracy, it is hardly surprising that reactions to the president's behavior fell along predictable party lines and counterarguments from both sides fell on deaf ears. In the never-ending campaign season, Republican senators played to the president's base with "deep state" conspiracy theories promoted by Fox News and conservative talk radio. Determined not to let a good business opportunity go to waste, Trump's campaign used the impeachment proceedings to motivate Republicans to open their pocketbooks. Ads poured out of the Republican National Committee (RNC) targeting the president's "most LOYAL supporters." Certain fundraising ads even permitted donors to jointly contribute to the accounts of Republican nominees in districts targeting vulnerable House Democrats who had voted to impeach the president.[49] During the last quarter of 2019, as the impeachment proceedings followed a predictable course, the president's campaign hauled in more than $46 million, including donations from 600,000 new donors, exceeding any previous record.[50] On the eve of the House's vote to impeach the first US president running for reelection, Trump's campaign manager practically celebrated: "That has put money in our bank. It has added volunteers to our field program. It's filled up the rallies easier."[51]

Nixon's pioneering and corrupt advance of executive-centered partisanship resulted in efforts to restore the "guardrails" of liberal democracy. One might hope that the Trump impeachment episode and its aftermath—in which the White House took retribution against career diplomats and civil servants in the Justice and State Departments as well as the intelligence agencies who testified in the impeachment investigations or waivered in their support of the president—might result in a renewed effort to restore constitutional norms and institutional constraints. But, as the final year of the Trump presidency and the early days of the Biden administration made all too clear, those who seek to restore the restraints or refinements of institutions must face the imposing obstacle of a government that for years has sacrificed responsible leadership to aggressive and resolute partisan administration. As Democrats and Republicans have come to rely on partisan administration to fulfill their collective goals, they have ceded greater authority to the White House.

This commitment to executive prerogative has gone hand in hand with the denigration of the bureaucracy as a site of policy expertise. The increasing consolidation of policy responsibility in the White House Office as well as the partisan and politicized shape of the federal government's senior appointments since the Nixon years are a visible corollary of the state in perpetual redeployment. It is an ineluctable implication of the "unitary executive" since presidents want to appoint civil servants who will deploy state resources in the president's preferred way.[52] As David Lewis points out, the civil service has been under assault at least since the Reagan presidency.[53] Moreover, the Trump administration, through savvy conservative populists like the West Wing's immigration czar Stephen Miller, installed handpicked political appointees across key departments and agencies, many recruited from conservative social movement networks and organizations, who exploited the ennui of the federal bureaucracy.[54] Although his network was not as extensive as Miller's, Peter Navarro, who headed the White House Office of Trade and Manufacturing, outflanked more moderate voices in the West Wing and regular departments and agencies in the formulation of the Trump administration's controversial trade policies.[55] Given the outsize influence of Miller and Navarro, the politics and policies pertaining to the pillars of Trump's America First agenda—immigration and trade—were insulated from regular bureaucratic procedures. And even though Trump, Miller, and Navarro no longer control these administrative levers, the Trump White House's influence might be indelible. The rapidity of change afforded to modern administration successfully produced real, tangible results; these were not plans; they were not proposals. Government acted, and lives changed. Moreover, Trump partisan administrators left an inestimable precedent for future administrators, who can act with similar speed and limited oversight.

Fear abounds that the Trump presidency has gone so far in hollowing out and intimidating valued political servants in many departments and agencies that restoring a measure of bureaucratic autonomy that moderates rancorous partisanship and constrains executive aggrandizement might prove impossible. Conservative Republicans have demonized civil servants since the Reagan administration. But in the past, civil servants could lie low and bide their time until a more supportive administration occupied the executive branch. The Trump administration sent a message that all career staff are suspect, indeed, enemies of the people, who should be forced out of the government or made completely subservient to political appointees.[56] The administration's hostility even extended to traditionally conservative agencies, such as the FBI. Characteristic of executive-centered partisanship, the Trump administration's "deconstruction of the administrative state" was selective—but conservative state-building in Homeland Security, the Defense Department, and Veterans Affairs emphasized empowering Trump loyalists and tasking career employees and civil servants with the unenviable task of maintaining their professional integrity amid disruptive and polarizing tactics that have fractured the nation.[57] The maintenance of professionalism was even a problem for the military establishment—the most respected government institution—which fretted over the possibility of losing its prized credibility while assuming the challenging task of explaining the president's bellicose tweets and controversial actions, such as the drone strike on Iranian general Qassem Soleimani, which risked a dangerous escalation of bellicosity between the United States and Iran.[58]

America at Low Ebb

Expressing the fears of many commentators in spring 2020, the distinguished *Washington Post* columnist, Dan Balz, observed an "America at its lowest ebb": "Pain and destruction strangle hopes and dreams of people across the country. People are dying—alone from a terrible virus or from a knee on the neck in full public view. Cities burn, destroying businesses and inflaming divisions. Tens of millions are out of work. The president makes it all worse."[59] Rather than unifying the country as a devastating pandemic infected 2 million Americans, the president targeted "deep state" public health experts such as the highly regarded Dr. Anthony Fauci, director of the National Institute of Allergy and Infectious Diseases (NIAID), pushing them to the sidelines so that he could hasten the reopening of the economy. Stoking his base with machoistic remonstrances in the face of a highly contagious and sometimes deadly virus, he refused to wear a face mask, which public health experts insisted was one of the few effective prophylactics that could slow the spread of infection. The Trump administration thus turned facecloth coverings into a polarizing symbol that sharply divided Red and Blue America. The face mask became a proxy for a polarizing struggle over how soon to lift the lockdown that had led to the worst recession since the Great Depression.

Political psychologists puzzled over surveys that showed conservatives, who in the past had shown greater fear of communicable disease that traveled across the border (obsessing about "purity"), such as the Ebola outbreak during the Obama administration, strongly backing the president's call to confidently—in scientists' understanding brazenly—return to normality. Summarizing a number of such studies that confirmed the power of executive-centered partisanship, *New York Times* columnist Thomas Edsall wrote, "The pandemic has become another example of Trump's mastery over his most loyal subjects, his ability to manipulate them into violating their own instincts. It is this power over a substantial bloc of the electorate that has put him in the White House—and continues to make him so dangerous."[60]

The potential danger became all too clear on Wednesday, April 15, when a demonstration formed outside the Michigan statehouse in Lansing, where a group of protesters—many of them wearing MAGA hats and brandishing menacing firearms (one waved a confederate flag)— demanded an end to the policy declared by that state's Democratic governor, Gretchen Whitmer, of locking down her state's homes, schools, and businesses to protect people from the spreading coronavirus that had ravaged her constituents. On the same day, smaller demonstrations were mounted in Virginia and Minnesota, but the movement spread rapidly across the country. By the weekend, rallies were being held in six other states, most of them led by Democratic governors but including Republican-led Texas and Maryland, where the governors had been cautious in their commitment to opening the economy. Maryland governor Larry Hogan—one of the rare moderates still standing in the Republican Party—had been especially harsh in his criticisms of the administration's failure to provide fiscal support to the states. Resembling the Tea Party demonstrations that erupted during Obama's first term, these rallies were in part the product of spontaneous groundswells of opinion on the part of citizens worried about the collapse of their states' economies and in part the result of behind the scenes orchestration by well-heeled interest groups. Whether there were formal organizations behind the protests became a moot question when the president, seizing the mantle of a popular leader at the vanguard of a revolt against the deep state, grabbed the attention of the media by strongly endorsing the protests, which took direct action against rules that reflected the guidelines of his own administration's Center for Disease Control and Prevention (CDC) for restarting the economy:

"LIBERATE MICHIGAN!" the president tweeted on Friday, April 17.
"LIBERATE MINNESOTA!"
"LIBERATE VIRGINIA," he concluded, adding that the protesters should also "save your great 2nd Amendment. It is under siege!"[61]

This call to arms—presaging the January 6 insurrection at the Capitol—seemed especially incendiary months later, when the FBI foiled anti-government vigilantes plotting to kidnap and execute Governor Whitmer.

As the battles raged for the right to define the appropriate response to the pandemic, President Trump used the levers of the administrative state to advance his Make America Great agenda. The White House had been criticized for its lax response to the crisis, with critics charging that it failed to act quickly enough to thwart the virus's spread and deflected responsibility to the states for ramping up testing and procuring critical medical supplies. Yet through the late spring and into the summer, the Trump administration aggressively imposed tighter restrictions on immigration, relaxed environmental regulations, advocated stricter curbs on voting, persisted in its efforts to undermine the Affordable Care Act, and continued its aggressive push to imprint the Trump brand on the judiciary. In some cases, Trump was using the country's preoccupation with a public health crisis to continue the deployment of administrative power for controversial conservative policies pushed by advocacy groups and favored by his base. In others, especially in matters pertaining to immigration, the president and key White House aides used the broad powers granted the executive branch amid a national crisis to pursue policy goals he had long sought but struggled to achieve. From the earliest days of the Trump administration, Steven Miller had tried repeatedly, without success, to use an obscure law to protect the nation from disease overseas as a justification to tighten borders. In imposing restrictions under the cover of the pandemic, he relied not only on the public health authority but also on section 221 (f) of the Immigration and Nationality Act that grants sweeping power to the executive—but under circumstances that set a high legal bar for its use. Following the mantra of former Obama White House chief of staff Rahm Emanuel to "never allow a crisis to go to waste," Miller took advantage of the pandemic to pursue policy goals, such as finding a way to quickly deport children who travel to the United States with a parent or guardian, without regard for the substantial due process requirements designed to ensure that deportation would not place them in harm's way.[62]

Trump's response to the pandemic thus continued the top-down, bottom-up strategy of executive-centered partisanship. Rather than attempt to reprise the modern executive as the steward of the public welfare that many journalists and public figures longed for in a national crisis of the highest order, he chose to follow the play book of partisan administration, bringing the fusion of executive prerogative and partisanship to a new and incendiary place as demonstrations broke out in response to George Floyd's death. While the protests spread throughout the country—and eventually the world—an overwhelming number of Americans supported the demonstrators and accepted a truth long denied, or resisted, that Floyd's death was a sign of systemic racial injustices. Predictably, Trump declared himself the president of law and order, praised most law enforcement officers as "great people," and threatened to treat protesters, portrayed as "terrorists," with overwhelming—"dominating"—force. Yet a Monmouth poll released a week after the protests began found that 57% of Americans—including a majority of White people—said the anger that led to the protests was completely justified. Even among self-described conservatives, 65% said the protesters' frustrations were at least partly justified. These sentiments were especially striking among younger individuals surveyed, with 52% of Republicans under 55 indicating they believed the killing of Floyd was evidence of a broader problem.[63]

Standing against this tide, Trump believed, as Richard Nixon did at the birth of a new Republican Party, that a "silent majority" supported his commitment to "traditional values." Living not just in rural and exurban areas but also in working-class suburbs like Macomb County outside of Detroit, these voters and potential voters, even if disgusted by police violence, were not joining the protests.[64] Although a declining part of the population, the "coalition of restoration" — blue-collar, religiously devout, and nonurban Whites — had already developed such an atavistic relationship with Trump that, as the 2016 election showed, they could amplify their influence in a presidential election, especially in the Electoral College that gives disproportionate influence to those areas of the country that support Trump.

In an episode confirming that the January 6 riot was not an isolated incident, Trump decided to make a direct appeal to his "most loyal customers." As demonstrations around the country took a militant turn on Sunday, May 31, racial justice protesters encamped in Lafayette Square—just north of the White House—grew so restless that the president was forced to briefly retreat to a bunker. Angered that the press painted a picture of him hiding from the cascading rebellion against police brutality and systemic racism, the president staged a dramatic rejoinder. Summoning the press to the Rose Garden the following afternoon, he declared himself an "ally of all peaceful demonstrators," but, more emphatically, "Your President of Law and Order." For emphasis, he berated state and local governments for failing to control demonstrations "gripped by professional anarchists, violent mobs, arsonists, looters, criminals, rioters, Antifa, and others"—and threatened to deploy the military to "dominate the streets." As an object lesson in force, just before Trump made his statement, a squadron of military police descended on peaceful demonstrators who had reassembled in Lafayette Square. An Inspector General's report later found that U.S. Park Police had a plan to clear the park, and that it did not communicate it with the White House. But, Secret Service agents arrived – who do not take orders from the U.S. Park Police – and, without warning, used pepper spray and tear gas to clear out a perimeter for what in effect was a choreographed photo-op, meant to depict the president as a strong defender of conservative values.[65]

Marching across the path cleared of dissenters, Trump strode to the patio of the historic St. John's Church, which had been slightly damaged by a fire in Sunday's unrest. He made no formal remarks, but held aloft the Bible his daughter Ivanka had pulled from her $1,540 Max Mara Bag—calling to mind Sinclair Lewis's Elmer Gantry assuring his avid followers, "We shall yet make these United States a moral nation." The president then gathered his accomplices—Ivanka; her husband Jared Kushner; Attorney General Barr; General Milley; and Secretary of Defense Mark Esper—for a group photo that did not include a single person of color. Having accomplished his purpose, Trump headed back to the White House—boasting on Twitter the next morning: "Many arrests. Great job done by all. Overwhelming force. Dominance." By Tuesday afternoon, however, the crowds were back and even bigger.[66]

The battle of Lafayette Square, not surprisingly, also divided religious leaders. Clergy of established churches, including Bishop Mariann Edgar Budde of the Episcopal Diocese of Washington, who was not consulted beforehand, were outraged over the use of an iconic religious site as a political backdrop to boast of squelching protests against racism. But the president's evangelical base was ecstatic over the president's counterdemonstration. As Robert Jefreess, a Dallas megachurch pastor, told the *Atlantic*, he thought the moment was "completely appropriate." "By holding up the Bible," he added, "[the president] was showing us that it teaches that, yes, God hates racism, it's despicable—but God also hates lawlessness."[67]

Conclusion

Throughout his four years in office, Trump exposed the inability, or unwillingness, of congressional Republicans or leaders in the statehouses to serve as gatekeepers of the party's collective responsibility; he also revealed during his first term how the national committee and state organizations could be readily captured by a president who has excoriated the party "establishment" in his ascent to the White House.

Obama constructed a parallel organization alongside the Democratic National Committee to advance his partisan objectives, thus subordinating party politics to presidential ambition; Trump engaged in a hostile takeover of the Republican Party, pushing the Republican Party's rearguard to the margins. Neither president was a champion of collective party politics; however, Trump's populist demagogy threatened to turn the Grand Old Party into a cult of personality.

Indeed, rather than stand apart from the Republican apparatus, Trump engaged in a determined effort to remake its national and state committees in his own image. To accomplish this, the campaign staff in Trump Tower and the RNC orchestrated a state-by-state assault on the party organization by placing Trump loyalists in powerful positions within the state party organizations, allowing them to more easily change party rules governing the selection of delegates for the national convention. Trump's selection of a former state party leader, Ronna Romney McDaniel, as the National Republican Chairwoman proved invaluable in this respect, as the Trump machine succeeded even in states where the president performed poorly in 2016. For example, the Trump-backed candidate for state party chairman in Massachusetts, Jim Lyons, defeated the candidate supported by the vocal Trump critic and Republican governor, Charlie Baker.

Through his heavy-handed approach to remove independently inclined Republican officeholders and dominate state party organizations, Trump went far to purge the remnants of the Never Trumpers who opposed his reelection and worked to support the election of more moderate Republicans to Congress or state and local governments. While some congressional and gubernatorial Republicans expressed concern about Trump's visceral partisanship in matters pertaining to the coronavirus, immigration, and the protests against unjust police practices, those voices were the frail vestiges of collective partisan responsibility. As Daniel Galvin has concluded in his careful study of Trump's relationship with the GOP, "although divisive issues that generate public dissent from Republicans will undoubtedly continue to emerge, the main storyline of Trump's party leadership through early 2020 has been his domination and personalization of the Republican Party."[68] So much was clear in primary battles down ballot, as elder Republican statesmen had to fend off insurgencies from self-styled Trump candidates in Republican strongholds, such as Alabama, Arizona, and West Virginia. In fact, even insurgents who succeeded in defeating more establishment candidates whom Trump supported in House Republican primaries—Robert Good of Virginia and Madison Cawthorn of North Carolina—proudly proclaimed that they were more Trump-like than the candidates Trump endorsed.

Leaving no doubt that the Republican Party had fully become the Party of Trump, the RNC passed a sycophantic resolution before the 2020 national convention that convened in Charlotte at the end of August. The resolution announced that for first time since its first presidential campaign in 1856, there would be no platform. Instead, the Resolution made clear its whole-hearted commitment to Donald Trump, pledging "to enthusiastically support the president's America-first agenda."[69]

Because Trump seemed to embrace rather than fall victim to the dynamics of executive-centered partisanship, one of the more hopeful signs about the future of American politics is that the Democratic Party has proved to be more resilient in the face of the populist challenges that have been roiling the nation since the late 1960s. The party activists who emerged with the civil rights and anti-war movements set in motion populist assaults on the separation of powers and party organizations—giving rise to the dismantling of the convention system, the weakening of the state and local party organizations, and the erosion of the linchpins that sustained an independent Congress as well as constitutional federalism. Yet this insurgency was given institutional effect by advocacy groups and elected officials who remained committed to remaking rather than dismantling the institutional arrangements of the New Deal state. Consequently, Obama—the lineal descendant of the civil rights movement—viewed his task as restoring the transcendent status of the modern executive. As shown by the pioneering information grassroots organization he formed, he sought to infuse the executive-centered administrative state with populist enthusiasm—to strengthen the coalition of the ascendant that represented the maturing of the Great Society. Obama's electoral and policy alliance with Organizing for Action (OFA) greatly upgraded the Democratic Party's voter outreach by expanding the national voter file started by the Democratic National Committee (DNC) in 2006. Moreover, the president's effective use of volunteers in campaigns and policy advocacy enlivened the party with an expanded grassroots presence. For example, the number of Democratic campaign volunteers rose from roughly 252,000 in 2004 to 2.2 million in 2012. This upgraded campaign capacity was joined to effective policy advocacy, as Obama and his information-age grassroots organization turned controversial issues, including immigration, gay rights, and climate change, to the Democrats' advantage. Although dedicated to pragmatic, compromised policies that fell short of the democratic socialist solutions championed by the party's intransigent left wing, such as the Affordable Care Act or the Wall Street Reform and Consumer Protection Act (Dodd-Frank), the first African American president developed a tense alliance with social movements that emerged in the wake of the Iraq War and the Great Recession.

As the 2016 election showed, however, Obama's popularity was not portable. Although Obama's two terms established him as the most popular politician in the Democratic Party—Obama's approval rating was almost 87%—the president's endorsement of the new Democratic flag-bearer carried little weight with his core constituencies. Hillary Clinton failed to ignite enthusiasm particularly among young and African American voters who Obama and his personal organization mobilized so effectively in 2008 and 2012. The president's fraught alliance with the Black Lives Matter movement further limited the party's collective position on behalf of racial justice. This uneasy relationship followed from Obama's tempered view of the presidency. Obama styled himself as a leader of a new progressive coalition, but he distinguished between social activism, on the one hand, and forging a consensus and governing, on the other. He thus presided over a party that had become more liberal on his watch but remained far more committed to practical policy solutions than the Republicans.[70] Obama thus began to construct a new left of center coalition—a new Democratic establishment—that responded to the populism represented by Sanders without being fully captured by it.[71]

It was the support of this nascent progressive establishment that enabled Obama's loyal vice president, Joe Biden, to withstand the populist insurgency of the Sanders revolution after a four-year hiatus. Biden's remarkable victory over Sanders and a large field of contenders for the 2020 Democratic nomination followed from his ability to rally the diverse coalition that Obama summoned, which was united by the pragmatic imperative of beating Donald Trump. Without such a polarizing figure in office to attack, the moderate position within the Democratic Party would not have been able to muster a viable message. Even with the galvanizing force of Trump, it still looked as though Sanders was poised to ride the momentum he built during 2016 and the early 2020 nomination contests in Iowa, New Hampshire, and Nevada to a first ballot nomination. But Biden's flagging campaign was resurrected by one of the few sites of institutional resilience in the Democratic Party—Representative James Clyburn's political organization in South Carolina. Clyburn—the House's Democratic Whip and a member of Congress since 1993—used his homestyle resources and connections to rally African American voters to deliver the former vice president's stunning 28-point victory. South Carolina set up a rapid domino effect that saw the leading moderate contenders—Pete Buttigieg and Amy Klobuchar—end their campaigns and endorse Biden, helping the former vice president consolidate left of center Democrats in the Super Tuesday contests and squelch the gilded age insurgency of former New York mayor and multi-billionaire, Michael Bloomberg. After Biden handily beat Sanders in Florida, Illinois, and Arizona, he became the presumptive Democratic nominee, thwarting the Democratic socialist's incursion much sooner and far more decisively than Hillary Clinton had done four years earlier. The imperatives of booting Trump from office motivated Sanders and his base to rally around Biden in the general election—a pragmatic impulse that failed to ignite four years earlier when Sanders's voters remained cold to Clinton, indeed, somewhat beguiled by Trump's economic nationalism.

When Biden won election over Donald Trump, most institutionalists breathed a sigh of collective relief. The guardrails of American democracy seemed to hold, proving surprisingly resilient after four years of the Trump administration's aggressive assault on the "establishment." Although the highly competitive and bellicose nature of the campaign and its hazardous conclusion point toward Trumpism's endurance, the peaceful transfer of power, no matter how fraught, and the election of a moderate, elder statesman might portend something good for America's governing institutions.

Such hopes are not without merit. As we have argued since the first chapter, populist insurgency has endued the Republican Party with messianic fervor while the Democratic Party has become a complex, combustible mixture of pragmatism and movement politics. Amid the massive disruption of 2020, however, the fate of Biden's coalition-building and the prospects of renewing the idea of a party system in American politics remained highly uncertain. As we discuss in the final chapter, the new president was confident that his administration could avoid the cauldron of partisan polarization that Trump so eagerly embraced. He promised a return to some sense of normalcy—a restoration of the modern executive as a transcendent institution that would moderate rather than incite rancorous party conflict. Yet George W. Bush and Barack Obama had also promised to be uniters rather than dividers only to see their presidencies engulfed by the fundamental battles over identity that made bipartisan leadership a chimera. In truth, Bush and Obama were not victims of the party wars. Amid confrontations that tested their mettle, they practiced the art of executive-centered partisanship that stoked the country's political divisions. Following in the wake of a president who relished partisan warfare and exploited the pathologies at the heart of contemporary American politics, we should be wary of the restorative potential of President Biden. The restoration of American democracy will require more than presidential leadership, not matter how savvy. Only a willingness to think institutionally can ameliorate the causes of our present discontents.

7

Conclusion

Executive-Centered Partisanship and the Future of American Democracy

Democracy is about winning and losing. And every four years, the rhythms of America's constitutional republic guarantee that one presidential candidate will win and another will lose.

Previous losers have sought relief in the courts to support their claims that critical ballots might not have comported with constitutional and legal requirements. Most dramatically, George W. Bush and Al Gore took their legal fight all the way to the Supreme Court in the 2000 election; after the Court in the appropriately named case of *Bush v. Gore* ruled against him, Gore stepped aside, and conceded defeat. Donald Trump never did, even after each of the 63 lawsuits challenging alleged election irregularities were thrown out of court for lack of evidence.

Most ex-presidents have been conciliatory in their loss; and some have conceded, not only to their opponents but to the "will of the people." On the night he lost to Bill Clinton, former President George H. W. Bush praised the "majesty of the democratic system"; on the Resolute Desk, he penned a note to the new president: "Your success now is our country's success. I am rooting hard for you. Good Luck."[1] Trump became the first outgoing president since Andrew Johnson to skip his successor's inauguration. Snubbing the ritual that has symbolized the resilience of American democracy since the Civil War, he and the First Lady, Melania Trump boarded a helicopter on the White House lawn in the early morning hours, the start of a journey to the former president's Elba, Mar-a-Lago, Florida.

Of course, not all transitions between administrations have gone smoothly. Before Franklin Roosevelt's fabled First One Hundred Days, Herbert Hoover regarded the "bold, persistent experimentation" that he promised during the 1932 campaign as portending the illegitimate use of presidential and federal power. Hoover insisted during the transition period that the incoming administration fend for itself. Still, Hoover did attend Roosevelt's inauguration as a sign of his reluctant but firm acceptance of a peaceful transition of power. In contrast, not only did Donald Trump refuse to attend his sucessor's inauguration; he also misused his managerial authority to delay the release of important government records and national security details to the incoming Biden administration until just weeks before he took office.

Trump and his allies were determined to do more than gum up the works. On January 6, 2021, the president stood in front of the White House and denounced the legitimacy of the election he lost decisively. His supporters, who had traveled across the country to attend a massive "Stop the Steal" rally, then descended on the Capitol building. For weeks, the president and his allies had concocted every conceivable tale of fraud and had twisted every possibility of voting irregularity to prop up the myth that Trump was the true winner. "We won in a landslide," he repeatedly claimed. "This was a landslide. They said it's not American to challenge the election. This [is] the most corrupt election in the history, maybe of the world. . . . With your help over the last four years, we built the greatest political movement in the history of our country and nobody even challenges that. . . . We fight like hell. And if you don't fight like hell, you're not going to have a country anymore."[2]

Marching on the Capitol, Trump's band of self-styled patriots, with far-right militia groups such as the Proud Boys at the vanguard, heeded the president's call. Brandishing Confederate flags, crowbars, knives, zip-tie handcuffs, and guns, the insurrectionists broke windows, overwhelmed police barricades, and stormed into the hallways of the Capitol as legislators met to certify the Electoral College votes. Startled viewers watched live coverage of an armed mob racing through the corridors of the People's House to hunt down individual members of Congress, including Speaker Nancy Pelosi and the presiding officer, Vice President Mike Pence, who had just received the brunt of the president's scorn on Twitter: "Mike Pence didn't have the courage to do what should have been done to protect our Country and our Constitution." Perhaps more than any of his predecessors, Trump revealed the power—and the potential peril—of the president's words. These provocations made history: Trump became the first president to use the "bully pulpit" to sow distrust in a free and fair election and overturn the constitutional process for ensuring a peaceful transition of power. Other presidents had stoked the base, fueled discord, and benefited from creating deep societal divisions. But Trump will always have the dubious distinction of being the first president to actively court a movement to "fight like hell," to win at all costs, even if it meant violence against the government.

Although unprecedented, the insurrection can be understood as a symptom of the developments we have charted in this book. We are not so bold as to claim that the theory of executive-centered partisanship would have enabled us to predict an unfathomable rebellion, led by a sitting president, to overturn the foundational rock of self-government. But Trump's incitement, and the political aftermath, cannot be understood without taking account of how presidential aggrandizement and movement politics have converged since the outbreak of the culture wars during the 1960s. Even after the president encouraged an insurrection to prevent the certification of a free and fair election, Trump's spell over the Republican Party persisted. Just hours after donning gas masks as police officers armed with automatic weapons escorted the vice president, Speaker of the House, and each member of Congress to secure and undisclosed locations in the Capitol, 139 House Republicans and eight Republican senators still voted against certifying some of the Electoral College votes. With unwavering loyalty to Trump—and a lot of posturing for the next presidential nomination—they persisted in their assault on the ramparts of democracy, on behalf of millions of Republican loyalists who had invested their political faith in a charismatic leader who presumed to embody their party.

Some Republicans defected. In the House, 10 members of the GOP voted to impeach the president for his incitement of the insurrection, and seven of their fellow partisans in the Senate voted to convict him, even though his term had expired. Trump departed office without a sound (Twitter had suspended the president's account, which might explain his uncharacteristic silence). But three days after his Senate impeachment acquittal—his second—nearly 60% of Republicans said they wanted Trump to remain active in the party; over half said that he was already their first choice in the 2024 primaries. As William Galston summarized in February 2021, "State and county Republican Party organizations across the country are censuring elected officials who broke with Mr. Trump to support his impeachment in the House and conviction in the Senate. The Trump base has anathematized even Trump loyalists such as former Vice President Mike Pence, who honored their oath of office. These supporters will not countenance anything short of unswerving fealty to Mr. Trump."[3]

Whether out of fear of facing the wrath of the Republican base or devotion to Trump's promise to make "America Great Again," party officials—leaders in name only—also fell into line. In early March, Trump was invited back to the annual Conservative Political Action Conference, where he stoked the base and derided Biden as having "the most disastrous first month of any president in modern history." He regularly entertained Republicans at Mar-a-Lago, demanding that they stop giving money to "RINOS"—Republicans in Name Only—who "will never lead us to Greatness."[4] Rarely in American history has a national party committee remained wedded to a vanquished incumbent president; yet the RNC continued to honor Trump, his message to defend America First, and his incendiary rhetoric in its fundraising materials. Two Republican senators with presidential ambitions, Ted Cruz and Josh Hawley, both of whom voted against certifying the voting results in swing states that Biden won, continued to peddle Trump's populist vision of a country torn asunder by politically correct elites. Their greatest contempt was reserved for those "woke" leaders of Major League Baseball and large corporations who opposed the post-election efforts by Republicans to keep Democrats from voting in future elections. In many Republican-controlled states, justified by the "Big Lie" that the 2020 election had been fraudulent, legislators enacted "reform" bills that would make it more difficult for Democratic constituencies, especially African Americans and Latinos, to vote. Speaking against the large corporations that had opposed the new laws, Hawley insisted that government should "bust them up."[5]

Trump, only the tenth president to be defeated in a reelection bid, nevertheless remained at the center of Republican politics. Part personality, part institutional decay—a toxic combination of raw power, polarization, and sectarian identity—the Trump presidency dramatically revealed how a populist demagogue could command a party with diminished organizational capacity. His polarizing response to the global pandemic, resistance to the racial reckoning brought on by George Floyd's murder, and refusal to concede electoral defeat were signs that the top-down, bottom-up strategy of executive-centered partisanship poses an existential threat to liberal democracy. As exceptional and rare a personality as Trump might be, his ascendance is unthinkable in the absence of the systemic changes that have remade political institutions and transformed partisanship over the past 60 years.

It remains to be seen, as some scholars have argued, whether the ferocious opposition to Trump's leadership offers an opportunity to ameliorate the pathologies that plague American political life.[6] His failure to win reelection, in a brutal and very closely contested campaign, leaves us with the question of whether Donald Trump's leadership has left an enduring imprint on the American polity. Have we reached the peak of executive-centered partisanship? Do the election and early days in office of Joe Biden—a leader who displays a studied aversion to self-aggrandizement—suggest a return to normality or the emergence of a different model of presidential power, party politics, and political gamesmanship? These are the pressing questions that now confront a polity that has been shaken at its core.

Realists, Romantics, and Institutional Imagination

In no way will Biden's presidency mirror that of Trump's. But it might display more continuities with his predecessor's style of leadership than partisans and pundits believe. At a personal level, Biden is the anti-Trump, but he is not immune from the systemic conditions presidents confront, which sustain the working arrangements of executive-centered partisanship. Some have suggested that Donald Trump's mismanagement of the worst national crisis since the Great Depression should have sentenced him to the fate of what Stephen Skowronek calls "a late regime affiliate"—like Herbert Hoover or Jimmy Carter—and resulted in a severe political reckoning: "the final repudiation of a bankrupt conservative political order and the rise of a new progressive regime."[7] And yet, while personally defeated, Trump still reigned over his party and reveled in the adulation of its base supporters. He received over 11 million more votes than he did when first elected, and Joe Biden could hardly claim a mandate from the slim majority of voters he won.

Transformative presidential leadership—the illusory vision of a unifying, transcendent leader—maintains its hold over scholars and columnists who, no matter how much they may disdain partisan polarization, cannot paper over the deep divisions sown into American society and which have grown wider since the late 1960s. Many commentators, especially political activists, when considering populist unrest, propose that the remedy to what ails democracy is more democracy; in effect, this might only further fracture the country and weaken national resolve. As the institutions and processes that once restrained democratic politics from its worst tendencies have been hollowed out over the last fifty years, populism has become a more regular and dangerous feature of self government tin the United States. "Although [democracy] has some theoretical affinity for liberty, equality and fairness," Robert Wiebe warned, "it does not provide reliable, concrete support for any of these grand concepts. Democracy. . . reveals our humanity, not our salvation. We may not like it."[8]

Our account of party development, especially since the 1960s, places us alongside a growing group of political scientists who are skeptical about the causal effects unleashed by democratic reform—a venerable tradition that dates back to the critics of the 1950s Political Science Association Committee (APSA) report on political parties.[9] On one level, we agree with many of these "realist" sentiments and prescriptions. Like Ray La Raja and Brian Schaffner, we agree that reforms to root out the corrupting influence of campaign contributions rarely, if ever, lead to less money in politics; instead, that money flows to outside groups that are less prone to compromise than an established political party.[10] We also agree with the analyses of the distinguished Congress scholars, Frances Lee and Sarah Binder, who show how efforts to make the legislative process more transparent and participatory have reduced Congress's capacity to negotiate and justify policy compromises to a now ever-watching constituency.[11] And, like Bruce Cain, we do not equate the spread of direct democracy through institutions like the open primary with the establishment of a fully participatory electorate; indeed, the reforms had the opposite effect: reducing participation rates and concentrating power among a very distinct minority of primary voters.[12]

Yet we also recognize that these calls to rethink the "romantic" conception of democracy can be inured to the seismic changes in American political life. It is tough to think that our political divisions would be healed if C-Span turned off the cameras every once in a while, or that an earmark here or there would unleash a tidal wave of legislative correctives from Congress—or even if such reforms would make a difference at the margins. More pointedly, many Americans, maybe most, embrace the romantic ideal of democratic empowerment and believe that the procedural reforms to get us closer to "pure democracy" have not gone far enough. If the "pragmatic" and insular politics of a previous era that proved indifferent to the stubborn tumor of Jim Crow and American adventurism abroad are the only thing the institutional realists can offer, they risk prescribing a cure that is worse than the disease of partisan polarization. As Mark Schmitt warns, the "nostalgia" for past party practices, is romanticized in its own way. History suggests that a political system that is closed to outside scrutiny and tightly managed by party and committee leaders, one that is also awash in unregulated and unknown money and driven by quiet deals for votes that benefit parochial interests, not only falls short of a democratic ideal but also fails by any measure of government effectiveness. That describes American politics in the Gilded Age of the

1890s and the Congresses of the 1950s, which were paralyzed in dealing with the urgent cause of civil rights.[13]

The debate between the romantics and realists will undoubtedly continue, and, as we describe later in the chapter, the impressive and awe-inspiring display of mass protest for racial justice is just the latest reminder that democratic participation can be valuable, necessary, and glorious. The demands for racial justice, even when they divide the nation, will not be spurned by calls for patience—nor should they be. Indeed, the debate between the romantics and realists suggests something problematic in how institutionalists have framed the contemporary crisis in American government. Realists ask what the system is doing poorly, and what institutional designs or procedures have produced more effective government in the past. Such a line of inquiry helps us to consider the merits of compromise and mediating institutions; but these appeals for consensus avoid the unavoidable and unanswerable question of evaluating what the less polarized government of the post–World War II era did not do. As the pioneering institutionalist Elinor Ostrom recognized, we must apply other criteria to evaluate government action or inaction as normatively good or bad, and those criteria exist outside the analytical model and description of a system of institutional arrangements.[14] Where one group of scholars sees compromise, another sees delay; where one researcher measures a successful logroll, another sees distributive injustice; where one activist celebrates higher turnout among the majority as a triumph for democracy, another claims that a victimized minority was disenfranchised. Most problematically, one person's "effective government" is another person's governmental nightmare. For example, R. Shep Melnick has argued, contrary to received wisdom, that "the constantly repeated 'gridlock' meme misdiagnoses our contemporary ills. . . . In a nutshell, our central problem is not that government 'can't get anything done' . . . but rather that we are doing so many things and responding to so many political demands that we are incapable of resolving the serious conflicts among them."[15]

If scholars cannot even agree on what they want, let alone how to get it, the debate between the romantics and the realists is a non-starter. So, instead of arguing that the political system is broken, we have argued that contemporary politics does one thing well—perhaps too well: modern American government works for partisan presidents and the movements that energize their base. The presidency has become the preeminent prize in American politics, and the country's political institutions and organizations are dedicated to securing or influencing it. In the mid-20th century, the famed presidency scholar Richard

Neustadt described a presidential institution seized by contradictory forces and an inescapable dilemma: "The same conditions that promote his [the president's] leadership in form preclude a guarantee of leadership in fact." As the Brownlow Committee envisioned, presidents had become responsible for leading the United States toward "the expression of our national will";[16] however, this obligation fell on the president with no assurance of "an influence commensurate with services performed."[17] Many scholars and students still try to understand the presidency through this lens, emphasizing how presidential responsibilities far exceed the powers of the modern executive office. But Neustadt's analysis does not apply to the current state of presidential politics. Presidents are no longer dependent on the power to persuade, which Neustadt believed was so critical to the dilemma he posed. In many instances, with strong attachment to their parties' core supporters and armed with the powers of the modern executive office, presidents can command. Congress and even the president's partisan brethren still resist executive dominion. But the joining of executive prerogative, social activism, and partisan politics creates the perception—and to an extent, the reality—that presidents can campaign and govern independently of the Congress, bureaucracy, and regular party organization. Since the late 1960s, in any case, presidents have demonstrated that partisan gridlock in Congress and the states can be circumvented by exploiting executive power for partisan purposes.

Most accounts of our present discontents have emphasized polarization in Congress and the dilemmas to collective governance that have accompanied its institutional development. But the modern executive has also been pulled into the caldron of partisan combat. The fractious politics in Congress have not only sharply divided Democrats and Republicans but have also created internal disputes within the legislative caucuses, making parties even more dependent on presidents to advance their objectives.

That both liberals and conservatives have embraced presidential power and administrative politics makes this contest for the soul of America especially unsettling. Once contested by conservative Democrats and Republicans as an existential threat to constitutional government, national administrative power gained acceptance on the right as liberalism expanded throughout the 1960s. As a consequence, partisanship in the United States is no longer a struggle over the size of the state. It is an executive-centered struggle for the services of national administrative power. Despite rhetorical appeals to "limited government," since the late 1960s conservatives have sought to deploy state power as ardently as liberals.

This is not to suggest that the conservative attack on government is un-important. Republicans' rhetorical assault on the liberal state is consistent with their persistent efforts to weaken social welfare programs and, more generally, to remake aspects of the administrative state through "privatiza-tion" and outsourcing. By the same token, less hostile to government than conservatives, liberals display a lingering commitment to the value of "en-lightened administration" that was the cachet of the administrative state forged during the New Deal. However, since the late 1960s, conservatives have pursued programs and policies that would restore traditional values and commitments that they alleged liberalism had weakened. There is a real sense in which this battle for the services of the administrative state is a struggle over the terms of the New Deal charter: Democrats have sought to uphold freedom from want while Republicans have embraced freedom from fear. Consequently, while liberals seek to build administrative capacity to design and implement social welfare policies, guided by the tools of so-cial science and mainstream economics, conservatives have sought to re-deploy and extend that power in pursuit of their own partisan goals (while often espousing anti-state sentiments and denigrating mainstream exper-tise): enhancing national defense, homeland security, border protection, and local policing; and establishing more market-oriented policies in education, climate change, and other social services.

Indeed, Republican presidents, especially Ronald Reagan and George W. Bush, pioneered the art of mobilizing partisan opinion and exploiting ad-ministrative power for their partisan objectives.[18] In that light, during the 2008 campaign, Barack Obama presented himself as a transcendent leader who could imbue the policy state with new causes and moral fervor. Yet, by the time he reached office, it no longer seemed possible for presidents to stand apart from partisan combat; more to the point, partisan polarization had come to so divide Congress and advocacy groups in Washington and the states that the Obama administration had strong incentives to take refuge and pursue progressive policies through the administrative presidency.

The End of Executive-Centered Partisanship?

Contrary to the conventional understanding at the time, Biden's tri-umph over Trump in 2020 was not a victory for the Democratic Party. The establishment's hold on the party's selection process was limited to a few, albeit critical, states like South Carolina, and the party faced hard challenges as the nomination season progressed to high-profile Senate and House races. Some down-ballot, establishment—Biden-like—candidates faltered, a harbinger perhaps of a tense relationship with a Democratic Congress, once the presidential honeymoon period comes to an end. For example, Eliot Engel, a 30-year veteran of the House who received endorsements from Hillary Clinton, Chuck Schumer, and Nancy Pelosi, lost to Jamaal Bowman, whom Elizabeth Warren and Bernie Sanders openly favored. No less stunning was Black Lives Matter activist Cori Bush's upset win over Lacy Clay, the incumbent, in Missouri's Democratic primary. A member of a local African American political dynasty, Clay had represented the district since 2001, having succeeded his father, Bill, who was first elected in 1968. In Kentucky, Amy McGrath, the establishment's hand-picked candidate to take on the Republican majority leader Mitch McConnell, emerged battered and weakened after Warren and Sanders endorsed a more progressive nominee in the state.[19]

These divisions within the Democratic Party were not just reflective of progressive candidates catching the wave of reform enthusiasm that swept over the nation in the midst of the twin crises of disease and police brutality. Throughout his presidency, Obama's grassroots organization, although it mobilized a formidable national coalition, did not strengthen the Democratic National Committee or the Party's state and local organizations; it further attenuated them. Indeed, Obama presided over a greater loss of congressional seats for his party than any two-term president since the Second World War. As Obama acknowledged after he left office, "Partly because my docket was really full here, so I couldn't be both chief organizer of the Democratic Party and function as commander in chief and president of the United States. We did not begin what I think needs to happen over the long haul, and that is rebuild the Democratic Party at the ground level."[20]

As Theda Skocpol has shown, some of that work began during the 2018 election; that was when grassroots organizations born of the nationwide Women's March that spearheaded the anti-Trump Resistance became involved in local and state politics. "Ordinary citizens, led by middleclass women, organized everywhere," she writes. "Unprecedented numbers ran for city and town offices, state legislatures and Congress, while tens of thousands went door to door to turn out voters for both moderate and progressive Democrats. Even candidates who lost provided choices and a voice in public discussions."[21]

With the start of the 2020 campaign, however, most Democratic presidential candidates emphasized executive-centered partisanship, arguing that Trump's bellicose partisanship had to be returned in kind. On the campaign trail, Biden promised to restore civility to American politics and celebrated his ability to broker legislative compromises with Congress. But he found himself on the defensive as ardent progressives Bernie Sanders and Elizabeth Warren promised to take aggressive executive action to jump start the transformation of American politics on day one. Even the more moderate self-styled outsider, Pete Buttigieg, insisted that "there is no back to normal" and warned that Democrats would have to play constitutional hardball after the election, most notably by following Franklin Roosevelt's playbook and enlarging a Supreme Court remade by Donald Trump.[22]

Following Biden's surprisingly decisive victory in the nomination contest, it remained to be seen whether he would be able to build a broad coalition that could win a Democratic victory—and restore a measure of collective party responsibility to American politics. Lacking the charisma of the president he served—and temperamentally suited to inclusiveness—Biden might be in a position to make partisan debate less ad hominem—to focus partisanship on competing principles rather than personal recrimination. Indeed, he immediately took significant steps to bring movement activists into his fold. Anxious to avoid the bitter antagonisms that plagued the 2016 election, he reached out to the Sanders campaign, assuring the Vermont senator that his supporters would be well represented on the floor of the convention and the major committees that would forge a party platform, the bedrock of the Democrats' message for the upcoming election and potential fodder for the Republican Party. Biden also made overtures to the progressive wing of the party by adopting a more aggressive plan to make college tuition free for middle- and low-income families at public universities and a bankruptcy policy championed by Elizabeth Warren. Finally, Biden's campaign brought new leaders aboard to enhance outreach to key constituencies of the Obama coalition that the Clinton campaign had failed to mobilize. It hired Karine Jean-Pierre, a former Obama administration official and chief public affairs officer for MoveOn, an influential progressive advocacy group, who was highly regarded by social activists and establishment Democrats such as South Carolina Representative James Clyburn. The campaign also added Julie Chavez Rodriguez as a senior advisor to help with its outreach to the Latino community, which was especially unenthusiastic about Biden's candidacy. Chavez Rodriguez, granddaughter of the iconic 1960s civil rights leader Cesar Chavez, was former Obama White House liaison to leaders in the LGBTQ, Asian American, Latino, veterans, youth, education, and labor communities; she also had the great respect of populist and mainstream Democrats. These measures encouraged Sanders, never known as a team player, to work harmoniously with the Biden campaign. He appeared to position the former vice president to build a winning coalition of voters that would draw from three key groups needed to improve on Clinton's performance: young and minority voters, suburban women, and disaffected Republican and Independent voters who backed Trump in 2016 or did not vote. Such a coalition, Democratic strategists argued, would not only enable Biden to win the presidency but would also bring a party victory that might retain the House and take control of the Senate.[23]

Consequently, against the despair of a pandemic, racial strife, and a sitting president determined to stoke the fires of division, Democrats approached the final months of a critical election with some glimmers of hope. Democrats did not do as well as they expected in House races, losing 11 seats and barely holding on the majority they achieved in the 2018 elections; however, they picked up three seats in the Senate, winning two remarkable special elections in Georgia, leaving the upper chamber evenly divided, with Vice President Kamala Harris the deciding vote in the event of a tie. Thus, for the first time since 2010, the Democrats controlled the White House and both chambers of Congress—albeit by the narrowest of margins in a country that remained sharply divided.

Moreover, the fate of Biden's coalition-building and the prospects of renewing the idea of a party system in American politics remains highly uncertain. The Democratic Party had already become a more decidedly left of center party since Obama left office. And then, as Biden was wrapping up the nomination, the country was roiled with extraordinary demonstrations, which extended beyond metropolitan areas to deep red small towns such as Shippensburg, Pennsylvania, and Danville, Virginia. These calls for racial justice challenged the 2020 campaign with demands for fundamental change in healthcare, the economy, and most demonstrably criminal justice. Black Lives Matter activists, supported by some local Democratic officials, called controversially for defunding the police. These powerful forces, clamoring for remedies to structural racism, aroused attention to the "unresolved policy issues from the 1960s movement," so labeled by Matthew Delmont, a scholar of African American history. The renaissance of '60s movement politics inspired many young African Americans and their "White allies" to renew the idealism that touched the civil rights and anti-war movements and to scorn the institutions that were part of a racist system.

At the same time, the surge of radical demands for change caused concern among more establishment Democrats that an antinomian surge might wash over the nascent, delicate collaboration between the Democratic president and activists to consolidate a new progressive party. Marjaan Sirdar, a Minneapolis activist who lives a few blocks from where George Floyd was killed, fiercely denounced progressive politicians, recalling the fiery determination of Black militant Stokely Carmichael in disparaging Lyndon Johnson and his Democratic allies in the 1960s. "The Democrats created this problem," Sirdar said. "Anybody can pay for a $200, $300 training and learn how to sound anti-racist. They learn the language of anti-racism and they just become better gatekeepers of white supremacy."[24]

It is debatable whether the Biden administration's actions in the name of racial justice will heal this divide within the Democratic Party. Biden promised that his appointments would "look like America," better representing the diversity of the country. Early signs were that this was not just rhetorical flourish. For example, both Karine Jean-Pierre and Julie Chavez-Rodriguez were appointed to positions in the White House: the former as White House deputy press secretary and the latter as special assistant to the president and senior deputy director of public engagement. More generally, paired with his choice of senior-level White House staff, Biden was on track after three months in office to have a more diverse administration than any past president.[25] Biden also appointed women and racial minorities to positions that have historically been held exclusively by White men. For example, Janet Yellen is the first woman to be named head of the Treasury Department; Deb Haaland, appointed secretary of the Department of the Interior, is the first Native American to serve in a president's cabinet; and Pete Buttigieg, appointed to head Transportation, is the first openly gay individual to be confirmed as a cabinet secretary.[26]

Nevertheless, social activists who remained outside the palace gates were concerned that many of Biden appointments, such as Yellen, were establishment figures who had served in the Obama administration and that Biden exceeded his predecessor in placing individuals with government experience in the White House Office and other federal agencies—individuals who were likely to pursue pragmatic rather than progressive solutions to racial and economic equality. As Autumn Dornfeld, manager of the ActLocal directory of more than 7,300 grassroots groups, put it, "We are going to keep after him [and other Democratic representatives] to move left, and maybe find some ways to make this democracy work for everyone."[27]

As difficult as it might be to balance the factions of the Democratic Party, the larger challenge the president faced was unifying a country that remained bitterly divided in spite of his efforts to avoid the culture wars that Trump had relished. Joe Biden, who has been described as the nation's consoler in chief, seemed to play that role adroitly as the nation reeled with the legacies of George Floyd's murder and the conviction of his murderer, Derek Chauvin. But Biden's comments before Chauvin's trial ended—that he was "praying the verdict is the right verdict"—sparked fierce backlash from Republicans and conservative media. Of course, we are not suggesting, in this instance, that a president cannot exercise moral leadership and take a strong, even divisive, stand on an issue as important to the country as racial justice. But the political backlash was a deluge of cold water on the hopes that Biden could unify the country around the issue on which progressives demand bold action and conservatives, still mobilized by the rally cry of law and order, will stubbornly resist.

As such, caught between the aspirations of the progressive wing of his party and the strident opposition of a not-so-loyal opposition still under the spell of its charismatic leader, Biden launched his presidency with a dramatic display of executive-centered partisanship. During the campaign, Democrats promised to issue new executive orders that would rescind the Trump administration's policies and advance progressive measures on a litany of issues ranging from climate change to immigration. Biden took a more measured tone, insisting that progress was best pursued through legislation, substantiated by bipartisan consensus. Yet during his first 100 days in office, Biden signed more executive actions than any other president since Franklin Roosevelt in the storied beginning of his first term. With a cascade of executive orders, memoranda, and other administrative actions, the president was especially intent on addressing many of the immediate concerns of his most progressive partisan allies. About half these actions were taken to reverse the most controversial policies of the Trump administration, with particular attention given to undoing his predecessor's immigration legacy by halting border wall construction, pausing most deportations from the interior of the United States, rescinding travel and immigration restrictions on several Muslim-majority countries, formally halting the effort to preclude undocumented immigrants from the census figures used to award states seats in Congress, and safeguarding the DACA protections for "Dreamers."

Beyond the swift action to undo Trump's most provocative measures, a number of Biden's action were new directives, in pursuit of substantive reform promised on the campaign trail.[28] Particularly noteworthy were the new administration's policies prohibiting discrimination on the basis of gender identity and sexual orientation, directing federal agencies to take affirmative steps to secure these rights; and developing measures to launch a new plan to battle the pandemic, including the creation of a COVID-19 coordinator, reporting directly to the president and managing efforts to produce and distribute vaccines and medical equipment.[29]

Predictably, Republican members of Congress attacked these orders, denouncing Biden for betraying his promise to foster a new spirit of bipartisanship. However, few of these orders aroused the public outcry that greeted the Trump administration's antagonizing measures that banned Muslims, eviscerated environmental regulations, and denigrated LGBTQ rights. To a point, some of the relative calm has to do with the fact that many, such as orders for "advancing racial equity," ensuring an "equitable pandemic response," and promising a "data-driven response to COVID-19," are, at least in the first instance, rhetorical commitments that leave uncertain what sort of policy might follow. Similarly, the decision to rejoin the Paris Climate accords, symbolizing a recommitment to fighting climate change, and President Biden's willingness to entertain the possibility of reforming the Supreme Court, appointing a presidential commission to study various possibilities, including the "membership and size of the Court," are additional nods to the party's base and its reliance on presidential power to advance progressive causes. Nevertheless, they have yet to bear fruit. In the very early days of his presidency, therefore, Biden avoided the most polarizing fights that executive-centered partisanship portends. Indeed, focusing like a laser on the pandemic, he gained the overwhelming support of his party, and considerable credit in the coin of public opinion, in enacting and administering the $1.9 trillion American Rescue Plan, passed on a party-line vote.

Still, turbulent waters lie ahead. Biden's approval rating at the 100-day mark of 54% was higher than Trump's 42% at the same benchmark; nevertheless, it was still lower than any other newly elected president going back to Dwight Eisenhower in 1953. Notably, the new president's tepid honeymoon with the American people testified to how polarized the country remained in the wake of Trump's disruptive four years in the White House. In fact, his approval rating had the largest gap between Democrats and Republicans in Gallup's presidential approval polling over the first 100 days of any recent president—the 85% point spread (with 96 percent of Democrats and 11 percent Republicans approving of his performance) even surpassed the partisan gap that divided the country during the disruptive start to Trump's presidency (77 percent).[30] Biden's prospects for a successful presidency, therefore, appeared to depend on his ability, not to reach to the center, which clearly lacked vitality, but to mobilize his fellow partisans for a bruising battle with conservative Republican lawmakers largely beholden to a right-wing populist base.

The prospects for such masterful partisan leadership, which could buttress a diverse coalition without arousing a countermobilization on the right that would deprive the Democrats of their thin majorities in the House and Senate, remain highly uncertain at this point. As was the case with Obama, the early criticism from the left wing of the Democratic Party points to some potential fault lines. Ardent progressives are disappointed that Biden did not include the cancellation of student loans with his flurry of executive actions. Advocacy groups and social activists also criticized the Biden administration for not pushing more aggressively for a $15 minimum wage to be included in the America Rescue Plan after the Senate parliamentarian determined that it could not be a part of a budget reconciliation package, the procedure Democrats used to enact the massive COVID relief package by a simple majority vote, thus obviating a certain Republican filibuster.

A less visible but potentially troublesome arena of conflict is national security. Biden will find it difficult to avoid the challenge of reconciling the progressive wing of his party to a foreign policy team composed largely of establishment figures, whose pursuit of world order is likely to agitate the neo-isolationist, anti-imperialist activists, the lineal descendants of the anti-war movement that crested during the national tragedy of Vietnam.[31] Grumbling could already be heard that the administration continues to cozy up to Saudi Arabia. Progressive activists' pressure was a factor in the White House decision to end the United States support for Saudi-led operations in Yemen; however, the Biden administration resisted the calls of movement organizations to defund militarization abroad in continuing to provide defensive support to Saudi Arabia against missile and drone attacks by Iranian-backed forces. More potentially fractious was Biden's handling of a volatile situation in the Middle East. When violence erupted between Israel and Hamas in Israeli and Palestinian territories, the president faced strong pressure from the left to intervene against the United States' strongest ally in the Middle East—and reverse the staunch pro-Israeli policy of the Trump administration. "We oppose our money going to fund militarized policing, occupation and systems of violent oppression and trauma," said Representative Cori Bush of Missouri, now in her first term in Congress, in her floor speech soon after the deadly conflict broke out. "Until all our children are safe, we will continue to fight for our rights in Palestine and in Ferguson."[32] Uncertainties also attended the pending withdrawal of the last American forces from Afghanistan, which Biden, like Trump, promised to accomplish in 2021.

Despite all these tensions, early reports paint a picture of a progressive wing largely satisfied with the access to and positive signals from the Biden administration. Time will tell, however, whether a more contentious partnership will emerge as Biden seeks to thread the needle between an aspiring left and an angry right. No issue poses more danger to the Biden administration than immigration. An early sign of potential conflict arose with an emerging crisis on the southern border. Facing strong pressure from immigration rights advocates, the Biden administration quickly retreated from a strategic decision *not* to rescind a Trump order pertaining to refugee and asylum seekers. As the president began his pitch for a near $2 trilllion infrastructure package and a $3.5 trillion spending bill, which contained a long list of progressive demands, he announced that he would keep the previous administration's limit of 15,000 refugees per year. It was a sincere effort to demonstrate to moderate Democrats and Republicans in Congress that the administration was a good-faith negotiator, and that it recognized that the growing surge of undocumented immigrants on the border was a political boon for his adversaries. The decision was framed as a temporary concession; but one that, even though revealed at the tail end of the Friday news cycle, aroused immediate and bitter condemnation. Within hours, Biden reversed course and sought to absolve his controversial decision as a "messaging mistake." For the moment, things settled down, but this was in all likelihood only the first shot fired across the president's bow—from a base that, as it demonstrated during President Obama's tenure, was not inured to the politics of policy management, even if those substantive compromises were linked to larger progressive goals.[33]

A Way Forward?

This book started with concern for the decline of a party system that was displaced by the unlikely alliance of a presidency-centered democracy and movement politics, leaving us with this puzzling situation of weak party organizations and angry partisanship—a rancorous, all-consuming battle for the levers of administrative power. Renewing party organizations, as mediators of the ongoing democratic struggle between populism and institutions, we argue, would be an important salve for the rancorous factionalism that rends the country. As La Raja and Rauch sensibly argue, restoring a measure of influence to elected officials and party leaders—for example, restoring a role for the misleadingly named "superdelegates" in the nomination process—"can provide expertise on the qualities and trade-offs necessary for governance" and empower voices who "can speak for the long-term interests of the party."[34]

It is unlikely, however, that stronger party organizations alone could restore the foundations of representative constitutional government— that newly anointed gatekeepers could convince both progressives and conservatives to compromise, make politics less personal, restore some balance between the central and local government, and reinvigorate the constitutional system of checks and balances. As the distinguished members of the 1950 APSA committee learned, proposing institutional solutions without attention to the common ground that sustains a vital center is calling into the wind. A truly vital center, as Arthur Schlesinger recognized, encourages fundamental struggles for the soul of America while preserving the principles that make a large and diverse group of individuals a country.

There is no panacea for the maladies that threaten democracy in the United States. Above all, as La Raja and Rauch acknowledge, we need "a new mindset"—although such a new understanding about the value of mediating institutions must go well beyond acceptance of "peer review" in the presidential selection process. The most dangerous tendencies of tribal politics, in our view, are sustained by an illusory vision of presidential leadership—a misplaced faith in the democratic potential of the modern presidency. Political realists usefully demonstrate how alternative institutional arrangements in American states and comparable nations might ameliorate Manichean politics and structure more effective collective action. Our proposals lack such precision, precisely because they are not yet empirically demonstrable. Indeed, this is what a historical perspective adds—it expands our institutional imagination to discover the root causes of the problems that plague American democracy and to craft new solutions to remedy a system that appears broken to so many, even as they revel in principles and tactics that have fractured the nation.

Our analysis has shown how joining populism, presidential aggrandizement, and partisan polarization has transformed the dynamic of politics and government. Executive-centered partisanship has created a dangerous pattern of rapid political action and reaction—one that creates dramatic openings for both significant democratic gains and authoritarian challenges to essential constitutional norms and democratic rights. The hard task that lies ahead is to restore a vital center that engages the country in the fundamental contest to define who We the People are—without undermining the constitutional norms and institutions that hold individual freedom and populist demand in delicate balance. In that spirit we propose reforms that might expand political participation, renew parties as mediating organizations and restore the rule of law. These proposals, although informed by the lessons of American political development, look forward, not backward to some illusory golden age of politics that proscribed spirited conflict, which is, after all, the essence of self-government.

Expand the Voting Base

Fierce partisan conflict in the United States is not new. Throughout American history, as we have shown, there have been polarizing struggles over fundamental questions relating to the meaning of the Declaration of Independence, the Constitution, and the relationship between the two. These struggles over ideals have become all-encompassing when joined to battles over what it means to be an American—the most perilous example being the conflict over slavery during the 1850s.

The periodic swells of populist fervor have traditionally given way to dramatic institutional reforms. It would be a mistake to label these all as "democratizing," if, by that term, democratization is supposed to expand access to the political system. Previous efforts to democratize the party system, as we have noted, have concentrated power, not diffused it. The McGovern-Fraser reforms displaced elected officials and party leaders who strove to build broad coalitions and instead empowered primary voters who pledge support for candidates seeking to build a personal following. The result is a plebiscitary, media-driven process that has inclined even more moderate candidates to appeal to the militant partisans—the base—who are disproportionately represented in the primary system. Reinforcing this factionalism, Republicans and Democrats have become anchored in distinct regions, states, and communities: the Republicans in the southern, border, and mountain states, especially in small towns and exurban enclaves; and the Democrats along the East and West Coasts, especially in the major metropolitan areas. The bitter 2016 election appeared to accentuate these trends: with Donald Trump winning states like Pennsylvania, Wisconsin, Ohio, and Michigan; and Hillary Clinton winning fast-growing and urbanizing states like Nevada, Colorado, and Virginia, the sharp cultural divide between Red and Blue America has become more pronounced. Red areas are becoming redder and blue areas bluer: notably, one-third of 700 counties in the country that voted for Barack Obama twice (mostly White and outside of major metropolitan areas) flipped for Trump in 2016. As the schism between Democratic and Republican voters in key battleground states like Georgia, Arizona, Wisconsin, Michigan, and Pennsylvania illustrated, the 2020 election reinforced the boundaries that separated liberal and conservative loyalists. In the last 30 years, only one candidate for office, Bill Clinton, has achieved broad-based support in both urban and rural America during the general election. There is little overlap in the types of places where presidential nominees succeed and the types of voters they attract. Having concentrated the authority for selecting nominees in the hands of ideologically united, activist bases, the system is less democratic, even though the number of individuals involved is greater.

The passionate factions that now dominate partisan politics testify to the unanticipated consequences of "democratic" reforms. But another contributing factor is perilously low voter turnout. Even in the high-stakes 2016 presidential election, just 59.2% of the voting eligible population, or 54.8% of the voting age population, showed up to the polls. In 2020, we were collectively proud of the fact that after a highly charged election and the expansion of early and mail-in voting amid the pandemic, "turnout soared": 66.2% of eligible voters showed up. By historical comparison, in fact, this was an impressive turnout. Not since 1900 has such a large percentage of the voting-age population cast a ballot in a presidential election.

But we might want to temper the celebration of the latest voter surge. In spite of the expanded opportunities to cast ballots, nearly 4 out of 10 eligible voters did not participate in a contest characterized, with good reason, by Joe Biden as a contest for the "soul of the nation." Moreover, voter turnout in primary, midterm, and state and local elections remains well below participation in presidential contests, a mark of the presidentialism that now encompasses political life in the United States.

To paraphrase the great civil rights activist John Lewis, who died during the 2020 battle for the identity of America, expanding the franchise would be disruptive, in a good way.

The current struggles over voting rights in Congress and the states cut to the heart of self-government. It is important that Americans believe in the integrity of the electoral system; however, efforts to suppress voter participation—targeting minority communities in the name of security—are toxic. As E. J. Dionne has written, "Functional partisanship depends, at the bare minimum, on commitments to abide by the results of free elections, to tell the truth about those elections, and to offer all citizens equal opportunities to participate in the electoral process."[35]

The Republican Party's embrace of the "big lie"—that Donald Trump won the 2020 presidential election—is symptomatic of the party system's decay. It has given rise to voter "reforms" to make Democrats less competitive in places like Georgia and Texas. But as mischievous and foundational as these "reform" efforts are, we urge both parties to shift their attention to measures that would bring more individuals—especially those who have traditionally not participated in elections—to the polls. Democrats should make this a part of their larger message of inclusivity; Republicans should live up to their claim to be a "populist" party. There is a silver lining in the 2020 turnout boost; it took place in the middle of a global pandemic that left many sheltered at home. But, with all-mail voting, and expanded early voting options, more Americans still showed up, and in support of *both* sides.

Still, although recent scholarly work has suggested that the move to all-mail voting does not advantage one party, any reform must be sensitive to concerns, no matter how ill founded, that it will.[36] Elections only work because they are seen as legitimate; moreover, figuring out a way to bring more people to the polls collectively might make elections truly a celebration of American democracy. Rather than emphasize voting methods that enable individuals to cast ballots separately, we propose making Election Day a holiday. The poet Walt Whitman, a partisan Democratic who celebrated America's national expression of democracy every four years, gave lyric expression to the festive nature of a vibrant national election—in a poem entitled "Election Day, November, 1884":

—This seething hemisphere's humanity, as now, I'd name—*the still small voice* vibrating—America's choosing day,

(The heart of it not in the chosen—the act itself the main, the quadrennial choosing,)

In a country still badly divided by the Civil War—indeed, in the process of reversing the revolution promised by the abolition of slavery—Whitman did not see North and South, Red and Blue. He was enchanted by the idea that no matter who won the election, the nation would go on, in search of the ever elusive More Perfect Union. In the spirit of Whitman's aspiration—in this time of a Cold Civil War—we should formally designate election day as a celebration of American democracy. There is no clear reason for making election day a Tuesday in November. Move it to Saturday. Or, give people a day off. Close the government, the banks, the schools, and the stock market. Give voters a sticker, and maybe even a tax break. If we are worried about ballot drop-off sites or signature irregularities, stop spending millions on ballot recount conspiracies and simply open up more polling places. Do not, as commanded in the mean-spirited voter suppression law that Georgia enacted after the 2020 election, prohibit providing refreshments to those who brave long lines to exercise the franchise; rather, encourage a festive atmosphere of food, drink, and music that celebrates America's Choosing Day. Take one day out of the presidential election year to celebrate not the warring factions, but the people who turn out to vote.

Re-Center the Party Organization

As we have argued, modern partisanship is nationalized. There are a few holdout states left where local political culture and personal histories seem to defy the pollsters and trendlines. For example, in the last two presidential elections, only one state chose a senator and a president of opposing political parties: Susan Collins of Maine. Democrats and Republicans have come to depend on presidents and presidential candidates to raise funds, mobilize grassroots support, articulate the party's message, and advance party programs. Presidents, their personas, and their beliefs dominate the image of party politics down-ballot. What can be done to restore what Martha Derthick celebrated as America's "Compound Republic"?[37]

Just as the 1950 APSA report on political parties found relief in the salutary role played by state and local party leaders, we too might find solace in reconsidering the way party leaders, representing their distinct communities come together to guide party politics. The APSA committee conceived a new

Party Council as "the most important link between the party of the President and his Administration." In effect, the committee hoped, the Council would facilitate give-and-take between the representatives of a multilevel party and the president in the formulation of a party program. Both parties briefly experimented with "Advisory Councils," but these mediating institutions were only effective when the party was out of power, thus anticipating the institutional combat agitated by divided government. In retrospect, it is difficult to imagine how an "advisory" board could, as Martin Van Buren prescribed, transform "personal preference" into "party principle." Such collective partisan responsibility presupposed an independent Congress and state governments that were not beholden to presidential candidates and presidents to advance partisan objectives.

Rather than establishing partisan councils that would seek to advise presidents—or empowering "superdelegates" that, if they checked the primary electorate, would be derided as illegitimate, political parties need to reestablish themselves as true "gatekeepers." Parties need independent power to hold presidents and members of Congress accountable to a collective party program. This is easier said than done, especially if parties are to retain their non-centralized character. Much attention has focused on the resources party leaders have at their disposal to whip recalcitrant members into line. Revising campaign finance reforms that limit how much money can be contributed to political parties also might serve the purpose of reinvigorating party life. Likewise, scholars of legislative behavior have emphasized the broken lawmaking process that risks exposing too much of each party's dirty laundry in the open. Sarah Binder and Frances Lee have put a fine point on the problem of open deliberations: "Transparency interferes with the search for solutions. Conducting negotiations of multidimensional, integrative solutions behind closed doors gives lawmakers more freedom to explore policy options."[38] We agree that reforming certain reforms would be a step in the right direction.

But if influence is key, what can be done to elevate collective partisan deliberations in a way that resonates with the public? One interesting solution is to reimagine the role of the party nominating conventions. Once the lifeblood of the nomination process, they now serve little function except to anoint and adorn the presidential nominee every four years. This coronation reached new heights at the abbreviated 2020 Republican Convention, where rather than approving a platform expressing party principles and commitments, the National Committee passed a Resolution pledging "to enthusiastically support the president's America-first agenda."

Party conventions could perhaps serve a very different role if instead of convening only at the end of the nominating process, party leaders would also congregate at the beginning. "One way out of the nomination mess," Dan Shea has argued, "might be to create a democratic process whereby enlightened partisans have a greater say."[39]

Of course, there is the possibility that no one would pay attention or take seriously deliberations that preceded the main event. But the nominating convention might retain influence if presidential hopefuls were required to attend and deliver speeches; and the delegates chosen by state and local organizations participated in a straw vote that expressed each state's candidate preferences and, more to the point, publicly debated the major resolutions of the party platform, which the eventual candidate for president could not ignore. Conventions that precede the party nomination contest might not garner the same attention as the spectacle that follows the primary and caucus contests, but it would bring together party leaders in a representative and less presidency-centered way. With this initial screening, the high drama accompanying early state nomination contests might be viewed from a broader perspective, all the while remaining important sites for would-be breakthrough candidacies. The 2020 nomination cycle offers hints at the sort of influence respected party leaders might have on the nomination contests. Joe Biden prevailed over the insurgent Sanders candidacy in spite of faring poorly in the highly salient Iowa and New Hampshire contests, because South Carolina's elder statesman, Jim Clyburn, endorsed him and deployed his strong organization to get his constituents to the polls. Clyburn, with close ties to party leaders and social activists, should not be viewed as the rearguard of the Democratic Party's "gatekeepers." Rather, he showed how a state party could still play a critical mediating role in the presidential selection process. Institutionalizing this influence and staging it as part of the national convention, party influence might have residual effects throughout the political system.

Giving the national conventions an important role in formulating the party program in a presidential election year might also re-center elections on contentious but principled debate. Democrats can, and should, disagree with fellow Democrats; Republicans can, and should disagree with fellow Republicans. But fellow partisans who compete for these party's nomination should have more in common with one another than the current candidate-driven presidential contest encourage. This type of persona-driven politics is reminiscent of the candidate-centered politics that destroyed "King

Caucus" in the early part of the 19th century; revisiting that period, as we do in Chapter 2, sheds light on the fragility of the pseudo-democratic partisan machinations of our own time. Being a Democrat or Republican should mean more than battling for the auspices of a hollowed-out organization that can merely certify winners and losers. The American people still remain quite ambivalent when it comes to the standard measures of political ideology.[40] They pretend to be devout conservatives or liberals, but attitudes toward the parties are driven more by social animosity, distrust toward the other side, and allegiance to political leaders. Parties can restore their collective purpose only by hammering out party commitments and facilitating principled debate. They should not sacrifice the painstaking but exalted task of platform writing to presidential fealty. They should not craft documents that largely go unread and list every possible promise to their party's principal stakeholders. There should be plans for action if the party achieves power. Give voters something to cast their ballot for or against instead of just a benign despot who renders any sense of collective responsibility a chimera.

The Administrative Presidency

Finally, as we have stressed, so many of the contemporary problems that threaten representative constitutional government follow from the presidentialism that has come to dominate partisan politics. As parties have come to rely on the White House to advance their objectives, presidents have been expected to use the administrative presidency to carry out programs and policies unilaterally. As institutional loyalties have given way to partisan allegiance, Congress has done little to prevent presidents from concentrating more power in the Executive Office of the President and politicizing the bureaucracy, thus undermining its commitment to "neutral competence." Central to this dynamic has been the illusion that presidents can represent the nation. Yet no diverse and diversifying country of over 300 million people can invest so much faith in one individual and call itself a democratic republic. Indeed, the ferocious partisan polarization that has emerged since the 1960s has made a sham of the ideal espoused by Theodore Roosevelt that the modern executive should be "the steward of the public welfare." The merging of executive prerogative and partisan polarization has hitherto encouraged Republicans and Democrats to support their own presidents' incursions on legislative prerogatives and to denounce the executive aggrandizement of presidents who represent their partisan opponents. Similarly, the parties' bases have viewed partisan administration with a jaundiced eye. Put simply, half the country hates the president while the whole nation loves the presidency.

In this instance, some reform to the reforms seems especially well advised. Congress knowingly, and with every possible good intention, delegated vast powers to the executive branch in the name of modernizing and democratizing the federal government. In the past, Congress has tried to claw back its power after learning the hard mistakes of congressional acquiescence. It has created institutions, such as the Congressional Budget Office, the Government Accountability Office, and the Congressional Research Service that can provide impressive expertise were Congress inclined to revitalize its role as chief legislator and live up to the promise of the Legislative Reorganization Act of 1946, enacted in response to the consolidation of the modern executive, to exercise "continual watchfulness" of the execution of the laws by administrative agencies. Some scholars have suggested enacting new measures that enable Congress to engage in constructive competition with the White House. For example, Stephen Skowronek, Desmond King, and John Dearborn urge Congress to rework the president's declaration of emergency powers, which Trump exploited when denied funding to build The Wall, by requiring legislative approval of any action lasting more than thirty days. The merit of such measures, they argue, is that Congress insists "on being more than just a watchdog or simply countering the president's claims to control. Instead, it envisions reworking institutional relationships, recruiting the presidency as a partner in new cooperative enterprises."[41]

The snake in this garden of new institutional partnerships is that executive-centered partisanship, fueled by social activism, invariably tears asunder cooperative enterprises. However, the constitutional struggle between Donald Trump and Speaker Nancy Pelosi over whether the president could give the 2019 State of the Union Message in the middle of a government shutdown dramatically highlighted how partisan and institutional struggles can be intertwined in ways that check executive aggrandizement. This impasse arose as a result of Trump's unwillingness to sign a bipartisan bill to keep the government open unless it included funding for his wall; Pelosi argued that it would be unseemly to invite the president to give his state of the union address while government workers and those who depended on them were the victims of the president's grandiose ambition. In the end, the president caved; he agreed to delay the annual message until the government shutdown ended. Although Trump contemplated giving his speech at an alternative site, he ultimately had to admit that "there is no venue that can compete with the history, tradition and importance of the House Chamber."[42]

Pelosi's stand on behalf of congressional Democrats did not succeed solely on the basis of her opposition to an "immoral wall." Rather, Pelosi's advantage followed from her savvy commitment to government effectiveness (government workers should not be held "hostage") and defending the House—and her office—as a coequal institution with the presidency. Her willingness to cancel the president's State of the Union message and the president's concession that the House chambers added essential luster to this address show that the institutional rivalry built into the Constitution still has some force, even if it remains badly beaten.

The contretemps over the State of the Union illustrates the need for Congress to engage the White House more regularly in legislative affairs. For example, the president and Congress could collaborate on a "grand bargain" that requires Congress to cede obstructionist tactics such as the routine use of the filibuster to thwart the president's program in exchange for the executive's agreement to anoint fewer "policy czars," as Mark Rozell and Mitchell Sollenberger call them: members of the White House Office with important policy responsibility who are insulated from legislative oversight (including Senate confirmation).[43] Constructive partisan engagement might also be encouraged by experiments in executive-legislative relations that would encourage the president and Congress to confront each other more constructively than is possible during the State of Union spectacle or the constitutional brinksmanship of impeachment. Something akin to the question period that the prime minister endures in the United Kingdom's parliament might lead to meaningful debates over current policy that divide and roil the nation. These events are likely to be rough and tumble in an age of partisan polarization; but the interaction would be healthy, an opportunity for the president and legislators, even when divided by parties, to meet each other face to face rather than lob bombs across Pennsylvania Avenue.

Of course, this all may be pie in the sky—the incentives for Congress and the president to partake of constructive engagement might be overwhelmed by the imperatives of executive-centered partisanship, which has become deeply entrenched in American politics. The motivation for the president to cooperate seems especially weak, as the administrative presidency allows the White House to do so much on its own. The time has come to recognize that the president no longer "needs help," as the Brownlow Committee report insisted in the 1930s. Let the president keep his press secretary and communications director. But if the goal is to encourage some inter-branch or intergovernmental interaction, it might be time to reduce the size of the Executive Office of the President. Let administrators justify their regulations before the oversight committees of Congress, instead of Office of Information and Regulatory Affairs, ensconced in the Office of Management and Budget. If presidents need technical expertise in cost-benefit analysis, place the actuaries back in regular executive department like Treasury or Commerce, not next door to the West Wing. Allow the president to have a chief policy advisor and director of legislative affairs, but the White House should not have policy czars like Stephen Miller whose power over immigration matters in the Trump administration circumvented the authority of the Department of Homeland Security and usurped Congress's legislative authority. The Office of Legal Counsel in the Department of Justice provides ample cover for presidential overreach, and the White House Counsel does little but to justify a ballooning set of presidential powers. Scaling these offices back will not make the president more likely to act "illegally." It will re-center the debate over the president's constitutional powers in the halls of the nation's representatives.

Additionally, we need to rework the budgeting process. The Office of Management and Budget has become a critical staff agency that gives direction to fiscal and regulatory policy; however, with the increasing use of reconciliation orders, it has abetted presidents in their quest to cut through the Gordian Knott of congressional budget and appropriation committees. Critics of federal budgeting thought the old, decentralized system of committee-crafted budget requests was a political thicket that protected irresponsible deficit spending. However, the promise that the president, with the support of the budget office, could impose order has not been fulfilled. Instead, Congress routinely fails to pass any meaningful fiscal policy, the president's budget is an annual symbolic reminder about how little the White House depends on Congress to achieve its goals, and the debt continues to grow.

Such proposals to renew the division of powers and collective responsibility within the federal government also presuppose moderating the powerful centripetal trends that have dominated American politics since the construction of the New Deal political order. Centralization and coordination are the lifeblood of presidential aggrandizement. As James Madison recognized very early on, the consolidation of the state governments into one large national government would invariably lead to a hereditary or, more insidiously, an elected monarchy. As he wrote in the *National Gazette*, a newspaper that rallied opposition to Hamilton's program of "consolidation," the "incompetency of one Legislature to regulate all the various objects belonging to the local governments, would evidently force a transfer of many of them to the executive department; whilst the encreasing splendour and number of its prerogatives supplied by this source, might prove excitements to ambition too powerful for a sober execution of the elective plan."[44] The 20th century made Madison's prophesies a reality, as presidents and federal administrators increasingly took charge of inter-governmental policy-making and set the terms for debate in the states: what local schools should teach, what training and armaments police need, who is required to work in order to receive certain benefits. In the name of "cooperative federalism," or "new federalism," executive power has grown with the objective of making government more unified, efficient, and egalitarian. Instead, the joining of executive power, social activism, and partisan conflict over the past 60 years has pulled the states into fierce partisan struggles centered in the national capital over American identity.[45]

There is no prospect of restoring the "dual federalism" that preceded the New Deal—the division of national and state authority in clearly defined terms, with state governments exercising powers reserved to them without interference from the national government. Nor should there be, for the return of power and autonomy to state and local governments will inevitably result in greater inequality: "federalism means inequality," as Aaron Wildavsky once acknowledged.[46] However, some of the largest efforts to resist executive aggrandizement during the Trump years came from the vestiges of the country's federal framework: it was state attorneys general who successfully blocked Donald Trump's most ambitious efforts to unilaterally impose new immigration standards, rewrite eligibility criteria for the Affordable Care Act, and aggressively use administrative power for partisan purposes.[47] Citizens, living in diverse communities, pressured their local governments to stop cooperating with Immigration and Customs Enforcement (ICE) officials, make federal grants to schools more equitable, reform local policing, and even commit themselves to international environmental standards, such as the Paris Climate Agreement.

This is not to say that the states can by themselves become the new gatekeepers of American politics. Nevertheless, as was especially evident throughout the COVID-19 pandemic, state and local governments can still play a consequential role in managing a national crisis of the first order. Moreover, it is noteworthy that the fracturing of the nation has encouraged Democrats and Republicans to embrace decentralized power when their party is out of power at the national level. To be sure, the nationalization of American politics ensures that neither Democrats nor Republicans cherish provincial liberties. Nevertheless, although the partisan defense of state and local autonomy might seem fragile—sustained by opportunism rather than principle—opposition to the White House that grows out of the states might be the last line of defense against executive-centered partisanship. To the extent that Americans—Democrats and Republicans—see their states as shelters that protect their values from national consolidation, the decades long accretion of power to the White House for managing every aspect of American life might no longer seem ineluctable.

Finally, as Hugh Heclo never failed to remind us, it is up to us to celebrate the virtuous actions of institutionalists, not just the institutions themselves. In this regard, it is not a fool's errand to mark and praise the forbearance of Joe Biden in the early days of administration. While it is not enough to rely on prudence (forbearing statesmen will not always be at the helm), part of renewing our collective faith in institutional processes is to note when acting institutionally supports constitutional principles and institutions. Of course, it is very early in Biden's term, and the flurry of executive actions he issued during his First Hundred Days raises doubts that the president, although a lifelong establishment figure, will continue to play the restrained elder statesman. But there is no gainsaying that although the collective tempera-ture in the room has not gone down, Biden's presence on the national stage has ameliorated the Twitter wars his predecessor relished; moreover, his ag-gressive use of executive power has not preempted efforts to advance par-tisan objectives legislatively. It is noteworthy that during the first month of the Biden presidency, the president and congressional Democrats navigated an ambitious $1.9 trillion package through the legislative process, which al-though unanimously opposed by Republican legislators, had strong bipar-tisan support in the public. Partisans can disagree on the America Rescue Plan's merits, and its contribution to national healing remains uncertain. But Biden has sought to lead a party that has moved significantly to the left since he served in the Obama administration while resisting the most militant populist demands for administrative actions to advance such causes as can-celing student loan debt, prosecuting financial firms, breaking-up "big tech," or declaring a national emergency on gun violence.

Reckoning with America's Past

The greatest challenge faced by those who would restore the vital center is coming to terms with the legacy of slavery and Jim Crow—the roots of systemic racism that is at the core of the party wars that fracture the country and weaken the national resolve. As we argued at the start of this book, most social movements that have struggled to redeem the rights of Black Americans have not been populist. Neither Abolitionists nor Civil Rights activists have sought to divide American society between the People and a demonized other. The peaceful protesters provoked by police killings of unarmed Black men and women did not presume to represent some reified concept of Americans; rather, they marched in solidarity with their White allies to demand the rights promised but still not fulfilled by the Declaration of Independence. To some, this is a radical force, but the widespread movement is not populist. Standing on the shoulders of their forebears, they are at the vanguard of a fundamental struggle to determine who We the People are.

Riven by a Cold Civil War, made all the more hazardous by the pathologies of executive-centered partisanship, Americans might take some small comfort from the reflections of the president who presided over the bloody, all-consuming struggle between North and South. Even during the darkest days of the Civil War, Lincoln never gave up on the proposition that most Americans, even those who supported slavery and refused to acknowledge its inhumanity, were part of a Union forged on the principles of the Declaration and Constitution. An intractably fractured nation, he warned, is vulnerable to demagogues—to those who presume to be champions of people only to betray their interests.

Addressing the Young Men's Lyceum in 1838 on the "perpetuation of our political institutions," Lincoln spoke to an audience whose own vital center was being torn apart, many of them young men who in 20 years would lose their sons in a bitter contest over what it meant to be an American. Lincoln foretold the dangers of a lawless society and, as many conservative witnesses of the social disorder that erupted in 2020 have noted, warned that as "the walls erected for the defense of the persons and property of individuals, are trodden down, and disregarded . . . the lawless in spirit, are encouraged to become lawless in practice." But to those who might simply equate lawfulness and order with the preservation of our political institutions, it is important to recall the context of Lincoln's warning. It came as an admonition against lynch mobs and, in particular, the lynching of a free Black man in St.

Louis, who was denied access to the country's justice system because of the color of his skin. While there was no question of his guilt in the murder of a prominent St. Louis resident, the spirit of lawlessness grew, not by the infliction of murder, but by the government's complicity with the citizenry who took the law into its own hands—the denial of the American creed to protect the liberties of all individuals. Lincoln foretold that by disregarding justice under the law, the group would become a mob, and "in the confusion usually attending such transactions, they will be as likely to hang or burn someone who is neither a gambler nor a murderer as one who is; and that, acting upon the example they set, the mob of tomorrow, may, and probably will, hang or burn some of them by the very same mistake. And not only so; *the innocent, those who have ever set their faces against violations of law in every shape, alike with the guilty, fall victims to the ravages of mob law; and thus it goes on, step by step.*"[48]

Like the Sirens calling out to Odysseus, the demagogues who exploit partisan rancor threaten to lure us all onto the rocks, as we each, step by step, inflict the same carnage on one another in disregarding the laws and norms that preserve free government. The party system, which Lincoln highly valued, forged during the early days of the republic to arbitrate the struggle to fulfill the rights promised by the Declaration, was an important but fragile institution in mediating the fundamental and angry contests that arise in any democracy. As the great abolitionist, Frederick Douglass, warned in his justly famous 1852 July 4th oration, "The cause of liberty may be stabbed by the men who glory in the deeds of your fathers."[49] It is telling that the party system designed to reconcile constitutional government and populist uprisings could not prevent a Civil War or the neutering of the 14th and 15th Amendments in its aftermath, or the rise of a strong reform movement by the end of the 19th century that would denigrate party organizations. That movement, framing American politics as a contest between Progressivism and Conservatism, began the bracing yet disruptive battle for America's identity that reverberates through our own time.

In the midst of political and cultural upheaval, it does little good to condemn polarization. For all its fury and tribalism, the current engagement of the citizenry is preferable to the ennui of administration that seemed to have taken root by the 1960s. As we think institutionally about the distemper loosed by the '60s, we must face the sobering truth that the vital center held in part until that reckoning because of the compromises that both the North and South, Democrats and Republicans made with America's original sin.

The civil rights revolution was so polarizing because it finally forced the United States to confront, after a century of false promises, the shameful limits of its grand experiment in self-rule. Only then did America begin to live up to its foundational principles.

It should not surprise us that the vital center fell apart as the democratic experiment took flight. "Few societies in history have managed to be both multiracial and genuinely democratic," Levitsky and Ziblatt write. "This is our challenge. It is also our opportunity. If we meet it, American will truly be exceptional."[50] The liberal struggle to forge a truly diverse—"rainbow"— coalition over the past six decades represents an impressive effort to meet this challenge. But the hope for an inclusive majority is a fool's errand unless there is some prospect, as Lincoln believed, that most Americans could be "touched by the better angels of our nature." Sustained by their faith that America is an exceptional nation, conservatives can join in this painful struggle to set things right; but only when they reject intolerant nationalism and acknowledge that American can only be a city on a hill—a lodestar to the rest of the world—when engaged in the never-ending struggle to bestow equal dignity on all its citizens.

The experience of the Revolution led to the birth of the foundational principles of the Declaration—"the ring-bolt to the chain of [our] nation's destiny," as Douglass put it. From then on, the political institutions adopted to frame the journey to live up to these ideals were reconstructed when leaders channeled populist protest into meaningful reform, in a collective engagement that placed the defense of principle above rank opportunism, and above the promises made by any one single individual or presidential aspirant. When both Democrats and Republicans engage in this search for common ground, we would have reason to hope for a "new birth of freedom," and a true renewal of a responsible party system.

Notes

Chapter 1

1. Ray Jenkins. April 7, 1968. "George Wallace Figures to Win Even if He Loses." *New York Times Magazine.*

2. Homar Bigart. October 25, 1968. "3,000 Police Ring Garden as Wallace Stages a Rally." *New York Times*, p. 1.

3. Thomas P. Slaughter. 1986. *The Whiskey Rebellion: Frontier Epilogue to the American Revolution.* New York, NY: Oxford University Press.

4. James McPherson. 2003. *Battle Cry of Freedom: The Civil War Era.* New York, NY: Oxford University Press; Barnet Schecter. 2006. *The Devil's Own Work: The Civil War Draft Riots and the Fight to Reconstruct America.* New York, NY: Walker..

5. Eric Foner. 1988. *Reconstruction: America's Unfinished Revolution, 1863–1877.* New York, NY: Harper and Row.

6. Bircherism and its founder Robert Welch were deemed so extreme that leading conservative intellectuals such as Russell Kirk and William F. Buckley went to great lengths to distance themselves from a man "so far removed from common sense." See William F. Buckley Jr. March 2008. "Goldwater, the John Birch Society, and Me." *Commentary.*

7. Donald Trump's Inauguration Speech. January 20, 2017. https://www.politico.com/story/2017/01/full-text-donald-trump-inauguration-speech-transcript-233907.

8. Stephen Levitsky and Daniel Ziblatt. 2018. *How Democracies Die.* New York, NY: Crown; Patrick J. Deneen. 2019. *Why Liberalism Failed.* New Haven, CT: Yale University Press.

9. Alexander Hamilton, James Madison and John Jay, *The Federalist Papers*, with an Introduction and Notes by Charles R. Kessler (New York, Signet Classics, 2003), No. 71, 430–432.

10. On the marginalization of the intellectual right by Schlesinger and other mid-20th-century liberals, see Kevin Mattson. 2004. *When America Was Great: The Fighting Faith of Postwar Liberalism* (rev. ed.). New York, NY: Routledge, 104–106.

11. Louis Hartz. 1955. *The Liberal Tradition in America.* New York, NY: Harcourt, Brace and World.

12. See especially John Patrick Diggins, ed. 2017. *The Liberal Persuasion: Arthur Schlesinger, Jr., and the Challenge of the American Past.* Princeton, NJ: Princeton University Press; Alan Brinkley. 2000. *Liberalism and Its Discontents.* Cambridge, MA: Harvard University Press; Richard H. Pells. 1989. *The Liberal Mind in a Conservative Age: American Intellectuals in the 1940s and 1950s* (2nd 3ed.). Middletown, CT: Wesleyan University Press.

13. Indeed, Schlesinger does not develop fully a defense of the New Deal party system. But given a central assumption of Schlesinger's politics that individuals are weak, fragile, and prone to mishap, the New Deal could not be sustained by new cultural norms alone. Moreover, as an ironist, Schlesinger recognized that to yearn or pray for strong liberal leaders to rescue American democracy is a chimera—especially in world faced with deep ideological divisions, none more dangerous to the project of free society than communism and fascism.

14. Arthur M. Schlesinger Jr. 1949/1998. *The Vital Center: The Politics of Freedom*. New Brunswick, NJ: Transaction, 244.

15. William A. Galston and William Kristol. November 29, 2016. "A New Center." *Brookings Institution*. https://www.brookings.edu/opinions/a-new-center/. Last accessed, April 18, 2017. See also William Kristol and William A. Galston. November 29, 2016. "In Defense of Liberal Democracy, a Joint Statement." *Weekly Standard*. http://www.weeklystandard.com/kristol-and-galston-in-defense-of-liberal-democr acy/article/2005580. Last accessed, April 18, 2017.

16. In his most comprehensive study of modern liberalism, Galston, like Schlesinger, recognizes the necessity of maintaining an open, free economy and in guaranteeing "expressive liberty," or the rights of free speech and free conscience. Moreover, his condemnation of democratic "squeamishness" or the refusal by some "virtuous" politicians to play "hardball" in defending their beliefs, we believe, supports our call for a strengthened, competitive party system. See William A. Galston. 2005. *The Practice of Liberal Pluralism*. Cambridge, UK: Cambridge University Press, 75–94.

17. An interesting study on the rise of "political hobbyism" suggests something similar about modern civic practice and the unequal participation rates among those who are advantaged by so-called movement politics. See Eitan Hersh. 2020. *Politics Is for Power: How to Move Beyond Political Hobbyism, Take Action, and Make Real Change*. New York, NY: Scribner.

18. For example, see Nancy Rosenblum. 2015. *On the Side of the Angels: An Appreciation of Parties and Partisanship*. Princeton, NJ: Princeton University Press; Russell Muirhead. 2015. *The Promise of Party in a Polarized Age*. Cambridge, MA: Harvard University Press; Jonathan Rauch. 2015. *How Hacks, Machines, Big Money and Back Room Deals Can Strengthen Democracy*. Washington, DC: Brookings Institution.

19. Daniel Schlozman and Sam Rosenfeld. 2019. "The Hollow Parties," in Frances Lee and Nolan McCarty, eds., *Can America Govern Itself?* New York, NY: Cambridge University Press.

20. Schlozman and Rosenfeld, "The Hollow Parties."

21. V. O. Key. 1964. *Politics, Parties, and Pressure Groups*. New York, NY: Crowell.

22. Daniel M. Shea. 2010. "The Road Less Taken: New Directions in American Party Politics," in L. Sandy Maisel, Jeffrey M. Berry, and George C. Edwards, eds., *Oxford Handbook of American Political Parties and Interest Groups*. New York, NY: Oxford University Press; Daniel M. Shea. 2003. "Schattschneider's Dismay: Strong Parties and Alienated Voters," in John C. Green and Rick Farmer, eds., *The State of the Parties: The Changing Role of Contemporary American Parties* (4th ed.). Lanham, MD: Rowman and Littlefield.

23. Rosenblum, *On the Side of the Angels*; Muirhead, *The Promise of Party in a Polarized Age*.

24. Sidney M. Milkis, Jesse H. Rhodes, and Emily J. Charnock. 2012. "What Happened to Post-Partisanship? Barack Obama and the New American Party System." *Perspectives on Politics* 10(1): 57–76; Sidney M. Milkis and Nicholas F. Jacobs. 2017. "'I Alone Can Fix It': Donald Trump, the Administrative Presidency, and the Hazards of Executive-Centered Partisanship." *The Forum* 15(3): 583–613.

25. Morton Keller. 2007. *America's Three Regimes: A New Political History*. Oxford, UK: Oxford University Press.

26. Muirhead, *The Promise of Party in a Polarized Age*.

27. On the differences between Democrats and Republicans, see Matt Grossmann and David A. Hopkins. 2016. *Asymmetric Politics: Ideological Republicans and Group Interest Democrats*. New York: Oxford University Press.

28. Richard Hofstadter. 1969. *The Idea of a Party System: The Rise of Legitimate Opposition in the United States, 1789–1840*. Berkeley: University of California Press..

29. Robert A. Dahl. Autumn 1990. "Myth of the Presidential Mandate." *Political Science Quarterly* 105: 355–372.

30. Among academics, see, for example, Samara Klar and Yanna Krupnikov. 2016. *Independent Politics: How American Disdain for Parties Leads to Political Inaction*. New York: Cambridge University Press.

31. As we make clear, the reaction against institutional rules and procedure—the almost instinctive turn toward further dismantling institutions—is the product of a long historical process, similar to what Hugh Heclo identifies as our "modern impasse" of "culture-based" distrust. See Hugh Heclo. 2008. *On Thinking Institutionally*. Oxford, UK: Oxford University Press.

32. Daniel Scholzman and Samuel Rosenfeld. 2017. "Prophets of Party in American Political History." *The Forum* 15(4): 685–709.

33. By group-referential or institutionally minded questions, Heclo specifies: "What expectations and conduct are appropriate to my position and the choice that I might make? What is it, larger than myself, into which I am drawn? And attracted by the light of its value, what *should* I want?"

34. Scholzman and Rosenfeld, "Prophets of Party," p. 64.

35. Alexis de Tocqueville. 1835/2000. *Democracy in America*, trans. Harvey Mansfield and Delba Winthrop. Chicago, IL: Chicago University Press, pp. 662–663.

36. Robert N. Bellah, Richard Madsen, William M. Sullivan, Ann Swidler, and Steven M. Tipton. 2007. *Habits of the Heart: Individualism and Commitment in American Life* (3rd ed.). Oakland, CA: University of California Press.

37. David Von Drehle. March 1, 2019. "Opinion: Where does America find such sad excuses for elected leaders?" *Washington Post*. https://www.washingtonpost.com/opinions/where-does-america-find-such-sad-excuses-for-elected-leaders/2019/03/01/9a221ade-3c5a-11e9-a06c-3ec8ed509d15_story.html; January 15, 2019. "Opinion: I don't usually relish the snow. But this time I found the beauty in it." *Washongton Post*. https://www.washingtonpost.com/opinions/i-dont-usually-relish-the-snow-but-this-time-i-found-the-beauty-in-it/2019/01/15/306e5d4a-18f2-11e9-8813-cb9dec761e73_story.html.

38. David Brooks. August 5, 2019. "Opinion: The Ideology of Hate and How to Fight It." *New York Times*. https://www.nytimes.com/2019/08/05/opinion/el-paso-dayton-shooting.html?rref=collection%2Fbyline%2Fdavid-brooks.

39. E. J. Dionne, Norman J. Ornstein, and Thomas E. Mann. 2017. *One Nation After Trump: A Guide for the Perplexed, the Disillusioned, the Desperate, and the Not-Yet Deported*. New York, NY: St. Martin's Press.

40. Alexander Hamilton, James Madison, and John Jay. *The Federalist Papers*, 75.

41. Jack N. Rakove. 1979. *The Beginning of National Politics*. New York, NY: Alfred A. Knopf.

42. Samuel Beer. 1993. *To Make a Nation: The Rediscovery of American Federalism*. Cambridge, MA: Harvard University Press, 86.

43. George Thomas. Fall 2016. "Madison and the Perils of Populism." *National Affairs*, 142–156.

44. James Morone. 1998. *The Democratic Wish: Popular Participation and the Limits of American Government* (rev. ed.). New Haven, CT: Yale University Press..

45. Bruce Ackerman. 1993. *We the People*, 3 vols. Cambridge, MA: Harvard University Press.

46. For a comprehensive and illuminating history on the development of voting rights in the United States is offered by Alexander Keyssar. 2009. *The Right to Vote: The Contested History of Democracy in the United States* (rev. ed.). New York, NY: Basic Books. See also David A. Bateman. 2018. *Disenfranchising Democracy: Constructing the Electorate in the United States, the United Kingdom, and France*. Cambridge, UK: Cambridge University Press.

47. Wilson Carey McWilliams. 1980. "Democracy and the Citizen: Community, Dignity and the Crisis of Contemporary Politics in America," in Robert A. Goldwin and William A. Schambra, eds., *How Democratic Is the Constitution?* Washington, DC: American Enterprise Institute, 79–101.

48. Abraham Lincoln. 1838. "Address to Young Men's Lyceum, January 27," in Don Fehrenbacher, ed., *Abraham Lincoln: Selected Speeches and Writing*. Boone, IA: Library of America Paperback Classics, 1992, 14.

49. Michael Kazin. 2014. *The Populist Persuasion: An American History* (rev. ed.). Ithaca, NY: Cornell University Press, 3.

50. Richard Hofstadter. 1955. *The Age of Reform*. New York, NY: Vintage Books.

51. Elizabeth Sanders. 1999. *Roots of Reform: Farmers, Workers, and the American State, 1877–1917*. Chicago, IL: University of Chicago Press.

52. Charles Postel. 2009. *The Populist Vision*. New York, NY: Oxford University Press.

53. Kurt Weyland. 2001. "Clarifying a Contested Concept: Populism in the Study of Latin American Politics." *Comparative Politics* 31(1): 1–22.

54. Sidney G. Tarrow. 2011. *Power in Movement: Social Movements and Contentious Politics* (3rd ed.). New York, NY: Cambridge University Press.

55. Gregory Koger, Seth Masket, and Hans Noel. 2016. "No Disciplined Army: American Political Parties as Networks," in Jennifer Nicoll Victor, Alexander H. Montgomery, and Mark Lubell, eds., *The Oxford Handbook of Political Networks*. Oxford, UK: Oxford University Press; David Karol. 2007. *Party Position Change in American Politics: Coalition Management*. Cambridge, UK: Cambridge University Press.

56. Kazin, *The Populist Persuasion*, 1

57. Pierre Rosanvallon. 2008. *Counter-democracy: Politics in an Age of Distrust*, trans. Arthur Goldhammer. New York, NY: Cambridge University Press, 266.

58. Rosanvallon similarly identifies the "populist temptation" as the tri-part culmination of "counter-democracy" pathologies: the politics of oversight (intense distrust of government), negative sovereignty (the failure to affirmatively state governing ends), and the politics of judgment (the emphasis placed on revenge as opposed to a concern for just distribution), see Rosenvallon, *Counter-democracy*, chapter 10, pp. 227–247.

59. Sidney M. Milkis and Daniel Tichenor. 2019. *Rivalry and Reform: Presidents, Social Movements and Changes in American Politics*. Chicago, IL: University of Chicago Press, chapter 2.

60. Hamilton, Madison and Jay, *Federalist* 49, 314; 10, 73.

61. Hamilton, Madison and Jay, *Federalist* 68.

62. James Q. Wilson. 1962. *The Amateur Democrat*. Chicago, IL: University of Chicago Press, 22.

63. Jonathan Rauch. Summer 2021. "Rescuing Compromise." *National Affairs* 48. https://www.nationalaffairs.com/publications/detail/rescuing-compromise.

64. Michael S. Lewis-Beck, Helmut Norpoth, William G. Jacoby, and Herbert F. Weisberg. 2008. *The American Voter Revisited*. Ann Arbor: University of Michigan Press.

65. Jennifer Wolak. 2020. *Compromise in an Age of Party Polarization*. New York, NY: Oxford University Press.

66. G. Calvin MacKenzie and Robert Weisbrot. 2008. *The Liberal Hour: Washington and the Politics of Change in the 1960s*. New York, NY: Penguin Books.

67. Stephen Skowronek. 2011. *Presidential Leadership in Political Time: Reprise and Reappraisal* (2nd ed.). Lawrence: University of Kansas Press, 108.

68. Bruce Miroff. 1993. *Icons of Democracy: American Leaders as Heroes, Aristocrats, Dissenters and Democrats*. New York, NY: Basic Books.

69. Suzanne Mettler. 2011. *The Submerged State: How Invisible Government Policies Undermine American Democracy*. Chicago, IL: University of Chicago Press.

70. Suzanne Mettler. 2018. *The Government-Citizen Disconnect*. New York, NY: Russell Sage Foundation.

71. Kimberly J. Morgan and Andrea Louise Campbell. 2011. *The Delegated Welfare State: Medicare, Markets, and the Governance of Social Policy*. Oxford, UK: Oxford University Press.

72. Theodore Lowi. 1979. *The End of Liberalism: The Second Republic of the United States* (2nd ed.). New York, NY: Norton, 107.

73. Hugh Heclo. 2005. "Sixties Civics," in Sidney M. Milkis and Jerome Mileur, eds., *The Great Society and the High Tide of Liberalism*. Amherst: University of Massachusetts Press.

74. Richard Harris and Sidney Milkis. 1996. *The Politics of Regulatory Change: A Tale of Two Agencies*. New York, NY: Oxford University Press.

75. Paul Pierson. 2007. "The Rise of Activist Government," in Paul Pierson and Theda Skocpol, eds., *The Transformation of American Politics: Activist Government and the Rise of Conservatism*. Princeton, NJ: Princeton University Press, 35.

76. Milkis, Rhodes, and Charnock. "What Happened to Post-Partisanship?"
77. Heclo, "Sixties Civics," 60. This combination of demands for more government while people trust it less dovetails with conceptions of the state as dysfunctional that scholars have identified. See Lawrence R. Jacobs and Desmond King, eds. 2009. *The Unsustainable American State*. New York, NY: Oxford University Press.
78. See, alternatively, Jacobs S. Hacker and Paul Pierson. 2005. *Off Center: The Republican Revolution and The Erosion of American Democracy*. New Haven, CT: Yale University Press; E. J. Dionne Jr. 2016. *Why the Right Went Wrong: Conservatism—From Goldwater to the Tea Party and Beyond*. New York, NY: Simon & Schuster.
79. Phillip Rucker and Robert Costa. February 23, 2017. "Bannon Vows a Daily Fight for 'Deconstruction of the Administrative State.'" *Washington Post*.
80. Sam Rosenfeld. 2018. *The Polarizers: Postwar Architects of Our Partisan Era*. Chicago, IL: University of Chicago Press.
81. Milkis and Jacobs, "'I Alone Can Fix It'"; Julia Azari. November 3, 2016. "Weak Parties and Strong Partisanship Are a Bad Combination." *Vox*. https://www.vox.com/mischiefs-of-faction/2016/11/3/13512362/weak-parties-strong-partisanship-bad-combination. Last accessed December 11, 2019.
82. We wish to draw attention, however, to Madison's own important role in correcting for perceived problems with the Constitution he had a hand in drafting. Put simply, Madison "evolves" on the issue of parties in a constitutional republic. See especially Stanley Elkins and Eric McKitrick. 1993. *The Age of Federalism*. Oxford, UK: Oxford University Press; and Sidney M. Milkis. 1999. *Political Parties and Constitutional Government*. Baltimore, MD: Johns Hopkins University Press. In contrast to James Ceaser's argument that the party system emerged in the mid-19th century as a complement to the framers' initial goal of moderating the ambition of presidential candidates and presidents—one that sees the party system as a "corrective" to the original Constitution—we view the party system as a fundamental constitutional re-form, one that presupposed ongoing and spirited party competition as a critical in-gredient of a vital representative government. See James Ceaser. 1979. *Presidential Selection: Theory and Development*. Princeton, NJ: Princeton University Press.
83. James Madison to Richard Henry Lee, June 25, 1824, in *Writings of James Madison*, ed. Gaillard Hunt, 9 vols. 1904. New York: Putnam, 9: 190-191.
84. Katherine Krimmel. 2017. "The Efficiencies and Pathologies of Special Interest Partisanship." *Studies in American Political Development* 31(1), 149-169.
85. David W. Rhode. 1979. "Risk-bearing and Progressive Ambition: The Case of the United States House of Representatives. *American Journal of Political Science* 23(1): 1-26; John Aldrich. 2011. *Why Parties? A Second Look*. Chicago, IL: University of Chicago Press.
86. For a quantitative demonstration of this point and an elaboration on "non-central-ization," see Nicholas F. Jacobs. 2020. "Polycentric Party Governance: Competition, Federalism, and the Production of Political Leadership in American Politics," in Peter Boettke, Bobbi Herzberg, and Brian Kogelmann, eds., *Exploring the Political Economy & Social Philosophy of Vincent and Elinor Ostrom*. Lanham, MD: Rowman and Littlefield.

87. Frances McCall Rosenbluth and Ian Shapiro. 2018. *Responsible Parties: Saving Democracy from Itself.* New Haven, CT: Yale University Press.

88. Walter Dean Burnham. 1970. *Critical Elections and the Mainsprings of American Politics.* New York: Norton.

89. Daniel DiSalvo. 2012. *Engines of Change: Party Factions in American Politics, 1868–2010.* New York, NY: Oxford University Press.

90. Arthur M. Schlesinger Jr. 1960. *The Politics of Upheaval: 1935–1936, the Age of Roosevelt*, vol. 3: 522.

91. Daniel Schlozman and Sam Rosenfeld. 2017. "Prophets of Party in American Political History." *The Forum* 15(4): 706–707.

92. On the reformist ambitions of the New Deal as it relates to the party system, see Sidney M. Milkis. 1993. *The President and the Parties: The Transformation of the American Party System Since the New Deal.* Oxford, UK: Oxford University Press.

93. See, for example, John Aldrich. 2011. *Why Parties? A Second Look.* Chicago, IL: University of Chicago Press.

94. Richard Hofstadter. 1965. *The Idea of a Party System: The Rise of Legitimate Opposition in the United States, 1780–1840.* Berkeley: University of California Press.

95. Gallup Polls. 2019. "Confidence in Institutions." https://news.gallup.com/poll/1597/confidence-institutions.aspx.

96. "Toward a More Responsible Two-Party System: A Report of the Committee on Political Parties, American Political Science Association," *The American Political Science Review* (Supplement: Vol. 44, September 1950, Number 3, Part 2)

97. Liliana Mason. 2018. *Uncivil Agreement: How Politics Became Our Identity.* Chicago, IL: University of Chicago Press; David A. Hopkins. 2017. *Red Fighting Blue: How Geography and Electoral Rules Polarize American Politics.* Cambridge, New York: Cambridge University Press; Dante J. Scala and Kenneth M. Johnson. 2017. "Political Polarization Along the Rural-Urban Continuum. The Geography of the Presidential Vote, 2000–2016." Annals of the American Academy of Political and Social Science 672(1): 162–184.

98. Heclo, *On Thinking Institutionally*, chapter 6.

Chapter 2

1. Hugh Heclo. 2005. "Sixties Civic," in Sidney M. Milkis and Jerome Mileur, eds., *The Great Society and the High Tide of Liberalism.* Amherst: University of Massachusetts Press, 53–82.

2. Steven Levitsky and Daniel Ziblatt. 2018. *How Democracies Die.* New York, NY: Broadway Books, chapter 2.

3. The concept of intercurrence is most fully elaborated on in Karren Orren and Stephen Skowronek. 2004. *The Search for American Political Development.* New York, NY: Cambridge University Press.

4. Stephen Skowronek. 1982. *Building a New American State: The Expansion of National Administrative Capacities, 1877-1920.* New York, NY: Cambridge University Press.

5. Barry D. Karl. 1983. *The Uneasy State: The United States from 1915-1945.* Chicago, IL: University of Chicago Press, 238.

6. James Pierson. 1982. "Party Government." *Political Science Review* 12: 2-52; Harry Jaffa. 1977. "A Phoenix from the Ashes: The Death of James Madison's Constitution (Killed by James Madison) and the Birth of Party Government." Prepared for delivery at the annual meeting of the American Political Science Association, Washington, DC

7. His task was made more difficult by Federalist machinations that sought to select Aaron Burr—the Democratic-Republican vice-presidential candidate—to lead the nation. Their maneuvers were made possible because the Constitution provided no mechanism for electors to distinguish between presidential and vice-presidential candidates, resulting in a tie between the two representatives of the Democratic-Republican ticket. This impasse left the final decision to the House, where the ambitious Burr and opportunistic Federalists conspired to thwart the clear verdict of the election. Hamilton, arguing that the unprincipled Burr was unfit to be president, persuaded enough Federalists to give up their conspiracy that Jefferson, after a prolonged constitutional crisis, was eventually elected to the executive mansion. With control of Congress and the states, the Democratic-Republicans added the 12th Amendment to the Constitution in 1804, allowing electors to cast separate votes for president and vice president. This amendment, Hofstadter notes, marks the first Constitutional recognition of parties.

8. Thomas Jefferson. March 4, 1801. *First Inaugural Address.* http://avalon.law.yale.edu/19th_century/jefinau1.asp. Last accessed February 16, 2017.

9. Alexis de Tocqueville. 1835/2000. *Democracy in America*, trans. Harvey Mansfield and Delba Winthrop. Chicago, IL: Chicago University Press,167.

10. Thomas Piketty and Gabriel Zucman. 2014. "Capital Is Black: Wealth-Income Ratios in Rich Countries, 1700-2010." *Quarterly Journal of Economics* 129(3): 1303.

11. Pauline Maier. 1999. "Early American Local Self-Government," in Martha Derthick, ed., *Dilemmas of Scale in America's Federal Democracy.* Washington, DC: Woodrow Wilson Center, 84-88.

12. Kathleen Smith Kutolowski. 1978. "The Janus Face of New York's Local Parties: Genesee County, 1821-1827." *New York History* 59(2): 146; see also Ronald P. Formisano. 1974. "Deferential-Participant Politics: The Early Republic's Political Culture, 1789-1840." *American Political Science Review* 68(2): 473-487. And, more generally, see David A. Bateman. 2018. *Disenfranchising Democracy: Constructing the Electorate in the United States, the United Kingdom, and France.* New York, NY: Cambridge University Press.

13. Ronald P. Formisano. 2012. *For the People: American Populist Movements from the Revolution to the 1850s.* Chapel Hill: University of North Carolina Press, 77-82.

14. Ronald P. Formisano. 1999. "The 'Party Period' Revisited." *Journal of American History* 86(1): 98.

15. Andrew R. L. Cayton. Summer 1982. "The Fragmentation of 'A Great Family': The Panic of 1819 and the Rise of the Middling Interest in Boston, 1818-1822." *Journal of the Early Republic* 2(2): 157.

16. Maurice G. Baxter. 2004. *Henry Clay and the American System*. Lexington: University Press of Kentucky, 38–42.

17. Steven C. Bullock. 1996. *Revolutionary Brotherhood: Freemasonry and the Transformation of the American Social Order, 1730–1840*. Chapel Hill: University of North Carolina Press.

18. Formisano, *For the People*, pp. 98–99.

19. Leonard L. Richards. 2000. *The Slave Power: The Free North and Southern Domination, 1780–1860*. Baton Rouge: Louisiana State University Press.

20. William Preston Vaughn. 2009. *The Anti-Masonic Party in the United States, 1826–1943*. Lexington: University Press of Kentucky.

21. See Michael F. Holt. 1999. *The Rise and Fall of the American Whig Party: Jacksonian Politics and the Onset of the Civil War*. New York, NY: Oxford University Press.

22. James W. Ceaser. 1979. *Presidential Selection: Origins and Development*. Princeton, NJ: Princeton University Press.

23. Lee Benson. 1961. *The Concept of Jacksonian Democracy: New York as a Test Case*. Princeton, NJ: Princeton University Press.

24. Benson, *the Concept of Jacksonian Democracy*.

25. Formisano, *For the People*, p. 113.

26. Formisano, *For the People*, pp. 149–154.

27. "Amendments to the Constitution of 1821," ratified September 1826, in *The Federal and State Constitutions*, ed. Francis Newton Thorpe, 7 vols. Washington, DC: Government Printing Office, 1909, 5: 2651.

28. Formisano, *For the People*, 147.

29. Martin Van Buren. 1867. *Inquiry into the Origin and Course of Political Parties in the United States*. New York, NY: Hudson and Houghton.

30. Martin Van Buren to Thomas Ritchie. July 13, 1827. *Martin Van Buren Papers*, Library of Congress. Washington, DC.

31. Both of these objectives fit within a much larger and historically rich account of modern republicanism that is beyond the scope of this study. Jackson's assault on national governing institutions, such as the 2nd Bank of the United States, and the Democratic Party's reliance on state party leaders nurtured the hallmark of America's participatory politics: the local community or township. Likewise, the restraining effect of party democracy helped to ward off the perpetual tormentor of democratic self-rule, the demagogue—the populist who, as Hamilton warned, "flatters . . . the people's . . . prejudices to betray their interests."

As James Ceaser has written, "In line with the Founder's aims, party competition would prevent personal factionalism and control popular leadership; discourage sectional divisions and encourage moderate, coalitional majorities; ensure the existence of candidates with broad national support and thus avoid the evils of Congressional selection; undo any unjust advantage to the oligarchic party deriving from unforeseen electoral influences; and restore at least a modicum of energy to the executive." Yet this concern to ameliorate a fractious populist politics was wedded to a fundamental reconsideration of the relationship between government and the citizenry—it was an institutional solution to the Constitution's failure to cultivate attention to, and participation in public affairs. The decentralized structure of the mass party would proscribe efforts to build up a strong national state that threatened to denigrate the dignity of the democratic individual.

32. Richard Hofstadter. 1970. *The Idea of a Party System: The Rise of Legitimate Opposition in the United States, 1780–1840*. Berkley: University of California Press, 225 (emphasis in original).

33. Stephen Skowronek. 1982. *Building a New American State: The Expansion of National Administrative Capacities, 1877–1920*. New York, NY: Cambridge University Press, 40.

34. Keller, *Affairs of State*, pp. 266–268.

35. Frances Lee. 2016. "Patronage, Logrolls, and 'Polarization:' Congressional Parties of the Gilded Age, 1876–1896." *Studies in American Political Development* 30(2): 116–127.

36. Richard Franklin Bensel. 2008. *Passion and Preference: William Jennings Bryan and the 1896 Democratic Convention*. New York, NY: Cambridge University Press.

37. James L. Sundquist. 1983. *Dynamics of the Party System: Alignment and Realignment of Political Parties in the United States* (2nd ed.). Washington, DC: Brookings Institution, 154–168.

38. Lawrence Goodwyn. 1978. *The Populist Moment: A Short History of the Agrarian Revolt in America*. New York, NY: Oxford University Press, 52.

39. Goodwyn, *The Populist Moment*, p. 56.

40. Goodwyn, *The Populist Moment*, p. 114.

41. Goodwyn, *The Populist Moment*, p. 60.

42. Robert C. McMath. 1992. *American Populism: A Social History, 1877–1898*. New York, NY: Hill and Wang, 98–99.

43. Donna A. Barnes. 1984. *Farmers in Rebellion: The Rise and Fall of the Southern Farmers Alliance and People's Party in Texas*. Austin: University of Texas Press.

44. Quoted in Goodwyn, *The Populist Moment*, p. 134.

45. Quoted in Goodwyn, *The Populist Moment*, p. 138.

46. Jeffery Ostler. 1993. *Prairie Populism: The Fate of Agrarian Radicalism in Kansas, Nebraska, and Iowa, 1880–1892*. Lawrence: University Press of Kansas.

47. Goodwyn, *The Populist Moment*, pp. 141–143.

48. Bruce Palmer. 1980. *Man over Money: The Southern Populist Critique of American Capitalism*. Chapel Hill: University of North Carolina Press.

49. Stephen Kantrowitz. 2000. *Ben Tillman and the Reconstruction of White Supremacy*. Chapel Hill: University of North Carolina Press.

50. Robert C. McGrath. 2011. *Populist Vanguard: A History of the Southern Farmers' Alliance*. Chapel Hill: University of North Carolina Press.

51. A full text copy of the Omaha platform is available in Randall E. Adkins. 2008. *The Evolution of Political Parties, Campaigns, and Elections: Landmark Documents, 1787–2007*. Washington, DC: CQ Press, chapter 21.

52. Michael Kazin. 1995. *The Populist Persuasion: An American History*. Ithaca, NY: Cornell University Press, 112–113; 43.

53. Gregg Cantrell. 2020. *The People's Revolt: Texas Populists and the Roots of American Liberalism*. New Haven CT, Yale University Press.

54. *New York Times.* 1896. "Bryan, Free Silver, and Repudiation." July 11.

55. Matthew Hild. 2007. *Greenbackers, Knights of Labor, and Populists: Farmer-Labor Insurgency in the late-Nineteenth-Century South.* Athens, GA, University of Georgia Press.

56. William Jennings Bryan, "Cross of Gold Speech." http://historymatters. gmu.edu/d/ 5354/. Last accessed April 3, 2016.

57. Kazin, *The Populist Persuasion*, p. 45.

58. Gil Troy. 1996. *See How They Ran: The Changing Role of the Presidential Candidate* (rev. and exp. ed.). Cambridge, MA: Harvard University Press, 105–106.

59. Walter Dean Burnham. 1981. "The System of 1896: An Analysis," in Paul Keppner, ed., *The Evolution of American Electoral Systems.* Westport, CT: Greenwood Press.

60. Kazin, *The Populist Persuasion*, p. 45.

61. Elizabeth Sanders. 1999. *Roots of Reform: Farmers, Workers, and the American State, 1877–1917.* Chicago, IL: University of Chicago Press, 147.

62. V. O. Key. 1948. *Southern Politics in State and Nation.* New York: Alfred A. Knopf; see also J. Morgan Kousser. 1974. *The Shaping of Southern Politics: Suffrage Restriction and the Establishment of the One-Party South, 1880–1910.* New Haven, CT: Yale University Press.

63. Theodore Lowi. 1985. *The Personal President: Power Invested, Promise Unfulfilled.* Ithaca, NY: Cornell University Press, 41; Eldon Eisenach, *The Lost Promise of Progressivism* (Lawrence: University Press of Kansas, 1994).

64. Woodrow Wilson. 1908. *Constitutional Government in the United States.* New York, NY: Columbia University Press, 179–180.

65. Daniel Rogers summarizes the difficulty in writing about the Progressive "movement" or "era" as such: "The trouble with comprehending 'progressivism' as a list of beliefs is that progressives did not share a common creed or a string of common values." Moreover, and providing further complication, "those whom historians had labeled progressives shared no common party or organization." Daniel T. Rogers. 1982. "In Search of Progressivism." *Reviews of American History* 10: 114–123. There was a Progressive Party, but it championed a program of direct democracy that disdained intermediary institutions such as party organizations.

66. Henry Adams. October 1876. "The Independents in the Canvas." *North American Review* 123: 436–464.

67. Barry Karl. 1983. *The Uneasy State: The United States from 1915 to 1945.* Chicago, IL: University of Chicago Press, 236. On the Progressive Party's importance and legacy, see Sidney M. Milkis. 2011. *Theodore Roosevelt, the Progressive Party and the Transformation of American Democracy.* Lawrence: University Press of Kansas.

68. Wilson devotes considerable space—nearly 60 pages—in his history to the intra-party weakness revealed by the question of free silver and the People's Party demands. While he views the Populists as radicals, he uses the narrative to defend his emerging theory of presidential government and responsible party leadership. See Woodrow Wilson. 1901. *A History of the American People: Reunion and Nationalization*, vol. 5. New York, NY: Harper and Brothers, 209–267.

69. Scott James. 2005. "The Evolution of the Presidency: Between the Promise and the Fear, in Joel Auberbach and Mark Peterson, eds., *The Executive Branch*. New York, NY: Oxford University Press, 19.

70. Wilson, *Constitutional Government in the United States*, pp. 18, 124, 123.

71. Eric Yellin, *Racism in the Nation's Service: Government Workers and the Color Line in Woodrow Wilson's America* (Chapel Hill: University of North Carolina Press, 2013).

72. Sean Beienburg. 2018. "Neither Nullification nor Nationalism: The Battle for the States' Rights Middle Ground During Prohibition." *American Political Thought* 7(2): 271–303.

73. Quoted in James P. Shenton. 1958. "The Coughlin Movement and the New Deal." *Political Science Quarterly* 73(3): 352.

74. Glen Jeansonne. 2012. "The Priest and the President: Father Coughlin, FDR, and 1930s America." *Midwest Quarterly* 53(4): 359.

75. This account is richly detailed in one of the first biographies written on Coughlin, published in 1933: Ruth Mugglebee. 1933. *Father Coughlin, the Radio Priest, of the Shrine of the Little Flower: An account of the Life, Work and Message of Reverend Charles E. Coughlin*. Garden City, NY: Garden City Publishing, 212–218.

76. Many of Coughlin's sermons have not survived, including his infamous description of Soviet life and communist connections to American business. These are detailed in Mugglebee, *Father Coughlin*, pp. 220–223.

77. Alan Brinkley. 1982. *Voices of Protest: Huey Long, Father Coughlin, and the Great Depression*. New York, NY: Random House, 97.

78. FDR to Baker. March 20, 1935. *President's Personal File*, 2332. FDR Presidential Library.

79. Brinkley, *Voices of Protest*, p. 108.

80. Coughlin's mindset is most fully revealed in the month's long back-and-forth with Hugh Johnson, FDR's first director of the National Recovery Administration: *Boston Daily Globe*. March 12, 1935. "Coughlin Hurls Back Charges," p. 1.

81. Rexford G. Tugwell. 1957. *The Democratic Roosevelt: A Biography of Franklin D. Roosevelt*. New York, NY: Doubleday, 349–350.

82. Brinkley, *Voices of Protest*, p. 113.

83. Brinkley, *Voices of Protest*, p. 121.

84. John M. Carlisle. October 29, 1933. "Priest of a Parish of the Air Waves." *New York Times Magazine*..

85. *New York Times*. June 15, 1933. "Radio Priest Urged as Adviser in London," p. 5.

86. *The New Republic*. April 24, 1935. "Father Coughlin's Program," pp. 299–300.

87. Kazin, *The Populist Persuasion*.

88. James T. Patterson. 1969. *The New Deal and the States: Federalism in Transition*. Princeton, NJ: Princeton University Press.

89. Ira Katznelson. 2005. *When Affirmative Action Was White: An Untold History of Racial Inequality in Twentieth-Century America*. New York, NY: W.W. Norton.

90. See, for example, Gareth Davies and Martha Derthick. 1997. "Race and Social Welfare Policy: The Social Security Act of 1935." *Political Science Quarterly* 112(2): 217–235.

91. George A. Condon. 1962. "The Politics of the Social Justice Movement." PhD dissertation, University of Tennessee, 168.

92. A. B. Magil. June 24, 1936. "Can Father Coughlin Come Back?" *New Republic*, 196–198.

93. Frank Kent. May 13, 1935. "The Great Game of Politics: The Coughlin Objective." *Wall Street Journal*, p. 2.

94. *New York Times*. March 11, 1935. "Third Party Talk Grows at Capital," p. 3.

95. Raymond Clapper. May 11, 1935. "Between You and Me: Bonus Heat Turned on Wrong Way." *Washington Post*, p. 2.

96. *Boston Globe*. June 3, 1935. "Fr Coughlin Sees Victory Ahead Now for New Deal," p. 4.

97. *New York Times*. March 4, 1935. "Coughlin Terms New Deal Failure," p. 2.

98. Marc Landy. 2002. "Presidential Party Leadership and Party Realignment: FDR and the Making of the New Deal Democratic Party," in Sidney Milkis and Jerome Mileur, eds., *The New Deal and the Triumph of Liberalism*. Amherst: University of Massachusetts Press.

99. *Boston Globe*. May 15, 1935. "Lippmann Declares Bonus 'Immoral' in Talk Here," p. 1.

100. James P. Shenton. 1958. "The Coughlin Movement and the New Deal." *Political Science Quarterly* 73(3): 352–373.

101. *Daily Boston Globe*. May 9, 1935. "Calls Patman Veto Suicide," p. 1.

102. *New York Times*. February 18, 1935. "Coughlin Offers Bill for a Central Bank," p. 2.

103. *New York Times*. March 12, 1935. "Father Coughlin Says Johnson Aids 'Money Changers,'" p. 1.

104. Kazin, *The Populist Persuasion*, p. 122.

105. Jonathan Mitchell. August 26, 1936. "Father Coughlin's Children." *New Republic*, pp. 72–74.

106. James A. Farley. 1948. *Jim Farley's Story: The Roosevelt Years*. New York, NY: McGraw-Hill, 52.

107. Charles J. Tull. 1965. *Father Coughlin and the New Deal*. Syracuse, NY: Syracuse University Press, 91–92.

108. John O'Connor. February 18, 1936. "O'Connor Denies Coughlin Charge." *New York Times*, p. 2.

109. *Los Angeles Times*. May 20, 1935. "Bonus Fight May Rest on Single Vote," p. 1.

110. Harold Ickes. *The Secret Diary of Harold Ickes: The First Thousand Days* (New York: Simon and Schuster, 1954).

111. *New York Times*. May 23, 1935. "23,000 Here Cheer Coughlin Attack on the President," p. 1.

112. *New York Times*. November 4, 1935. "Coughlin to Expose 'Benedict Arnolds,'" p. 3; *Daily Boston Globe*. November 4, 1935. "Open Season on Congress Declared by Fr Coughlin," p. 5.

113. *New York Times*. November 18, 1935. "Coughlin Breaks with Roosevelt," p. 15; *Los Angeles Times*. November 18, 1935. "Priest Raps Plutocracy," p. 4.

114. *Los Angeles Times*. November 19, 1935. "Coughlin on Roosevelt," p. A4.

308 NOTES TO PAGES 89-100

115. Raymond Clapper. September 13, 1935. "Between You and Me: Reporters at Hyde Park Miss Coughlin Visit." *Washington Post*, p. 2.

116. T.R.B. August 21, 1935. "Washington Notes." *New Republic*, p. 46.

117. Kazin, *The Populist Persuasion*, p. 124.

118. Arthur Krock. October 6, 1936. "Close Race Likely in Massachusetts." *New York Times*, p. 8.

119. Tull, *Father Coughlin and the New Deal*, p. 166.

120. Murphy had the added appeal of not only being a widely supported elected official but as one who had made inroads with Michigan's organized labor movement. See Charles W. Hurd. October 6, 1936. "Says 90% of Labor Is for Roosevelt." *New York Times*, p. 1.

121. Kazin, *The Populist Persuasion*, 127-133.

122. Eric Schickler, *Racial Realignment: The Transformation of American Liberalism: 1932-1965* (Princeton, New Jersey: Princeton Univerity Press, 2016).

Chapter 3

1. Stanley High. February 6, 1937. "Whose Party Is It?" *Saturday Evening Post*, 10-11, 34-37.

2. Historians have generally divided FDR's first term into two periods, each identified by a flurry of legislative activity lasting approximately 100 days. The first period (1933-34) was a response to FDR's call for "bold, persistent experimentation" to meet the great emergency at hand. The second period (1935-36) brought laws that converted emergency programs, such as the Social Security Act and the National Labor Relations Act, into ongoing obligations of the national government, beyond the vagaries of public opinion and the reach of elections and party politics. Scholars have given inadequate attention, however, to the institutional program of Roosevelt's second term, when FDR pursued a program to thoroughly reconstruct the institutions and practices of constitutional government in the United States. This Third New Deal presupposed that programmatic rights, such as Social Security and collective bargaining, would not amount to much unless new institutional arrangements were established that would comport with Roosevelt's redefinition of the social contract. For a discussion of FDR's constitutional program, see Sidney Milkis. Spring 2014. "Ideas, Institutions, and the New Deal Constitutional Order." *American Political Thought*. Symposium on American Political Development and Political Thought, 167-176.

3. Louis Brownlow. Final Edited Manuscript, vol. 2, chapter 30 ("We Report to the President"), 20. Louis Brownlow Papers, John F. Kennedy Library, Boston, MA.

4. Herbert Coly. 1914. *Progressive Democracy*. New York: Macmillan, 364

5. Stephen Skowronek. 1982. *Building A New American State: The Expansion of National Administrative Capacities, 1870-1920*. New York, NY: Cambridge University Press.

6. James T. Sparrow. 2013. *Warfare State*. New York, NY: Oxford University Press.

7. Franklin D. Roosevelt. 1941. "Introduction." *Public Papers and Addresses*, vol. 7 (1938 volume), ed. Samuel I. Rosenman. New York, NY: Macmillan, xxviii–xxxii.

8. For a broad critique of electoral realignments, see David R. Mayhew. 2004. *Electoral Realignments: A Critique of an American Genre*. New Haven, CT: Yale University Press.

9. Eric Schickler. 2016. *Racial Realignment: The Transformation of American Liberalism, 1932–1965*. Princeton, NJ: Princeton University Press, chapter 3.

10. Herbert Croly. 1914. *Progressive Democracy*. New York, NY: Macmillan, 15.

11. Franklin D. Roosevelt, September 23, 1932. *Campaign Address on Progressive Government at the Commonwealth Club in San Francisco*. https://www.presidency. ucsb.edu/documents/campaign-address-progressive-government-the-commonwea lth-club-san-francisco-california. Last accessed, February 16, 2017.

12. Roosevelt, *Campaign Address*.

13. Edward J. Flynn. 1948. *You're the Boss*. New York, NY: Viking Press, 153.

14. Paul Van Riper. 1958. *History of the United States Civil Service*. Westport, CT: Greenwood, 327.

15. Cited in Martha Derthick. 1983. *Policymaking for Social Security*. Washington, DC: Brookings Institution, 230.

16. William V. Nessly. November 7, 1938. "C.I.O. Backs Friends." *Washington Post*. See also *Los Angeles Times*. November 13, 1938. "Lewis Urges Purge of Party"; *Los Angeles Times*. September 13, 1938. "Downey Given CIO Support"; *Los Angeles Times*. June 30, 1938. "CIO Fights for Liberals."

17. When asked whether he thought the solid South would stay Democratic very long, Roosevelt replied: "I think the South is going to be a more intelligent form of democracy than has kept the South, for other reasons, in the democratic column all these years. It will be intelligent thinking, and, in my judgment, because the South is learning, it is going to be a liberal democracy." *Complete Press Conferences of Franklin D. Roosevelt*. April 21, 1972. New York, NY: Da Capo Press,, 1938m no. 452-B, 11: 338–340. In the end, the New Deal political realignment did not succeed in displacing White supremacy with economic liberalism—and once the New Deal state, pressured by a rising civil rights movement, extended its reach to matters of social justice under Harry Truman, John Kennedy, and especially Lyndon Johnson, the South moved to the Republican Party, which had become a solidly right of center party by the 1980s.

18. Raymond Clapper. October 1938. "Roosevelt Tries the Primaries." *Current History* 49: 16.

19. Ernest Cuneo. n.d. "The Eve of the Purge," 23. Unpublished manuscript found in the Ernest Cuneo Papers, Box 111. Franklin D. Roosevelt Library, Hyde Park, NY.

20. *Humphrey's Executor v. United States*, 295 U.S. 602 (1935); *Schechter Poultry Corp. v. United States*, 295 U.S. 495 (1935).

21. William Leuchtenburg. 1996. *The Supreme Court Reborn: Constitutional Revolution in the Age of Roosevelt*. New York, NY: Oxford University Press.

22. William E. Leuchtenburg. 1985. "FDR's Court-Packing Plan: A Second Life, a Second Death." *Duke Law Journal*, 673–689.

23. Felix Belair Jr. August 16, 1938. "Roosevelt Drives for the Completion of the New Deal." *New York Times*, 2.

24. *Congressional Record*, 75th Congress, 3rd session, April 8, 1938, 521.

25. Matthew Dickinson. 2005. "The Executive Office of the President: The Paradox of Politicization," in Joel D. Aberbach and Mark A. Peterson, eds., *The Executive Branch*. New York, NY: Oxford University Press.

26. Brian Balaough. 2009. *A Government Out of Sight: The Mystery of National Authority in Nineteenth-Century America*. Cambridge, UK: Cambridge University Press; Oscar Kraines. 1958. *Congress and the Challenge of Big Government*. New York, NY: Bookman Associates.

27. Louis Brownlow. 1958. *A Passion for Anonymity*. Chicago, IL: University of Chicago Press, 392.

28. *Report of the President's Committee on Administrative Management*. 1937. Washington, DC: Government Printing Office, 53.

29. *New York Times*, January 17, 1937.

30. *Time Magazine*, April 18, 1938, 16.

31. Franklin D. Roosevelt. March 29, 1938. Letter on the Reorganization Bill. https://www.presidency.ucsb.edu/documents/letter-the-reorganization-bill.

32. Luther Gulick. September 1939. "Politics, Administration, and the New Deal." *Annals* 169: 64.

33. Carter Glass to Ernest Stack. August 1937. Box 380, Carter Glass Papers, Accession #2913, University of Virginia Library, Charlottesville, VA.

34. Gulick quoted in Clinton Rossiter. 1960. *The American Presidency*, 2nd edition. New York: Harcourt, Brace and World, 129.

35. The term *administrative presidency* is drawn from Richard Nathan's book on the use of administrative strategies by modern presidents to pursue their policy objectives. See Richard Nathan. 1993. *The Administrative Presidency*. New York, NY: Wiley.

36. Sidney M. Milkis. Spring 2014. "Ideas, Institutions, and the New Deal Constitutional Order." *American Political Thought* 3(1): 167–176.

37. Daniel P. Carpenter. 2002. *The Forging of Bureaucratic Autonomy: Reputations, Networks, and Policy Innovation, 1862–1928*. Princeton, NJ: Princeton University Press.

38. Sidney M. Milkis. 1993. *The President and the Parties: The Transformation of the American Party System Since the New Deal*. Oxford, UK: Oxford University Press.

39. Karen Orren and Stephen Skowronek. 2017. *The Policy State: An American Predicament*. Cambridge, MA: Harvard University Press.

40. Herbert Croly, in criticizing Wilson's own presidency-centered views of the party system remarked, "The party that submits to such a dictatorship, however benevolent, cannot play its own proper part in a system of partisan government. It will either cease to have any independent life or its independence will eventually assume the form of a revolt." Several pages later, Croly would also note that greater executive power—and the decline of the party system—was "an indispensable condition of the success of progressive democracy." Herbert Croly. 1915. *Progressive Democracy*. New York, NY. Macmillan, 345–346, 348.

41. Theodore Lowi. 1979. *The End of Liberalism: The Second Republic of the United States* (2nd ed.). New York, NY: Norton.

42. Schlesinger, while admiring the "quantitative liberalism" of the New Deal generation was nevertheless a critic of what he came to see as its myopic focus on economic stability and growth. After he published *The Vital Center*, Schlesinger devoted his political energies to promoting an alternative "qualitative" liberalism that "moved beyond" the politics of the New Deal—programs and government interventions concerned with the public's "spiritual uncertainty and anxiety" and which could bring about a "new dedication of public purposes." Many of these concerns anticipate the new left's critique of the New Deal in the 1960s. In other words, we find some tension with the "vital center" described by Schlesinger in 1949 and the liberal reforms he advocated and promoted in later years. The "ends" or vision of both types of liberalism are not incommensurate, but the structural form they often take is difficult to reconcile. On qualitative versus quantitative liberalism, see Kevin Mattson. 2004. *When America Was Great: The Fighting Faith of Liberalism in Post-War America.* New York: Routledge, 143–169.

43. Schlesinger, in his three-volume account of the New Deal (1933–1937), is largely responsible for reifying the notion of a "first" and "second" New Deal. Interestingly, he never published a final volume or set of volumes on what some scholars have called the "Third New Deal," dedicated to strengthening the government's administrative capacities. On these distinctions and the historiography of New Deal scholarship see John W. Jeffries. 1990. "The 'New' New Deal: FDR and American Liberalism, 1937–1945." *Political Science Quarterly* 105: 397–418. After witnessing the indiscretions of the Johnson and Nixon years, Schlesinger wrote in 1973, "In the last years presidential primacy, so indispensable to the political order, has turned into presidential supremacy. The constitutional presidency, as events so apparently disparate as the Indochina War and Watergate affair showed—has become the imperial presidency and threatens to be the revolutionary presidency." Arthur M. Schlesinger Jr. 1973. *The Imperial Presidency.* New York, NY: Popular Library, 10.

44. Nicole Rae. 2007. "Be Careful What You Wish For." *Annual Review of Political Science* 10: 169–191.

45. E. E. Schattschneider. 1945. "Party Government and Employment Policy." *American Political Science Review* 39(1): 48.

46. Committee on Political Parties. 1950. American Political Science Association. "Toward a More Responsible Two-Party System." *American Political Science Review* 54(1): 24–25.

47. E. E. Schattschneider. 1942. *Party Government.* New York, NY: Farrar and Rinehart, 163.

48. Schattschneider, *Party Government,* p. 22.

49. Louis Brownlow. January 27, 1943. "Perfect Union." Appendix to Official Files 101 and 101b, 38–39. Franklin Roosevelt Papers, Franklin Roosevelt Library, Hyde Park, New York. Elliott's manuscript, entitled "The President's Role in Administrative Management," can be found in the Papers of the President's Committee on Administrative Management, Roosevelt Library (our emphasis).

50. E. E. Schattschneider. 1974. "The Struggle for Party Government," in *The Party Battle*. New York, NY: Arno Press, 40.

51. Committee on Political Parties, "Toward a More Responsible Two-Party System," 56.

52. Jerome M. Mileur. 1992. "Epilogue: Prospects for Party Government," in John Kenneth White and Jerome M. Mileur, eds., *Challenges to Party Government*. Carbondale: Southern Illinois University Press, 219–220.

53. Committee on Political Parties, "Toward a More Responsible Two-Party System," pp. 93–95 (emphasis in original).

54. Committee on Political Parties, "Toward a More Responsible Two-Party System," pp. 37.

55. Committee on Political Parties, "Toward a More Responsible Two-Party Sytem," pp. 90

56. Committee on Political Parties, "Toward a More Responsible Two-Party System," pp. 61–62. See alternatively Daniel Stid. September 21, 2015. "Political Science and the Challenge of Congressional Reform." Prepared for American Enterprise Institute, Conference on Congress, the Constitution, and Contemporary Politics. Washington, DC.

57. Committee on Political Parties, "Toward a More Responsible Two-Party Sysem," pp. 39–44 (emphasis in original).

58. Both the Democratic and Republican parties experimented with "Advisory Councils," but the Democrats implemented and relied on theirs when Eisenhower, a Republican, was in the White House, and Republicans followed suit when Kennedy and Johnson were president. Therefore, these national leadership councils never had the counter-vailing power the APSA report prescribed, because the party lacked control of the presidency. On the recommendation, see Committee on Political Parties. "Toward a More Responsible Two-Party System," 43 (emphasis added). The Democratic Party experimented with a midterm national convention in the 1970s. The first, held in 1974 when Gerald Ford was president, adopted a charter for the national party and served as a staging area for those considering a run for the party's presidential nom-ination two years later. The second, meeting in 1978, gave progressive Democrats a chance to criticize President Jimmy Carter's attempt to push the party toward the center. Most significantly, however, it served as a launching pad for the 1980 challenge by Massachusetts senator Edward Kennedy to Carter's nomination. The conference, therefore, became a fractious rather than a unifying forum and was soon relegated to history. See Mileur, "Epilogue," p. 226.

59. Committee on Political Parties, "Toward a More Responsible Party System," Foreword.

60. Committee on Political Parties, "Toward a More Responsible Party System," p. 48.

61. Committee on Political Parties, "Toward a More Responsible Party System," p. 54.

62. Committee on Political Parties, "Toward a More Responsible Party System," p. 58.

63. Arthur Schlesinger Jr. March, 1951. Review of *Toward a More Responsible Two Party System*. A Report of the Committee on Political Parties. *Annals of the American Academy of Political and Social Science* 274: 222.

64. Schlesinger, *Review of Toward a More Responsible Two Party System*.

65. See, for example, Frances McCall Rosenbluth and Ian Shapiro. 2018. *Responsible Parties: Saving Democracy from Itself*. New Haven, CT: Yale University Press.

66. Hugh Heclo. 2005. "Sixties Civic," in Sidney M. Milkis and Jerome M. Mileur, eds., *The Great Society and the High Tide of Liberalism*. Amherst: University of Massachusetts Press, 60, 64. This combination of demands for more government while people trust it less dovetails with conceptions of the state as dysfunctional that scholars have identified. See Larry Jacobs and Desmond King. 2009. *The Unustainable American State*. New York: Oxford University Press.

67. Richard A. Harris and Sidney M. Milkis. 1996. *The Politics of Regulatory Change: A Tale of Two Agencies, revised edition*. New York: Oxford University Press.

68. Paul Pierson. 2007. "The Rise of Activist Government," in Paul Pierson and Theda Skocpol, eds., *The Transformation of American Politics: Activist Government and the Rise of Conservatism*. Princeton, NJ: Princeton University Press, 35.

69. E.E. Schattschneider. 1935. *Politics, Pressures and the Tariff*. New York: Prentice-Hall.

70. On the idea of interrogating, lauding, and remaking institutions to enact political change, see Hugh Heclo. 2008. *On Thinking Institutionally*. Boulder, CO: Paradigm.

71. Schlesinger elaborates on this peculiar problem of heroic leadership in modern democratic society in the first essay of his collected anthology, *The Politics of Hope* (1963), first published in 1960 under the title, "On Heroic Leadership and the Dilemma of Strong Men and Weak Peoples." We return to this essay in the closing chapter where we elaborate on the connection between Schlesinger's vital center and party democracy.

72. David O'Brien. 1986. *Storm Center: The Supreme Court in American Politics*. New York, NY: W.W. Norton.

73. Heclo, "Sixties Civics," 62.

74. Gary C. Jacobson. 2019. *Presidents and Parties in the Public Mind*. Chicago, IL: University of Chicago Press.

Chapter 4

1. The first Kennedy-Nixon Debate, September 26, 1960. https://www.debates.org/voter-education/debate-transcripts/september-26-1960-debate-transcript/.

2. Alexander Keyssar. 2009. *The Right to Vote: The Contested History of Democracy in America*. New York, NY: Basic Books, 264.

3. The term, "Faustian bargain," describing the Democratic Party's neglect of civil rights to win southern votes, is the core theme of Ira Katznelson. 2005. *When Affirmative Action Was White: An Untold History of Racial Inequality in Twentieth-Century America*. New York, NY: W.W. Norton; John F. Kennedy. January 20, 1961. Inaugural Address. http://www.presidency.ucsb.edu/ws/index.php?pid=8032&.

4. Papers of John F. Kennedy. Pre-Presidential Papers. Presidential Campaign Files, 1960. Speeches and the Press. Speeches, Statements, and Sections, 1958-1960. Defense and disarmament: Missile gap, John F. Kennedy Library, Boston, Massachusetts.

5. Eric Schickler. 2017. *Racial Realignment: The Transformation of American Liberalism: 1932–1965*. Princeton, NJ: Princeton University Press.

6. John F. Kennedy. 1988. Speech to the National Press Club, Washington, DC, January 14, 1960, in Theodore C. Sorenson, ed., *"Let the Word Go Forth": The Speeches, Statements and Writings of John F. Kennedy*. New York: Delacorte, 17–23.

7. Allen J. Matusow. 1984. *The Unraveling of America: A History of Liberalism in the 1960s*. New York, NY: Harper and Row.

8. Johnson used this term in invoking Kennedy's inaugural address and its defense of the Cold War during his (Johnson's) nationally televised speech announcing he would not run for a second full term. See Lyndon B. Johnson. March 31, 1968. "Remarks on Decision Not to Run for Re-election." https://millercenter.org/the-presidency/presidential-speeches/march-31-1968-remarks-decision-not-seek-re-election.

9. Hugh Heclo. 2005. "Sixties Civics," in Sidney M. Milkis and Jerome Mileur, eds., *The Great Society and the High Tide of Liberalism*. Amherst: University of Massachusetts Press.

10. For a review of the GI Bill's economic and political effects, see Suzanne Mettler. 2005. *Soldiers to Citizens: The G.I. Bill and the Making of the Greatest Generation*. Oxford, UK: Oxford University Press.

11. Pub.L. 79–304

12. *New York Times*, March 29, 1958, p. 1.

13. "The Economy: We Are All Keynesians Now." December 31, 1965. *Time Magazine*.

14. The idea of a "countervailing" power is given its mid-20th-century expression by the noted Keynesian economist and political theorist, John Kenneth Galbraith. 1952. *American Capitalism—The Concept of Countervailing Power*. New York, NY: Houghton Mifflin.

15. Matusow, *The Unraveling of America*, p. 33.

16. The most thorough description of Franklin Roosevelt's political economy is detailed in his "Campaign Address on Progressive Government at the Commonwealth Club in San Francisco, California." September 23, 1932, https://www.presidency.ucsb.edu/documents/campaign-address-progressive-government-the-commonwealth-club-san-francisco-california. See especially how Roosevelt contrasts his administration with earlier Progressives, like Woodrow Wilson.

17. M. J. Rossant. "Business and Politics." August 17, 1964. *New York Times*, p. 37.

18. Schlesinger's critique of corporate capitalism is most fully explored in Arthur M. Schlesinger Jr. May 3, 1956. "The Challenge of Abundance." *Reporter.*. Galbraith's more famous call to renew public spending is found in John Kenneth Galbraith. 1958. *The Affluent Society*. New York, NY: Houghton Mifflin. For a general discussion of this distinction between quantitative and qualitative liberalism, see Kevin Mattson. 2004. *When America Was Great: The Fighting Faith of Liberalism in Post-War America*. New York, NY: Routledge.

19. For an example of Kennedy's "partial revision" to the New Deal political economy, see Nicholas Jacobs and James Savage. 2018. "Kennedy's Keynesian Budgetary Politics and the 1962 Public Works Acceleration Act." *Journal of Policy History* 30(1): 522–551.

20. Bruce Miroff. 1976. *Pragmatic Illusions: The Presidential Politics of John F. Kennedy.* New York: David McKay.

21. Michael Harrington. March 1966. "Reactionary Keynesianism." *Encounter.*

22. Students for a Democratic Society (US). 1962/1990. The Port Huron Statement. Chicago, IL: C. H. Kerr.

23. On the origins of the concept of a Great Society, see Sidney M. Milkis. 2005. "Lyndon Johnson, the Great Society and the 'Twilight' of the Modern Presidency," in Milkis and Jerome M. Mileur, eds., *The Great Society and the High Tide of Liberalism.* Amherst: University of Massachusetts Press.

24. Lyndon B. Johnson. 1964. "Remarks at the University of Michigan, May 22." Online by Gerhard Peters and John T. Woolley. The American Presidency Project, https://www.presidency.ucsb.edu/documents/remarks-the-university-michigan.

25. Julian Zelizer. 1998. *Taxing America: Wilbur D. Mills, Congress, and the State, 1945–1975.* New York, NY: Cambridge University Press.

26. Students for a Democratic Society (US), The Port Huron Statement.

27. Robert A. Nisbet. 1953. *Quest for Community.* New York, NY: Oxford University Press.

28. Economic Opportunity Act of 1964, Title 2, Part A, Section 202 (a).

29. Report to Accompany H.R. 11377, Economic Opportunity Act of 1964. US House of Representatives, Committee on Education and Labor. 88th Congress, 2nd Session, Report No. 1458, p. 10.

30. Cited in Michael B. Katz. 2005. "The New African American Equality." *Journal of American History* 92: 75–108; see also Francis Fox Piven and Richard A. Cloward. "The Politics of the Great Society," in Sidney M. Milkis and Jerome M. Mileur, eds., *The Great Society and High Tide of Liberalism.* Amherst: University of Massachusetts Press, 259: 253–269,.

31. Matusow, *The Unravelling of Liberalism*, p. 245.

32. Sidney M. Milkis and Daniel J. Tichenor. 2019. *Rivalry and Reform: Presidents, Social Movements, and the Transformation of American Politics.* Chicago, IL: University of Chicago Press, 166–174.

33. Marjorie Hunter. April 18, 1965. "Shriver Defends Antipoverty Aid." *New York Times*, p. 46; see also Tom Littlewood. April 19, 1965. "War on Poverty Brings Political Skirmishing," *Chicago Sun Times*, p. A4.

34. Daniel P. Moynihan. 1969. *Maximum Feasible Misunderstanding: Community Action in the War on Poverty.* New York, NY: Free Press (emphasis in original).

35. Hubert H. Humphrey to Lyndon B. Johnson. August 26, 1965, in *White House Central Files: Local Government*, Lyndon B. Johnson Library, Box 1; U.S. Conference of Mayors. 1965. *Special Report: The Office of Economic Opportunity and Local Community Action Agencies*, in *White House Central Files: Executive, WE9*, Lyndon B. Johnson Library, Box 26 Austin, Texas.

36. John G. Wofford. 1969. "The Politics of Local Responsibility: Administration of the Community Action Program," in James L. Sundquist, ed., *On Fighting Poverty: Perspectives from Experience.* New York, NY: Basic Books, 90–93.

37. Charles Haar. 1975. *Between the Idea and the Reality: A Study in the Origin, Fate and Legacy of the Model Cities Program.* Boston, MA: Little, Brown; Bernard J. Frieden and

Marshall Kaplan. 1975. *The Politics of Neglect: Urban Aid from Model Cities to Revenue Sharing.* Cambridge, MA: MIT Press.

38. *Examination of the War on Poverty*, prepared for the Subcommittee on Employment, Manpower and Poverty of the Committee on Labor and Public Welfare, United States Senate. Washington, DC: Government Printing Office, 1967, V, 1238, 1241–1242.

39. Sanford F. Schram. 2015. *The Return of Ordinary Capitalism: Neoliberalism, Precarity, Occupy.* New York, NY: Oxford University Press.

40. Mark Landler. October 6, 2011. "Protests Offer Obama the Opportunity to Gain, and Room for Pitfalls." *Washington Post.* https://www.nytimes.com/2011/10/07/us/polit ics/occupy-wall-street-protests-offer-obama-opportunity-and-threats.html.

41. On the long civil rights movement, see Eric Arnesen. April 2009. "Reconsidering the 'Long Civil Rights Movement.'" *Historically Speaking* 10(2): 265–288.

42. Barack Obama received 91% of all votes cast from Black Americans, while his Republican opponent, Mitt Romney, received just 6%. We relied on a consistent, multi-year measure for these comparisons. See Alex Tyson and Shiva Maniam. 2016. "Behind Trump's Victory: Divisions by Race, Gender, Education." *Pew Research Center.* http://www.pewresearch.org/fact-tank/2016/11/09/behind-trumps-victory-divisions-by-race-gender-education/.

43. William H. Frey. November 12, 2020. "Exit Polls Show Both Familiar and New Voting Blocs Sealed Biden's Win." *Brookings Institution.* https://www.brookings.edu/resea rch/2020-exit-polls-show-a-scrambling-of-democrats-and-republicans-traditional-bases/.

44. David Bateman, Ira Katznelson, and John S. Lapinski. 2018. *Southern Nation: Congress and White Supremacy after Reconstruction.* Princeton, NJ: Princeton University Press.

45. Democratic Party Platforms: "1948 Democratic Party Platform," July 12, 1948. presi-dency.ucsb.edu/documents/1948-democratic-party-platform

46. C. P. Trussell. July 15, 1948. "South Beaten on Race Issue as Rights Plank Is Widened." *New York Times*, p. 1.

47. Thurmond received all the electoral votes from Louisiana, Mississippi, Alabama, and South Carolina, and one faithless electoral vote from Tennessee, for a total of 39 elec-toral votes, and 2.4% of the popular vote.

48. And in the 1960 election, Alabama and Mississippi once again sent electors pledged to a protest Southern candidate—this time the architect of massive resistance in the South, Virginia Senator Harry F. Byrd. To be sure, Texas too went for Kennedy likely due to the presence of its senior senator, Lyndon Johnson, on the ticket.

49. Executive Order 11063, issued toward the end of 1962, banned racial discrimina-tion in the sale, leasing, or rental of federally funded housing; however, it excluded all existing housing and applied only to new housing that the federal government directly owned or financed. William E. Leuchtenburg. 2005. *The White House Looks South: Franklin D. Roosevelt, Harry S. Truman, Lyndon B. Johnson.* Baton Rouge: Louisiana State University Press, 416.

50. King cited in Nick Kotz. 2006. *Judgement Days: Lyndon Baines Johnson, Martin Luther King, Jr., and the Laws That Changed America.* New York: Houghton Mifflin, 324.

51. Matusow, *The Unraveling of America*, pp. 360–362

52. *Violence in the City—an End or a Beginning?* December 2, 1965. A Report by the Governor's Commission on the Los Angeles Riots, pp. 5, 82. https://www.lc.edu/uploadedFiles/Pages/Services/Reid_Memorial_Library/McCone%20Commission%20Report%20Violence%20in%20the%20City%20Watts%20Neighborhood.pdf.

53. Kerner Commission, National Advisory Commission on Report on Civil Disorders, p. 1. https://www.ojp.gov/ncjrs/virtual-library/abstracts/national-advisory-commission-civil-disorders-report.

54. Ernest Boynon. September 16, 1967. "Has White U.S. Learned or Lost?" *Chicago Defender*, p. 11.

55. James H. Cone. 1991. *Martin & Malcom & America*. Maryknoll, NY: Orbis Books, 221.

56. Kotz, *Judgment* Days, 204–205

57. Johnson combined persuasion and ruthless methods, including the use of FBI wiretaps on civil rights leaders, in resolving the Mississippi Freedom Democratic Party (MFDP) dispute. See Kotz, *Lyndon Baines Johnson, Martin Luther King, Jr., and the Laws that Changed America*, 206–218.

58. Memorandum, White to Johnson, August 13, 1964; E-mail to authors from Sherwin J. Markman, a Johnson White House aide, who was heavily involved in resolving the MFDP controversy, January 13, 2004, LBJ Library.

59. Johnson also was concerned, even at this early stage of his presidency, that an unruly convention might open the door to a Robert Kennedy candidacy. Former White House aide Sherwin Markman, written communication with the authors.

60. Kotz, *Judgment Days*, 220–221.

61. Stokeley Carmichael and Charles Hamilton. 1967. *Black Power: The Politics of Liberation in America*. New York, NY: Vintage Books, 1967, 40 (emphasis in original), 93.

62. Stokely Carmichael, with Ekwueme Michael Turin. 2003. *Ready for Revolution: The Life and Struggles of Stokely Carmichael*. New York, NY: Scribner, 527 (emphasis in original).

63. For an excellent, contemporaneous commentary on the challenge Black nationalism posed to the party establishment, see Tom Wicker. July 21, 1966. "White Moderates and Black Power." *New York Times*, p. 25.

64. Raymond S. McCann. September 2, 1967. "LBJ Deferred Negro Dreams: Dr. King." *Chicago Defender*, p. 1.

65. Martin Luther King, "Beyond Vietnam: A Time to Break Silence," Speech at the Riverside Church, New York City, April 4, 1967. https://www.americanrhetoric.com/speeches/mlkatimetobreaksilence.htm.

66. "LBJ Losing Black Backing: Leader." October 24, 1967. *Chicago Daily Defender*.

67. Harold Cruse. 1987. *Plural but Equal*. New York, NY: Quill, 346.

68. Elizabeth Drew. 1989. *Election Journal: Political Events of 1987–1988*. New York: William Morrow, 155–156.

69. Jesse L. Jackson. 1991. "For the Democrats, a Strategy of Inclusion." *Washington Post*, p. A21. Jackson, in the op-ed, is responding to this column in the preceding week's

paper: Richard Cohen. May 14, 1991. "From Jesse Jackson, Strategies That Would Divide." *Washington Post*, p. A19.

70. Alert R. Hunt. November 1, 1988. "Jackson Says Woes of Democrats Stem from Trying to Placate Conservatives." *Wall Street Journal*, p. A30.

71. Memorandum, Sherwin Markman, for the President, February 1, 1967, LBJ Library.

72. For an excellent account of the strategies and ideologies of feminist and gay rights groups, see Robert O. Self. 2012. *All in the Family: The Realignment of American Democracy Since the 1960s.* New York, NY: Hill and Wang.

73. Jamelle Bouie. August 17, 2015. "Black Lives Matter Protests Matter." *Slate.* http://www.slate.com/articles/news_and_politics/politics/2015/08/black_lives_matter_and_bernie_sanders_why_the_protesters_are_so_hard_on.html.

74. In opposition to this idea—that pragmatic electoral concerns outweigh these types of protest tactics—Jamil Smith of *The New Republic* has argued that "the idea that Black Lives Matter protesters are hurting their cause by challenging candidates, even those considered allies, is based in the notion that the burden of making change is on them. It isn't. Too many Sanders supporters appear to be caught up in their feelings when a protester rubs them the wrong way. They ask, Why are the protesters so rude, or annoying, or targeting the "wrong guy"? In response, I ask simply, Since when are protest tactics designed to make the people whom they are targeting feel more comfortable and less annoyed?" Such an exchange—while thought provoking—perhaps elides an answer to the question of where to draw the line. See Jamil Smith. August 10, 2015. "Black Lives Matter Protesters Are not the Problem." *New Republic.* https://newrepublic.com/article/122510/blacklivesmatter-protesters-are-not-problem.

75. On the change of attitudes toward Black Lives Matter, see Michael Tesler. 2020. " The Floyd protests have changed public opinion about race and policing. Here's the data." *Washington Post: Monkey Cage Blog.* https://www.washingtonpost.com/politics/2020/06/09/floyd-protests-have-changed-public-opinion-about-race-policing-heres-data/.

76. John F. Kennedy. October 18, 1960. "Speech of Senator John F. Kennedy, American Legion Convention, Miami Beach, FL." https://www.presidency.ucsb.edu/documents/speech-senator-john-f-kennedy-american-legion-convention-miami-beach-fl.

77. Franklin D. Roosevelt. December 29, 1940. "Fireside Chat." https://www.presidency.ucsb.edu/documents/fireside-chat-9.

78. Aaron L. Friedberg. 2002. "American Antistatism and the Founding of the Cold War State," in Ira Katznelson and Martin Shefter, eds., *Shaped by War and Trade: International Influences on American Political Development*. Princeton, NJ: Princeton University Press.

79. Daniel Ford. February 6, 1965. "Vietnam Convoy." *New Republic.*

80. Bernard B. Fall. October 9, 1965. "Vietnam Blitz: A Report on the Impersonal War." *New Republic.*

81. Richard M. Pious. 1979. *The American Presidency*. New York: Basic Books, 399.

82. Senate Foreign Relations Committee. "National Commitments." Senate Report 797, 90th Congress, 1st Session, 1967, 21–22, *Congressional Record*.

83. John W. Finney. December 23, 1967. "Fulbright Confirms Senate Panel Is Studying 1964 Gulf of Tonkin Incidents." *New York Times*, p. 4.

84. Jake Foisie. December 26, 1965. "Our Numbers Game Isn't Working." *Los Angeles Times*, p. E1; William Tuohy. October 29, 1967. "The Interpretation Gap." *Los Angeles Times*, p. E1.

85. "Text of Fulbright's Statements and Excerpts from Morse's on Tonkin Incidents." February 22, 1968. *New York Times*, p. 14.

86. "The Gulf of Tonkin, the 1964 Incidents, Hearing before the Committee on Foreign Relations." February 20, 1968. United States Senate, 90th Congress, 2nd Session, *Congressional Record*.

87. "McCarthy to Run Against LBJ." December 1, 1967. *Los Angeles Times*, p. 1.

88. Philip E. Converse, Warren E. Miller, Jerrold G. Rusk, and Arthur C. Wolfe. 1969. "Continuity and Change in American Politics: Parties and Issues in the 1968 Election." *American Political Science Review* 63(3): 1092, 1087 (emphasis in original).

89. Norman Mailer. 1968. *Miami and the Siege of Chicago: An Informal History of the Republican and Democratic Conventions of 1968*. New York, NY: World Publishing, 191.

90. George McGovern, Speech Accepting the Democratic Nomination at the Democratic National Convention, Miami, Florida, June 14, 1972. https://www.presidency.ucsb.edu/documents/address-accepting-the-presidential-nomination-the-democratic-national-convention-miami.

91. Arthur M. Schlesinger Jr. 1973. *The Imperial Presidency*. Boston, MA: Houghton Mifflin, 206.

92. See Kathryn S. Olmstead. 1996. *Challenging the Secret Government: The Post-Watergate Investigations of the CIA and FBI*. Chapel Hill: University of North Carolina Press.

93. Select Committee to Study Governmental Operations. April 26, 1976. "Final Report: Foreign and Military Intelligence." *U.S. Senate*. Washington, DC: US Government Printing Office. Stock No. 052-071-00470-0.

94. It is a tough case to suggest that Carter was a Cold Warrior in the vein of Truman, Kennedy, or Johnson. Carter's pursuit of a pro-human rights foreign policy was primarily rhetorical and did not engender the types of humanitarian interventions that we associate with such a posture under Clinton; he negotiated the return of the Panama Canal to Panama, in spite of deep opposition among conservative Republicans and Democrats; he signed nuclear arms reduction agreements with the Soviet Union (Salt II); he continued to open up trade with China; and, most significantly, he brokered what has amounted to a lasting peace deal, the Camp David Accords, between Israeli Prime Minister Menachem Begin and Egypt's President Anwar Sadat.

95. Full text of Edward Kennedy's remarks at Georgetown University printed in the *Washington Post*, January 29, 1980, p. A4.

96. For a remarkably prescient analysis of student activists, identity politics, and the appeal of anarchism in the late 1990s, see Franklin Foer. May 1, 2000. "Meet the New New Left: Bold, Fun, and Stupid." *New Republic*, 21–23.

97. Clinton's vote was highly symbolic, but her substantive view on foreign policy, before and after the vote, was also toxic. For example, leading up to her 2000 Senate election in New York, Clinton argued, "There is a refrain . . . that we should intervene with force only when we face splendid little wars that we surely can win, preferably by overwhelming force in a relatively short period of time. To those who believe we should become involved only if it is easy to do, I think we have to say that America has never and should not ever shy away from the hard task if it is the right one." See Michael Crowly. April 2, 2007. "Hillary's War." *New Republic*, 18–25; Michael Crowly. May 7, 2008. "Barack in Iraq." *New Republic*, 27–31.

98. Nelson Lichtenstein. 2005. "Pluralism, Postwar Intellectuals, and the Demise of the Union Idea," in Sidney M. Milkis and Jerome M. Mileur, eds., *The Great Society and High Tide of Liberalism*. Amherst: University of Massachusetts Press.

99. Hugh Heclo. 1996. "The Sixties False Dawn: Awakenings, Movements, and Postmodern Policymaking," in Brian Balogh, ed., *Integrating the Sixties*. University Park: Pennsylvania State University Press, 55–60.

100. Bruce Miroff. 2007. *The Liberals' Moment: The McGovern Insurgency and the Identity Crisis of the Democratic Party*. Lawrence: University of Kansas Press.

101. George McGovern. 1977. *Grassroots: The Autobiography of George McGovern*. New York, NY: Random House.

102. Editorial. July 22, 1968. "Mississippi Again." *Chicago Daily Defender*.

103. *Report of the Commission on the Democratic Selection of Presidential Nominees*, reprinted in *Congressional Record*, vol. 114, 90th Congress, 2nd Session, 1968, 31546.

104. *Report of the Commission on the Democratic Selection of Presidential Nominees*, 31546.

105. Austin Ranney. 1975. *Curing the Mischiefs of Faction: Party Reform in America*. Berkeley: University of California Press, 184.

106. Warren Weaver Jr. July 1, 1972. "Panel Denies Convention Seats to 59 Dailey Delegates." *New York Times*. https://www.nytimes.com/1972/07/01/archives/panel-denies-convention-seats-to-59-daley-delegates-their-places.html.

107. Byron Shafer. 1983. *Quiet Revolution: The Struggle for the Democratic Party and the Shaping of Post-Reform Politics*. New York, NY: Russell Sage Foundation.

108. David Truman. 1985. "Party Reform, Party Atrophy, and Constitutional Change: Some Reflections." *Political Science Quarterly* 99(4): 638.

109. James Ceaser. 1982. *Reforming the Reforms: A Critical Analysis of the Presidential Selection Process*. Cambridge, MA: Ballinger, 186.

110. In December 1977, a chastened Carter appeared at a dinner honoring Hubert Humphrey. The president wondered how Senator Humphrey "gets younger and younger" while he grew grayer and older. Senator Humphrey, Carter explained, answering his own question, "has been here in Washington long enough to know how to handle the political scene and I haven't learned yet." "Remarks of the president at ceremony honoring Senator Hubert H. Humphrey, Washington Hilton Hotel, December 2, 1977. https://www.presidency.ucsb.edu/documents/dinner-honoring-senator-hubert-h-humphrey-remarks-the-dinner.

111. James Ceaser. 1978. *Presidential Selection: Theory and Development*. Princeton, NJ: Princeton University Press, 283.

112. La Raja, R. J. 2008. *Small Change: Money, Political Parties, and Campaign Finance Reform*. Ann Arbor: University of Michigan Press; Samples, J. 2006. *The Fallacy of Campaign Finance Reform*. Chicago, IL: University of Chicago Press; P.Wallison and J. Gora. 2009. *Better Parties, Better Government: A Realistic Program for Campaign Finance Reform*. Washington, DC: American Enterprise Institute.

113. Morton Keller. 2007. *America's Three Regimes: A New Political History*. Oxford, UK: Oxford University Press, 246.

114. Byron E. Shafer. 1988. *Bifurcated Politics: Evolution and Reform in the National Party Convention*. Cambridge, MA: Harvard University Press, 114.

115. Thomas E. Mann. 1985. "Elected Officials and the Politics of Presidential Selection," in Austin Ranney, ed. *The American Elections of 1984*. Washington, DC: American Enterprise Institute.

116. Thomas Byrne Edsall and Mary D. Edsall. 1991. *Chain Reaction: The Impact of Race, Rights, and Taxes on American Politics*. New York, NY: Norton, 14–15.

117. Donna Brazile's bombshell memoir encapsulates this never-ending circle of anti-party critiques and power-yielding elites. Yet Brazile cut her political teeth in the insurgency of Jesse Jackson's campaign. Far from being "co-opted," her career success, culminating as chair of the Democratic Party, is attributable to these institutional changes. See Donna Brazile. 2017. *Hacks: The Insider Story of the Break-ins and Breakdowns that Put Donald Trump in the White House*. New York, NY: Hachette Book Group.

118. The DLC had articulated this set of concerns throughout the 1980s but then formed the Progressive Policy Institute to better motivate them. In its first report, these criticisms reflect the three myths found among liberal Democrats: the "myth of mobilization," the "myth of liberal fundamentalism," and the "myth of the Congressional Bastion." In William Galston and Elaine C. Kamarck. 1989. *The Politics of Evasion: Democrats and the Presidency*. Washington, DC: Progressive Policy Institute.

119. Kenneth S. Baer. 2000. *Reinventing Democrats: The Politics of Liberalism from Reagan to Clinton*. Lawrence: University Press of Kansas.

120. Wilson Carey McWilliams. 1996. "Conclusion: The Meaning of the Election," in Gerald M. Pomper, ed., *The Election of 1996: Reports and Interpretations*. Chatham, NJ: Chatham House, 258–259.

Chapter 5

1. Barry Goldwater. 1964. "Speech Accepting the Republican Nomination, July 16, San Francisco, California." http://www.washingtonpost.com/wp-srv/politics/daily/may98/goldwaterspeech.htm. Last accessed January 3, 2018.

2. Lydia Saad. January 3, 2017. "U.S. Conservatives Outnumber Liberals by Narrowing Margin." *Gallup*. http://news.gallup.com/poll/201152/conservative-liberal-gap-contin ues-narrow-tuesday.aspx?g_source=link_NEWSV9&g_medium=TOPIC&g_campa

ign=item_&g_content=U.S.%2520Conservatives%2520Outnumber%2520Liber als%2520by%2520Narrowing%2520Margin. Last Accessed: August 20, 2017.

3. See, for example, John Micklethwait and Adrian Wooldridge. 2004. *The Right Nation: Conservative Power in America*. New York, NY: Penguin.

4. Goldwater. "Speech Accepting the Republican Nomination."

5. Richard H. Rovere. September 25, 1964. "The Goldwater Campaign." *The New Yorker*. https://www.newyorker.com/magazine/1964/10/03/the-campaign-goldwater.

6. Barry Goldwater. 1960. *The Conscience of a Conservative*. Shepherdsville, KY: Victor.

7. Nicholas Jacobs. 2017. "After the White House: The Politics of the Post-Presidency." *Presidential Studies Quarterly* 48 (Dec 2018): 711–740.

8. David W. Reinhard. 1983. *The Republican Right Since 1945*. Lexington: University Press of Kentucky, 203–204.

9. Richard Nathan. 1983. *The Administrative Presidency*. New York, NY: Wiley.

10. Willard Clopton. April 6, 1968. "4000 Troops Move into District After Day of Looting and Arson." *Washington Post*, p. A1.

11. United Press International. April 5, 1968. "A Long, Hot Summer Predicted by Powell."

12. The 50th anniversary of the Kerner Commission Report produced an outpouring of new scholarship. We recommend Andrew Hacker. 1992. *Two Nations: Black and White, Separate, Hostile, Unequal*. New York, NY: Simon & Schuster.

13. Kevin P. Phillips. 1969. *The Emerging Republican Majority*. New Rochelle, NY: Arlington House, 25.

14. Robert D. Novak. 2008. *The Prince of Darkness: 50 Years Reporting in Washington*. New York, NY: Three Rivers, 225.

15. On the passage of this law and its connection to the broader Great Society, see Daniel J. Tichenor. 2016. "Lyndon Johnson's Ambivalent Reform: The Immigration and Nationality Act of 1965." *Presidential Studies Quarterly* 46(3): 691–705.

16. Matthew Lassiter. 2007. *The Silent Majority: Suburban Politics in the Sunbelt South*. Princeton, NJ: Princeton University Press.

17. Lassiter, *The Silent Majority*.

18. https://www.census.gov/newsroom/press-releases/2018/estimates-cities.html.

19. *Wall Street Journal*. September 10, 1968. "Law and Order," p. 20.

20. Whitney Young. October 26, 1968. "To Be Equal: Law and Order." *New Journal and Guide*, B12.

21. *New Journal and Guide*. September 5, 1964. "Law and Order."

22. Elizabeth Hinton. 2016. *From the War on Poverty to the War on Crime: The Making of Mass Incarceration in America*. Cambridge, MA: Harvard University Press, 15. See also Vesla Weaver. 2012. "The Significance of Policy Failures in Political Development: The Law Enforcement Assistance Administration and the Growth of the Carceral State," in Jeffery Jenkins and Eric Patashnik, eds., *Living Legislation: Durability, Change, and the Politics of American Lawmaking*. Chicago, IL: University of Chicago Press.

23. Philip Warden. May 10, 1967. "Honors Daley as Democrat of the Year." *Chicago Tribune*, p. 1.

24. Floyd McKissick. July 19, 1969. "From a Black Point of View: 'Law and Order' Candidates." *New York Amsterdam News*, p. 17.

25. Vesla M. Weaver. Fall 2007. "Frontlash: Race and the Development of Punitive Crime Policy." *Studies in American Political Development* 21: 230–265.

26. Byron E. Shafer and Richard Johnston. 2006. *The End of Southern Exceptionalism: Class, Race, and Partisan Change in the Postwar South*. Cambridge, MA: Harvard University Press.

27. Ronald Reagan. September 28, 1981. "Remarks in New Orleans, Louisiana, at the Annual Meeting of the International Association of Chiefs of Police." Online by Gerhard Peters and John T. Woolley. The American Presidency Project. http://www.presidency.ucsb.edu/ws/?pid=44300.

28. George W. Bush and Michael Herskowitz. 1999. *A Charge to Keep*. New York, NY: William Morrow.

29. Michelle Alexander. 2012. *The New Jim Crow: Mass Incarceration in the Age of Colorblindness*. New York, NY: New Press.

30. Desmond King and Rogers Smith. 2011. *Still a House Divided: Race and Politics in Obama's America*. Princeton, NJ: Princeton University Press.

31. Frances M. Shattuck and Charles A.H. Thomson. 1960. *The 1956 Presidential Campaign*. New York: Praeger; Robert Mason. 2013. "Citizens for Eisenhower and the Republican Party, 1951–1965." *Historical Journal* 56(2).

32. George H. Gallup. 1972. "Semi-Final Election Analysis," *The Gallup Poll Public Opinion 1935–1971* vol. 2. New York: Random House, 1438-9; Samuel Lubell. 1957. "The Future of the Negro Voter in the United States." *Journal of Negro Education* 26(3), 408; Samuel Lubell. 1956. "Why Negroes Switched to Ike." *Jet* 11(3).. Microform in Library of Congress.

33. Richard M. Nixon. September 1, 1968. "Remarks on the NBC and CBS Radio Networks: 'The Nature of the Presidency,'" 9. Online by Gerhard Peters and John T. Woolley. The American Presidency Project. http://www.presidency.ucsb.edu/ws/?pid=123874.

34. Norman Mailer. 1968. *Miami and the Siege of Chicago: An Informal History of the Republican and Democratic Conventions of 1968*. New York, NY: World Publishing, 37.

35. Richard Nixon. August 8, 1968. "Address Accepting the Presidential Nomination at the Republican National Convention Miami Beach, Florida." https://www.presidency.ucsb.edu/documents/address-accepting-the-presidential-nomination-the-republican-national-convention-miami.

36. Howard L. Reiter and Jeffrey M. Stonecash. 2012. *Counter Realignment: Political Change in Northeastern United States*. New York, NY: Cambridge University Press.

37. On the persistence of this cultural divide, see Mark D. Brewer and Jeffrey M. Stonecash. 2015. *Polarization and the Politics of Personal Responsibility*. New York, NY: Oxford University Press.

38. Phillips, to his credit, did recognize that all politicking involved some perverse degree of picking in-groups and out-groups. In the same interview, he suggested that his "Southern Strategy" had become so reviled, in part, because of its transparency: "Had one of Franklin D. Roosevelt's brain trusters promulgated in 1932 a thesis that

explained how Democrats were conniving to build a majority coalition out of plantation owners and urban Negroes, Ku Kluxers and immigrants, courthouse gangs in the South and corrupt war machines in the North, anti-union farmers and antifarmer laborers, he would have been drummed out of the party and his name would today be as reviled as is Machiavelli's." See James Boyd. May 17, 1970. "Nixon's Southern Strategy: 'It's All in the Charts.'" *New York Times*, p. 215.

39. *The Washington Post*. November 29, 2016. "2016 Election Exit Polls: How the Vote Has Shifted." https://www.washingtonpost.com/graphics/politics/2016-election/exit-polls/. Last Accessed, August 15, 2018; *Election Polls—Vote by Groups, 1960–1964*. Gallup. https://news.gallup.com/poll/9454/election-polls-vote-groups-19601 964.aspx. Last Accessed, August 15, 2018.

40. Irving Kristol. August 20, 1973. "The Ironies of Neo-Isolationism." *Wall Street Journal*.

41. Irving Kristol. September 25, 1983. "What's Wrong with NATO? *New York Times Magazine*. https://www.nytimes.com/1983/09/25/magazine/what-s-wrong-with-nato.html.

42. Woodrow Wilson. April 2, 1917. "Address to a Joint Session of Congress Requesting a Declaration of War Against Germany." Online by Gerhard Peters and John T. Woolley. The American Presidency Project. http://www.presidency.ucsb.edu/ws/?pid=65366.

43. Goldwater, *The Conscience of a Conservative*.

44. Robert A. Taft. 1946. "A Return to Liberty: Address before the Missouri Republican Club in Kansas City on February 12." Reprinted in the *Congressional Record*, 79th Cong., 2nd sess., pp. A1047–A1049.

45. Nixon, "Remarks on the NBC and CBS Radio Networks."

46. Peri Arnold. 1998. *Making the Managerial Presidency: Comprehensive Reorganization Planning, 1905–1996* (2nd ed. rev.). Lawrence: University of Kansas Press.

47. Richard M. Nixon. November 3, 1969. "Address to the Nation on the War in Vietnam." Online by Gerhard Peters and John T. Woolley. The American Presidency Project. http://www.presidency.ucsb.edu/ws/index.php?pid=2303.

48. Clyde Haberman. July 1, 2020. "The Day the White Working Class Turned Republican." *New York Times*. https://www.nytimes.com/2020/07/01/books/rev iew/the-hardhat-riot-david-paul-kuhn.html?action=click&module=Editors%20Pi cks&pgtype=Homepage.

49. For more on the "hard hat riots" see Philip S. Foner. 1989. *U.S. Labor and the Vietnam War*. New York, NY: International.

50. Quotations and depictions taken from Karl E. Meyer. May 21, 1970. "N.Y. Rally of 100,000 Backs War." *Washington Post*, p. 1; Homer Bigart. May 21, 1970. "Huge City Hall Rally Backs Nixon's Indochina Policies." *New York Times*, p. 1; Francis X. Clines. May 21, 1970. "For the Flag and for Country." *New York Times*, p. 22.

51. Jill Lepore. May 4, 2020. "Blood on the Green." *New Yorker*, pp. 70–75.

52. On working-class whites and Richard Nixon's presidency, see David Paul Kuhn. 2020. *The Hardhat Riot: Nixon, New York City, and the Dawn of the White Working-Class Revolution*. New York, NY: Oxford University Press.

53. John Andrew III. 1997. *The Other Side of the Sixties: Young Americans for Freedom and the Rise of Conservative Politics*. New Brunswick, NJ: Rutgers University Press.

54. Robert Mason. 2011. *The Republican Party and American Politics from Hoover to Reagan*. Cambridge, UK: Cambridge University Press.

55. Gerald Ford. 1979. *A Time to Heal*. New York, NY: Harper and Row, 334.

56. Ronald Reagan. October 27, 1964. "A Time for Choosing," in Richard M. Scaife. ed., *Ronald Reagan Talks to America*. Old Greenwich, CT: Devin Adair, 4–5.

57. Ronald Reagan. July 17, 1980. "Republican National Convention Acceptance Speech." Ronald Reagan Presidential Library. https://www.reaganlibrary.gov/7-17-80.

58. Lawrence J. Haas. 2016. *Harry and Arthur: Truman, Vandenberg, and the Partnership That Created the Free World*. New York, NY: Potomac Books.

59. Ronald Reagan. August, 18, 1980. "Speech before the Veterans of Foreign Affairs Convention." Chicago, Ill. https://www.reaganlibrary.gov/8-18-80.

60. Raymond Coffey. May 21, 1981. "America's Neglected War Vets." *Chicago Daily Tribune*, p. 19; Denise Kersten Wills. November 1, 2007. "The Vietnam Memorial's History." *Washingtonian*.

61. Charles Krauthammer. May 23, 1981. "Washington Diarist: Memorials." *New Republic*, 43.

62. *The National Review*. September 18, 1981. "Stop that Monument," 1064.

63. *The National Review*. November 26, 1982. "That Vietnam Monument," 1461.

64. Quoted in Spencer Ackerman. October 9, 2006. "The Other Vietnam Syndrome: Warniks." *New Republic*, 10.

65. National Commission on Terrorist Attacks upon the United States. 2004. *9-11 Commission Report*. Washington, DC: US Government Printing Office; James A. Baker and Lee Hamilton, eds. 2004. *Comprehensive Report of the Special Advisor to the DCI on Iraq's WMD*. Washington, DC: US Government Printing Office.

66. "Vital Statistics on Congress, Updated September 2017." *Brookings Institution*. Washington, DC. https://www.brookings.edu/multi-chapter-report/vital-statistics-on-congress/.

67. Heidi A. Urben. 2010. "Civil-Military Relations in a Time of War." PhD dissertation, Georgetown University.

68. "War and Sacrafice in the Post-9/11 Era." October 5, 2011. *Pew Research Center*. http://www.pewsocialtrends.org/2011/10/05/war-and-sacrifice-in-the-post-911-era/.

69. Ronald Reagan. 1981. "Inaugural Address, January 20." http://www.presidency.ucsb.edu/ws/?pid=43130. Last accessed January 3, 2018.

70. Charles E. Walcott and Karen M. Hult. 1999. "White House Staff Size: Explanations and Implications." *Presidential Studies Quarterly* 29(3): 638–657.

71. Bert Rockman. 1988. "The Style and Organization of the Reagan Presidency," in Charles O. Jones, ed., *The Reagan Legacy: Promise and Performance*. Chatham, NJ: Chatham House, 10.

72. For a fuller discussion of conservative "redeployment" and its relationship to other theories of American state building, see Nicholas Jacobs, Desmond King, and Sidney Milkis. 2019. "Building a Conservative State: Partisan Polarization and the Redeployment of Administrative Power." *Perspectives on Politics* 17(2): 453–469.

73. Carol Felsenthal. 1981. *Sweetheart of the Silent Majority*. New York, NY: Doubleday; John Fund. September 6, 2016. "Phyllis Schlafly: 'The Sweetheart of the Silent Majority.'" *National Review*.

74. Phyllis Schlafly. 1964. *A Choice Not an Echo*. Alton, IL.: Pere Marquette Press

75. On the success of the anti-ERA movement and its influence on public opinion within targeted states, see Donald T. Critchlow and Cynthia L. Stachecki. 2008. "The Equal Rights Amendment Reconsidered: Politics, Policy, and Social Mobilization in a Democracy." *Journal of Policy History* 20(1): 157–176; Jane Mansbridge. 1984. "Who's in Charge Here? Decision by Accretion and Gatekeeping in the Struggle for the ERA." *Politics & Society* 13(4): 343–382.

76. Clyde Wilcox. 1995. *Onward Christian Soldiers*. Boulder, CO: Westview Press.

77. Marjorie J. Spruill. 2017. *Divided We Stand: The Battle over Women's Rights and Family Values That Polarized American Politics*. New York, NY: Bloomsbury Press.

78. Sidney M. Milkis and Daniel J. Tichenor. 2019. *Rivalry and Reform: Presidents, Social Movements, and the Transformation of American Politics*. Chicago, IL: University of Chicago Press, chapter 5.

79. Milkis and Tichenor, *Rivalry and Reform*, chapter 5.

80. Jerry Falwell. August 1979. "Why the Moral Majority?" *Moral Majority Newsletter*, 1, Moral Majority Papers, Series 2, Liberty University Archives.

81. Joseph Crespino. 2009. *In Search of Another Country: Mississippi and the Conservative Counterrevolution*. Princeton, NJ: Princeton University Press; see also Nancy Burns. 1994. *The Formation of American Local Governments: Private Values in Public Institutions*. New York, NY: Oxford University Press.

82. William Martin. 1996. *With God on Our Side*. New York: Broadway, 71.

83. Jack White. December 15, 1975. "Segregation Academies." *Time*, 60; David Nevin and Robert Bills. 1976. *The Schools That Fear Built: Segregationist Academies in the South*. Atlanta, GA: Acropolis Books; Peter Skerry. Fall 1980. "Christian Schools Versus the IRS." *National Affairs*. https://www.nationalaffairs.com/public_interest/detail/christian-schools-versus-the-irs.

84. Martin, *With God On Our Side*, pp.70–71.

85. Randall Balmer. 2014. *Redeemer: The Life of Jimmy Carter*. New York: Basic Books, pp. 104–105; Crespino, *In Search of Another Country*, pp. 237–252; Nevin and Bills, *The Schools That Fear Built*.

86. In a prescient analysis, the eventual Supreme Court justice and liberal icon Ruth Bader Ginsberg would comment in 1985, "*Roe,* I believe, would have been more acceptable as a judicial decision if it had not gone beyond a ruling on the extreme statute before the Court. The political process was moving in the early 1970s, not swiftly enough for advocates of quick, complete change, but majoritarian institutions were listening and acting. Heavy-handed judicial intervention was difficult to justify and appears to have provoked, not resolved, conflict." See Ruth Bader Ginsberg. 1985. "Some Thoughts on Autonomy and Equality in Relation to *Roe* v. *Wade*." *North Carolina Law Review* 63: 375–386.

87. Nixon, "Remarks on the NBC and CBS Radio Networks."

88. *Mapp v. Ohio*. 1961. 367 U.S. 643.

89. *Gideon v. Wainwright.* 1963. 372 U.S. 335.

90. *Miranda v. Arizona.* 1966. 384 U.S. 436.

91. Ronald Kahn and Ken I. Kersch. 2006. "Supreme Court Decision Making and American Political Development," in Ronald Kahn and Ken I. Kersch, eds., *The Supreme Court and American Political Development.* Lawrence: University Press of Kansas.

92. Robert B. Semple Jr. May 22, 1969. "Warren E. Burger Named Chief Justice by Nixon." *New York Times*, p. 1.

93. *Eugene R. Frazier*, Appellant, *v. United States of America*, Appellee. 1969. 419 F.2d 1161 (D.C. Cir.).

94. Steven M. Teles. 2008. *The Rise of the Conservative Legal Movement: The Battle for Control of the Law.* Princeton, NJ: Princeton University Press.

95. Republican Party Platforms. July 15, 1980. "Republican Party Platform of 1980." Online by Gerhard Peters and John T. Woolley, The American Presidency Project. http://www.presidency.ucsb.edu/ws/?pid=25844.

96. Richard P. Nathan. 1975. *The Plot That Failed: Nixon and the Administrative Presidency.* New York, NY: John Wiley, 62.

97. William A. Niskanen. 1971. *Bureaucracy and Representative Government.* Chicago, IL: Aldine-Atherton; E. S. Savas. 1982. *Privatizing the Public Sector: How to Shrink Government.* Chatham, NJ: Chatham House.

98. Kimberly J. Morgan and Andrea Louise Campbell. 2011. *The Delegated Welfare State: Medicare, Markets, and the Governance of Social Policy.* Oxford, UK: Oxford University Press, 4.

99. James Savage. 1988. *Balanced Budget and American Politics.* Ithaca, NY: Cornell University Press.

100. Eric A. Posner and Adrian Vermeule. 2011. *The Executive Unbound: After the Madisonian Republic.* Oxford, UK: Oxford University Press, 11.

101. Mary Dudziak. 2012. *War Time: An Idea, Its History, Its Consequences.* Oxford, UK: Oxford University Press.

102. Personal interview with Grover Norquist, interviewed by Sidney M. Milkis, and Jesse H. Rhodes, August 3, 2004.

103. Cited in: Daniel K. Williams. 2010. *God's Own Party: The Making of the Christian Right.* New York, NY: Oxford University Press, 181.

104. Antonin Scalia. February 7, 1981. "Regulatory Reform: The Game Has Changed." *Regulation: AEI Journal of Government and Society.* (https://www.aei.org/publicat ion/regulatory-reform-the-game-has-changed/). Last accessed January 3, 2018.

105. Fred Barnes. August 17, 2003. "Big-Government Conservatism." *Weekly Standard.* Last accessed August 20, 2018. https://www.weeklystandard.com/fred-barnes/big-government-conservatism.

106. Patrick J. Buchanan. November 10, 1974. "The Republican Prospect." *Washington Post*, C1.

107. Stephen Skowronek. 2009. "Conservative Insurgency and Presidential Power: A Developmental Perspective on the Unitary Executive." *122 Harvard Law Review 2070.* See also Jeremy D. Bailey. 2008. "The New Unitary Executive and

Democratic Theory: The Problem of Alexander Hamilton." *American Political Science Review* 102(4): 453–465.

108. Sidney M. Milkis, Jesse H. Rhodes, and Emily J. Charnock. 2012. "What Happened to Post Partisanship: Barack Obama and the New American Party System." *Perspectives on Politics* 10(1): 57–76.

109. For contemporaneous accounts of this divide, see Lou Cannon. August 15, 1972. "Seating Realignment Argued." *Washington Post*, p. A1.

110. Lou Cannon. December 6, 1974. "GOP to Meet Quietly on Reform." *Washington Post*, p. A1.

111. Chilton Williamson. June 9, 1978. "Country and Western Marxism: To the Nashville Station." *National Review*, p. 715..

112. Stephen Skowronek. December 12, 2016. "Barack Obama and the Promise of Transformative Leadership." Presented at conference on Obama's Legacy: Tensions and Reconfigurations after the Presidential Elections, Paris, France.

113. These reforms were a combination of legally binding changes (The Legislative Reorganization Act of 1970) and the party's own internal rules for governing caucus procedures. For example, funding for more staff was a legislatively enacted change. By 1973, both Democrats and Republicans had agreed to subject committee chairmanships to secret votes, effectively ending seniority norms. The Democrats adopted a new "subcommittee bill of rights" that limited the ability of committee chairmen to select, create, and choose chairs of the various subcommittees.

114. R. Shep Melnick. November 1985. "The Politics of Partnership." *Public Administration Review*, 45: 655.

115. Donald R. Wolfensberger. 2013. "A Brief History of Congressional Reform Efforts." Paper prepared for use by the Bipartisan Policy Center, Washington, DC, and the Princeton School of Public and International Affairs (formerly Woodrow Wilson Center), Princeton University, Princeton, NJ ; Daniel J. Palazzolo. October 2015. "Return to Deliberation? Politics and Lawmaking in Committee and on the Floor." Paper prepared for Congress and the Constitution Conference, American Enterprise Institute, Washington, DC.

116. Stanley I. Kutler. 1992. *The Wars of Watergate: The Last Crisis of Richard Nixon* (rev. ed.). New York, NY: W. W. Norton.

117. Quoted in Bob Woodward and Carl Bernstein. 1974. *All the President's Men*. New York, NY: Simon and Schuster, 162.

118. Theodore Lowi. 1985. *The Personal President: Power Invested, Promise Unfulfilled*. Ithaca, NY: Cornell University Press, 171, 175.

119. Frances Lee. 2009. *Beyond Ideology: Principles, and Partisanship in the U. S. Senate*. Chicago, IL: University of Chicago Press; Matthew Glassman. 2012. "Congressional Leadership: A Resource Perspective," in Jacob R. Straus, ed., *Party and Procedure in the United States Congress*. Lanham, MD: Rowman and Littlefield.

120. The dynamics of the Congress-Party relationship are most comprehensively explored in John H. Aldrich and David W. Rohde. 2001. "The Logic of Conditional Party Government: Revisiting the Electoral Connection." In Lawrence C. Dodd and

Bruce I. Oppenheimer, eds., *Congress Reconsidered*. Washington, DC: CQ Press, 269–292.

121. Frances E. Lee. 2016. *Insecure Majorities: Congress and the Perpetual Campaign*. Chicago, IL: University of Chicago Press.

122. Barbara Sinclair. 2011. *Unorthodox Lawmaking: New Legislative Processes in the U.S. Congress* (4th ed.). Washington, DC: CQ Press.

123. Andrew Rudalevige. 2016. "The Broken Places: The Clinton Impeachment and American Politics," in Michael Nelson, Barbara Perry, and Russell Riley, eds., *42: Inside the Clinton White House*. Ithaca, NY: Cornell University Press.

124. Sidney M. Milkis and Jesse Rhodes. 2007. "George W. Bush, the Republican Party, and the 'New' American Party System." *Perspectives on Politics* 5(3): 461–488.

125. Michael Pence. September 8, 2005. "Funding to Rebuild After Hurricane Katrina." Printed in the *Congressional Record*, 109th Cong., 1st sess., 19738; see also Michael D. Tanner. 2007. *Leviathan on the Right: How Big-Government Conservatism Brought Down the Republican Revolution*. Washington, DC: Cato Institute.

126. Leo Gerard. 2013. "Why The Tea Party Loves Medicare But Hates Obamacare," *In These Times*, October 12. https://inthesetimes.com/article/the-tea-partys-misconception-of-medicare.

127. Wilfred M. McClay. 2016. "A Distant Elite: How Meritocracy Went Wrong." *Hedgehog Review* 18(2).

128. Matthew Continetti. November 16, 2009. "The Palin Persuasion." *Weekly Standard*. https://www.weeklystandard.com/matthew-continetti/the-palin-persuasion. Last accessed, August 20, 2018.

129. Theda Skocpol and Vanessa Williamson. 2016. *The Tea Party and the Remaking of Republican Conservatism* (rev. ed.). New York, NY: Oxford University Press.

130. Kathy Goldschmidt. 2017. *State of the Congress: Staff Perspectives on Institutional Capacity in the House and Senate*. Washington, DC: Congressional Management Foundation. http://www.congressfoundation.org/storage/documents/CMF_Pubs/cmf-state-of-the-congress.pdf. Last accessed August 20, 2018.

131. Christopher Demuth. October 19, 2015. "The Decline and Fall of Congress." *Wall Street Journal*, p. A15.

132. Daniel Cox. December 26, 2017. "On Immigration, the Tea Party Remains an Important Outlier." https://www.huffpost.com/entry/on-immigration-the-tea-pa_b_5485363. Immigration was the central issue in the shocking upset of Republican House Leader, Paul Cantor, a conservative from central Virginia, who was defeated in a 2014 primary by David Brat, an economist from Randolph Macon College. Bratt's campaign, which Tea Party activists championed, accused Cantor, a former darling of the Right, for being soft on undocumented immigrants. Cantor opposed comprehensive immigration reform but supported a path to citizenship for those brought to the United States as children. Jeremy Peters. November 25, 2014. "After Obama's Immigration Action, a Blast of Energy for Tea Party." *New York Times*. https://www.nytimes.com/2014/11/26/us/obamas-immigration-action-reinvigorates-tea-party.html.

133. Support for the Tea Party is not synonymous with support for the Christian Right. But survey analysis has shown that Tea Party supporters tend to have conservative opinions about not just economic issues but also about abortion and same sex marriage. Pew Forum on Religion and Public Life, the Tea Party and Religion, February 23, 2011, https://www.pewforum.org/2011/02/23/tea-party-and-religion/.

134. Ronald Brownstein. November 21, 2012. "The Coalition of Transformation Versus the Coalition of Restoration." *The Atlantic.* https://www.theatlantic.com/politics/archive/2012/11/the-coalition-of-transformation-vs-the-coalition-of-restoration/265512/.

135. George Hawley. 2016. *Right-Wing Critics of American Conservatism.* Lawrence: University Press of Kansas.

136. Donald Trump's full remarks available in "Full Text: Donald Trump 2016 RNC Draft Speech Transcript." July 21, 2016. *Politico.* http://www.politico.com/story/2016/07/full-transcript-donald-trump-nomination-acceptance-speech-at-rnc-225974.

137. The classic statement of a new conservative majority arising from a backlash against the Great Society is Mary Edsall and Thomas Edsall. 1992. *Chain Reaction: The Impact of Race, Riots and Taxes on American Politics.* New York: Norton,.

138. Jacob S. Hacker and Paul Pierson. 2005. *Off Center: The Republican Revolution and the Erosion of American Democracy.* New Haven, CT: Yale University Press. In contrast with our thesis, Hacker and Pierson subscribe to a different theory of how parties and political opinion *are supposed* to interact in the American constitutional system. We emphasize how beholden parties have become to public opinion, while they argue that "our political leaders are supposed to obey the dictates of surveys and focus groups, afraid to run afoul of the all-powerful oracle of public opinion. Our parties are supposed to be weak, fragmented, and ineffective. Our electoral structure is supposed to encourage two major parties vying for the center, not a majority party heading for the fringes" (p. 2).

139. Richard H. Pildes. 2011. "Why the Center Does Not Hold: The Causes of Hyperpolarized Democracy in America." *California Law Review* 99(2): 273–333.

Chapter 6

1. Steven Levitsky and Daniel Ziblatt. 2018. *How Democracies Die.* New York: Broadway Books, 37.

2. Randolph Bourne. 1918. "The State." http://fair-use.org/randolph-bourne/the-state/). Last accessed January 3, 2018.

3. Nicholas F. Jacobs, Desmond King, and Sidney M. Milkis. June 2019. "Building a Conservative State: Partisan Polarization and the Redeployment of Administrative Power. *Perspectives on Politics* 17(2): 453–469.

4. Daniel P. Carpenter. 2001. *The Forging of Bureaucratic Autonomy: Reputations, Networks, and Policy Innovation in Executive Agencies, 1862–1928.* Princeton, NJ: Princeton University Press.

5. Kenneth Lowande and Sidney M. Milkis. 2014. "'We Can't Wait': Barack Obama, Partisan Polarization, and the Administrative Presidency." *The Forum* 12(1): 3–27.

6. News Conference of Immigration Advocacy Leaders, White House, February 25, 2015, SM. https://docs.google.com/presentation/d/11CrmZF0MLxxLH-EUrG7aOWTFggD FKI62WxD5U4w3xQ/edit#slide=id.p. The DAPA initiative was blocked by the courts until the Trump administration repealed it. Muzaffar Chishti and Faye Hipsman. June 29, 2016. "Supreme Court DAPA Ruling a Blow to Obama Administration, Moves Immigration Back to the Political Realm." *Immigration Information Service.* https:// www.migrationpolicy.org/article/supreme-court-dapa-ruling-blow-obama-adminis tration-moves-immigration-back-political-realm.

7. Sidney M. Milkis and John W. York. 2017. "Barack Obama, Organizing for America, and Executive-Centered Partisanship." *Studies in American Political Development* 31(1): 1–23.

8. Jamiles Lartey. November 14, 2016. "Obama Made Progress on Criminal Justice Reform. Will It Survive the Next President?" *The Guardian.* https://www.theguard ian.com/us-news/2016/nov/14/barack-obama-criminal-justice-reform-prison-sen tencing-police.

9. Lartey, "Obama Made Progress."

10. Ta-Nehisi Coates. January/February 2017. "My President Was Black." *The Atlantic.*

11. Ronald Brownstein. April 17, 2015. "The Clinton Conundrum." *The Atlantic.* https:// www.theatlantic.com/politics/archive/2015/04/the-clinton-conundrum/431949/.

12. Brownstein, "The Clinton Conundrum."

13. For Donald Trump's full remarks, "Read: Full transcript of Trump's rally speech in Florida." February 18, 2017. *Palm Beach Post.* http://www.palmbeachpost.com/news/ national/read-full-transcript-trump-rally-speech-florida/DeDCpoNEKLQmWcI KndWB0M/.

14. Michael C. Bender. October 22, 2019. "Trump Rallies Are No Longer Side Shows. They Are the Campaign." *Wall Street Journal.* https://www.wsj.com/articles/trumps-rallies-arent-just-part-of-his-campaign-they-are-the-campaign-11571753199.

15. Kellyanne Conway. 2016. "Transcript: Interview with Jim Gilmore on December 8, 2016." *Frontline.* http://apps.frontline.org/trumps-road-whitehouse-frontline-intervi ews/transcript/kellyanne-conway.html. Last accessed May 29, 2019.

16. Interview with White House Aide, not for attribution, May 28, 2019.

17. Katie Glueck. November 25, 2016. "Christian Leaders See Influence Growing on Trump." *Politico..*

18. Jerry Falwell Jr. September 27, 2016. Interview on Fox Business News.

19. Douglas McAdams and Karina Kloos. 2014. *Deeply Divided: Racial Policies and Social Movements in Postwar America.* New York: Oxford University Press.

20. Nolan McCarty. 2016. "Polarization and American Political Development," in Richard M. Valelly, Suzanne Mettler, and Robert C. Lieberman, eds., *Oxford Handbook of American Political Development.* New York, NY: Oxford University Press.

21. *Growth and Opportunity Project,* 2013. Republican National Committee. http:// goproject.gop.com/rnc_growth_opportunity_book_2013.pdf.

22. The percentage of Americans indicating immigration as the most important problem was so small in 2016 that Gallup did not record a partisan differential. Information on 2016 and 2018 numbers were documented in the Internet Archive. www.gallup.com. See also Frank Newport. July 18, 2018. "Immigration Surges to Top of Most Important Problem List." *Gallup*.

23. "Declaring a National Emergency Concerning the Southern Border of the United States." Proclamation 9844, February 15, 2019. *Federal Register* 84(34): 4949–4950.

24. Erica Werner and John Wagner. February 28, 2019. "GOP Opposition to Emergency Declaration Grows as Trump Warns Lawmakers." *Washington Post*. https://www.was hingtonpost.com/politics/trump-republicans-who-cross-him-on-national-emerge ncy-are-at-great-jeopardy/2019/02/28/07d3d334-3b6a-11e9-a2cd-307b06d0257b_ story.html.

25. Scott Wong and Alexander Bolton. March 13, 2019. "GOP's Tillis Comes Under Pressure for Taking on Trump." *The Hill*. https://thehill.com/homenews/senate/433 929-gops-tillis-comes-under-pressure-for-taking-on-trump.

26. For example, during the 2016 presidential campaign, Pew tracked a massive drop in the share of Republicans and Republican-leaning independents claiming that free trade agreements had been a "good thing" for the United States from 56% in early 2015 to 29% in October 2016; see Ashley Parker. March 25, 2018. "A Sturdy Plank in the GOP Platform: Trumpism." *Washington Post*, pp. A1, A21. Trump also managed during his first two years in office to make the Wall the core of Republican immigration policy, a partisan symbol of their support for border security. Colby Itkowitz. January 15, 2019. "Republicans Spent Two Years Resisting Trump's Border Wall. What Happened?" *Washington Post*. https://www.washingtonpost.com/politics/2019/ 01/15/republicans-spent-two-years-resisting-trumps-border-wall-what-changed/ ?utm_term=.2a2eed8bcf78.

27. Toluse Olorunnipa. June 3, 2019. "Trump's Frenetic Immigration Approach Becomes a Central Part of the 2020 Bid." *Washington Post*, p. A2.

28. Toluse Olorunnipa. July 6, 2019. "'A Willingness to Fight': Win or Lose, Trump's Push for Citizenship Question in the Census Is Red Meat for the Base." *Washington Post*. https://www.washingtonpost.com/politics/a-willingness-to-fight-win-or-lose-tru mps-push-for-a-citizenship-question-in-the-census-is-red-meat-for-his-base/2019/ 07/06/4950889c-9f5c-11e9-b27f-ed2942f73d70_story.html.

29. US Census Bureau. June 23, 2020. "Statement from Census Bureau Director Dr. Steven Dillingham." Release Number CB20-RTQ.20. https://www.census.gov/newsroom/ press-releases/2020/statement-new-staff.html.

30. Dartuinnoro Clark. July 21, 2020. Trump Signs Memo to Omit Undocumented Immigrants from Census Apportionment Count." https://www.nbcnews.com/polit ics/white-house/trump-sign-executive-order-aimed-omitting-undocumented-imm igrants-census-count-n1234228.

31. Nina Totenberg. December 18, 2020. "Supreme Court Punts Census Case, Giving Trump Iffy Chance to Alter Numbers." https://www.npr.org/2020/12/18/946875796/ supreme-court-punts-in-census-case-says-its-premature-to-decide-the-issue.

32. Department of Homeland Security v. Regents of the University of California. 591 U.S. (2020).

33. Matt Keenley. June 20, 2020. "Trump Says 'We Won on DACA' at Tulsa Rally after Supreme Court Ruling. *Newsweek*. https://www.newsweek.com/trump-says-we-won-daca-tulsa-rally-after-supreme-court-ruling-1512364.

34. A. M. Kurta. October 13, 2017. "Memorandum: Military Service Suitability Determinations for Foreign Nationals Who Are Lawful Permanent Residents." Office of the Secretary of Defense.; Sarah Holder. August 13, 2019. "How Rule Changes About Public Benefits Could Affect Immigrants." *City Lab*. https://www.citylab.com/equity/2019/08/public-charge-rule-legal-immigration-welfare-services-dhs/595987/; Nick Miroff. December 20, 2019. "Under Secret Stephen Miller Plan, ICE to Use Data on Migrant Children to Expand Deportation Efforts." *Washington Post*. https://www.washingtonpost.com/immigration/under-secret-stephen-miller-plan-ice-to-use-data-on-migrant-children-to-expand-deportation-efforts/2019/12/20/36975b34-22a8-11ea-bed5-880264cc91a9_story.html.

35. Immigrant Defense Project. 2019. " Safeguarding the Integrity of Our Courts: The Impact of ICE Courthouse Operations in New York State." https://www.immigrantdefenseproject.org/wp-content/uploads/Safeguarding-the-Integrity-of-Our-Courts-Final-Report.pdf.

36. Erica L. Green. July 7, 2017. "DeVos's Hard Line on Education Law Surprises States." *New York Times*. https://www.nytimes.com/2017/07/07/us/politics/devos-federal-education-law-states.html?mcubz=0.

37. "Enforcing Statutory Prohibitions on Federal Control of Education," Executive Order 13791. April 26, 2017. *Federal Register*. https://www.federalregister.gov/documents/2017/05/01/2017-08905/enforcing-statutory-prohibitions-on-federal-control-of-education.

38. US Department of Education. September 22, 2017. "Department of Education Issues New Interim Guidance on Campus Sexual Misconduct." https://www.ed.gov/news/press-releases/department-education-issues-new-interim-guidance-campus-sexual-misconduct.

39. https://www.ed.gov/news/press-releases/secretary-devos-takes-historic-action-strengthen-title-ix-protections-all-students.

40. Michael Stratford. May 9, 2017. "Education Department Forges Ahead with Loan Servicing Overhaul." *Politico*. https://www.politico.com/tipsheets/morning-education/2017/05/education-department-forges-ahead-with-loan-servicing-overhaul-220209; Danielle Douglas-Gabriel. May 3, 2017. "Trump Administration Welcomes Back Student Debt Collectors Fired by Obama." *Washington Post*. https://wwwwashingtonpost.com/news/grade-point/wp/2017/05/03/trump-administration-welcomes-back-student-debt-collectors-fired-by-obama/?utm_term=.7bc1472cd35d.

41. Katie Benner. September 3, 2018. "Trump's Justice Department Redefines Whose Civil Rights to Protect." *New York Times*. https://www.nytimes.com/2018/09/03/us/politics/civil-rights-justice-department.html.

42. Sara Horwitz and Emma Brown. August 1, 2017. "Justice Department Plans New Project to Sue Universities over Affirmative Action Policies. *Washington Post*. https://

www.washingtonpost.com/world/national-security/justice-department-plans-new-project-to-sue-universities-over-affirmative-action-policies/2017/08/01/6295eba4-772b-11e7-8f39-eeb7d3a2d304_story.htmn.

43. https://www.kff.org/medicaid/issue-brief/medicaid-waiver-tracker-approved-and-pending-section-1115-waivers-by-state/#Table2.

44. The Trump administration's attempt to remake the Medicaid program is modeled on the playbook for welfare reform that the Clinton White House and a Republican-controlled Congress enacted in 1996, replacing cash payments for low-income households with temporary, strict work requirement-based assistance. The Trump presidency envisioned using a similar strategy in remaking the federal government's principal nutrition program. Toward the end of 2019, the administration issued a rule that would require "able-bodied" adults without dependents to work at least 20 hours a week to keep their Supplemental Nutrition Assistance Program benefits (formerly known as food stamps). Margarette Purvis. December 20, 2019. "The SNAP Rule Will Cause More Hunger Than We Can Handle." New York Times. https://www.nytimes.com/2019/12/12/opinion/trump-snap-food-stamps.html.

45. Center for American Progress, April 25, 2019. https://www.americanprogress.org/issues/lgbt/news/2019/04/25/468377/hhs-budget-fund-discrimination-expense-civil-rights-enforcement/. The religious conscience rule was blocked by a New York district court ruling, which the Trump administration appealed: https://news.bloomberglaw.com/health-law-and-business/trump-administration-appeals-religious-health-care-rule-decision. The fate of the rule hung in the balance as the Biden administration considered how to reverse the Trump administration's rules pertaining to religious rights.

46. For an excellent analysis of the anti-Trump Resistance, see Sidney Tarrow. 2018. "Rhythms of Resistance: The Anti-Trumpian Movement in a Cycle of Contention," in David S. Meyer and Tarrow, eds., The Resistance: The Dawn of the Anti-Trump Movement. New York: Oxford University Press, 187–206.

47. Jonathan Martin and Alexander Burns. May 19, 2019. "Abortion Fight or Strong Economy: Cultural Issues Undercut 2020 Message." https://www.nytimes.com/2019/05/19/us/politics/republicans-abortion-economy-issues.html.

48. Nicholas Jacobs and Sidney M. Milkis. Forthcoming. "Our 'Undivided Support': Donald Trump, the Republican Party, and Executive-Centered Partisanship," in Eric Patashnik and Wendy Schiller, eds., Partisanship in the Age of Trump. Lawrence: University Press of Kansas; Sabrina Tavernese and Robert Gebeloff. October 26, 2019. "Are the Suburbs Turning Democratic? It Depends on Which Ones." Washington Post, pp. A1, A12.

49. Alex Isenstadt. September 25, 2019. "GOP Cashes in on Impeachment." Politico..

50. Josh Dawsey and Michelle Ye Hee Lee. January 3, 2020. "Trump and the RNC Raised Almost Half a Billion Dollars Last Year and Still Had Nearly $200 Million Heading into 2020." Washington Post..

51. Toluse Olorunnipa. December 12, 2019. "'This Lit Up Our Base': Trump Campaign says Impeachment Will Help Him Win Reelection." Washington Post..

52. Milkis, *The President and the Parties*, 132–134; Joel Aberbach and Bert A. Rockman. 2009. "The Appointments Process and the Administrative Presidency." *Presidential Studies Quarterly* 39(1): 38–59.

53. David Lewis. July 2019. "Deconstructing the Administrative State." *Journal of Politics* 81(3). https://www.journals.uchicago.edu/doi/full/10.1086/703443.

54. Nick Miroff and Josh Dawsey. August 18, 2019. "The Advisor Who Scripts Trump's Border Policy." *Washington Post*, pp. A1, A20–21.

55. Josh Dawsey and Damien Paletta. June 12, 2019. "'My Peter': Rising Influence of Controversial Trade Advisor Worries Critics." *Washington Post*. https://www.washing tonpost.com/politics/my-peter-rising-influence-of-controversial-trump-trade-advi ser-navarro-concerns-his-critics/2019/06/12/e4fcb81c-8b96-11e9-b162-8f6f41e c3c04_story.html.

56. Brad Plumer and Coral Davenport. December 28, 2019. "Science Under Attack: How Trump Is Sidelining Researchers and Their Work." *New York Times*. https://www. washingtonpost.com/national-security/in-aftermath-of-ukraine-crisis-a-climate-of-mistrust-and-threats/2019/12/24/03831e3e-2359-11ea-a153-dce4b94e4249_st ory.html.

57. For an illuminating study of how presidents since the 1960s have weakened bu-reaucratic autonomy and expertise, see Stephen Skowronk, John A. Dearborn, and Desmond King. 2021. *Phantoms of A Beleaguered Republic: The "Deep State" and the "Unitary Executive."* New York: Oxford University Press.

58. Brian Bender and Jaqueline Feldsher. January 8, 2020. "'It's Terrible': Fear Grows that Trump Is Kneecapping the Pentagon." *Politico*. https://www.politico.com/news/2020/ 01/08/donald-trump-created-pentagon-credibility-problem-096146.

59. Dan Balz. May 31, 2020. "America Is at a Low Ebb, Shaken by Multiple Blows, and the President Adds to the Distress." *Washington Post*. https://www.washingtonpost.com/ politics/america-is-at-low-ebb-shaken-by-multiple-blows-and-trump-adds-to-the-distress/2020/05/31/2becbd02-a35c-11ea-b619-3f9133bbb482_story.html.

60. Thomas Edsall. May 20, 2020. "When the Mask You Are Wearing Tastes Like Socialism." *New York Times*. https://www.nytimes.com/2020/05/20/opinion/coro navirus-trump-partisanship.html?smid=em-share.

61. Sidney Tarrow. April 21, 2020. "There Go the People." *Public Seminar*. https://public seminar.org/essays/there-go-the-people-trump-whitmer/.

62. Toulouse Olorrunnipa. April 9, 2020. "Trump Forges Ahead with Broader Agenda Even as Coronavirus Upends the Country. *Washington Post*. https://www.washing tonpost.com/politics/trump-coronavirus-immigration-environment-inspectors-general/2020/04/08/bc1590e2-79b9-11ea-b6ff-597f170df8f8_story.html;   Caitlin Dickerson and Michael D. Shear. May 3, 2020. "Before Covid-19, Trump Aide South to Use Disease to Close Borders." *New York Times*. https://www.nytimes.com/2020/ 05/03/us/coronavirus-immigration-stephen-miller-public-health.html.

63. Maggie Haberman and Katie Rogers. June 12, 2020. "As Americans Shift on Racism, President Digs In." *New York Times*. https://www.nytimes.com/2020/06/11/us/polit ics/trump-on-race.html.

64. David Siders. June 3, 2020. "Trump Bets His Presidency on a 'Silent Majority.'" *Politico.* https://www.politico.com/news/2020/06/03/trump-suburbs-reelection-nixon-296980.

65. Office of the Inspector General, U.S. Department of Interior. June 8, 2021. "Review of U.S. Park Police Actions at Lafayette Park." Report Number 20-0563.

66. Peter Baker et al. June 2, 2020. "How Trump's Idea for a Photo Op Led to Havoc in a Park." *New York Times.* https://www.nytimes.com/2020/06/02/us/politics/trump-walk-lafayette-square.html.

67. Mia Jankowitz. June 4, 2020. "Trump's Evangelical Base Is Ecstatic over His Bible Photo-Op." *Insider.* https://www.insider.com/the-christian-right-loved-trumps-bible-photo-op-outside-church-2020-6.

68. Daniel Galvin. May 5, 2020. "Party Domination and Base Mobilization: Donald Trump and the Republican Party in a Polarized Era." Working Paper Series. Northwestern Institute for Policy Research. https://www.ipr.northwestern.edu/documents/working-papers/2020/wp-20-18-rev.pdf.

69. https://prod-cdn-static.gop.com/docs/Resolution_Platform_2020.pdf?_ga=2.165306300.2055661719.1598124638-455285808.1584478680.

70. The liberal wing of the Democratic Party has about doubled in size since the Clinton years to 51%; 34% of Democrats identify as moderate and 13% as conservative. In comparison, 73% of Republicans identify as conservative, 22% as moderates and 4% as liberals. https://news.gallup.com/poll/245813/leans-conservative-liberals-keep-recent-gains.aspx.

71. Peter Beinart. March 4, 2020. "The Democratic Party Wasn't Ripe for a Takeover." *The Atlantic.* https://www.theatlantic.com/ideas/archive/2020/03/regular-democrats-are-just-fine-establishment/607417/.

Chapter 7

1. Alex Horten. December 1, 2018. "George H.W. Bush Left a Letter for Bill Clinton: It's an Artifact of Political Humility." *Washington Post.* https://www.washingtonpost.com/history/2018/12/01/george-hw-bush-left-note-bill-clinton-its-an-artifact-political-humility/.

2. Brian Naylor. February 10, 2021. "Read Trump's January 6 Speech, a Key Part of Impeachment Trial." National Public Radio. https://www.npr.org/2021/02/10/966396848/read-trumps-jan-6-speech-a-key-part-of-impeachment-trial.

3. William Galston. February 16, 2021. "The GOP Won't Purge Trump." *Wall Street Journal..*

4. Domenico Montanaro. March 9, 2021. "'No More Money for RINOs': How Trump's Fight with the GOP Is All About Control." National Public Radio. https://www.npr.org/2021/03/09/975341543/no-more-money-for-rinos-how-trumps-fight-with-the-gop-is-all-about-control.

5. Greg Sargent. April 9, 2021. "Josh Hawley's Ugly Rant Unmasks the Fraudulence of the Anti-'wokeness' Crusade." *Washington Post.* https://www.washingtonpost.com/opinions/2021/04/09/josh-hawley-fox-news-rant-woke-corporations/.

6. Sidney Tarrow. 2021. *Movements and Parties: Critical Junctures in American Political Development.* New York: Cambridge University Press.

7. Richard Kreitner. October 12, 2020. "What History Tells Us About Trump's Implosion and Biden's Opportunity." *The Nation.* https://www.thenation.com/article/politics/interview-stephen-skowronek/.

8. Robert H. Wiebe. 1996. *Self Rule: A Cultural History of American Democracy.* Chicago, Illinois: University of Chicago Press, 9.

9. Austin Ranney. 1975. *Curing the Mischiefs of Faction: Party Reform in America.* Berkeley: University of California Press; Austin Ranney and Willmoore Kendall. 1956. *Democracy and the American Party System.* New York: Harcourt, Brace.

10. Raymond La Raja and Brian F. Schaffner. 2015. *Campaign Finance and Political Polarization: When Purists Prevail.* Ann Arbor: University of Michigan Press.

11. Sarah A. Binder and Frances Lee. 2013. "Making Deals in Congress," in Jane Mansbridge and Cathie Jo Martin, eds., *Negotiating Agreement in Congress.* Washington, DC: American Political Science Association.

12. Bruce E. Cain. 2014. *Democracy More or Less: America's Political Reform Quandary.* New York, NY: Cambridge University Press.

13. Mark Schmitt. Spring 2015. "Democratic Romanticism and Its Critics." *Democracy* 36. https://democracyjournal.org/magazine/36/democratic-romanticism-and-its-critics/?page=all.

14. Elinor Ostrom. 1986. "An Agenda for the Study of Institutions." *Public Choice* 48(1): 3–25; Michael D. McGinnis and Elinor Ostrom. 2012. "Reflections on Vincent Ostrom, Public Administration, and Polycentricity." *Public Administration Review* 72(1): 15–25.

15. R. Shep Melnick. 2014. "The Conventional Misdiagnosis: Why 'Gridlock' Is Not Our Central Problem and Constitutional Revision Is not the Solution." *Boston University Law Review* 94: 767–793.

16. *Report of the President's Committee on Administrative Management,* 1937. Washington, DC: Government Printing Office, 53.

17. Richard Neustadt. 1990. *Presidential Power and the Modern Presidents: The Politics of Leadership from Roosevelt to Reagan* (4th ed.). New York: Free Press, 8–9.

18. Daniel J. Galvin. 2010. *Presidential Party Building: Dwight D. Eisenhower to George W. Bush.* Princeton, NJ: Princeton University Press; Daniel Galvin. March 2014. "Presidents as Agents of Change." *Presidential Studies Quarterly* 44(1): 95–119.

19. The Democratic Senatorial Campaign Committee (DSCC) was unusually aggressive in the 2020 primaries, endorsing more moderate and well-financed candidates in nearly every race that could be competitive in the fall. It is notable that all of the endorsed candidates won; however, the national party organization faced hard-fought campaigns in many states and faced backlash from other candidates.

20. Chris Cillizza. January 9, 2017. "President Obama Finally Admitted He Didn't Pay Enough Attention to the Democratic Party." *Washington Post.* https://www.washing

tonpost.com/news/the-fix/wp/2017/01/09/president-obama-finally-admitted-he-didnt-pay-enough-attention-to-the-democratic-party/.

21. Theda Skocpol. July 28, 2018. "Democrats Had a Winning Playbook in 2018; They Should Use It to Beat Donald Trump in 2020." *USA Today*. For a detailed study of this locally rooted resistance, see Lea Gose and Theda Skocpol. 2019. "Resist, Persist and Transform: The Emergence and Impact of Grass Roots Resistance Groups Opposing the Trump Presidency." *Mobilization: An International Journal* 24(3): 293–317.

22. David Siders. May 4, 2019. "Democrats Preview Post-Trump Plan: Executive Orders." *Politico.* https://www.politico.com/story/2019/05/04/democrats-executive-orders-2020-1301633; Sean Sullivan. June 3, 2019. "Liberals Take Biden to Task to Blunt Candidacy." *Washington* Post, pp. A1, A4; Chelsea Jane. October 3, 2019. "Democrats Hate Trump's Executive Orders; Why Are They Promising So Many of Their Own?" *Washington Post.* https://www.washingtonpost.com/politics/democrats-hate-tru mps-executive-orders-why-are-they-promising-so-many-of-their-own/2019/10/03/ 9f065c08-d800-11e9-a688-303693fb4b0b_story.html.

23. John Verhovek and Molly Nagle. April 30, 2020. "Biden Campaign Reaches Deal to Allow Bernie Sanders to Retain Hundreds of Delegates, Maintain Influence over the Party Platform." ABC News. https://abcnews.go.com/Politics/biden-campaign-reaches-deal-bernie-sanders-retain-hundreds/story?id=70428518; Molly Nagle, John Verhovek, and Zohreen Shah, "Biden Campaign Focuses on Diverse Coalition Building With New Senior Leadership, ABC News, May 21, 2020, https://abcnews. go.com/Politics/biden-campaign-reaches-deal-bernie-sanders-retain-hundreds/ story?id=70428518.

24. Franklin and Sirdar quoted in Cleve R. Wootson Jr. June 14, 2020. "Protest Organizers Skeptical of Politics." *Washington Post*, pp. A1, A9.

25. Brett Samuels. March 17, 2021. "Biden's Big Difference: Diversity?" *The Hill*. https:// thehill.com/homenews/senate/543539-bidens-big-difference-diversity.

26. Kathryn Dunn Tenpass. May 3, 2021. "Biden's Commitment to Diversity in the First Hundred Days." *Brookings.* https://www.brookings.edu/blog/fixgov/2021/05/03/president-bidens-commitment-to-diversity-in-the-first-100-days/.

27. Micah L. Sifrey. October 27, 2020. "Grass Roots Democrats Are Preparing to Swarm the Biden Administration." *New Republic.* https://newrepublic.com/article/159696/grassroots-democrats-preparing-swarm-biden-administration.

28. https://www.presidency.ucsb.edu/analyses/biden-action-the-first-100-days.

29. https://www.presidency.ucsb.edu/analyses/biden-action-the-first-100-days.

30. Geoeffrey Skelly. April 28, 2021. "Biden's First Hundred Days Shows How Partisan Things Have Become." *FiveThirtyEight.* https://fivethirtyeight.com/features/bidens-first-100-days-show-how-partisan-things-have-become/.

31. Maria J. Stephan. February 25, 2021. "How Domestic Civic Movements Could Reshape US Foreign Policy." *Just Security.* https://www.justsecurity.org/74877/how-domestic-civic-movements-could-reshape-us-foreign-policy/.

32. Lisa Lerer and Jennifer Medina. May 15, 2021. "Tensions Among Democrats Grow as the Left Defends Palestinians." *New York Times.* https://www.nytimes.com/2021/05/15/us/politics/democrats-israel-palestinians.html?smid=em-share.

33. https://www.nytimes.com/2021/04/20/us/politics/biden-refugees.html.

34. Ray La Raja and Jonathan Rauch. January 31, 2020. "Voters Need Help: How Party Insiders Can Make Presidential Politics Safer, Fairer and More Democratic." *Brookings Report*. https://www.brookings.edu/research/voters-need-help-how-party-insiders-can-make-presidential-primaries-safer-fairer-and-more-democratic/.

35. E. J. Dionne Jr. February 24, 2021. "In Defense of Partisanship—the Right Kind." *Washington Post*. https://www.washingtonpost.com/opinions/not-all-partisanship-is-bad/2021/02/24/c51410b2-76dc-11eb-8115-9ad5e9c02117_story.html.

36. Adam Bonica, Jacob M. Grumach, Charlotte Hill, and Hakeem Jefferson. May 4, 2020. "All-Mail Voting in Colorado Increases Turnout and Reduces Turnout Inequality." Draft Working Paper. http://voteathome.org/wp-content/uploads/2021/04/Color ado-All-Mail-Voting-in-Colorado-Increases-Turnout-and-Reduces-Turnout-Ine quality.pdf.

37. Martha Derthick. 2001. *Keeping the Compound Republic*. Washington, DC: Brookings Institution Press.

38. Sarah Binder and Frances Lee. 2015. "Making Deals in Congress," in Nathan Persily, ed., *Solutions to Political Polarization in America*. New York, NY: Cambridge University Press.

39. Daniel Shea. 2019. *Why Vote? Essential Questions About the Future of Elections in America*. New York, NY: Routledge Press, 240.

40. Donald R. Kinder and Nathan P. Kalmoe. 2017. *Neither Liberal nor Conservative: Ideological Innocence in the American Public*. Chicago, IL: University of Chicago Press.

41. John Dearborn, Desmond King, and Stephen Skowronek. March 16, 2021. "How to Tame the Presidency After Trump." *New York Times*..

42. Molly Olmstead. January 24, 2019. "President Trump Caves on the State of the Union. What Happened?" *Slate*. https://slate.com/news-and-politics/2019/01/trump-pelosi-state-of-the-union-timeline-shutdown.html.

43. Mitchel A. Sollenberger and Mark J Rozell. 2012. *The President's Czars: Undermining Congress and the Constitution*. Lawrence: University Press of Kansas.

44. James Madison. December 5,1791/1999. "Consolidation." *National Gazette*. In *James Madison: Writings*. New York, NY: Library Classics of the United States..

45. Nicholas F. Jacobs and Connor M. Ewing. 2018. "The Promises and Pathologies of Presidential Federalism." *Presidential Studies Quarterly* 48(3): 552–569.

46. Aaron Wildavsky. 1985. "Federalism Means Inequality." *Society* 22(6): 42–49.

47. John Dinan. 2020. "The Institutionalization of State Resistance to Federal Directives in the 21st Century." *The Forum* 18(1): 3–23.

48. Abraham Lincoln, "Lyceum Address," January 27, 1838. http://www.abrahamlincol nonline.org/lincoln/speeches/lyceum.htm (Our emphasis).

49. Frederick Douglass. "What to the Slaves Is the 4th of July," July 5, 1852. https://teac hingamericanhistory.org/library/document/what-to-the-slave-is-the-fourth-of-july/.

50. Steven Levitsky and Daniel Zinblatt. 2019. *How Democracies Die: What History Reveals About Our Future*. New York, NY: Crown, 231.

Index

For the benefit of digital users, indexed terms that span two pages (e.g., 52–53) may, on occasion, appear on only one of those pages.

Page numbers followed by *f* indicate figures. Numbers followed by n indicate notes.